The Theory of the Accommodation Based Consumerist Economic System

3rd Edition

By Michael Salaniuk

Paperback available for purchase online at : https://lulu.com/spotlight/salaniukmichael

Comment and follow the commentary on this economic system at Michael Salaniuk's blog here:
https://accommodationbasedconsumeristesystem.blogspot.com/

Distribution Inquiries may be made here, and please email questions, comments, criticism and suggestions regarding this Economic System to Michael Salaniuk and his marketing team at :
tTotABCES@gmail.com

Watch for more information and developments, as well as criticize, make comments, present questions and make suggestions on the website at :
https://sites.google.com/view/ttotabces

Cover art by **Paul Tomas**: http://www.lulu.com/spotlight/tomaspaul
Formatting by **David Foster** : https://sites.google.com/site/vid932008/

the theory of the accommodation CHARTS 2019-02-18 058 final .odt
Monday, February 18, 2019 05:59 PM

ISBN 978-1-9994758-0-2
9 781999 475802
90000

Dedications

This book is dedicated to Valdimort for inspiring me.

Acknowledgements

I would like to thank my parents, Anna and Andrzej for their support. I also value the encouragement of my brother Tom and sister Andrea. Thanks also go out to Paul Tomas for his wonderful artistic contributions. David Foster contributed his formatting expertise as well.

About the Author

Michael Salaniuk is a theoretical economic philosopher from Oakville Ontario Canada. He was born in Opole, Poland in 1982 but moved to Canada with his family in 1989. He graduated with a Bachelor of Science degree from the University of Toronto in 2012. Michael is also interested with Mathematics, Philosophy, Physics and Psychology. He also likes to learn foreign languages. As a hobby he plays the guitar, mandolin and harmonica.

Table of Contents

Introduction

Dear distinguished economists, honorable statesman and interested readers:

This is the solution to human poverty. It is a grand third alternative to capitalism and communism.

Currently there are two general theories regarding economic systems. On one side there is the capitalist free-market system and on the other there is the socialist command system. The free-market system is designed to benefit the "capitalists"- those who own the means of production. The socialist command system is designed to benefit the state- the community as a whole. Many of the countries under the free-market system in Africa (Chad, Madagascar) are impoverished and getting poorer. This is the strongest argument against the free-market system- it doesn't always work and it doesn't work everywhere. Then there is the dreaded business cycle of booms and recessions which has produced the infamous Great Depression, one of the greatest non-violent man made misery we ever created for ourselves. Many of the countries under the command system around the world (i.e. the U.S.S.R.) have had their economies collapse and were forced to change their economic system. This is the main argument against the command system. It will eventually collapse due to a lack of incentives. Experience has taught us that neither of these systems is perfect and that they each have their own problems.

Can we do better? Right now the free enterprise system is the best we can muster. The only alternative to it is some kind of socialist or communist system. Thus we are caught between a rock and a hard place. But there is a third alternative- accommodation based consumerism. Accommodation Based Consumerism is a third alternative to free-market and communist systems. Thus it is incorrect to categorize it as a purely socialist system just because it is not completely free enterprise.

The consumerist system, as its name suggests, is designed to benefit the consumerists- the class of people who consume goods and services. Since everyone is a consumerist, the system benefits everyone. The whole system revolves directly or indirectly around the consumerist to promote his interests. Yet it also promotes the other actors, namely producers, employers and investors. It is not a utopic invention. It is firmly rooted in reality, having all the ingredients and incentives to make it function. There are incentives for workers to work, employers to employ and investors to invest.

It makes little or no sense to dissolve the free-enterprise system in countries where it is working well. These countries include the U.S., France, Canada, Germany and Great Britain among others. Right now these nations do not need another economic system. Yet it is unknown whether the free-market system will eventually collapse sometime in the future or not. It would be good to have something to hold onto in case everything falls to pieces and we can't put the pieces back together again. Consumerism is good to keep as a device of last resort. Yet even now there are many dozens of countries worldwide that would flourish and prosper if they were given the methodology to do so. The consumerist economic system would lift these countries into economic splendor.

Accommodation based consumerism is not a political system, nor does it have anything to do with the law. The system could work alongside almost any type of political structure with the exception of communism. It works well under democracy, parliamentary monarchy and even autocracy. Democracy and the free-market system, although they usually go hand in hand, are not inseparable. Many officials and policy makers try to defend the free-market system by defending democracy. Yet one is an economic system and the other is a political system. This fallacy is similar to defending cats by providing the virtues of dogs or talking about apples by speaking about bananas.

This treatise explains what accommodation based consumerism is, how it works and how it is to be applied to society. Many of the numbers and variables are exemplary and need not be followed exactly as set out. They will be duly mentioned. Other parts must necessarily be followed as prescribed. They will also be noted accordingly. If certain areas do not work as intended, it may be necessary to make some adjustments.

I must now iterate what this system offers. It offers the end of poverty, homelessness, misery and all the ills that go along with them. The business cycle and the depressions and recessions that are tied to it are no more. There is no inflation (for the most part) and unemployment is low or nonexistent. Not only is it impossible for the stock market to collapse but all investors are guaranteed to make a profit. There are no taxes in the sense that we generally think of them. Those who purchase items are able to purchase the finest things available. Yet rights like private property are protected. There are incentives for firms to do business in the consumerist nation, employing workers in the process. In short, consumerism is not about the pursuit of happiness but about the actual attainment of it.

Prelude to the System

In order to do anything we need a place to start. Therefore to develop our system we must begin somewhere. Our system must have some grand purpose to satisfy and the system should satisfy that purpose.

What is the purpose of our system? The purpose is to increase the material wealth and quality of life of the people under the system. Such a setup offers the highest level of happiness. A traffic system of lights, roads and signs is designed to benefit automobile drivers. Who else? A political system whether it is democracy, monarchy, communism or autocracy is designed to benefit someone or a group of people. Who it benefits is different for each system.

Why should we strive under the system to benefit all the people with a high quality of life? A high quality of life is what everyone universally wants. Those who have a high quality of life and an abundance of material wealth enjoy life much more than people who do not.

Now that we have a place to start, the first question is: how do we increase the material wealth and quality of life of people? This is done by giving people goods and services and giving them enough leisure time to enjoy these. We will use the term possessions to denote property, food and objects. By services we mean such things as the help of a mechanic and access to health care and the police. The more possessions and services, the greater is the material wealth of people and the better is their quality of life.

How do we give people lots of possessions and services? In order to give lots of potatoes to people, it is necessary to produce lots of potatoes and make them easy to obtain for people. How do we give a cat a lot of cat food? We make a lot of it available in a bowl and make it easy for the cat to obtain it. How do we give a horse a lot of water? We would provide him with a lot of water and make it easily available for him. Therefore if we provide a lot of possessions for people and make the possessions easily available for people to obtain them, the people will have a lot of possessions.

However, if we do not provide a lot of goods to people then there is a limit to the accumulation of goods of our people. In addition, if goods are not easily accessible then it is hard to get the people to obtain goods and increase their wealth.

How do we give people a lot of services such as teaching? People who want to be taught karate must have someone to teach them. The teacher must know what she is teaching. Suppose it is necessary for a dog to be taken on a walk. For this to transpire there must be someone willing to do this. He can't carry the dog or ride a car and let the dog run behind. In order for a cat to be spayed, there must be someone to do this, a veterinarian, or else the job will not be done properly or not at all. Therefore to obtain services, people must have someone to provide the services to them and that person must be someone who knows how to perform the service. If people have no one to provide the service, the service won't be done because a service can't be done by itself. If people have no one who knows how to perform that service that service won't be done well. To have services of the highest quality, he or she who performs the service must be very competent in performing it. The more trained a surgeon is and the more experience he has the better he will perform the surgery. A taxi driver who knows all parts of a city and has been driving for 15 years is better than one who does not have these qualities.

The next logical question is: what is the best way of producing lots of possessions, i.e. houses, cars, TV's? How do we produce a lot of potatoes? We would grow them in huge numbers on a farm.

How would we produce a lot of trees? We would plant large quantities of seeds or saplings in a fertile area. How would we produce a lot of coal? We would do this by digging a lot of it out from a place where it is found, i.e. mine. The best way to produce lots of possessions is by creating, building, growing or manufacturing a particular kind of possession in an area suitable for its production. The possessions should be produced in special areas because certain areas will allow for the greatest production of possessions while others will allow for lesser production of possessions. For example, it is hard to grow corn in a plutonium mine because corn will not grow there and the conditions for growing it there are not suitable. Likewise for manufacturing chairs on a farm. The place is not suitable for the purpose. It's best to create chairs in a factory because it is easiest to produce them there. Likewise for growing tomatoes on a farm. It is easier to produce tomatoes on a farm than anywhere else. Some things are easy to produce in one area, location, building etc. while some things are hard to produce in other areas, locations, buildings etc.

To produce lots of possessions, the possessions should be created in vast numbers in the easiest way possible that can create a lot of a kind of a possession. Potatoes should be grown in such a manner that the most potatoes are produced. This implies that they have enough water, correct spacing and fertile soil. Trees should be produced in such a way that most trees grow. This implies enough sunlight and proper spacing. Coal should be mined such that the maximum amount of coal is mined. This implies using good equipment and working during optimal conditions. Possessions should be created such that the maximum amount of them is produced in a certain area, location or building. This will maximize the production of possessions.

What is the best way to make possessions easily available for people? What is the best way to make grass easily available to a cow? It would be to give the cow the ability to get it. We would put her into a situation where she can consume it. This is done by putting grass in front of her nose and letting her eat it. What is the best way to make water easily available for a horse? It would be to put the water near the horse and letting him drink it. The best way to make possessions easily available to people is to put the people into a position where they can take them and by giving people the ability to obtain them. This means giving the possessions directly to a person and allowing him to take it, just as we would put grass in front of a cow's nose. That is to give it to her or put it on the ground in front of her.

Let's return our focus back on services. What is the best way to obtain people who know how to perform the service they are supposed to perform? What is the best way to obtain someone who knows how to walk a dog? It would be to show him how to do it. What is the best way to obtain someone who can teach French? It would be to teach him French and show him how to teach it. What is the best way to obtain someone who is a veterinarian? It would be to teach him about animals and how to treat them. What is the best way to obtain someone who is a dentist? It would be to teach her about teeth and how to fix them when there is something wrong with them. Therefore, to obtain someone who can perform a service it must be the case that he or she is made competent in the area of his or her expertise by education, training and experience.

How do we obtain a lot of people who can perform a service? How do we obtain a lot of people who can fix teeth? We would do so by encouraging people to do this and making them interested in the art of fixing teeth. How do we obtain a lot of people who walk dogs? We would do so by making lots of people want to walk dogs. How do we obtain a lot of people who mow lawns? We would do so by making people want to mow lawns. Therefore, we would obtain a lot of people who can perform a service by making them want to perform the service or by encouraging them to do so thus making them interested in it.

People need a reason to do something and the fewer the number of people that want to do something the fewer there are that do it. If people have a reason to perform a service such as wanting to do the service then more people would be inclined to do the service. Therefore there will be a lot of people who perform a particular service.

Let's return to possessions. How do we make people produce, manufacture, create or grow a lot of possessions? How would we make people grow a lot of trees? We would give them a reason or purpose for doing so. How would we make people mine a lot of coal? We would give them a reason to dig and make their digging worth their while. How would we make people grow a lot of potatoes? We would give them a reason to want to do it. Therefore, we would make people produce a lot of possessions by giving them a reason to want to produce them or a purpose for doing so. Thus people will be encouraged to produce possessions.

What is the best reason that can be given to people to make them want to produce something? What is the best reason that we can give a person to plant trees? It would be to give the person something in return for his actions and to reward the person. If happiness is the only reason for productivity then the interest will soon fade as the worker looses motivation. Eventually indifference stalls progress. Happiness should be part of the reason for producing things and working but not the only one. What is the best reason that we can give a person to mine coal? It would be to reward him in return for his work with either possessions or services. What is the best reason we can give a person to grow wheat? It would be to give the person possessions or services in return. The best reason we can give people to make them want to produce something is to give them something in return for their actions. If this is the case then their material wealth and quality of life will be raised at the same time that they are raising the quality of life and material wealth of the people whom they are providing with possessions. This is the purpose of the system.

How should people be rewarded for their work? Their reward should be proportional to the work done. If a person who grows corn receives less of a reward or none of it if he grows four hectares of corn rather than three, he will lose his reason for working. If a person who mines coal receives less of a reward or none of it for digging for 8 hours rather than 6 he will also have no motive for working. The reward must be proportional to the work done because there must be a reason to do more work rather than less of it.

We need an economic system that will ensure that producers produce more goods, that workers will provide more services and that those who provide have an incentive to do so. The following is that system. It is called accommodation based consumerism. We will call the people who receive and utilize goods and services, "consumerists".

The Ideals of Accommodation Based Consumerism

The accommodation based consumerist economic system has a set of ideals that belong to it. By ideals we mean truths that we hold sacred due to the beauty of their meaning. These ideals are a testament of the goals of accommodation based consumerism. They are:

1) The quality of life of a human being is a nation's most important priority

2) There must not exist material poverty

3) No one should be homeless

4) Progress is a virtue

5) An economy must be both productive and efficient

6) The consumerist dream is to own a palace or a mansion

7) One should have the opportunity to be able to have any profession one wishes to have

8) One should have the opportunity to be able to become anyone desires they desire to become

9) One should have the opportunity to be able to have anything one wants to have

10) Hard work should be rewarded. The more one works the more one should earn

11) One should be able to keep all the money one earns to spend as one desires to spend it

12) One has the right to own private property

13) One has the right to do what one wishes with one's land possessions as long as it is within the law

14) All should have an equal opportunity to dream of, pursue and attain happiness

These are the ideals of accommodation based consumerism. They are the goals the system wants to accomplish. This treatise explains how we make these ideals real.

Axioms and Suppositions of General Economics

In order to make our theory logically sound we must list several fundamental axioms and suppositions. A supposition is something we take to be true without bothering to prove its validity. An axiom is a fact that we recognize as being obviously true simply by thinking about it. In this section we discuss the axioms and suppositions of economics in general and accommodation based consumerism in particular.

We suppose that the system applies to an actual country and is not a mere theoretical invention. All rules, parameters and ideals are applicable to a large group of people. The bigger the group, the better. Although the system can be adequately applied to smaller scenarios, it makes the most sense for it to be adopted by a country. For the greatest utility, the system ought to be adopted by a whole country or a group of nations.

We suppose that there are people in the country under the system. It is hard for a country not to be populated. There must be people in our country. A country is defined as an area where people live. Every country, including the one under our system, must have people living in it. It is the people of a nation whose best interests we are promoting.

The people would rather be happy than miserable. No one wants to live in misery, poverty and poor living conditions. Happiness gives meaning to life. The material happiness of our people is the ultimate goal of our system. Compared to misery everyone would instead want to live a happy life. In developing this system, our main goal to keep in mind is to make our citizens as happy as possible.

The people are capable of doing work. By work we mean things like building, cleaning and managing. An able bodied person has tremendous potential if he or she applies himself or herself. The harder people work the better. With effort people have the power to do work. The ability to do work is a fine attribute of a human being.

People look favorably on progress. This implies that people would rather see things improve than worsen. It is almost universally held that there will be progress in the future. Countries that have a higher level of progress in some sense have a higher standard of living and better quality of life. People want progress to continue. Progress is a positive goal.

Now let's look at several important axioms. They are all general and apply to all economies not just accommodation based consumerism. They are universal in nature. These axioms must be preserved when creating an economic system. Usually most treatise begin with a logical set of axioms.

Everything must have a reason or else there must be a reason why it does not. This implies that everything in economics must have meaning and purpose. For everything we talk about in economics it must be clear why it is so. A reason has to belong to all the expositions we make. Where it doesn't it must be clear why not.

People always look to promote their own self interests. People do what benefits them. They seek to obtain or become what suits them the most. They would rather have something positive than not have it. In general, everyone wants as much of the economic pie as possible. This is due to greed. Everyone thinks that they are entitled to the most. Whenever the economic pie is split among the members of society, each individual battles his counterparts for the most. This is the greed principle.

Many people are guided by a principle that I have arbitrarily named Bronson's Principle. This is an entirely arbitrary naming that does not reference any thing or any person, living or dead. This principle states that people are constantly comparing themselves to their neighbors. Suppose that there are two workers, both cashiers. One works 20 hours while the other works 80. The person working 20 hours earns $5 000.00 while the other who works 80 hours earns $ 1 000.00. The second person, instead of being happy that he earned a thousand dollars is infuriated that he made less than the other worker who worked less doing the same job. People sometimes care more about how much they earn in relation to another worker than about how much they actually earn themselves. This is Bronson's principle.

Another important principle is at the foundation of any economic system. It is that people do what is moral and legal. Of course, in particular cases it is violated and theft, bribery and exploitation appear. Yet most citizens are honest most of the time. If all people were dishonest, property rights would be violated and every economic system would fall apart. Most people expect others to act justly and legally and strive to do so themselves; at least in most situations. This is the honesty principle.

People need incentives to do anything. If people have a reason to do something they are more likely to do it. A reward of some kind motivates people to act. An incentive is a means for getting people to do things. The more of an incentive a person has to do something, the more likely he is of doing it. This is the incentive principle.

The greater the output of a society in terms of goods and services, the better off that country is. A country that produces more things is in better shape economically compared to one that produces less. It is very favorable to increase output as much as possible. In general, the total level of output of an economy is one of the measures of the nations standing among other nations. Thus it is clear that the output of a society should be as high as possible. This is a very important principle called the *output maximization principle*.

The amount of goods that can possibly be produced at any one time is limited. This is due to the scarcity of the resources used for production. Either the economy uses its resources to produce one thing or another or a limited combination of both. There is a maximum as to how much goods can be produced in a society. People always want more than there is available. Only in utopia, which is unattainable, is scarcity nonexistent.

The economy must be constructive. That is, it must benefit some people, some groups of people or the group itself. An economic system must have some positive rather than negative purpose. It must benefit someone or some entity.

An economic system is the means by which society produces and redistributes goods and services. There may be several ways to create an economic system and decide how people are to go about producing goods and services. The way goods and services are produced in a society depends on the economic system and how the system works. Likewise, the redistribution of goods and services in a society is a function of the efficacy of the economic system. These are the primary functions of an economic system.

Competition drives progress. Generally speaking competition refers to people or groups struggling with each other to excel in a particular parameter; for example lowest price. The more competition we have in a society, the better it functions. Through competition, technology growth and wealth increase. Progress is assured by competition. Competition can take several forms, including price, quality and quantity.

Trade is necessary to increase well being whether individually or collectively. Through trade, new goods can be acquired. Also something can be gained from selling goods as well. By trading, each person increases his material wealth. Furthermore, when nations trade with each other, both nations as well as their people prosper.

Exchange is the essence of an economy. Although direct exchange is possible, a medium of exchange facilitates the process. A medium of exchange can be coins, paper bills or precious metals like gold and silver. Exchange can also be in the form of bank entries. The ability to exchange one good or service for another spurs the growth of an economy. An economy works due to the people's ability to exchange goods.

In order to work, an economy must have some means of production. An economy must have a way of making goods and services. The production of goods is the way to gaining prosperity. There are many theories of the means of production each peculiar to an economic system. If an economy cannot produce goods and services, it cannot function. However, if an economy produces many goods and services, the better off it is in terms of functioning.

There are two fundamental principles that appear when formulating an economic system. These are the principles of ambiguity and rigidity. These two principles tear at each other. The principal of ambiguity states that ideas must be clear, well defined and well elaborated on as opposed to given in general and non specific terms. However the principal of rigidity states that if the ideas are two concrete and specific one has little room making adjustments that may arise when trying to put things into place. If too many details are dictated then there is little room to maneuver. One must strike a perfect balance between these two important principles.

We just described some key suppositions and axioms that relate to economics. They apply to our system and to most other economic systems. Our discussions in the upcoming sections are hinged on these rules.

The Three Questions

There are three very important general economic questions that must be answered regarding an economic system. The first question is: "What goods and services should be produced?" The second question is: "How do we go about producing these goods and services?" The third question is: "How do we go about dividing the output of the economy, these goods and services, among ourselves?"

The answer to the first question is that we produce those goods and services that the consumerists in our economy want and need. We want to produce as much of these as possible. In cases where we cannot, we produce those goods and services that are most important and vital. That is, those that are most desired. The goal is to increase the material wealth of the consumerists. Sometimes we must produce things like factories that are necessary for material wealth. We produce things of the highest quality possible.

The answer to the second question is this. We produce things in a manner that will maximize productivity and efficiency. Workers will do the jobs that they are the best at or enjoy doing the most. Production is carried out in institutions that are best suited for producing that good or service. We call these firms.

The answer to the third question is this. As regards the third question, there is no single answer. Materially speaking, all non institutionalized consumerists are granted a certain equivalent of money, with those who work getting more than those who do not. This the consumerists can spend on material goods and services. Those who contribute more to the economy earn more accommodational and laissez-faire money depending on their contribution to it. What this is will be further discussed in later sections. So in one sense there is no gap between the rich and the poor, yet in another sense there is an enormous gap between the rich and poor. The rich own palaces while the poor own apartments.

So, these are the answers to the three basic questions. Knowing them we have a general idea of how this system works. The answers to these 3 questions guide the formulation of Accommodation Based Consumerism.

Wealth

In our system we want our citizens to be wealthy. First we must know what it means to be "wealthy". We have three hypotheses as to what wealth is: A) A large amount of money, B) A large amount of assets and access to services; and C) Assets and services of the highest quality. Let's compare two people; a rich person and a poor person to see what the real difference between them is.

While the rich man may have a large fancy car or sport car, the peasant may have a bike. They both have goods used for the same purpose – transportation- but the difference is in the quality of the asset. Although the rich man has better cars he does not necessarily have a large quantity of them (unless he collects them).

A rich man may have a well prepared fancy dinner with fine ingredients such as shark, steak and caviar. He may eat anything he wants. At the same time the peasant eats bread and potatoes. They both have food but the real difference is in the quality of the food. The rich man probably will not have 1000's of pounds of shark or fish. He has just enough to satisfy himself.

The rich man may have about a dozen tuxedos and outfits made by famous designers. The peasant on the other hand has two or three white shirts and a plain pair of pants. They both have clothes but again the difference is in the quality or prestige of the commodity. The rich man will probably not have more than 30 suites.

The rich man may have a very large television set, a home theatre and several stereos. The peasant may only have a newspaper and a simple ham radio. Each person has a form of entertainment but the difference is in the quality.

Finally, the rich man may have several sofas, some couches, some loveseats and several of the best built chairs and tables. The peasant may have a poorly built small table and a pair of chairs. Both people have furniture but the furniture differs in quality.

The question now is, would a rich man choose quantity or quality when choosing a good. If the rich man was offered 25 bicycles or a limousine, he would still want the limousine. If the rich man was offered 15 loaves of bread or a lobster and steak dinner, he would choose the later. If the rich man was offered 50 plain white shirts or a single tuxedo he would still prefer the tuxedo. If the rich man was offered 25 news papers or a wide screen TV, he would still choose to have the TV. Thus the difference between a rich and a poor person is not the quantity of goods that counts but the quality of these goods and services.

For clarity and concreteness, what is the difference between living in a prison camp and in a luxurious palace/mansion? The person in the prison camp has a deck of cards to entertain himself while the rich man swims in a pool or watches movies. Both have entertainment yet the difference is clearly in quality. The man in the prison camp has rags to clothe himself while the rich man has the most fashionable and comfortable clothes possible. Both have clothing yet the difference is again in quality. The man in the prison camp has to walk to wherever he wants to go while the rich man goes from place to place in a limousine. Both have transportation but the difference is in the quality of the transportation. We can extend this sort of argument to any area of the lifestyle of the man in the prison camp and the one in the mansion. Therefore, we are entitled to conclude that true "wealth" lies in the quality of the goods and services that a human being possesses.

Imagine the following thought experiment. We have a person, Bob, with a lot of money, $ 1, 000, 000. He goes to a supermarket that sells poor quality goods. Rotten apples cost $0.50/kg, stale bread costs $1.00 per loaf and the beef is rancid and costs $2.00/kg. The milk is sour and costs $2.00 per litre. If Bob spends the million dollars he would buy a very large quantity of goods. However no matter how much he buys he will still be poor because what he bought is poor quality. Despite his monetary wealth he lives in misery. A homeless person could have obtained the same items by rummaging through garbage cans.

Let's run another thought experiment. Suppose Jack walks into a store similar to the one above. He has $100.00. The only difference is that the second store has goods of better quality. The apples are fresh. The bread is crispy. The beef is tender and fresh. The pop is bubbly. The fish is good. The milk is tasty. If Jack spent all of the $100.00 in the store and bought similar types of things as Bob, he would be better off than Bob since what he has is of higher value than what Bob has. The denominator is what is preferred. The second case is preferred to the first.

There is an interesting point in the meaning of wealth. If we are talking about a particular type of asset, it is better to have a larger quantity of it than less of it. Given a choice between two lobsters or four, a person would pick four lobsters. One would pick 8 tuxedos over five of them. A person would rather have two wide screen TV's than just one.

Sometimes wealth is measured in terms of money. Although this is good for quantitative purposes, it has several problems. Suppose someone has a million dollars. Is he rich or poor? If a hamburger costs $200, 000 and a car costs 100 million dollars, then he is poor. However when the inflation is small, the amount of money can be helpful in comparing the degree of wealth of an individual.

Suppose we ask a capitalist or capitalist professor, "What is 'Wealth'?" He may respond by saying that wealth is something like the financial assets one owns- how much money one has. But if we questioned him again we ought to ask him if the financial assets make one rich or is it the goods and services that these financial assets can be exchanged for. Most capitalists will concede the latter. Now, when it comes to what one may buy, is wealth more a function of "quality" or "quantity"? Clearly when considering goods and services of the same type- identical ice cream cones, identical T- shirt- the capitalist, using his common sense will say that more is better. However, when comparing items (goods and services) that differ in quality- a tuxedo vs. a poorly made blouse, a sports car vs. an economy car- it is very likely he will agree with us that it is better to own a higher quality good or have access to a higher quality service. It is also very, very likely that our capitalist will choose a limited amount of a higher quality item than a large supply of a very poor quality item. Thus his views will be consistent with what we have derived.

What conclusions can we draw from this analysis? We will call "wealth" the possession of goods and services of high quality. Fundamentally, wealth is qualitative, subjective and relative as opposed to purely objective, absolute and quantitative. We can compare wealth between two individuals by how much of the same asset they have. That is, a person is said to be wealthier if he has more of the same asset as another person. However, measurement in terms of money is not completely useless. We will call the possession of a lot of money, "prosperity". Due to the way we defined wealth, our system must be designed such that the people who consume, the consumerists, obtain goods and services of the highest quality.

Economic Taxonomy

In this section we introduce the concept of economic taxonomy. Like almost anything else in this treatise it is an original idea regarding economics. We can proceed in one of two ways. Either we discuss the purpose of the concept first and discuss what it is later or vice versa. But then if we try to talk about the concept without defining it, we wouldn't know what we are talking about and proceeding in this fashion would be impossible. Therefore we will first talk about what economic taxonomy is and after doing so we will talk about its importance.

Economic taxonomy is a concept similar to biological taxonomy. Biologists try to organize all organisms on Earth into taxons or sets of hierarchical classifications. Economic taxonomy is the idea of organizing all goods, services and inputs produced by the economy into a hierarchical system of classification.

Biologists classify all organisms into categories that become smaller and more and more specific. Thus they organize all organisms into one of three domains. These are then divided into kingdoms and these are divided into phyla. Phyla are divided into classes and classes are divided into orders. Orders are divided into families which are divided into geneses. Finally geneses are divided into species. Species are the most specific. This system classifies all the organisms found on Earth. Once again, the ordering of classifications is:

Domain

Kingdom

Phylum

Class

Order

Family

Genus

Species

In economic taxonomy the idea is similar. The economy is divided into sectors. Each sector is divided into industries. Each industry is divided into classes. Each class is divided into categories. Each category is divided into families. Each family is divided into a product/service. Each product/service is given a designation. Each successive level of classification is called a taxon. Schematically, the hierarchy looks like this:

Economy

Sector

Industry

Class

Category

Family

Product/Service

Designation

As can be seen, there is considerable congruence between the two classification systems. There is one main difference. In the biological system, all classifications are in Latin. In economic taxonomy the classifications need not be so. They are in English (in English speaking countries)

The economy is divided into four sectors- the materialist sector, the accommodational sector, the laissez-faire sector and the governmental sector. The materialist sector is the biggest in terms of the number of products and services that are included in it. The most important industries found in the materialist sector are:

- Hospitality

- Transportation

- Entertainment

- Furniture

- Hygiene

- Information

- Apparel

- Health

- Education

- Synthetics

- Manufacturing

The most important industries found in the governmental sector are:

- Education

- Administrative

- Law enforcement and protection

- Infrastructure

- Community centers

- Public transportation

- Health care

- Gambling

The most important industries found in the accommodational sector are:

- Land

- Housing

- Utilities

- Appliances

- Home accessories

- Leisure

- Adult entertainment

- Alcohol and tobacco

The most important industries found in the laissez-faire sector are:

- Entertainment

- All auctions

- Apparel

- Gifts and gratuities

- Works of art

- Insurance

- Legal payments

- Gambling

A key point is that some industries can belong to several sectors so that some goods and services in one industry can belong to one sector while other goods and services in an industry may belong to a different sector.

The output of an economy can only belong to one of two classes. They are "good" and "service". A product can only belong to one of three designations. It can be called "retail". This means that it is a final good sold at stores that sell directly to consumerists. Examples include crackers and chips sold at a grocery store. It can also be a "final good". This means that it is a good made at a factory or production facility and is sold to vendors. Examples include cars made at a factory and chairs made at a factory. It can also be an "input". An input is a good used to make a final good. Examples include steel for making cars and flour for making cake. All services are designated "service".

Goods and services are classified in this system based on their similarity of usage. The highest taxons (sector, industry) are general in terms of the usages or purposes of the goods and services that they classify. Each successive taxon gets less and less general and products and services with increasingly more specific similarities of uses become grouped together. Thus goods and services in a family have a similarity of use that is more general than the similarity of use for outputs in the group "products/services".

We will use a particular example to illustrate this. Take the product bananas. They are in the materialist sector. They share this position with cars. They are in the hospitality industry. They share this position with an ice cream cake. They are in the goods class. They share this position with pots. They are in the food category. They are grouped along with steaks. They are in the tropical fruit family. They share this characterization with pineapples. Finally they are in the bananas product section along with other sizes of bananas.

Each taxon or level of organization must have a definition of its essence. That is it must be specified what is required for something to belong to a particular taxon. For example, the taxon of the category "drink" would be, "a liquid taken internally that is useful for the body". The taxon of the family "soft drink" would be, "a sweet carbonated liquid taken internally". The same idea applies to all other taxons at all levels of classification.

The classification of a product, input or service into its taxons is called a taxonomic structure. In what follows we give examples of many taxonomic structures. In doing so, we will develop a sub-discipline of economics. We cannot make taxonomic structures for all services and products here. Doing so will take a lot of time. It remains for inspired economists to finish this work that we have begun. Economists working for a branch of the government are given the task of completing this.

1) Product- binder

    Economy

    Sector- materialist

    Industry- educational

    Class- good

    Category- learning utensils

    Family- note taking aid

    Product- binder

    Designation- retail

2) Product- oranges

    Economy

    Sector- materialist

    Industry- hospitality

Class- good

Category- food

Family- citrus fruits

Product- oranges

3) Service – wheel alignment

Economy

Sector- materialist

Industry- transportation

Class- service

Category- automotive

Family- car repairment

Service – wheel alignment

Designation- service

4) Product – root beer

Economy

Sector- materialist

Industry- hospitality

Class- goods

Category- drink

Family- soft drink

Product- root beer

Designation- retail

5) Product- limousine

   Economy

   Sector- materialist

   Industry- transportation

   Class- good

   Category- automotive

   Family – automobile

   Product- limousine

   Designation –final

6) Product- wooden table

   Economy

   Sector- materialist

   Industry- furniture

   Class- good

   Category- dinning furniture

   Family- table

   Product- wooden table

   Designation- final

7) Product- study desk

   Economy

   Sector- materialist

   Industry- furniture

   Class- good

   Category- business furniture

   Family- desk

   Product- wooden studying desk

Designation- final

8) Product- kitchen chair

Economy

Sector- materialist

Industry- furniture

Class- good

Category- dining furniture

Family- chair

Product- kitchen chair

Designation –final

9) Product- blueberries

Economy

Sector- materialist

Industry- hospitality

Class- good

Category- food

Family- berries

Product- blueberries

Designation- retail

10) Product- carrots

Economy

Sector- materialist

Industry- hospitality

Class- good

Category- food

Family- root vegetables

Product- carrots

Designation- retail

11) Product- potatoes

Economy

Sector- materialist

Industry- hospitality

Class- good

Category- food

Family- root vegetables

Product- potatoes

Designation- retail

12) Product- wide screen television set

Economy

Sector- materialist

Industry- entertainment

Class- good

Category- electronics

Family- TV's

Product- wide screen television set

Designation- retail

13) Product – 64 bit video game console

Economy

Sector- materialist

Industry- entertainment

Class- good

Category- electronics

Family- video game system

Product- 64 bit video game console

Designation- retail

From what we have observed, some products were either "retail" or "final" as regards their designation. It is usually the case that most goods are both "final goods" and "retail". If a good is retail it must have also been a final good because it must have been produced somewhere. Similarly, all "final" goods must be sold and they must be sold to retailers like department stores or grocery stores.

All "inputs" are automatically in the accommodation sector. This is because material/governmental/laissez-faire goods are goods that are immediately available to consumers. If a good is used as an input than it is definitely one that belongs to the accommodation sector.

It is possible that the same good may have more than one use. An example is the computer. A computer may be a form of entertainment or a business tool. Thus it may have two taxonomic structures each being equally valid. Neither taxonomic structure is more valid than the other. This is similar to the idea of resonance structures in chemistry. Thus the two taxonomic structures are called "resonance taxonomic structures". The following is an example of resonance taxonomic structures:

14) Product- PC computer

   Economy

   Sector- materialist

   Industry- entertainment

   Class- good

   Category- electronics

   Family- computer

   Product- PC computer

   Designation- retail

15) Product- PC computer

   Economy

   Sector- materialist

   Industry- information

Class- good

Category- electronics

Family- computer

Product- PC computer

Designation- input

The same idea applies to books. Books can be information or entertainment depending on how they are used. So the following are another example of taxonomic resonance structures:

16) Product- book "**Drawn & Courted**" by R. David Foster

Economy

Sector- laissez-faire

Industry- *information*

Class- good

Category- books

Family- art instruction

Product- book "**Drawn & Courted**" by R. David Foster

Designation- retail

17) Product- book "**Drawn & Courted**" by R. David Foster

Economy

Sector- laissez-faire

Industry- *entertainment*

Class- good

Category- books

Family- art instruction

Product- book "**Drawn & Courted**" by R. David Foster

Designation- retail

18) Service- news broadcast

    Economy

    Sector- materialist

    Industry- information

    Class- service

    Category- media

    Family- television news broadcast

    Service- news broadcast

    Designation- service

19) Service- internet service

    Economy

    Sector- materialist

    Industry- information

    Class- service

    Category- media

    Family- computer service

    Service- internet service

    Designation- service

20) Product- modern tank

    Economy

    Sector- governmental

    Industry- defense

    Class- good

    Category- military

    Family- tank

Product- modern tank

Designation- final

21) Product- heavy duty dishwasher

Economy

Sector- accommodational

Industry- appliances

Class- goods

Category- kitchen appliance

Family- dishwasher

Product- heavy duty dishwasher

Designation- retail

22) Product- microwave

Economy

Sector- accommodational

Industry- appliance

Class- good

Category-kitchen appliance

Family- cooking appliance

Product- microwave

Designation- retail

23) Service- optometrist appointment

Economy

Sector- governmental

Industry- health

Class- service

Category- medical

Family- doctor's appointment

Service- optometrist appointment

Designation- retail

24) Service- family doctor's appointment

Economy

Sector- governmental

Industry- health

Class- service

Category- medical

Family- doctor's appointment

Service- family doctor's appointment

Designation- service

25) Service- heart operation

Economy

Sector- governmental

Industry- health

Class- service

Category- medical

Family- emergency internal surgery

Service- heart operation

Designation- service

26) Service- cavity check up by dentist

Economy

Sector- governmental

Industry- health

Class- service

Category- medical

Family- dentist's appointment

Service- cavity check up

Designation- service

27) Product- industrial screw

Economy

Sector- accommodational

Industry- manufacturing

Class- good

Category- metallic goods

Family- industrial fasteners

Product- screw

Designation- input

28) Product- hammer

Economy

Sector- materialist

Industry- manufacturing

Class- good

Category- tools

Family- household tools

Product- hammer

Designation- retail

29) Product- ammonia

    Economy

    Sector- accommodational

    Industry- synthetics

    Class- good

    Category- chemicals

    Family- industry chemicals

    Product- ammonia

    Designation- input

30) Product- blue paint

    Economy

    Sector- accommodational

    Industry- home improvement

    Class- good

    Category- decorational item

    Family- wall covering

    Product- blue paint

    Designation- retail

31) Product- carpet

    Economy

    Sector- accommodational

    Industry- home improvement

    Class- good

    Category- floor furnishings

    Family- floor covering

    Product- carpet

Designation- retail

32) Product- tiles

Economy

Sector- accomodational

Industry- home improvements

Class- good

Category- floor furnishings

Family- floor coverings

Product- tiles

Designation- retail

33) Product- toothbrush

Economy

Sector- materialist

Industry- hygiene

Class- good

Category- oral hygiene

Family- teeth cleaning brush

Product- toothbrush

Designation- retail

34) Product- tooth paste

Economy

Sector- materialist

Industry- hygiene

Class- good

Category- oral hygiene

Family- teeth cleaning cream

Product- tooth paste

Designation- retail

35) Service- lecture by biology professor

Economy

Sector- government

Industry- educational

Class- service

Category- instruction

Family- service of a university professor

Service- lecture by biology professor

36) Service- instruction by a physic's teaching assistant

Economy

Sector- government

Industry- educational

Class- service

Category- instruction

Family- instruction by a university teaching assistant

Service- instruction by a physic's teaching assistant

Designation- service

37) Service- protection by a campus police officer

Economy

Sector- governmental

Industry- law enforcement and correction

Class- service

Category- police protection

Family- protection by a police patrol officer

Service- protection by a campus police officer

Designation- service

38) Service- firefighting team ladder operation

Economy

Sector- governmental

Industry- defense and protection

Class- service

Category- internal protection

Family- firefighting

Service- firefighting team ladder operation

Designation- service

39) Product- hot water

Economy

Sector- accommodational

Industry- utilities

Class- good

Category- household utility

Family- hot water

Product- hot water

Designation- final

40) Service- Defense Legal representation by a private lawyer

Economy

Sector- Laissez-faire

Industry- Legal

Class- Service

Category- Legal representation

Family- Private representation

Service- Defense Legal representation by a private lawyer

Designation- Service

In addition to the economic taxonomy system we have just developed there is a corollary system of classifying goods and services. It is called the numerical economic taxonomy system. The taxons are replaced by numbers. Every good and service would have a sequence of numbers that correspond to its taxonomical structure. The first number designates the sector of the good or service. It can only be 1, 2, 3 or 4. The next sequence of numbers designates the industry. Two numbers indicate the industry the good or service is in. For example, 02 could mean hospitality and 31 could mean transportation. The third number in the sequence refers to the class. It is either 1, referring to goods or 2 referring to services. The next number is a three digit number describing the category. Each category in the industry has an original three number sequence. Something similar applies to the next eight digit number which describes the family of the good or service in the particular category. The next taxon is product/service. It may have up to twelve digits. Each good or service has twelve digits describing what it is in the family. Finally the last number describes the good's or service's designation. 1 stands for retail, 2 for final product, 3 for input and 4 for service. An example illustrates the idea. Let's find the numerical economic taxonomy number for a hammer. First recall the taxonomic structure. It is the following:

Sector- materialist

Industry- manufacturing

Class- good

Category- tool

Family- household tool

Product- hammer

Designation- retail

It may have the following numerical economic taxonomy description:

1 – 17- 1 – 412- 00097774- 340001255513-1

We need to explain the above number. The 1 stands for the sector, in this case the materialist sector. 17 stands for the industry, in this case manufacturing. The next 1 stands for class, in this case goods. The 412 corresponds to the category, the category being "tools". 00097774 represents the family, which here is "household tools". The product is identified by the number 340001255513, which corresponds to "hammer". Finally, the last digit, 1, designates the hammer as being a retail commodity. Thus operates the numerical economic taxonomic system.

In this numbering system, a good or service can have the same number in its classification as long as the numbers before it are different. For example, 1- 17 …. and 2-17 refer to two different items. The "17" after "1" refers to a different industry than the "17" after the "2". The same reasoning applies to all classifications in the numerical taxonomy system.

Now that we know what economic taxonomy and numerical economic taxonomy are and have numerous examples of taxonomic structures, it would be good to discuss the importance of economic taxonomy. Economic taxonomy simplifies our understanding of the economy. We begin to grasp the relationships between various goods and services. By looking at taxonomic structures we can know what our economy produces and the services that people can do for each other. As we will see later on there is a particular price or wage function for each family of products or services. This greatly simplifies shopping as the consumerist knows exactly how much everything costs. Classifying products and services informs us of their relationships. We might want to know the relationship between goods and services in order to know how various goods were invented and how innovations came about. Also these relationships might help inventors come up with newer and better goods and ways of doing things. Since this classification is based on similarity of usage, studying it will help us know how similar goods are in terms of use. An economic taxonomy book (or an App on a cell phone), similar to a phone book will be a useful tool for all, listing all products, services and the price. Such a book (or app) would greatly simplify shopping. This notion of taxonomic organization is very useful for the Accommodation Based Consumerist Economic System. We will see its many applications in the forthcoming sections. That is the reason why we began this treatise with it.

We discussed what economic taxonomy and what numerical economic taxonomy are. We gave many examples to illustrate these concepts. We gave reasons why these concepts are important. The proceeding sections will fully incorporate what we have discussed here.

What is Accommodation Based Consumerism?

Accommodation based consumerism is a general economic system. It is neither completely a market economy nor a purely command economy. However, depending on the wishes of the people under the system, the system can have a quasi free-market or quasi socialist orientation. By itself, it is more general and has certain command and certain free-market elements. The means of production, although not completely, are in the hands of firms. The central bank sets certain parameters and is in charge of decisions as to prices and wages. The firms make most of the production decisions. That is, they decide what to produce, how to produce it and how to use resources such as labor. In this capacity the system resembles the free-market system. free-market capitalism is actually a special limiting case of Accommodation Based Consumerism where the laissez-faire sector is very large, the governmental sector is smaller and the materialist and accomodational sectors are very small or non-existent. There are some differences like for example how to raise taxes for the governmental sector. Nevertheless, Accommodation based Consumerism collapses (to some degree) into free-market capitalism.

In a few ways the system standouts. First, there are four sectors. There are three currencies. There are three partitions. The society is cashless. The government does not have sweeping powers to tax everything. There is only one tax. There is no inflation or business cycles of boom and recessions in three of the four sectors. Most workers own their jobs. There are also many other differences that we will discuss later.

Why is the system called "accommodation based"? As mentioned before, there are four sectors. One of them is the accommodational sector. By contributing to the economy in general, the consumerists earn profit to spend in the accommodational sector, on things like real estate, utility bills and leisure. The accommodational sector is the incentive for working.

Why is the system called "consumerism"? The system is designed to benefit the consumerist. The consumerist is the person who acquires goods and services. Everything else works directly or indirectly to benefit the consumerist. This system revolves around consumerists. Of course, producers, workers and investors are also promoted but differently.

The system has the following form. The consumerist society functions like a soccer team. The team wins games as a team regardless of who scores goals, who assists on these goals and who saves goals. Thus if the team wins the world cup, everyone on the team wins the world cup. However there are also individualistic rewards for individual players on the team. Players who score more goals are usually played more. The more saves a goalie successfully makes the more likely he is to get some kind of bonus. There are other rewards too- most valuable player, highest scorer, best rookie, etc. - which individual players dream to win. In trying to benefit the team, they also benefit themselves and in trying to benefit themselves, they benefit the team. The accommodation based consumerist system works the same way. Consumerists strive for individual wealth and in doing so increase the prosperity of the entire society. At the same time, when society's prosperity is raised all consumerists reap the rewards. This causes a spiral of prosperity that we will talk about later in detail.

These are some of the characteristics of the accommodation based consumerist system. How it works precisely follows. The following is a simplified model of the system.

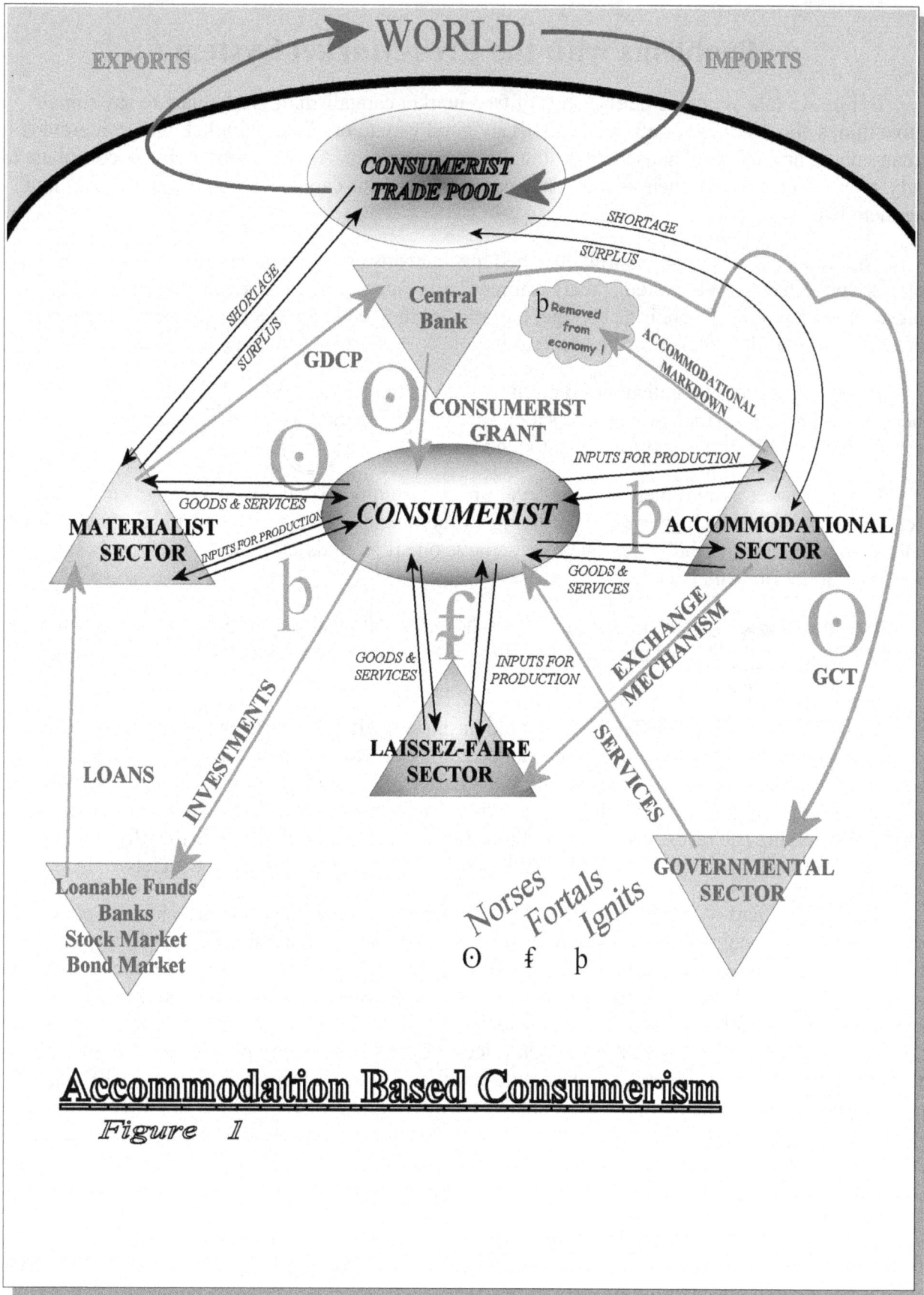

Accommodation Based Consumerism

Figure 1

Figure 1

43

Problems with the Free-Market System

Before we talk about the deficiencies of free-market capitalism, it is adequate to say some positive things about it. First of all, it is a relatively good way to organize a market. One can provide for the many needs and wants of households using the market system. As long as households contribute to society, they gain capital for their efforts. They can exchange this capital for goods and services that make them happy.

The free-market system has well designed mechanisms to fight certain kinds of shortages and surpluses. In the free-market system, "market forces" alleviate problems associated with shortages and surpluses. For example, if there is a shortage, the price of the good or service increases. If there is a surplus, the price of the good or service decreases.

Also, free-market capitalism has built in incentives to make it work. The profit motive that is the cornerstone of the free-market system gives a reason for employers to employ workers, for investors to invest, for households to buy and for banks to lend money.

In free-market nations there is some level of "opportunity". If one finds a way to contribute to society, then he can have a high standard of living. Although no one is guaranteed a high quality, happy life, there remains the possibility that one may achieve one if he finds a way how. So there is at least the hope of becoming rich and famous.

The free-market system is far from perfect, however. The majority of economists agree that there are several fundamental internal problems with the free-market system. Here we will have a look at them.

Perhaps the most profound difficulty is the business cycle. There seems to be a never ending cycle of recessions and booms. A recession is an economic downturn where the G.D.P., that is the general output of the economy, decreases over two quarters. A boom is a period where the economy gains momentum over two quarters. Recessions are bad for everyone; workers, capitalists, consumers and the government. The recessions are periodic and unavoidable. All we know is that they will happen sometime. No one has yet found a way to stop the business cycle in a free-market society.

The scariest part of the free-market is the existence of depressions. A depression is a period of time in which the economy falls into severe trouble. Besides war, a depression is one of the greatest forms of man-made misery. Unemployment skyrockets. The output of the economy crashes greatly. Stock prices drop tremendously. Businesses close or lose a lot of money and many banks go under. Real G.D.P. fell by around 30% in most countries between 1929 and 1933. In Canada, unemployment rose by 25 %. Price levels decreased by 15% and stock prices dropped 90%. Many people who lost everything committed suicide. Usually depressions last quite a while. The Great Depression of the 1930's lasted almost 10 years. There is no natural mechanism to get out of a severe depression. In systems other than the free-market, depressions and business cycles do not occur, indicating that these are free-market phenomenon. The frightening thing about the modern free-market system is that we do not know when the next depression will hit and whether or not it will be more severe than the one in the 1930's.

The free-market system, left to its own devices, quite often fails to give an equitable distribution of well being. The free-market system promotes those that have the ability to provide goods and services that other people will compensate for these things. The free-market system does not assure that all people's quality of life is equal. For example, the managers of companies have a higher standard of living than artists like musicians and writers who are not well known.   (Kneebone, R.D. 2002)

The free-market has a stock market with several problems. It is guided by the forces of supply and demand and the prices of stock can increase or decrease. This leads to the possibility of a crash or a sudden drop in prices. If this happens, stocks loose all their value and investors loose all their money. Something similar happened during the great depression. A tremendous stock market crash can wreck havoc on an economy.

All economists agree that monopolies in a free-market system are a problem. A monopoly is a firm or organization that doesn't have much competition in terms of providing a good or service. A monopoly provides an inefficient amount of a good or a service than it would if the market were more competitive. We say that there is "dead weight loss". That is, the economy looses production compared to what is otherwise achievable. Also a monopoly confers tremendous profit to the owner. There is a debate as to how this profit should be distributed. Monopolies produce difficulties in the free-market system.

Some contend that the free-market system contributed to the start of the Second World War. The war was about more than power. It was about money and economic domination. Each of the nations that fought wanted more money and going to war was a method for attaining that purpose. The Second World War was brought about at least in part by economic factors.

Sometimes the forces of supply and demand lead to economic absurdity. In Brazil, some coffee growers have destroyed their crops so as to raise the price of their coffee. Yet there are 100's of millions of people in third world countries that can only dream of coffee. In general, in the free-market, producers often restrict the supply of the product to raise its price, often by destroying the product. The people who lose out are those who do not get the good.

Few people who pay taxes actually like doing so yet the existence of taxes is a necessary part of the free-market system. Many people think that they are unavoidable. Hard working people pay a lot of their earnings in the form of taxes. There are several dozens of ways that the government has cleverly devised to steal people's money. Taxes also hurt the economy as they cause deadweight losses. Although it is impossible to avoid paying taxes in a free-market system, it is not impossible to get rid of them in another economic system.

Under the free-market system, only those things that can be marketed are produced. There is a general loss of philosophy, art, poetry, music and culture. Many public things are not provided without aid from the government. We lose the priceless things that give society its beauty.

Exchange rate crises are possible under the free-market system. In an exchange rate crisis, due to speculation, a currency is forced to be devalued or the interest rate drastically increased, thus destroying the economy. Exchange rate crisis have destroyed many currencies and have broken up many unions including the European Monetary Fund. This is a serious problem of the free-market system.

We now point out the Communist objection to the free-market system. Communists argue that workers are exploited. This applies especially to workers in the third world. Some workers earn only enough to subsist. Communists point out that workers work extremely hard, under inhuman conditions and get next to nothing for it. Meanwhile the capitalists keep all the profit. This was certainly true during the birth of the industrial revolution. Yet there are still sweat shops in poor countries where little children are forced to work.

Poverty exists in all free-market countries. There is a group, the poor, who lead miserable lives and cannot enjoy the same goods and services as their neighbors. Although the suffering is bad in itself, these people sometimes resort to crimes like robbery and drug trafficking to provide for themselves. The free-market economy always has an impoverished group.

Unemployment plagues most free-market systems. People have no work and fall into poverty. In most economies, unemployment is possible but not that dangerous if it is small. If the unemployment rises over 20%, then the economy is in bad shape. Unemployment can ruin the lives of the unemployed in particular and society in general. The unemployed lose their self worth in addition to their income. Certainly, the existence of unemployment is a failure of the free-market system.

A very important problem of the free-market economic system is that there is market failure. In some cases these appear as externalities and market power. Externalities are of the positive and negative type. A good example of a positive externality is a researcher producing a new model of a disease that helps many people. An example of a negative externality is a production facility that produces many cars and car parts but also gives off green house gases. These two examples are troublesome from an effectivity and efficiency perspective (Kneebone R.D. 2002)

Inflation exists in the free-market system. In some cases inflation can be excessively great as has occurred in the German economy in the early 1920's, where the Mark decreased in value millions of percent. The well known Phillips curve tells us that there exists a trade-off in the short run between unemployment and inflation. Clearly, under capitalism, in the short run, we must choose between inflation and high unemployment. Clearly this is a fault of the free-market system.

A free-market system can be destroyed or crippled by bank runs. A bank run is the occurrence when people want their money from the bank and the bank doesn't have it, resulting in the collapse of all firms the bank lent to. If a bank run happens, everyone loses. The possibility of a bank run is a critical fault of the free-market system.

A free-market economy can experience stagflation. Stagflation is the occurrence of both high unemployment and high inflation. It brings only misery to all those involved. Stagflation sometimes persists for quite a while before it is fixed. It exists specifically in the free-market system.

We saw the problems of the free-market system. We saw why certain issues are problematic. In designing our system, we must not have these problems in our economy.

Problems with the Command System

Before talking about the faults of the command system it is good to point out some positive attributes of the command system. This system allows the central planners to focus on the production of any good it sees necessary to make. If the central planners want to make more cars, they can use workers to make them. If they want to make more farms, they can use workers to make them.

A positive attribute of the command system is the strong social net. Although the odds are high against you being extremely rich, the command system is designed so you do not become overwhelmingly in need of goods and services. Almost everyone has enough to subsist. The command system is designed so that no one is impoverished.

The command system does not have a business cycle like the one in the free-market system. There does not exist a perpetual cycle of booms, downturns, recessions and expansions. Thus it appears that the economy is always growing. In fact of all major nations, the USSR was the only one to avoid the economic collapse of the 1920's.

Clearly most households organize themselves under some kind of mutual general command system. Someone does the dishes, someone vacuums, someone cooks dinner, and someone walks the dog while someone else does the grocery shopping. The household works for the greater common good of the family and benefit of everyone and everyone works together. It would be problematic if everyone in the family charged for their contribution to the household. Someone would not make lunch unless they were paid 6.00$ a plate. The kids would not make their beds unless they were paid 4.00$ for making their beds. And whoever walks the dog would not do so until he was paid 5.00 $ for doing so. Clearly, most households are organized under a mutual command system. The main problem occurs when the command system generalizes to too many people; i.e. it gets too big. In such case, problems of greed make it less effective than it is in theory.

Now it is time to make a critique of the command system. The point here is to expose the weaknesses of the command system. We will examine the problems of the command system one by one.

About a century ago in some places people thought the command system was a brilliant idea. There was constant talk of revolution. Some proclaimed that once the capitalists were gotten rid of and workers were given power, everything would be better. Yet they did not know how everything would be better. There wasn't a coherent, well thought out plan of an economic system. All there was, was rhetoric.

It was as if the communists were expecting a baby. They thought that as soon as the baby was born everything would all of a sudden change and life would be better. But having a baby requires having responsibility and work and things weren't all that rosy.

Communism may have worked on paper but not in reality. It wasn't practical. Most of the countries that have experimented with it have seen its folly. Most of them have collapsed. Among these were the Soviet Union and the Eastern European countries.

Communism puts the community before the individual. If one has the greatest, strongest, most powerful and influential ship on the sea, it is of little good if the crew is miserable, hungry and sick. The needs of the individual are the most important. A community with happy, well off people is happy and well off because then the people have something to defend and the will to defend it.

Communism has another fault. People do not succeed due to merit or hard work. They succeed due to political shrewdness. An uncreative, uneducated, lazy man can become the owner of a factory just because he has friends in important political positions. People advance for the wrong reason.

One very important element is missing in the command system. This is incentive. People need an incentive to work and be efficient. This the command system lacks. It assumes that people will operate unselfishly.

Communism is both inefficient and ineffective at a grand level. The central planners are not able to effectively deal with shortages and surpluses. The central planners are unable to respond to the demands of the people. Things are produced that no one needs and things that people need are not produced. The resources and inputs are mismanaged. They are not used to the maximum potential or are overused.

Coordinating all production in a large country under the command system is extremely hard or even impossible. The literally millions upon millions of production decisions cannot be practically made by a central government. The management of all economic decisions under a command system is inefficient and impractical.

We saw some of the issues that make the command system in general and communism specifically, troublesome. We discussed why they are so. In designing our system we must be careful that we do not run into any of these problems. However it is a good idea to borrow some of the positive ideas of the command system.

Benefits of Consumerism

There are several benefits that consumerism has over the free-market and command systems. Here we give a brief description of them. The rest of the treatise is dedicated to explaining the consumerist system.

In consumerism we incorporate the positive attributes of free-market and socialist paradigms. Meanwhile, we discard all the problems and discrepancies these two economic systems have. Of course, as we shall see, there is a lot more to accommodation based consumerism than free-market and socialist ideas. The majority of this system is founded on new concepts.

In accommodation based consumerism there is no material poverty. The central bank grants money (Norses) to all members of society regardless of their occupation. Those not working or not in the work force are granted less money to give them an incentive to find work. Those in institutions are not granted money as they are taken care of directly by transfers from the government. The working all receive the same amount if they contribute over a certain threshold to the economy. There is no gap between the rich and the poor (materially speaking) as long as they are working.

There is no inflation or deflation and prices in 3 of the 4 sectors cannot increase or decrease. They are fixed permanently by the central bank. The central bank cannot print money at random like in the free-market system. All prices and wages remain fixed.

There is no business cycle. The free-market experiences business cycles because at the boom demand outstrips the supply and inflation starts rising rapidly. To combat this, the free-market central bank raises interest rates to offset the rising inflation and a recession starts. With no inflation possible, the possibility of a recession evaporates. The free-market business cycle of recession and expansion does not exist. The business cycle is replaced by the consumerist spiral of prosperity. At the point where the demand begins to outstrip the supply, instead of their being inflation, there is a surge in the supply side. The economy works like a tornado, constantly perpetuating itself. The more people buy, the more people sell, the more people make money and more people receive goods and services. The economy grows exponentially. First it grows quite slowly. As soon as it picks up momentum, it grows at a faster and faster rate. This effect will be discussed in detail later.

In the free-market economy, a lot of students are infuriated about ever increasing tuition costs for their education. In consumerism tuition is paid by the government. The government of a consumerist nation, whether federal or provincial, pays for a student's education. Education at all levels is free.

There are no real taxes in consumerism. The money the government earns does not come out of anyone's pockets. There are no corporate, income, property or sales taxes. The government does need money but it receives it not from consumerists but from the central bank. The average person does not pay taxes to the government.

There are two general types of stock markets. The consumerist stock market, due to the way it is set up, cannot collapse. All stocks in the "market" are of the same price regardless of the firm they are from and how many shares the firm issued. Prices do not fluctuate. If they do not fluctuate, they cannot depreciate in value and hence the stock market cannot crash.

It is impossible to lose money while investing in the consumerist stock market. All investors earn a profit from stocks via dividends based on the profit of the firm and how much of the total shares an investor has. In a free-market society, if a firm bankrupts the investor who had the company's stock loses all his money. However in the consumerist society if a firm bankrupts it has to pay the investors the value of the shares they own, essentially buying them back. If it doesn't have the money after selling off its assets, a bankruptcy insurance firm steps in to pay the investors.

There can be no depression. An essential part of a depression is a decrease in prices and wages. Since wages and prices are fixed, there cannot be a depression. Depressions are impossible.

The goods and services are of the highest quality. There is an incentive for producers to produce goods of the finest quality. Since all prices for a type of good are fixed the net effect is that most people have luxurious goods and top quality professional services. This is called *quality selection*.

The consumerists are granted money from the central bank. They are granted this money for being citizens. They can spend it on goods and services they desire in the materialist sector. This includes things like TV's, cars, clothes and pets. Why do they receive this? So they can have the best life possible.

Consumerism does not resort to the rhetoric of a revolution. This treatise is a rather complete description of a consumerist society, omitting only specific details. It does not promote revolution but suggests an alternative economic system which intelligent people will judge to be better than anything before it. Consumerism appeals to reason whereas the communist system appeals to rhetoric and emotion.

The individual is put ahead of the state. The most important maxim of the system is that the quality of life and well being of the consumerist should be increased. Everything is done to help the consumerist. The state is only as valuable as its people. Merits are rewarded. Those that put effort into life and help society are those that get ahead. Political shrewdness isn't much of an asset as this system is workable with democracy. The right qualities of a person are rewarded.

The idea of an incentive to motivate people to work and be efficient and productive is present in consumerism. The incentive is the profit motive. The higher one's contribution to society, the more profit one earns for the accommodational sector and laissez-faire sectors to buy things like houses or vacations. The more someone contributes to society, the more prosperous he is in terms of the accommodational and laissez-faire sectors.

The problems that result from grand central planning like shortages and misallocation of resources do not exist. Firms are the means of production. Firms will ensure that resources are used as best as possible. The means of production are used more effectively when in the hands of firms as opposed to the hands of central planners. However the benefits of central planning are extracted when we put normally idle workers to work to counteract unemployment.

A monopoly is not that much of a problem in consumerism. The reason being that the prices charged by monopolists are, like all other prices, fixed. The monopolist cannot charge any price he wants. Thus there is less deadweight loss. In consumerism a monopoly is just like any other firm except that it has no competitors.

The laws of supply and demand do not apply to consumerism in 3 of the 4 sectors. The absurdities relating to them do not exist. The case of Brazilian coffee growers would be resolved differently in consumerism. The prices of the coffee beans would be the same regardless of supply and demand and thus none of the crops would be destroyed. If there are too many coffee beans, they would be exported to countries that need them.

The fine things in life are kept alive by the government. The government sponsors art, philosophy and poetry through the command partition. In a free-market economy they would not exist yet we would be at a loss to lose them.

Exchange rate crisis do not occur. The exchange rate is not determined by the market. It is calculated using real exchange rates and the amount of goods being traded between two countries.

Workers are not exploited. Firms cannot pay their workers whatever they wish. The central bank determines each worker's wage. These wages are designed such that at the least each worker gets by. In other jobs workers can make a handsome profit. This is the communist objection to the free-market system and here it disappears.

There is no disparity between the wages of women and men. All wages are set by the central bank. A worker, whether a woman or a man, receives the same pay for doing the same job. There is no economic discrimination by sex in consumerism.

Unemployment is minimized. Employers have an added incentive to hire new workers. Workers buy jobs from their employers and are guaranteed a certain salary. Firms are paid a bonus from the government for making a profit thus attracting more firms to the consumerist nation and providing more work. The government reimburses a portion of a worker's wages so that firms have a greater incentive to hire more people. Due to these measures and several more that will be discussed in detail later unemployment should be drastically reduced.

Bank runs are impossible. In order for there to be a bank run, people must want their money from a bank. But consumerism is a cashless society. There is no money in cash (paper bills) or coins. All currency is in bank accounts and saving accounts. Therefore there cannot be bank runs.

These are the benefits of consumerism. They stand opposed to the problems of the communist and free-market systems. In the rest of this exposition we will explore these benefits in greater detail.

Axis 1: The Consumerist Quatrotomy

A key feature of this system is that it is divided into four major sectors- accommodational, materialist, laissez-faire and governmental. Although there is only one economy, there are four separate semi-independent sectors. It is this setup that makes this system unique.

The communist system has one sector. Everything is run by the government. Communism and the variations of socialism subscribe to such an arrangement. This type of system is characterized by central planning.

The free-market system has two sectors. These are the private and public sectors. The private sector consists of all firms and enterprises owned by persons or shareholders trying to make a profit. In contrast, the public sector is there to provide services that the private sector could not. The public sector functions to promote the well being of society rather than a single person. Things like the army and schools are in the public sector. A two sector economy is the cornerstone for all modern free-market and mixed economies.

If society could produce everything how would it produce it? In order for there to be goods and services in an economy, someone must produce them. But in a Utopia people can have everything without working. If no one works nothing could be produced and therefore a Utopia is impossible.

Now the question is how to give people as many goods and services as possible? People must work and they must have an incentive to work in order to produce these goods and services. The solution is accomplished by dividing the economy into sectors. One sector, the materialist sector provides materialist goods and services to consumerists as much as possible. The governmental sector provides government services and goods to consumerists. These goods and services in the governmental sector are such that they are provided best publicly. The accommodational sector as well as the laissez-faire sector give consumerists the incentive to contribute to society through either the materialist, governmental, accommodational or laissez-faire sectors. This is the consumerist quatrotomy.

When the system is being applied in an actual setting, that is a country adopts the system, it is important to understand the relative sizes of the four sectors. The most efficient and productive possibility is where:

materialist sector > accommodational sector > governmental sector > laissez faire sector

Ideally, either the materialist sector or accommodational sectors should be the largest. The governmental sector should be third in relative size while the laissez-faire sector should be the smallest. Such an arrangement will allow us to make do with only one tax – the Grand Consumerist Tax. If we have a smaller materialist sector and a proportionally larger laissez-faire sector, then it is necessary to create "creative taxes" (for example income tax and corporate tax) on the accommodational and laissez-faire sectors and complicate the system.

Nevertheless, the relative sizes of the four sectors can be manipulated to whatever the founding fathers – and thus the government- desire. Although, ideally, either the materialist or accommodational sectors should be the biggest, it is quite possible that the laissez-faire sector could be the largest. The laissez-faire sector could compromise anywhere from 5 % to 95 % of the economy. Clearly, if the government finds a system organized by the laws of supply and demand favorable, they will opt for a very large laissez faire sector and keep the other 3 sectors much smaller.

Although the founding fathers of the system have the final say as to the relative sizes of the four sectors, we can make several good suggestions. The lassez-faire sector should be 5 to 20 percent of the overall economy. The governmental sector should be about 10 to 25 percent of the economy. The materialist sector should be about 25 to 55 percent of the economy whereas the accomodational sector should be about 25 to 55 percent of the economy.

Of the four sectors we can group three together as they are of a somewhat different nature than the fourth. We will call the governmental, accommodational and materialist sectors the *GAM sectors* in distinction from the Laissez-faire sector. In the GAM sectors prices and wages are set by the central bank while in the laissez-faire sector they are set by the interaction of firms and consumerists. Also inflation is a real problem in the laissez-faire sector as opposed to the GAM sectors.

Accommodation based consumerism must allow the possibility for extreme "richness" and be seen as a land of opportunity. All consumerists that contribute to the economy, regardless of what sector of the economy, earn Ignits that have the potential of being converted into Fortals. Those that find a way to contribute, earn more and more of these types of money. So some people have the opportunity of living in enormous mansions (palaces), taking extremely pleasant and lengthy vacations and wear the most expansive jewelry.

We saw that the accommodation based consumerist system is divided into four sectors and why. In the following sections we will see what we mean by materialist goods and services, governmental goods and services and accommadational goods and services and laissez-faire goods and services.

Axis II: The Consumerist Trichotomy

Besides dividing the economy into four sectors, we can divide it into three partitions. The three partitions of the accommodation based consumerist economic system are the governmental partition, the natural partition and the command partition. All three are equally important for a properly functioning accommodation based consumerist economic system.

The governmental sector and governmental partition are one. The idea behind the governmental partition/sector is to provide services that are best provided by a general public entity rather than a private firm or enterprise. Good examples include health care; that is medical services for all consumerists and the police service that protects all consumerists. There are many others. These types of services are better provided publicly; that is by a centralized system rather than a profit maximizing entity.

The natural partition is by far the largest part of the consumerist economic system. The natural partition involves firms trying to earn a profit in the materialist, accommodational and laissez-faire sectors. The essence of the natural partition is that the means of production is organized in the hands of firms. These firms have constraints that are set by the central bank and government; for example wage functions, input functions and price functions (in the materialist and accommodational sectors) but in the end they want to earn a profit.

The command partition is a special part of the accommodation based consumerist system. It involves the same sectors and industries under the direction of the natural partition. The main difference is that these businesses are under the control of a centralized government entity called the *Human Resource Management Commission (HRMC)*. The main purpose of this partition is to give employment to individuals that cannot find a job under the natural partition and the governmental partition, and who would otherwise be unemployed and not doing anything productive. The profits from the command partition go directly to the government as an alternative source of revenue and this helps fund social programs like health care, defense and education. Furthermore if organizations run by the command partition function in the materialist sector, this is good because it increases the consumerist grant given to working and non working consumerists as well as adding to the Grand Consumerist Tax. More on this later.

All three partitions are important. The governmental partition functions to provide services that are best provided publicly. The other two partitions do not differentiate as to what goods and services are provided to consumerists. Rather the difference between these two partitions is how goods and services are provided to consumerists. In the natural partition goods and services are provided by profit maximizing firms. In the command partition goods and services are provided by organizations whose goal is to provide employment for consumerists as well as making a profit.

The laissez-faire, materialist and accommodational sectors can be either in the natural or command partition. Thus there is a natural-laissez faire sector, a natural-accommodational sector, a natural-materialist sector, a command-laissez-faire sector, a command-accommodational sector and a command-materialist sector.

Thus there are three partitions in accommodation based consumerism. Each gives a means of providing goods and services. Dividing accommodation based consumerism into partitions is a good way to organize it.

The Materialist Sector

The materialist sector is one of the four sectors of the consumerist economy. It is identified as everything non-governmental that does not belong to the accommodational/laissez-faire sectors. This sector has the distinguishing feature that consumerists receive the goods and services in this sector just for being consumerists. Each working consumerist regardless of age, sex or profession receives Norses (Θ), one of the currencies from the central bank to exchange for anything they desire in this sector. The non working non institutionalized consumerists also receive Norses from the central bank but a little bit less. They must be granted less in order to maintain an incentive to work. Every working consumerist – that contributes to society above a threshold- is granted an equal amount of Norses and all non-working non-institutionalized consumerists are also granted an equal amount of Norses relative to one another. No one is left with an absence of money.

In this section we attempt to analyze the materialist sector. However due to the enormous multitude of goods and services in this sector in existence, this analysis will not be exhaustive. First let's list the industries in the materialist sector. They are:

Transportation

Apparel

Hospitality

Entertainment

Information

Synthetics

Hygiene

Educational

Furniture

Medical

Now let's list some of the categories in each industry. Note that this is neither complete nor exhaustive.

1) Transportation- automobile, passenger movement

2) Apparel- clothes, foot wear, swim wear, winter wear, costume

3) Hospitality- restaurant food, grocery food

4) Entertainment- electronic entertainment, social entertainment

5) Information- electronic, written, media

6) Synthetics- cleaning, building

7) Hygiene- oral, facial, internal

8) Educational- scientific, literary, school, personal knowledge

9) Furniture- dining, sleeping, studying, relaxation

10) Medical- drugs

Here is a list of goods and services that could be found in the materialist sector. Once again this list is neither exhaustive nor is it of necessity.

- running shoes

- widescreen TV

- CD player

- radio

- PC computer

- lab top computer

- a bed

- dishwashing liquid

- insect repellent

- a sports car

- a jet

- a dog

- a winter jacket

- a T-shirt

- a piece of paper

- a spoon

- a desk

- a pair of jeans

- plates

- a map

- a cup of coffee

- a bowl of spaghetti

- a pizza

- a bowl of soup

- a cat

- a guitar

- a pair of skis

- a tape

- a doughnut

- a carton of eggs

- a jug of milk

We have talked about the materialist sector of the economy. We gave some examples of industries, categories and products and services in this sector. It is important to note that these lists were neither complete nor total. What is important is that the division of industries and categories among sectors is not fixed. It is up to the government of a consumerist nation to define the division between the materialist, accommodational, laissez-faire and governmental sectors. We have just provided a workable yet effective setup.

The Accommodational Sector

The next sector of the consumerist economy is the accommodational sector. To give people an incentive to work and produce goods and services they must earn something that is proportional to their contributions to the economy. We must come up with certain goods and services that people would be willing to work for as a reward for their contribution to society. As consumerists exchange the Norses they obtained from the central bank for goods and services in the materialist sector, those that produce these goods and services or helped to do so earn Ignits, one of the other currencies. The same concept applies to the governmental sector. For working for the government and serving the public, people earn Ignits. Likewise for the accommodational sector- those that contribute to it earn Ignits. With these Ignits consumerists purchase goods and services made available in the accommodational sector.

What are the goods and services in the accommodational sector? The most important is land. Almost every war in history was fought over land. World War II saw the Germans taking over land by attacking their neighbors. WWI was also about land as hundreds of thousands of soldiers died for only several miles in the western front. The Napoleonic wars and the crusades were focused on the acquisition of land from others. Even in ancient times, wars were aged over land. The Romans expanded their vast empire by subduing their neighbors. It seems like land is highly valued and it would be reasonable to include it as one of the rewards for contributing to society.

Another important part of the accommodation sector is accommodation (hence the name). In any system, accommodation, the place one lives in, is the most expensive possession one owns and it should be something to work for. Those who work hard and produce a lot for society live in large mansions while those who do not have to settle for apartment buildings. Accommodation is the essence of the accommodational sector and is the reason for the name of the system itself.

To make sure that everyone participates in contributing to the economy, it would be good to include the utility industry in the accommodational sector. Since the utility industry is so essential, including it under the accommodational sector will surely motivate even the least hard working consumerist into action.

The leisure industry is also included in the accommodational sector. This means that the more productive workers have the better vacations. All consumerists want some enjoyment in life and some time to relax; not just work all the time. To have a chance to "get away from it all", the consumerist must contribute to society.

The appliance and home accessory industries are affiliated with the accommodation sector. This means that in order to have a stove, microwave or a washing machine one must contribute to society. To improve the accommodation one lives in- by buying paint, carpet or wall paper- one must contribute to society. The appliance and home accessory industries are good motivators for working unless someone doesn't mind living without vital possessions like an oven and a dishwasher.

All business interactions are considered part of the accommodational sector. This includes paying workers, purchasing firms, factories or stores as well as buying consumerist stock. All of the financial industry, with several notable exceptions, is affiliated with the accommodational sector.

Since adult entertainment is strictly pleasure it would make more sense to include it in the accommodational rather than materialist sectors. Adults who enjoy this type of entertainment should be given it the more they contribute to society. People who desire this commodity should work for it. In order to obtain adult entertainment some people would work very hard. Thus they will contribute to society.

Finally we have alcohol and tobacco. This is also something few people really need but some enjoy it once in a while or a little more often. It would also make more sense to put this under the accommodational rather than the materialist sector. If a heavy smoker doesn't have cigarettes he will work very hard to buy them. Thus to buy them he works and contributes to society.

The exact definition of the "accommodation sector" is hard to find as the industries in the sector are quite varied. Initially it was meant to be a sector having to do with "accommodation". That is, the things having to do with living arrangements. Eventually other industries like the leisure industries were added in order to strike a balance between the accommodational and materialist sectors. Now the only thing that the industries under the accommodational sector have in common is the fact that Ignits as a currency are used. This will have to suffice as a definition.

The main industries in the accommodational sector are:

- Land

- Accommodation

- Utility

- Appliances

- Home accessories

- Leisure

- Financial

- Adult entertainment

- Alcohol and tobacco

Here is a list of some of the categories under some of the industries. This list is not exhaustive as there could be more categories that are not mentioned.

- Land- agricultural, residential, industrial, commercial, recreational

- Accommodation- house, apartment, condominium, mansion

- Utility- household utility, entertainment utility

- Appliances- laundry appliance, kitchen appliance, household appliance

- Home accessory- floor furnishings, decorational items, lights, wall furnishings

- Leisure- domestic vacation, international vacation

- Financial- stock market, bond market, banking, wages, salaries, corporate

- Adult entertainment- video, magazine

- Alcohol & Tobacco- tobacco, alcohol

Here is a list of a number of goods and services found in the accommodational sector. This list does not include everything and could be slightly altered depending on how the government wants to manage the economy.

- a bungalow

- a palace

- a mansion

- a condominium

- an apartment building

- industrial land

- residential land

- commercial land

- rural land

- electricity

- hot water

- heating

- a dishwasher

- an oven

- a washing machine

- a drier

- a carpet

- a rug

- lamps

- yellow paint

- wall paper

- tiles

- floor

- windows

- plumbing service

- Jacuzzi

- cable setup

- shower head

- new faucet

- drapes

- a trip to Jamaica

- a trip to France

- stay at a hotel

- visit to a spa

- visit to an amusement park

- visit to a circus

- visit to a movie theatre

- visit to a rock concert

- purchase of consumerist stock

- purchase of a consumerist bond

We examined the accommodational sector. We described why certain industries should belong to this sector rather than the materialist one. We listed the categories in each industry. Finally we listed a number of goods and services that might be found in this sector.

The Governmental Sector/Partition

The governmental sector is one of the four sectors of the accommodation based consumerist economy. With a number of important differences, it is similar to the free-market public sector. The governmental sector can also be conceptualized as the governmental partition.

There are three levels of government- federal/central, provincial/state and municipal. There are several revenue streams for the various levels of government. One way the government makes money is by taking a percentage of the Gross Domestic Consumerist Product- what this is will be explained shortly. The percentage that is taxed is spread equally among the three levels of government. The government can be of any political alignment. It could be very socialist or it could be very right wing (conservative). The percentage of the Gross Domestic Consumerist Product (GDCP) that is taxed is reflective of the political ideology. A socialist government would tax a higher percentage and provide many social services for its people. A right wing government would tax very little of the GDCP and let the various firms in the economy provide goods and services. There are also governments in between. The government that is elected (assuming we have a democracy) decides how socialist or right wing the government is. This depends upon the wishes of the people.

There are many services that the government is supposed to provide. As consumerists, everyone deserves access to 1) free health care, 2) free education and 3) free clean drinking water. Of course there are a lot more that could be added to this short list. However these are among the most basic.

The governmental sector provides certain goods and services for consumerists. We will talk about them shortly. First we must discuss the source of revenue of the three levels of the government. One source of revenue depends on the output of the materialist sector called the GDCP. The government puts a tax on this called the Grand Consumerist Tax (GCT). We will talk about the determination of the Grand Consumerist Tax in another section. Suppose that the GDCP is 15, 000 Θ and the GCT is 30% Therefore 4, 500 Θ go to the government. The central government receives 1/3 of this. The provincial/state governments receive 1/3 of this based on their populations. The municipal governments also receive 1/3 of this based on their populations. Thus in our example the federal government receives 1, 500 Θ. There are five provinces. They have populations of 10 000, 20 000, 30 000, 40 000 and 50 000. The 1, 500 Θ is spent among the provinces in a ratio of 1:2:3:4:5. The provinces with the greatest populations receive the most and the provinces with the least people receive the least. The same applies to the municipalities but is a bit more complicated. The 1, 500 Θ is split according to population. Each municipality receives a percentage of the 1, 500 Θ equal to the percentage of the population of the whole country that the municipality has. For example there are, for simplicity, ten municipalities. They have populations in terms of percentage of the whole country equal to 10%, 20%, 5%, 5%, 10%, 30%, 5%, 5%, 5%, 5%. The municipality with 30 % of the country's population receives 30 % of the revenue for the municipalities or 450 Θ. The municipality with 5% of the country's population receives 5 % of the tax for municipalities.

The 3 levels of government function with all three types of currency. They function with Norses and Ignits and when there is a source of revenue in the form of Fortals, these are converted to Ignits. So the government can pay for services in different ways. Here's an example: If the federal government has 10 000 000.00 Θ and wants to pay for a hospital, the Norses are converted to Ignits to pay those who build the hospital and those who operate it. So the 10 000 000.00 Θ are deducted from the governments bank entry and the equivalent of Ignits is added to the bank accounts of those who built the hospital. In the case when the government has 10 000 000.00 þ, they can pay directly as the 10 000 000.00 þ are deducted from the government's Ignit account and the equivalent in the form of Ignits is added to the bank accounts of those who created the hospital. If the government has Fortals to spend, these are first exchanges to Ignits and with these the government pays for services.

There is something called the Inter-Governmental Transfer. This means that one level of government can give money to another level of government. If the federal government made an abundance of money it can give some of it to a province that is running into debt. Also, the provincial government can transfer some money to municipalities within the province if they are short in money.

Now we present the industries that are found in the governmental sector. They are

- education

- health

- protection/defense

- parks and recreation

- water/sanitation

- support services

- infrastructure

- public transport

- research

- community centers

- land marks

- beurocracy

We try to list some categories of goods and services that belong to the governmental sector. However trying to list all categories would be too tedious. A word of note: The industries and categories presented here as being under the governmental sector need not necessarily be so. This is a proposition. In a real application, the governmental sector would be relatively bigger under a quasi-socialist society and relatively smaller under a quasi-free-market society. So it is possible that some of the industries or categories of goods and services will be found under the accommodational, laissez-faire or materialist sector. Also some industries may have goods and services that are in different sectors. For example, an elementary education would be found under the governmental sector while a karate school would be under the materialist sector

- Education- elementary, secondary, post secondary

- Health- treatment facilities, medical procedures, information

- Protection/Defense- internal defense, external defense

- Parks and Recreation- parks, nature trails

- Water/ Sanitation- water purification, water recycling, solid waste management

- Support services- youth programs, transfer payments to needy

- Infrastructure-public transportation infrastructure, pedestrian transportation infrastructure

- Public Transport- public human transport

- Research- medical research, scientific research, military research

- Community Centers- information centers, sports centers

- Land Marks- statues, buildings, sights which attract tourists

- Beurocracy- parliament members, government officials, social servants

Here is a list of several goods and services that belong to the governmental sector:

- sidewalks

- roads

- hospitals

- a fountain

- a statue of a famous person

- a library

- a swimming pool

- a heart transplant

- physical rehabilitation services

- kidney transplant operation and nursing

- bus transportation

- trains

- AIDS research institute

- payment to mayor

- payment to members of government

- research into more accurate theories of the universe

- courthouse

- judges salary

- medium security correctional facility

- garbage pickup

- recycling services

- water purification

- operation of an elementary school

- operation of a secondary school

- national defense

- police officers

- fire fighting officers

- benches

- street lights

- pension plan

- welfare payments

- parks

This is not an exhaustive list nor is it a list of necessity. There are many goods and services not mentioned here. Also there are many goods and services here that the government in power could move to one of the other three sectors.

Each level of government has different responsibilities. The services provided are peculiar to a level of government. However we will not mention which industries or categories are under the jurisdiction of which hierarchy of government. This is more of a matter for politics than economics.

Some services provided through the governmental sector could be classified as "government assisted" services. These include public transit (buses, trains, and underground railway), passes to the skating rink or swimming pool, access to public galleries and museums, application for driver's license or passport and several others. The government has two options. It can give access to these without payment. In that case, consumerists do not have to pay to board a bus or train or visit the museum. Also the government can charge consumerists for access to these services. However the government provides government assisted services depends on the wishes of the government and the people.

We talked about the governmental sector of the accommodation based consumerist economic system. We talked about the sources of revenue for the levels of government. We also talked about which categories belong to which industries in this sector. We ended with a short list of several goods and services that could belong to this sector.

The Laissez-Faire Sector

The laissez-faire sector is one of the key sectors of the accommodation based consumerist economy. Amongst other things, it is distinguished because it has a separate currency and prices are dictated by supply and demand, thus leaving the possibility of inflation. The means of production in the laissez-faire sector is in the hands of profit maximizing firms.

In the laissez faire sector we have things that it does not make sense to fix price functions. Quality selection- this term will be discussed shortly- is not feasible and it is simply better to price goods and services using the laws of supply and demand. Instead of having prices determined by the central bank, prices are set by free-market forces.

Under this sector we have things like paintings, precious metals, gold, silver, antiques and jewelry. These are part of the laissez-faire sector. The same goes for tips for waitresses, donations for charities, gifts, books, collector's items and memorabilia like hockey cards. How do we fix a price function for art (paintings)? Can we compare a 3rd graders picture (or an art students) to a Leonardo da Vinci or a Picasso? It is better to use the market forces of supply and demand. Speculative stocks and speculative bonds are also in the laissez-faire sector.

The prices of antiques, paintings, etc... are determined by the interaction of consumerists and producers via the laws of supply and demand. The higher the price, the lower the quantity demanded but the higher the supply. The lower the price the higher the demand and lower supply.

Bankruptcy insurance is part of the laissez-faire sector. Firms compete to insure companies so more "risky" firms have to pay more to be insured. As stated in other sections when a company bankrupts, first all of its assets are liquidated and then the bankruptcy insurance firm steps in. This puts the default risk in the hands of the insurance company not the investor.

In the laissez-faire sector, goods should be only final goods not inputs for other goods, like for example wheat or oil. If they were inputs this would affect (fixed) prices in other sectors. Goods should only be the final goods that are directly provided to consumerists.

The laissez-faire sector should not involve markets that are monopolies or oligopolies. This would result in a monopoly with market power. Accommodation based consumerism is so arranged that all monopolies and oligopolies are in the GAM sectors where price/wage and input functions are fixed. This kills a monopoly's market power.

Generally, laissez- faire firms are those where it makes more sense for them to compete through price rather than quality. Sometimes it is hard to tell if they compete in quality (sports watches, books, and works of art). If it is possible for things to compete both in price and quality, these things are not in the laissez-faire sector but rather in the GAM sectors. However, when in doubt about fixing price functions, it is advisable to put the good or service in the Laissez-faire sector.

Merchant capitalists and those that thrive in the free-market capitalist system will really enjoy the laissez-faire sector of Accommodation Based Consumerism. The laissez-faire sector is capitalism in its purest form, where goods and services are exchanged using a pricing system based on supply and demand. However, the main advantage this sector has over capitalism in free-market countries is that in the laissez-faire sector there is no tax – no sales tax, no income tax and no corporate tax. Perhaps the only drawback is that the whole system isn't organized this way.

Some of the families of goods and services found in the laissez-faire sector include:

- actor in a TV commercial

- goalie in a NHL hockey team

- gold necklace

- stock in the speculative stock market

- bonds in the speculative bond market

- baseball card

- tips to a waitress in a French restaurant

- a monetary gift to another consumerist

- a donation to a charity that saves abused dogs

- a painting by a well known artist

- anything sold at an auction

- movie star

- silver earrings

- musician

- books

- antiques

- services of artist

- antique repair and restoration

- service of a private attorney

- comic books

- credit unions

- mortgages

- service of paralegal

- private school

- souvenirs

- mowing of neighbor's lawn

- lemonade stand

- selling chocolate bars door to door

The above list is not exhaustive. There could be many, many more families of goods and services depending on how quasi-free-market or how quasi-socialist the government is. Furthermore, some of the goods and services in the above list could be moved to another sector while other goods and services in the other 3 sectors could be brought to the laissez-faire sector.

We described briefly, how the laissez-faire sector functions. We noted its main attributes. Together with the other 3 sectors, the laissez-faire sector ensures that the consumerist economy works productively and efficiently.

The Natural Partition

As mentioned previously, there are three partitions in accommodation based consumerism. These are the governmental partition, the command partition and the natural partition. The natural partition is perhaps the largest partition in terms of how many economic transactions take place in that partition.

We define the natural partition as "all firms in the materialist, accommodational, and laissez-faire sectors trying to make a large profit, run by entrepreneurs and corporations under the stipulations of fixed price, wage and input functions in the GAM sectors and the laws of supply and demand in the laissez faire sector."

Firms in the natural partition are run by "merchant capitalists". These are individuals whose goal is to make a profit. Although there are capitalists in the free-market system, these same capitalists would find the accommodation based consumerist system, and its natural partition, preferable as there are no "disincentives" like those in the free-market system. For example, in accommodation based consumerism there does not exist corporate, sales, income, property tax or any other tax.

By definition, the natural partition does not involve the governmental sector/partition. Thus things in this partition cannot include things like hospital visits, protection from police or elementary school education. The natural partition does not involve things that would better be provided collectively by the government.

The natural partition does, however, involve things in the materialist, accommodational and laissez-faire sectors. Clearly, this involves a wide variety of industries and families of goods and services. It includes things like houses, cars, restaurants, grocery stores, clothes, toys, beer, newspapers etc. Almost everything not provided by the governmental partition can be provided via the natural partition.

The key idea behind the natural partition is that goods and services provided to consumerists are done so through profit-maximizing firms. These firms are entities that offer goods and services to consumerists while trying to maximize the difference between revenue and cost (profit) in doing so. If a firm can earn a profit while providing goods and services to consumerists it is more likely to flourish in the natural partition specifically and accommodation based consumerism in general.

All three currencies are involved in the natural partition. The natural partition can operate within the materialist, accommodational or laissez-faire sectors. Thus in the natural partition there can be Norses, Ignits or Fortals.

We introduced the natural partition of accommodation based consumerism. Of the three partitions it is the largest and most important. Most of the businesses in consumerism are part of the natural partition.

The Command Partition

The Command partition is an important section of the economy. It is essentially a branch of government that decides how to employ workers that would not normally be hired through the natural or governmental partitions. A branch of the government, we will call the Human Resource Management Commission (HRMC), has an obligation to put people to use that would otherwise be unemployed. This is similar to free-market concept of "work-fare" but taken to a much higher level.

The Command partition is linked to the Socialist Labor Pool, an important entity that will be fully described in another section. The workers that work in the Command partition are called *auxiliary workers*. These workers can work in the Materialist, Accommodational or Laissez-faire sectors but they cannot work in the governmental sector. In some sense, this has similarities to Chinese state capitalism, but it is at a much grander scale.

We previously didn't have too many positive things to say about a centrally run economic system such as the one in communist countries. True, a command economy is hard to manage on a grand scale. However, when small, it can be beneficial. Firms run through a command system can be made to produce anything that the government wants them to produce. So, if statistics show that there is a housing shortage, these firms can be used to build more apartment buildings. If it seems that people have not enough food to eat, they can set up several farms or grocery stores. Furthermore on a scale as small as a single household it actually works very well. In most families, chores and duties like vacuuming, doing the dishes and walking the dog are organized without any money being exchanged. These actions are performed through a system of mutual cooperation.

Of note is the fact that of all industrialized countries, the Soviet Union was the only one that avoided a Depression in the 1920's. Thus a command economy is incapable of having a stock market crash like other countries had.

As stated, the HRMC cannot create jobs in the government sector. Otherwise the government would cut government jobs and fill them with auxiliary workers. For example, the government would fire teachers and police officers and replace these with auxiliary workers because they get paid less.

No matter how inefficiently a government puts people to work, it is better than if these people did nothing. It is better if a 100 people dug a hole and another 100 filled it up than to have 200 people sit around and do nothing. Even if a HRMC run firm makes a profit of only 1000 þ per month, this adds up with a large number of these firms.

It is important that the HRMC enterprises are efficiently and productively run. It is common opinion that government operated institutions are very inefficient- but is this because they are run by the government or because they have poor management? It is possible that people with business knowledge may be unemployed. This refers to people with a business degree or experience in management. These people should be put in charge of running the firms we are referring to.

The HRMC creates subsidiary firms that hire auxiliary workers. These HRMC firms compete with firms in the accommodational, materialist and laissez-faire sectors that belong to the natural partition. The prices in the materialist and accommodational sectors are fixed while those in the laissez-faire sector are determined by the interaction of consumerists and firms- which in this case are HRMC firms operated in the command partition.

The Human Resource Management Commission would build factories, farms, foundries, mines, stores and use auxiliary workers as human input. If auxiliary workers would get a payment for doing nothing anyways, it is better if they did something. The profits from these HRMC enterprises go to the government budget as a profit. Thus in our system, the "welfare" system actually makes money. Also if the HRMC enterprises contribute to the output of the materialist sector, the GDCP increases, which increase the General Consumerist Grant as well as the GCT, increasing government revenue even further. We will talk more about this later.

The HRMC can create several firms that act as bankruptcy insurance firms. Thus they can affect how much businesses pay for bankruptcy insurance. So the government, in an indirect way, has some control over the bankruptcy insurance rate premium.

The HRMC represents firms that are run by an organization whose goal is to find employment for people while still making a profit. It ensures that there are no homeless. It is a program designed to give all consumerists some kind of shelter and everyone is guaranteed a job.

The mandate of the Human Resource Management Commission is to:

1) Find employment for all who seek it

2) Make a profit

3) Discourage people from belonging to the Socialist Labor Pool

No person, no matter how lazy, slow, irrational, uneducated, inexperienced or mentally ill or undeveloped shall be turned down from a job by the HRMC. The only question is what job he will be given

It is hard to coordinate an entire economy using the command system due to the many decisions that have to be made. It is more practical if we are dealing with a small portion of the population – those who cannot find jobs. If we have a country like Canada with 30, 000, 000 and 4% are unemployed after all unemployment reducing measures, this is only 1, 200, 000 people.

One of the goals of the Command partition is to create Wonders of the World. There is prestige in having the largest (tallest) building in the world, having a stadium so big that it can seat a million people, a restaurant so big that it can accommodate 100, 000 people or perhaps putting a human on Mars. There is value in some things beyond the need to satisfy the consumerists.

Those that run the Command partition have the power to assign work for a large number of workers. For example, auxiliary workers can be assigned to clean a 100 m section of a street. Their job would be to keep it totally clean and a supervisor would be assigned to make sure of that.

There are 3 levels of workers in the command partition. Level 1 workers perform jobs. Level 2 workers make sure level 1 workers do their job properly and level 3 workers make sure that level 2 workers do their job properly.

Auxiliary workers are paid by how much they work. Vs. how much they should work. If the Human Resource Management Commission sets for a worker to work 35 hours for 600 þ and 300 f and the worker works that much he gets 600 þ and 300 f. However if he works 17.5 hours (50% of what he should) he gets 300 þ and 150f. Another way of restating this is that if an auxiliary worker works, he earns 17.14 þ per hour and 8.57 ƒ per hour. So if the worker works 17.5 hours he earns 300 þ and 150 ƒ per week. Auxiliary workers are still entitled to a vacation.

Another use of the command partition is to support the arts like poetry, philosophy, music etc. In a purely free-market economy, it is very difficult for anyone to make a profit writing poetry. One has to be extremely, exceptionally good at what he does. A lot of culture is lost as brilliant philosophers, poets and musicians are forced to find work where they will make more money. Fortunately, accommodation based consumerism preserves things like poetry and philosophy. If the human resource commission comes to the conclusion that someone has the ability or aspiration for the arts then that person should spend his time in that endeavor. The alternative is that he would be receiving welfare checks for not doing anything. The only outstanding issue is how these people would be paid. Instead of paying them for the hour, it is better if they were paid weekly.

The command partition is one of the three partitions of accommodation based consumerism. Its primary goal is to find employment for workers who would otherwise be idle. It should also make some profit. Together with the natural and governmental partitions, it allows the consumerist economy to work smoothly.

Interaction of the Sectors and Partitions

The four sectors interact with the three partitions in a special way. The governmental sector and governmental partition refer to the same thing. The laissez-faire sector, the materialist sector and the accommodational sector can be in either in the command partition or the natural partition. The following diagram illustrates the concept:

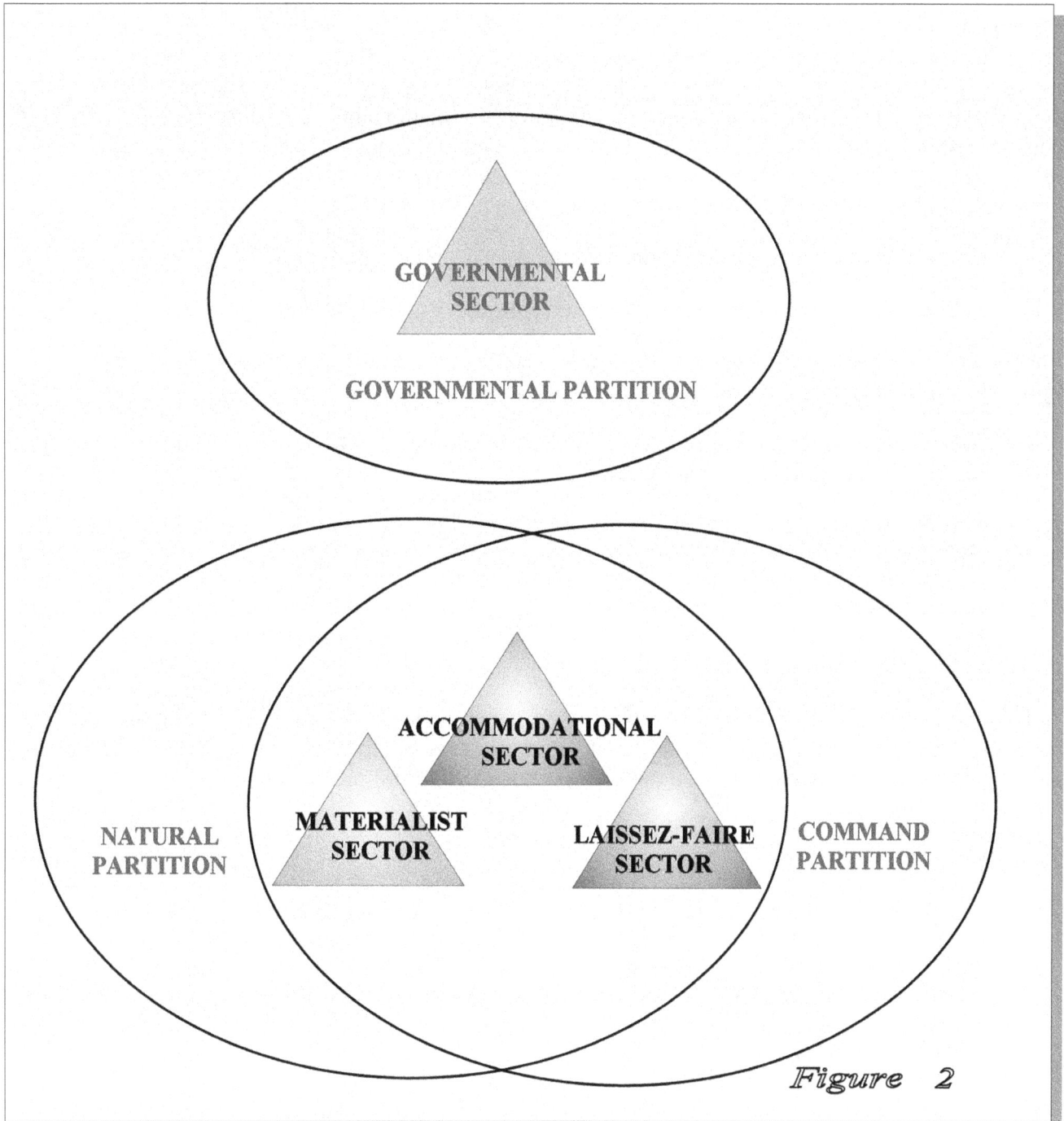

Figure 2

73

Parameters of the System

In this section we introduce the different parameters that come into play in accommodation based consumerism. By parameter we mean a variable that is determined by an individual or a group that effects the functioning of the system. In addition to parameters we include terms and determinants that are unique to this system. We will not describe these parameters and terms in detail here. We will simply define them and state who is in charge of that parameter or term. It is to the great advantage of the system that it has many rather than few parameters. A cook with a large selection of spices can make a tastier meal than one who only has salt and pepper. The free-market system is severely limited in its number of parameters. It only has fiscal policy and monetary policy. Besides interest rates, the money supply, taxes and spending there aren't too many options for manipulating the economy. The consumerist system has a lot of parameters that can be used to promote the well being of the system. The following are the parameters and unique terms of the accommodation based consumerist economic system. Included is what body or individual manipulates it.

Firm- an organization that transforms inputs into goods and services that people want

FR- firm revenue- the income, in Ignits, a firm earns through its transactions

Population- the growth or decline of the number of people in the nation. Determined by how many immigrants are permitted into the country- government

Materialist Demand- the desire for more goods and services. The want for things made in the materialist sector like TV's and cars- consumerists in the materialist sector

Accommodational Demand- the desire for more goods and services produced in the accommodational sector. The want for such things as houses and vacations- consumerists

Materialist Supply- the ability to provide consumerists with goods and services in the materialist sector. The willingness to impart consumerists with goods and services in the materialist sector- materialist producers directly, consumers indirectly

Accommodational Supply- The ability to provide consumerists with goods and services in the accommodational sector. The willingness to impart consumerists with goods and services in the accommodational sector- accommodational producers directly, consumers indirectly

Norses- one of the three currencies in the system. Used in the materialist and the governmental sectors. Have the symbol ☉

Ignits- one of the three currencies in the system. Used in the accommodational and governmental sectors. Have the symbol þ

Fortals- one of the three currencies in the system. Used in the laissez-faire sector. Have the symbol ƒ

Gross Domestic Consumerist Product (GDCP) - the total value of all goods and services sold or put into a position to be sold in the materialist sector during a period of time. Expressed in Norses- firms in the materialist sector.

Individual Domestic Consumerist Product- the total value a specific firm in the materialist sector contributes to the Gross Domestic Consumerist Product total in a period of time. Expressed in Norses- particular firm in the materialist sector

Grand Consumerist Tax (GCT) - a portion of the GDCP that is given to various levels of government. Used to provide governmental goods and services- the three levels of government

Accommodational Markdown- during certain transactions in the accommodational sector, a percentage of the transaction that is taken away from the seller and destroyed. Controls the over accumulation of Ignits in the accommodational sector- central bank

Retail Markup- a percentage increase in the price of retail goods in the materialist and accommodational sectors that the retailer can charge above the original price of the good. Allows retailers to make a profit- central bank

Price Functions- the cost of buying a good or service in the economy. Can be expressed in terms of Norses or Ignits per a certain quantity of good- central bank

Wage/ Salary Function- a function describing the amount a worker is paid for a service. Expressed in Ignits- central bank

Consumerist Universal Stock Price (CUSP) - the cost of buying a unit of consumerist stock. Expressed in Ignits- central bank

Extra Work Transfer- the amount of accommodational goods and services – like housing and utilities- that an unemployed person receives in order to subsist. It also involves money in the form of Ignits and Fortals that the welfare recipient can use to promote his interests- the government

Employment Reimbursement Transfer (ERT) - the money paid to firms as a reward for hiring more employees. Used to combat unemployment. Expressed as a percentage. - The government

Capital Investment Transfer (CIT) - the money paid to firms to cover the costs of purchasing capital to encourage investment. Used to combat unemployment. Expressed as a percentage- the government

Profit Reward Transfer (PRT) - a reward a firm makes for making a profit. Used to encourage investment and combat unemployment. Expressed as a percentage- the government

Interest Rate Stimulus (IRS) - a percentage of a loan that is paid to creditors by the government to encourage investment and decrease unemployment – the government

Quality Selection- the occurrence where firms compete with one another to provide the most desirable goods and services in a market where prices of goods and services are fixed

Consumerist Spending Reimbursement (CSR) - a reward from the government to consumerists for buying goods and services. Used to stimulate the economy and reduce unemployment. Expressed as a percentage- the government

Working Grant Threshold- the threshold that differentiates between a "working" and "non-working" consumerist. In terms of hours worked as well as Ignits/Fortals earned. Those above the threshold earn the general consumerist grant while those below it earn the non working consumerist grant- the government

Real Estate Profit Percentage (REPP) - the percentage of the transaction a real estate firm earns during a transaction involving real estate property. Expressed as a percentage- central bank

Adjusted Revenue Price Duration (ARPD) - the price of purchasing a business from a former owner. Based on the revenue it earns in a certain length of time- central bank

Political Ideology- whether the society is left wing/quasi-socialist or right wing/quasi-free-market. Whether the GCT is small or large. How big the governmental sector is compared to the materialist, laissez-faire and accommodational sectors- the government indirectly, the consumerists directly

Rental Equivalence Duration (RED) - how long it will take a renter to pay the cost of the building he rents. A calculation of how much rent a consumerist must pay for his accommodation when renting- central bank

Insurance Premium Rate- A monthly payment to an insurance company – life, car, house- in return for coverage in that area- interaction of firms and those wishing to be insured

Input Price Function- a function describing the cost of buying an input for a product. How much the producer must pay for certain factors of production- central bank

Delivery Price Function- a function describing the cost of delivering certain goods over a distance calculated by a base time in addition to a price per kilometer. It is of the form $w\þ + y\þ$ where w is a base fee and y is a fee per kilometer- central bank

Yearly Vacation Duration Period (YVDP) - the amount of paid free time from work a worker is entitled to. Expressed as hours/days per year- government

Timing of Vacation- When a worker can take his vacation and leave work for several days or weeks- interaction of firms and workers

Yearly Sick Leave Exemption Period (YSLEP) - the number of days a worker is allowed to skip from work due to illness. Expressed in days per year- government

Maternity Leave Duration Period- How long a pregnant woman can take time off from her work to take care of her baby- government

Injury Severance Payment- How much a worker or his family receives from a firm in case of an injury that disables him from working. Expressed in Ignits-central bank

Economic Taxonomy- the organization of all goods and services and things produced into coherent categories. Similar to biological taxonomy- government

Externality Regulations-the set of rules about how to deal with positive and negative externalities. Designed to eliminate externalities- government

Means of Production- the method used to produce things. The determination of what inputs are used- firms

Interest Rates- the cost of borrowing or lending a number of Ignits. Applicable to business and private loans as well as mortgages- central bank

Job Contract Price (JCP) - the amount of money required to buy a contract for work. This contract gives the worker the right to work at a particular job and a sense of job security– central bank

Adjusted Monthly Income Percentage (AMIP) - how much more a worker will earn in income than he originally had to pay for his JCP. Represented in terms of percent per month- central bank

Adjusted Yearly Income Percentage (AYIP) - how much more money a worker will earn than he had to pay for his job contract. Represented in terms of percent per year- central bank

Adjusted Income Earnings (AIE) - the amount of money a worker earns at the end of his contract minus the cost of the JCP and the interest to the bank for buying the JCP. Expressed in Ignits- central bank

Part –time Character- how much work a particular worker does relative to the full time. Expressed in terms of a percentage- worker and firm

Rental Repayment Value (RRV) - the cost of renting a good or service in the accommodational or materialist sectors of the economy. Set as a percentage. - The central bank

Consumerist Trade Pool- a trading fund where excess profits from exporting and importing are used to subsidize the importing and exporting of other goods. Allows us to export things we don't need and import things we do without affecting prices- central bank

Nominal Exchange Rate- the price of one unit of currency in terms of another foreign currency calculated using exports, imports and real exchange rates- central bank

The Consumerist Quatrotomy- how goods and services are divided among the four sectors- accommodational, materialist, laissez-faire and governmental. A reflection of the political ideology of the country- government

Supply of Norses Issued- the amount of Norses put into the economy is always equal to the GDCP. It goes directly to the government or is distributed among the consumerists- central bank

Distribution of Land- how land should be divided. Land can be divided into residential, industrial, commercial, agricultural, recreational, conservational, protected etc- government

Work Schedule- the minimum amount of hours a worker is entitled to work as a consequence of owning a job contract. Calculated using the JCP, the wage function, the length of a worker's contract and the AMIP- central bank

Industry patent period- the length of time a person or firm has the right to be the sole producer of a product or service. Different patent period for each industry- government

Minimum Retirement Age- the minimum age at which a worker can retire. At this age a worker is entitled a pension- government

Retirement Pension Allowance- the amount of money granted to a retiree by the government. Expressed in Ignits. – The government

WC- number of working non institutionalized consumerists

NWC- number of not working non- institutionalized consumerists that are still in the labour force

General Consumerist Grant- the amount of money –in Norses – employed non-institutionalized consumerists are granted each period by the central bank. Expressed in Norses- central bank

Non-Working Consumerist Grant Markdown- how much less non-working non-institutionalized consumerists are granted relative to working consumerists. Expressed as a percentage- government

Non-Working Consumerist Grant- the amount of money, in Norses, unemployed, non-working non-institutionalized consumerists are granted by the central bank as well as those not in the labour force and those working below a certain threshold, expressed in Norses- central bank

GDCP per capita- the GDCP divided by the number of people in the society- a statistic

Gross National Product (GNP) - the value of the final output of the accommodational sector. Expressed in Ignits- a statistic

General Bond- a form of investment where there is a promise to payback a certain amount of money after a length of time called a maturity. Exist as consumerist and speculative general bonds

Profit Bond- a form of investment that takes into account a firm's profit and revenue. Exist as consumerist and speculative profit bonds

Consumerist General Bond Interest Rate (CGeBIR) - the interest rate on a consumerist general bond. Expressed as a percentage- central bank

Consumerist General Bond Interest Repayment Frequency (CGeBIRF) - how often an investor is paid his interest from owning a consumerist general bond – central bank

Consumerist Profit Bond Interest Rate (CPBIR) - the interest rate on a consumerist profit bond. Expressed as a percentage- central bank

Consumerist Profit Bond Interest Repayment Frequency (CPBIRF) – how often an investor is paid his interest from owning a consumerist profit bond – central bank

Consumerist Governmental Bond Interest Rate (CGoBIR) - the interest rate on a consumerist government bond. Expressed as a percentage – government

Consumerist Government Bond Interest Repayment Frequency (CGoBIRF) - how often an investor is paid his interest from owning a consumerist government bond – government

Speculative General Bond Interest Rate (SGeBIR) - how much interest rate an investor receives on a speculative general bond. Expressed as a percentage – interaction of investors and firms

Speculative Profit Bond Interest Rate (SPBIR) – the interest rate an investor earns from owning a speculative profit bond- interaction of investors and firms

Speculative Government Bond Interest Rate (SGoBIR) - the interest rate an investor earns from owning a speculative government bond- government

Profit Bond Investment (PBI) - the size of a profit bond- the interaction of firms and consumerists

Speculative Bond Interest Repayment Frequency (SBIRF) - how often an investor is paid his interest from owning a bond. Applies to speculative general bonds, speculative profit bonds but not speculative government bonds. May fluctuate – interaction of bond sellers and consumerists

Speculative Government Bond Interest Repayment Frequency (SGoBIRF) - how often an investor is paid his interest from owning a speculative government bond. May fluctuate- government

Length of Bond Maturity- the length of time in days, months or years until a bond has to be repaid to an investor by a firm- interaction of investors and firms

Size of Bond- the value of a bond. How much money, in Ignits, an investor lends to a firm in exchange for interest payments- interaction of investors and firms

Consumerist Central Bank Stock- A special type of stock issued by the central bank to decrease the number of Ignits in circulation in the accommodational sector. Used as an anti-inflationary measure- central bank

Consumerist Central Bank Stock Interest Rate (CCBSIR) - How much profit one earns from owning Consumerist Central Bank Stock- central bank

Speculative Central Bank Stock – A special type of stock issued by the central bank to control the money supply by limiting the number or Fortels in circulation in the laissez-faire sector. Used as an anti-inflationary measure- central bank

Supreme Firm Director- the owner of a corporation. In charge of most of the decisions made by a corporation- picked by shareholders in the natural partition and by the human resource commission in the command partition

Grand Chairman- an important member of the central bank. Responsible for many key decisions in the economy

Deputy Grand Chairman- person who replaces the Grand Chairman in case of a crisis.

Bankruptcy Insurance Premium Rate (BIRP) - how much an insurance company earns monthly from insuring a company by bailing it out in the case of a bankruptcy. The insurance company pays the bankrupting firm's debts to shareholders, bond holders and workers if the firm can't do so. The premium rate is expressed in terms of the money insured- firms

Post- Reinvestment Profit- The profit a firm makes minus its reinvestment in itself (to expand production). Used to calculate earnings from owning stock.

Command Partition- one of the three partitions of the system characterized by firms trying to make a profit while hiring as many unemployed workers as possible

Natural Partition- one of the three partitions of the system characterized by firms guided by the profit motive

Human Resource Management Commission- a body created by the government whose goal is to oversee the functioning of the command partition- command partition

Socialist Labor Pool- the collection of workers who are unemployed but are put to work in the command partition

Auxiliary workers- workers in the socialist labor pool and the laissez-fare labor system

Auxiliary Worker Reimbursement Deduction (AWRD) - how much less a person in the socialist labor pool receives per month for being in the socialist labor pool. Expressed as a percentage- government

Unemployment Assistance Repayment (UAR) – how much money a worker has to repay the government when he finds a job in either the natural or government partition. Expressed as a percentage- government

Government Bond Pool- A special fund for collecting Fortals and Ignits from selling government bonds, either speculative or consumerist. Used as an anti-inflationary measure to control the money supply – the government

Consumerist Anti- Inflationary Pool- An anti-inflationary (money supply controlling) tool used to limit the number of Ignits circulating in the accommodational sector- central bank and government

Speculative Anti- Inflationary Pool- An anti-inflationary (money supply controlling) tool used to limit the number of Fortals circulating in the laissez-faire sector- central bank and government

Fortal- Ignit Exchange Mechanism – an arrangement for converting Fortals into Ignits and Ignits into Fortals. An anti-inflationary measure used to control the money supply – central bank

Employment Agency- a firm that works to find workers for firms (in exchange for a fee) and also work for the unemployed

Inter- Governmental Transfer- The movement of money from one level of government to another or to another jurisdiction at the same level where one level of government has more funds than another jurisdiction that needs money

Work for Freedom Program- An arrangement where an inmate does supervised work in exchange for time off his sentence

Work/Freedom Incentive Ratio (WFIR) - How much time off his total sentence an inmate receives in exchange for doing productive work- interaction of firms, judge, attorneys and inmate

Recycle for Pay Program- A system where consumerists bring useless items (paper, cans, glass) in exchange for a payment. This the government then sells this to input processing firms – government

Recycle for Pay Percentage (RFPP) – How much a consumerist is paid for bringing useless items to be recycled and converted to inputs. Expressed as a percentage of the value of the raw material- government

Employment Assistance Program- A system where the government pays a firm for hiring workers. Later this worker must pay the government (with interest) for the service – government

Employment Assistance Program Interest Rate (EAPIR) - the profit in terms of interest the government receives from workers in exchange for helping them find employment – government

Laissez – Faire Labor System- An anti-unemployment measure where workers wages are partially paid by firms in the Laissez-faire sector and partially by the government- government and firms in laissez-faire sector

Accommodational Award- the granting of some kind of accommodation to all consumerists (who need it) so as to eliminate homelessness- government

Accommodation Award Repayment Percentage (AARP) – how much a person receiving the accommodation award has to repay the government when he finds another form of accommodation, expressed as a percentage- the government

Materialist Overdraft – the grant of extra Norses to consumerists during a set period when the consumerist is drastically short of Norses to pay for essential items- the government

Materialist Overdraft Limit- the maximum amount of Norses a consumerist can be granted during a set period when he is short of money for essential items- the government

Materialist Overdraft Interest – How much (in terms of a percentage) a consumerist has to pay the government for providing him with the materialist overdraft- the government

Consumerist Grant Distribution Schedule – At what point in time consumerists receive their General and Non-Working Consumerist Grants- the Government

Universal Consumerist Card- a card that all consumerists are given which they can use to purchase items in the materialist, accommodational and laissez-faire sectors- all consumerists

Industry Specific Chairman- A member of the central bank in charge of some decisions regarding wages and prices for a specific industry

Industry Specific Deputy Chairman- A central banker whose role is to replace the industry specific chairman if he is unable to fulfill his duties

Industry Specific Commissioners- A group of central bankers in charge of some decisions regarding wages and prices for a specific industry

Resonance Price Functions – Description of prices in different terms.

Principal of Maximum Utility – the idea that an employment position should match the abilities of the individual seeking the employment

Accommodational Overflow Calamity – the occurrence where more and more Ignits enter the accommodational sector and are unable to leave

Consumerist Savings Bond- Special bonds issued to raise money for governmental services when the government is experiencing a deficit- the three levels of government

Consumerist Savings Bond Interest Rate- the interest paid on consumerist savings bonds – the three levels of government

Consumerist Savings Bond Interest Repayment Frequency- how often investors are paid their interest on consumerist savings bonds – the three levels of government

These are the various parameters of Accommodation Based Consumerism. We made a thorough list of many ideas and concepts that are prominent in this system. We gave a brief description of each parameter. Additionally, we mentioned which group or identity has control over that parameter.

Consumerism and the Government

The theory of the accommodation based consumerist system is not a theory of politics or a functioning of the government. This theory stays as far as possible from the government. Politics is one subject where everyone and no one is an expert. However we give some suggestions that may be of some use in this area.

The economic system could work alongside any political system. The only exceptions are communism and anarchy. There cannot be a communist government and a consumerist economic system at the same time.

This economic system works well under democracy regardless who is leader. The leader could be a president, prime minister or a chancellor. This system could also work under a constitutional monarchy.

We now introduce a new concept into the theory of government. This is the concept of the *public veto*. Suppose that the government passes a law or act or any form of legislation. If 50% + 1 of the population sign a petition against this, the law is repelled or vetoed. This framework gives power back to the people. It ensures a more equitable system of checks and balances. A public veto strengthens the democratic system.

The government should promote trade as much as possible. Generally speaking, the more goods imported or exported the better. The reason behind this is that the more goods consumerists import the more choice they have in purchasing. Also they will have the ability to purchase goods of better quality. Trade is discussed later on.

An important function of the government is to regulate some industries. Some regulation, as long as it is not excessive, is necessary so that products are up to standard. For example, water for drinking must meet certain requirements before it can be sent to consumerists. Also meat must be inspected to insure that it is disease free. To this end the government must establish certain agencies to regulate firms for the well being of consumerists.

The government is responsible for issuing licenses and permits. These include fishing licenses, building permits and business or vendors licenses. This is done to regulate certain areas and ensure quality.

The government is responsible for the following parameters. All are discussed more fully later on.

- Population

- Grand Consumerist Tax

- Yearly Vacation Duration Period

- Sick Leave Exemption Period

- Maternity Leave Duration Period

- Extra-Work Transfer Payments

- Political Ideology

- Externality Regulations

- The Consumerist Quatrotomy

- The Distribution of Land

- Industry Patent Period

- Minimum Retirement Age

- Retirement Pension Allowance

- Non-Working Consumerist Grant Markdown

- Economic Taxonomy

- Employment Reimbursement Transfer

- Capital Investment Transfer

- Profit Reward Transfer

- Consumerist Spending Reimbursement

- Interest Rate Stimulus

- Working Grant Threshold

- Government Bond Pool

- Consumerist and Speculative Government Bonds

- Auxiliary Worker Reimbursement Deduction

- Unemployment Assistance Repayment

- Work for Freedom Program

- Recycle for Pay Program

- Recycle for Pay Percentage (RFPP)

- Employment Assistance Program

- Employment Assistance Program Interest Rate (EAPIR)

- Laissez-Faire Labor System

- Accommodation Award

- Accommodation Award Repayment Percentage (AARP)

- Materialist Overdraft

- Materialist Overdraft Limit

- Materialist Overdraft Interest

- Consumerist Grant Distribution Schedule

- Consumerist Savings Bonds

- Consumerist Savings Bond Interest Rate

- Consumerist Savings Bond Interest Repayment Frequency

The government takes care of retirees. It sets the minimum retirement age; i.e. the minimum age at which a worker can retire. It also fixes a retirement pension allowance. This is how much money, in Ignits, a retired person receives from the government.

The government takes concrete steps to limit or eliminate unemployment. It creates and manages the Laissez-Faire labor system. It works in conjunction with firms in the laissez-faire system to create jobs that would not normally exist as they would be outsourced to another country. The government also runs the Employment Assistance Program to help workers buy jobs. The Employment Assistance Program Interest Rate (EAPIR) is dictated by the government. This is the extra income in terms of interest that the government receives from helping workers through the Employment Assistance Program.

The government takes care of those not working. The government makes Extra-Work Transfer payments. There is money involved and also the government provides minimal accommodation and the provision of utilities for those who do not contribute to society but are able to. The government also sets a non-working consumerist grant markdown. This is how much less those who are not working receive in the form of grants of Norses from the central bank. If it is set at 100% all non-institutionalized consumerists are granted an equal amount of Norses. The government may make this lower in order to provide an incentive to work or it may keep it high to fight poverty. In addition the government creates the Working Grant Threshold. This is essentially a definition of what it means to be a "working" consumerist. Let's say it is 200.00 þ per week or 40 hours per week. If a consumerist makes 550.00 þ per week then he is entitled to the General Consumerist Grant. If a consumerist earns 80.00 þ per week, he will get the Non-Working Consumerist Grant. If a consumerist works 45 hours per week then he is entitled to the General Consumerist Grant.

The government takes care of those not working in another way too. It sets the Auxiliary Worker Reimbursement Deduction (AWRD). This concerns how much less someone on welfare is given for being on welfare. This is set as a percentage. The government also creates the Unemployment Assistance Repayment (UAR). This indicates how much income a worker must repay the government after he finds employment in a partition other than the command partition. This is also set as a percentage.

The government provides help for those who are homeless. It gives all homeless and those with low Ignit income a place to live- for example a condominium or small apartment. This we call the Accommodation Award. However, after making use of this program, the consumerist is subject to the Accommodation Award Repayment Percentage (AARP). This means, basically how much of the value of the accommodation the consumerist must pay the government.

The levels of government pay for all consumerist's education. Every consumerist is entitled to a primary, secondary as well as a university/college education. However, as we will soon discuss, it is necessary to buy a job in certain sectors of the natural partition. This stands as the opposite of free-market capitalism where, essentially, a human being has to pay for their post secondary education but it is not necessary to purchase employment.

The Consumerist Grant Distribution Schedule is in the hands of the government. The government decides what day of a 2 week cycle –we are assuming that the Consumerist Grants are granted every 2 weeks- each consumerist is granted either the General or Non Working Consumerist Grant. This helps us avoid problems caused by everyone getting money on the same day and rushing into malls to be the first to buy goods.

The government takes care of the population. It determines how many immigrants are allowed to settle in the nation. How many people to let in depends on how well the economy is doing. If the economy is growing then it is a good idea to let in some immigrants.

The government has influence over both the Yearly Vacation Duration Period and the Sick Leave Exemption Period. It sets how many days in a year a worker can take time off for purposes of vacation or illness.

The government also sets the Maternity Leave Duration Period. That is it dictates how long a person can take time off work to care for a newborn child.

All three levels of the government contribute to the creation of the Grand Consumerist Tax. This is the percentage of the GDCP that the levels of government receive to provide governmental services. Each level of government receives 1/3 of the total and among the different levels it is spread out by population; i.e. the states/provinces with more people are granted more of the tax.

Political ideology is determined through the government by the people. The government picks whether it is quasi-left wing or quasi-right wing. This effects spending and taxation.

The patent period for each industry in a sector is created by the government. The government sets how long a firm has to be the sole producer of an innovation or invention. There is a different patent period for every industry.

The government is in charge of distributing land. It determines how land should be used. Whether land is designated as rural, residential, industrial, recreational, commercial etc depends on the policies of the government.

The government sets out how to regulate externalities. These include procedures on how to handle positive and negative externalities. The goal is to eliminate the externality as much as possible without hurting the economy.

One of the government's main responsibilities is the consumerist quatrotomy and the economic taxonomy. The government decides which industries and which families of goods and services go to each sector. Also a branch of the government is assigned the specific task of compiling the consumerist economic taxonomy. That means that it classifies all goods, services, inputs and wages into the appropriate classifications.

The government has control of several measures used to fight unemployment that will be discussed fully later on. These are the Employment Reimbursement Transfer (ERT), the Capital

Investment Transfer (CIT), the Interest Rate Stimulus (IRS), the Profit Reward Transfer (PRT) and the Consumerist Spending Reimbursement (CSR). These are set in terms of a percentage. The money for these transfers is taken from the government budget. As these measures are directly used to combat unemployment, they are some of the best things the government can spend its money on.

Another one of the roles of the government is to regulate the Governmental Bond Pool. This is an anti-inflationary measure regarding both consumerist and speculative government bonds.

The government works with government bonds; both of the speculative and consumerist kind. It decides how much to sell of these. To do so it manipulates certain parameters. These include: Consumerist Government Bond Interest Rate (CGoBIR), Consumerist Government Bond Interest Repayment Frequency (CGoBIRF), Speculative Government Bond Interest Rate (SGoBIR), and the Speculative Government Bond Interest Repayment Frequency (SGoBIRF).

During government budget deficits, the government may issue Consumerist Savings Bonds. These may be issued by either the Federal, Provincial or Municipal governments. Thus there are Federal Savings Bonds, Provincial Savings Bonds and Municipal Savings Bonds. The governments sell these at a particular interest rate to raise revenues for social services. The interest paid on savings bonds is dictated by a parameter called the Consumerist Savings Bond Interest Rate and this is set by the various levels of government. How often investors are paid on their savings bond is determined by the Consumerist Savings Bond Interest Repayment Frequency. This parameter is also set by the various levels of government.

The government has control over the work for freedom program. It works with judges, attorneys, inmates and firms to find suitable work for those convicted of crimes. Firms pay the government for the work of the inmate so this program is a source of revenue for the government. The inmate gains as he has a reduced sentence. Also society gains as production (total output) is increased. The work for freedom program will be discussed more fully in another section.

The government has jurisdiction over the recycle for pay program. This is also a source of governmental revenue as the government buys material that would otherwise be thrown out and sells it to firms that use it to make material for input for other products. The consumerists also benefit as they get money for ordinarily useless things like cardboard, cans, newspapers, glass bottles etc. Thus it has the side effect that it can provide some income to some consumerists. Furthermore, the government sets the Recycle for Pay Percentage (RFPP). This basically refers to the amount of money that consumerists are paid to bring useless items to "recycling stores".

The government provides help to those consumerists that ran short of money given to them through either the Non Working or General Consumerist Grant. This may be due to some unforeseen emergency or other reason. The government provides these consumerists with the Materialist Overdraft. This is extra money (in Norses) to help out a desperate consumerist. The Materialist Overdraft is subject to the Materialist Overdraft Limit. This parameter, set by the government, indicates the maximum in terms of a percentage of the General or Non Working Grant that the consumerist can be granted at any period of time. For providing the Materialist Overdraft, the government makes money, in terms of interest on the Materialist Overdraft. This is set by the government and is called the Materialist Overdraft Interest.

We should briefly mention the various sources of revenue that the levels of government have. We mentioned some previously, we discussed some in this section and we will encounter more in other sections. They are:

- The GCT- a general tax on the GDCP based on the output of the materialist sector

- Selling of land – when the government sells land for various uses to consumerists it makes money

- Gambling profits- the government makes money operating casinos and selling lottery tickets

- Work for freedom program- firms pay the government for work done by prison inmates

- Recycle for pay program- the government makes money buying waste and recyclable items and selling them to firms that process inputs

- Employment Assistance Program- the government charges prospective workers an interest for helping them find a job

- Unemployment Assistance Repayment (UAR) – those working for the command partition or Laissez-faire labor system pay a portion of the money granted to them as part of their extra-work transfer

- Accommodation Award Repayment – those receiving the accommodation award pay the government for taking advantage of the accommodation award once they find a job in the natural or governmental partitions

- The command partition- a division of the economy where all profits go directly to the government

- Issuing Savings Bonds- the levels of government sell savings bonds in exchange for money used to pay for public goods and services

- Interest for investing in various bonds and stocks

- Revenue from government assisted programs – consumerists pay a fee to board a bus or train or to visit a museum or for processing of a passport

- Selling things like marijuana; assuming these are made legal

- Advertising on public property- firms pay the government to put ads on things like buses, trains or bus stop shelters

- Interest payments from consumerists for taking advantage of the materialist overdraft.

Of all these sources of revenue, the GCT should be the one used least and it should contribute the least as a source of revenue. This is because money taken trough the GCT could otherwise be given to the consumerist grant, either working or not working.

We talked about the functioning of a government in general terms. We described the parameters that the government has control over. From this it can be gathered that the government has strong influence on how the economy progresses.

Consumerism and the Judiciary System

The theory of the accommodation based consumerist economic system is a purely economic theory. It is not concerned with the law, what crimes are and how those who brake then should be punished unless these crimes are purely economic transgressions. Thus this theory is not interested with murder, arson or assault; how these crimes are defined and how those who commit them are persecuted.

There are other crimes that are predominantly economic. These include theft, destruction of property, embezzlement and the braking of contracts. This treatise will not suggest punishments for those who commit these except to say that these crimes must be deterred if the system is to work. Most of the crimes that must be identified are similar to those in any other economic system; i.e. theft, braking of contracts.

Since there is no real tax in our system, there is no need to punish people for tax evasion. It is impossible to commit tax evasion because one does not need to pay any taxes out of his own pocket.

There are some offences peculiar to consumerism. One is the over-reporting of how many goods and services one has sold or has been able to sell. This crime is serious because it disrupts the economic system. This crime is similar in gravity to under-reporting one's taxes for tax purposes in the free-market system. Laws should be made to eliminate the over statement of the value of sold and unsold goods and services. There should be something in consumerism what an audit is in the free-market system.

Some of the most serious crimes are charging a price different for a good or service than that set by the central bank for the GAM sectors. Over selling is charging a price higher than the fixed price. Under-selling is charging a price lower than the price set by the central bank. These are serious crimes because they disrupt the proper functioning of the economic system.

Other crimes include paying workers more or less than the wage function set by the central bank for the GAM sectors. Essentially, any instances of setting rates, values or functions different than those set by the central bank must be forbidden in the GAM sectors.

A very serious crime is using currency from one sector to purchase goods and services in another sector. For example, if someone tries to buy a materialist good, like an apple, with Fortals, this is considered fraud. This is regarded as serious as check or credit card fraud is in free-market capitalism.

Other crimes are not fundamentally economic and are not mentioned here. There is no more mention of them in this section so as to avoid the danger of this treatise becoming a theory of jurisprudence. This theory is wholly economic.

We make one brief note about the justice system that is general in nature. That is, regardless of the crime a consumerist is accused of committing, he or she is entitled to the service of a free legal aid lawyer. No one should be punished or sent to prison simply because they cannot afford legal representation. However if they do want a private lawyer, they are permitted to find one in the laissez-faire sector and pay for the service using Fortals.

We briefly talked about some important crimes that occur in all economic systems. We mentioned a few crimes that were specific to consumerism. We did not go in to detail about these crimes or suggest punishments for breaking them to avoid creating a system of law.

Political Ideology

The politics of economics can be put on a spectrum. Originally this spectrum was just a line. On the far right was free-market capitalism- where there is free enterprise and minimum government involvement. On the far left there was communism with its supreme command system and total government control of all aspects of the economy. Near the center are forms of socialism and less extreme capitalism.

The 20th century saw the emergence of Nazi Germany and Stalinist Soviet Union. These two systems had more similarities than differences so the economic spectrum was changed. It was turned into the shape of a horse shoe, where the extreme left is near the extreme right.

Where does accommodation based consumerism fit in? This system is very general and could be either quasi-free-market or quasi-socialist. We are now forced to remodify the politico-economic spectrum once again. We add a second dimension. It still has a horse-shoe shape but now it has depth. It looks like a rainbow. In the center are unattainable and attainable systems. The bottom represents ideal-realistic systems while the top represents unattainable systems which include utopias.

The closer one gets to the outer perimeter, the unattainable one, the more one is dealing with utopic conditions. These are characterized by people having to do no work and everyone having plenty of everything. The closer one gets to the inner attainable perimeter, the more one is dealing with barter conditions, where things are exchanged for other goods or for a currency. These are characterized by the exchange of goods for other things and work. These two conditions are essentially opposites. In essence, attainability measures whether a system will fall apart due to lack of incentives (or other things) or whether it will last. The accommodational based consumerist economic system can be closer to the attainable line or closer to the unattainable line. This depends on the consumerist quatrotomy. The larger is the materialist sector, the closer the system reaches unatainability. The larger the accommodational sector, the closer the system reaches attainability. If there was no accommodational sector and there were only the materialist and governmental sectors the system would be an unattainable utopia. However if there was no materialist sector and there was only an accommodational, laissez-faire and governmental sectors, the system would be capitalist or communist depending on the relative sizes of the accommodational, laissez-faire and governmental sectors.

This system can be more or less socialist or free-market. This depends on how big the governmental sector is and how much tax the government levies. Under a quasi- free-market structure there is a relatively small government sector and the tax is small. The government spends only on the most essential, most basic services. Under a quasi-socialist structure there is a high tax and a relatively large governmental sector.

The attainability does have an impact on the type of government or economy. All Communist systems are equally far to the left. However they differ in how unattainable or attainable they are. Chinese communism is more attainable than Cuban communism which is more attainable than Soviet communism

All the political ideologies relating to this system have been examined. We have seen that the accommodation based consumerism system, being general, can be anywhere on the revised econo-political spectrum. Where it ends up in practice depends on the people and the government they choose. The following is the New Econo-Political Spectrum .

The New Econo-Political Spectrum

UTOPIA   IDEAL

unattainable   unattainable

Centre 4

5   UNATTAINABLE

Left Wing 10   16   11   .9   Right Wing
12   .8
ATTAINABLE
14   13
15

IDEAL
ATTAINABLE
PERFECTION

7

Socialism 1   Conservatism
2
3   *17*
TYRANNY
18

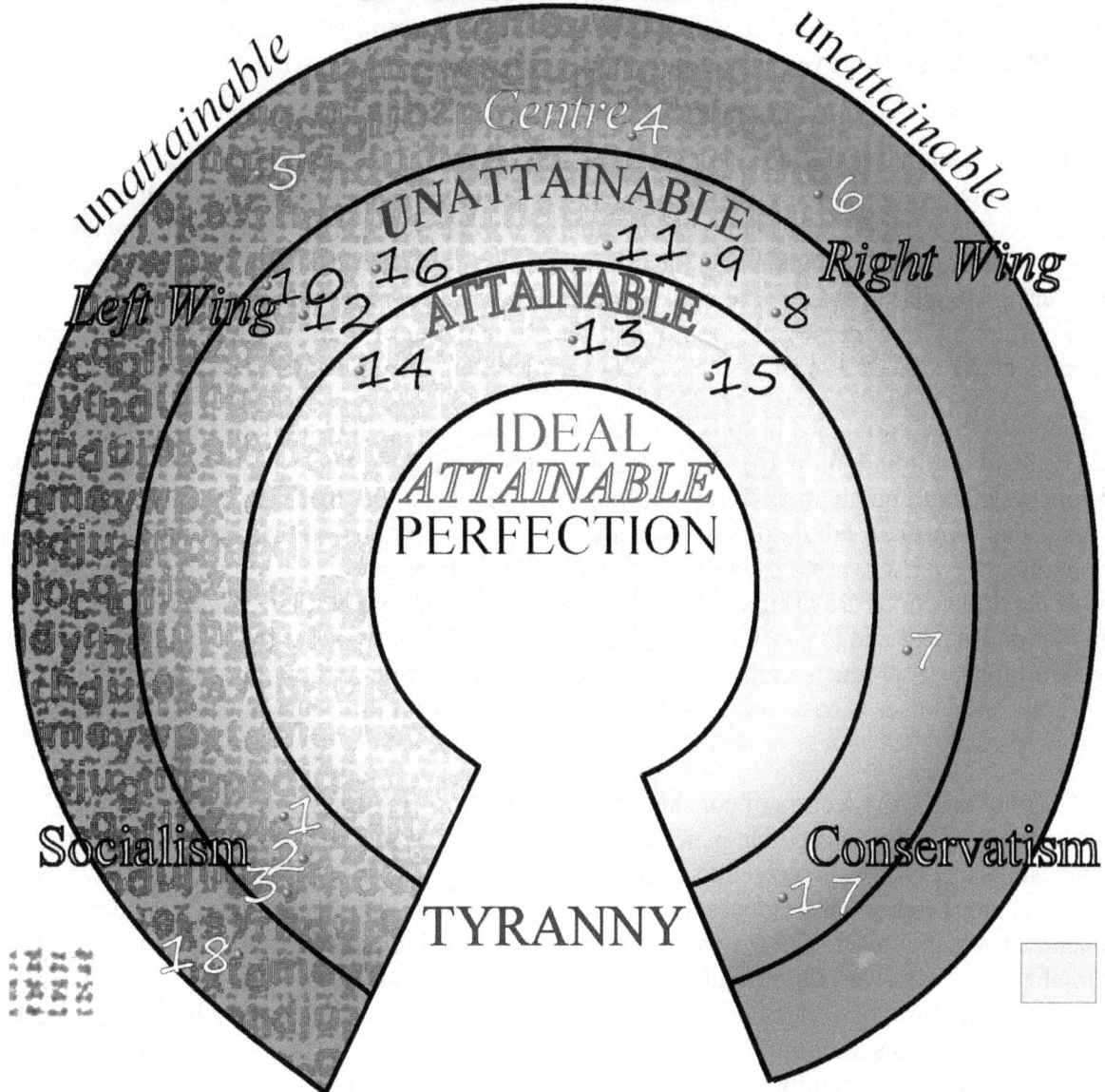

1	Chinese Communism	10	Government of Bill Clinton
2	Cuban Communism	11	Government of Paul Martin
3	Soviet Communism	12	Government of Tony Blair
4	Central Consumerism	13	Central Consumerism
	(*Large materialist sector*)		(*Large accommodational sector*)
5	Quasi-left wing Consumerism	14	Quasi left-wing Consumerism
	(*Large materialist sector*)		(*Large accommodational sector*)
6	Quasi-right wing Consumerism	15	Quasi right-wing Consumerism
	(*Large materialist sector*)		(*Large accommodational sector*)
7	Benito Mussolini's Government	16	Government of Juan Peron
8	Government of George Bush	17	Hitler's Nazism
9	Government of Steven Harper	18	Anarchy

Figure 3

Figure 3

Money

The accommodation based consumerist economic system works differently at a very basic level than its free-market counterpart. The free-market system economy uses one currency whereas the consumerist uses three types of currency. Like the free-market system, money is used to buy things and as a means of exchange. However, in consumerism there is a schism as to what each currency can purchase.

Accommodation based consumerism is a cashless society. There are no coins or bank notes. All money is in private bank accounts and is transferred between individuals and firms using checks, debit cards and a special card called the *Universal Consumerist Card* (UC Card). There are many advantages to a cashless society. One is convenience. Paper bills are not permanent. They can be destroyed, cut or damaged during laundering. A check or card that is lost or damaged does not present a loss. Then there is the problem of theft. Paper money can be stolen during a mugging or theft. Whereas a check can be stopped and a card replaced. For these reasons and many others the consumerist society is cashless.

There are three currencies in consumerism. There are Ignits, there are Norses and there are Fortals. The symbol for an Ignit is (þ). The symbol for a Norse is (Ө). The symbol for a Fortal is (ƒ). The symbol follows the number in an expression of money. The reason that there are three different currencies is that they are used to buy things in different sectors. Norses are used to buy final goods and services in the materialist sector. Also the government uses Norses and Ignits to pay for its expenditures. The rest of the transactions are in Ignits or Fortals. Ignits are used to pay salaries and wages in the accommodational sector and to pay for the inputs to any sector. Consumerist stocks and bonds are purchased in Ignits. All products in the accommodational sector are bought with Ignits. The separation between Ignits and Norses is based on what they can purchase. Fortals are prominent in the laissez-faire sector.

Money in the GAM sectors of consumerism, unlike most free-market economies, is not fiat money- this means that it is more than paper that we agree to have value. It is exactly equal to the GDCP. The supply of Norses is pegged to materialist goods and services, giving the money actual value. Whatever the materialist sector produces in the span of one month is granted to the consumerists and the government. This is in Norses. Every two weeks, the central bank grants all working non-institutionalized and non-working non-institutionalized consumerists a sum of money in Norses. This grant is in either the form of a check or direct deposit in the private bank account which all consumerist are assumed to have. Thus the central bank grants Norses to consumerists to spend on anything they wish in the materialist sector and it grants the government Norses to pay for goods and services it provides.

Private bank accounts are of three basic forms. They can be either Norse accounts, Ignit accounts or Fortal accounts. Even though one Norse is worth exactly one Ignit, no one can directly exchange an Ignit for a Norse or a Norse for an Ignit. This stipulation is crucial. Firms that provide material goods and services can provide accommodational goods and services although it must use different currency for goods and services in different sectors. These two sectors must be separate. Thus a department store can sell TV's, computers and ovens at the same time but use different currencies in specific situations since the first two items are in the materialist sector while the third is in the accommodational sector.

To purchase materialist things like clothes, TV's or computers, the consumerist spends the Norses the central bank granted him and that are now in his bank account. At the moment of purchase, a consumerist receives a good or service and the materialist producer provides the good or service. At the same time, the price of that good or service is deducted from the consumerist's Norse bank account and the equivalent number of Ignits is added to the producer's bank account. This is the idea behind the conversion of Norses to Ignits during a transaction of goods and services.

An example will illustrate the process. A consumerist, let's call him Bob, wants to buy a hat from Ultra-Z-Supermarket. The hat costs 5.00 Θ. Bob writes a check for 5.00 Θ to Ultra-Z-Supermarket and Ultra-Z-Supermarket gives Bob the hat. Ultra-Z-Supermarket takes the check to a private bank where for simplicity both Bob and Ultra-Z-Supermarket have accounts. Bob had a balance of 790.00 Θ on his Norse account. Ultra-Z-Supermarket had a balance of 20 500 þ on its Ignits account. Upon getting the check the bank subtracts 5.00 Θ from Bob's account leaving him with 785.00 Θ and adds 5.00 þ to Ultra-Z-Supermarket's account leaving them with 20 505 þ. Bob could have also used a debit card. This is accomplished when Bob swipes a card through a machine and enters a password (maybe more identification needs to be required for security reasons). This way the bank directly credits Ultra-Z-Supermarket with 5.00 þ and deducts 5.00 Θ from Bob. This is an example of a simple purchase in the materialist sector.

Let's look at a transaction in the accommodational sector. In this example the consumerist Bob, has earned 500.00 þ. With this he can make a purchase in the accommodational sector. He wants to buy tickets to a basketball game costing 50.00 þ. The ticket company gives Bob the ticket and Bob swipes his UC card. When the information is received at the bank, the bank deducts 50.00 þ from Bob's Ignit account leaving him with 450.00 þ. The ticket company receives 50.00 þ which are added to their Ignit bank account. This is an example of a simple purchase in the accommodational sector.

Let's entertain another example. The government is granted Norses as part of the GCT. Suppose that the federal government is granted 100 000.00 Θ. It wants to pay for a heart operation for a consumerist. Doctors must perform this operation. The price of an operation of this type is 2 500 þ. The doctor receives 2 500.00 þ when he performs this operation. The 2 500.00 Θ are deducted from the government's Norse bank account and 2 500.00 þ are added to this doctor's account. This is an example of a simple transaction in the governmental sector.

The exchange of money in the laissez-faire sector is similar to that in the accommodational sector. John wants to buy a book worth 10.00 ƒ from a bookstore. He has 450.00 ƒ in his Fortal account while the bookstore has 800 000.00 ƒ in its Fortal account. John swipes his special debit card, the UC Card, entering a code, and the cashier gives him the book to take home and read. At that time 10 ƒ are deducted from his account leaving him with 440.00 ƒ and 10 ƒ are credited to the bookstore leaving them with 800 010.00 ƒ.

As mentioned, the currency in the laissez-faire sector is Fortals. To combat inflation, which the laissez-faire sector is prone to, we have the Ignit- Fortal exchange mechanism. Normally 1ƒ = 1þ and 1þ = 1ƒ. However, if we want to decrease the money supply, these exchange rates can be different so that one loses money when converting back and forth between Fortals and Ignits. For example the exchange rate could be 1ƒ = 10þ and 100þ = 1ƒ. So if we started with 600 þ, this converts to 6 ƒ and if we convert this 6 ƒ again we get 60 þ. Note that these exchange rates are not necessarily inverses of each other. Trading Fortals into Ignits and back again is the surest way to lose money. However it may be necessary to exchange currencies to buy goods and services in another sector. It is crucial to understand that one cannot trade Norses to Fortals or Fortals into Norses.

The consumerist economy is cashless and functions with three types of currencies. These are needed to service a quatro-sectoral economy. This is a major difference from any economic system in existence or any that has ever been thought up.

Prices

No economic system would exist if there were no prices. Prices indicate the value of goods and services. It is almost universally agreed that it is impossible to set prices without a market system. Yet it is possible to create a coherent system of prices in the consumerist system. This is called the *democratic* or *consumerist* method of setting prices. First we discuss pricing under the free-market system and then talk about pricing under accommodation based consumerism.

In the free-market, prices fluctuate. There is competition among firms in terms of price. A key maxim is to buy at a low price and sell at a high price. The market system uses prices to determine the equilibrium cost and the equilibrium quantity sold of a certain good. Certain factors can cause the equilibrium price and equilibrium quantity to fluctuate. These fluctuations are governed by the laws of supply and demand.

The consumerist system, for the most part, does not rely on a fluctuating-price market system. Prices in consumerism (in the GAM sectors) are permanently fixed. They are fixed by a panel of economists working at the central bank. Once a price has been fixed it must not be changed lest an absolute emergency or producers can demonstrate to the central bank that it is impossible to make a profit under the fixed price function. If prices do fluctuate, unnecessarily or too much, the consumerist system will surely collapse.

There are several benefits to fixing a price. It eliminates the possibility of a depression. One of the reasons for the depression of the 1930's was that the prices of commodities such as wheat fell substantially. They fell so low that it was impossible to make a profit from growing wheat. The result was that people became unemployed and very poor.

One of the greatest faults of the free-market system is the business cycle. It is an inherent part of the system. There are periods of recessions, booms, expansions and downturns. This is bad. It can be completely avoided by fixing prices. Recessions are characterized by a relatively low level of prices. Booms are associated with inflation.

Inflation is a problem of the free-market system. However it does not exist in consumerism (with the exception of the laissez-faire sector). The essence of inflation is that prices of goods gradually increase over the years. Inflation has the effect that things today have a higher price than they did in the 1910's. The phenomenon of inflation will be discussed in detail later. Since prices are fixed in consumerism (in the GAM sectors) there can be no inflation.

Deflation is another possible problem of the free-market economy. The essence of deflation is that prices of goods fall over time. Deflation will be discussed in detail later. Although it is not as common as inflation, it could still hurt the economy. In consumerism, for the most part, there can be no deflation because prices are permanently fixed in the GAM sectors.

A fixed price function system eliminates the idea of predatory pricing. That is firms do not excessively undercut their competitors in terms of price only to greatly increase their prices after eliminating their rivals.

Having fixed prices confers another advantage. It adds simplicity to the economy. Consumerists know exactly how much they must pay for a good or service. Also producers know exactly how much to charge for their goods and services. Thus fixed prices make the economy work more smoothly.

Yet another advantage of a fixed price system is the tremendous simplicity in terms of purchasing. It is conceivable that a shopper will know most if not all of the prices of goods and services in an economy. Imagine walking to a supermarket and being confronted not with tens of thousands of prices for items but just several hundred of them. This makes budgeting and smart shopping more possible.

It is kind of a mistake to say prices are fixed by the central bank. What the central bank does is that it sets *price functions* on families of goods and services. Goods and services that are in the same family (see the section on taxonomy) have the same price function. In consumerism goods and services that are substitutes or are very similar to each other are given the same price per quantity regardless of their quality. Here are some examples. Note that all prices in this section and throughout this treatise are simply examples and need not be the same in an actual economy. Cola/lemonade/iced tea (soft drinks) could be 0.50 ☉ /100 mL. All T-shirts could be 10.00 ☉/unit. All wines could be 0.80 þ /litre. All C.D.'s could be 10.00 ☉/unit. All computer games could be 25.00 ☉ /unit. All vine fruit (i.e. tomatoes) could be 0.50 ☉ /kg. All tropical fruits (i.e. bananas) could be 0.25 ☉ /kg. Some things have more complicated price functions. Agricultural land => 100.00 þ/m^2. Housing => 200.00 þ/m^2 + x200.00 þ + y 2500.00þ + z10000.00 þ. Where x = # of washrooms, y= # of bedrooms, z = # of floors. The price of a dwelling / house/ mansion/ apartment is very hard to arrive at because dwellings are the main incentives for consumerists to produce for society.

How are price functions set? The central bank has 102 officials for every particular industry. There is an industry specific chairman, an industry specific deputy chairman and 100 industry specific commissioners. For example in the entertainment industry there is an entertainment industry chairman, an entertainment industry deputy chairman and 100 entertainment industry commissioners. These people are appointed not elected. For every family of goods or services that exists in the economy (with the exception of those in the laissez-faire sector) the industry specific chairman sets the form of the price function. For example he may set the form of the price function for automobiles as αx. The x stands for money and the α stands for units. He may set the form of price functions for chocolate bars as x/100 grams. The x stands for money. Thus the price of cars would be set in terms of numbers of units (how many cars). The price of chocolate bars is set in terms of its weight (how many grams)

Now the industry specific commissioners vote on the value of the monetary variable (x). The 25 highest and 25 lowest votes are discarded and the middle 50 are averaged. This is done so that the industry specific commissioners set a reasonable price and do not make extreme prices. (i.e. 0.01 ☉ for a car or 1 000 000 000.00 ☉ for a gram of chocolate) In our case let's suppose that the industry specific commissioners set a price of 12 129.00 ☉ for a unit of car and 0.25 ☉ for a 100 g of chocolate. Thus the price function for a chocolate bar is 0.25 ☉/100 g and that of automobiles is 12 129.00 ☉/car. So if a producer of chocolate makes chocolate bars in 500 g sizes it would seem he should charge the retailer 1.25 ☉ for each bar. It would also seem that the automobile producer would charge a car dealer 12 129.00 ☉ for a car. But this is not true. Only consumerists pay Norses for products and they can only do so at the retail level. Producers charge retailers in Ignits. The chocolate producer would actually charge 1.25 þ for the 500 g chocolate bar from a convenience store owner. The car manufacturer would actually charge 12 129 þ for the car from the car dealer.

If one person were to pick a price that would be good for both consumerists and producers, he would surely overvalue or undervalue the good or service. However with 100 economists voting on a price of a good or service, the price being determined democratically, there is more confidence that these prices are reasonable.

In some cases it may be necessary to introduce *resonance price functions*. These are prices that are fixed with respect to a different parameter. For example pizzas can be priced per units of pie or per slices. There may be price functions like Θ8.00/unit pizza or Θ1.00 per pizza slice. So when pizza producers compete with each other they can sell their pizza per whole pizza or per individual slice.

Fixing price functions also confers two more important advantages to members of the consumerist economy. Producers gain the security that the price of their product will never drop to levels where they cannot make a profit. For example, say the price of a bushel of wheat is usually $5.00. In the free-market system, there could arise a tragedy like a stock market crash, a terrorist attack or violent catastrophe where the price drops to $0.25 per bushel. No matter how much wheat the farmer sells, he cannot make a living. In consumerism, farmers and all other producers gain the valuable security that the price of their product will never drop.

Also, consumerist themselves gain stability and security from the fixing of prices. In the free-market system a cup of coffee that cost $0.60 fifteen years ago now costs $2.00. The coffee didn't become any better. However, in consumerism, the consumerist will benefit from the fact that if a medium cup of coffee cost Θ1.00 today, it will cost the same tomorrow, next week, next year and fifteen years from now. This peace of mind is very valuable.

Remember from biology the concept of natural selection. Species that are adapted best to their environment are those that survive and produce offspring. In consumerism we have *quality selection*. All goods and services in a family (similar or close substitutes) have the same price function. The way that producers compete is through quality. The best made products are sold. Those goods that consumerists think are best are bought and produced. If all automobiles cost 10 000.00 Θ, then wouldn't everyone want to own a limousine or a fancy sports car? Of all cars limousines would be made most of all. Other car makers must make their cars better in the eyes of consumerists. They may do this by adding new features like more powerful car engines or they may make their cars roomier, faster and safer. Manufacturers will strive to invent things that will please consumerists and make a consumerist buy that car. The net effect of this quality selection is that whoever owns a car not only has a car, but has the finest, most luxurious one made.

If all shoes are 45.00 Θ then only the most comfortable, most durable, best made shoes are bought. The net result is that every consumerist who has a pair of shoes not only owns a pair of shoes but has the best shoes available.

In the free-market economy only about 0.01 % or 1 in 10 000 people own a limousine (in most jurisdictions). Most people own average cars. These cars work but there are finer ones on the market. There are also quite a number of people in the free-market economy who own extremely mediocre cars that are either old or poorly made. In consumerism the picture looks different. In the case where the price of a good or service exceeds a consumerist's budget (for example an automobile or a jet) the firm that sells such an expensive product may wish to charge by installment. However the total price may not exceed the price set by the central bank. Example: Suppose an automobile costs 15 000.00 Θ. This is set by the central bank. Suppose a consumerist has a budget of 8 000 Θ/ month. This is how much he is granted by the central bank. The car dealer can charge a payment plan of 750.00 Θ a month for 20 months. However there can be no interest on the payment.

The fixing of prices also helps producers and sellers in that they no longer have to find an optimal price for their product or service. The price for their product that the central bank provides may be better than one they could come up with on their own. Producers no longer have to adjust their prices to maximize profit by balancing price and quantity sold.

The set of price functions set by the central bank compromise part of what is called the consumerist constitution. If it turns out that the price of something in practice is incredibly unreasonable (i.e. the steel required to make a car costs more than the car itself) the central bank can vote again on the price function of goods in question. The central bank must be presented with a petition from a large number of unhappy consumerist producers. However this must not happen too often.

Sometimes fixed prices can be a problem for producers. This happens if the cost of producing a good is more than the revenue for that product. For example, suppose that a litre of milk is 2.00 þ, a bucket of ice cream contains a litre of milk and the bucket of ice cream sells for 1.00 Θ. Clearly, the ice cream maker is losing money. However they can appeal to the central bank with a form describing their financial situation. If the central bank accepts this appeal they simply vote again on the price of the ice cream. For this to happen there must be appeals from several ice cream producers. When the central bank votes on the new price function, the original price function is the minimum that they can vote.

The way this concept of fixing price functions (for GAM sectors) means that there can be no "discounts". There can be no "sales" or "special events" where the price of a good is a certain percentage lower than before. So if running shoes are set by the bank to cost 60.00 Θ, there cannot be a special reduction to attract more consumerists.

The whole concept of budgeting in consumerism is the opposite of that of capitalism. In capitalism one walks into a store knowing roughly what to buy and tries to find the best price for these items. In consumerism one walks into a store knowing roughly how much he has to spend and tries to find the best goods he can get for that price.

We saw the nature of prices in the economy and how they are set. We contrasted the free-market and consumerist price systems. In what follows we will see how prices make the consumerist system work.

Quality Selection

We started discussing the concept of quality selection in the last section. Here we will elaborate a little bit on it. Quality selection refers to the idea that producers compete with one another not by undercutting each other in price and producing products and services of the cheapest kind but rather by making products and services that have the most value in the eyes of consumerists. It is one of the most wonderful results of the theory of accommodation based consumerism.

Let's take the family of frozen desserts. To this family would belong various kinds of ice creams and frozen yogurts. In the free-market system, competition pertaining to this market would involve the firms trying to sell cheaper and cheaper frozen desserts. Every brand would have a different price and buyers would usually buy the ice cream that costs the least. In consumerism the idea is different. All products in this family cost the same. Suppose the central bank set the cost of all frozen desserts at 1.00 Θ/1 L and the retail markup at 25%. Thus when a consumerist goes to a grocery store he would have to pay 1.25 Θ for every litre of frozen dessert. Since all frozen desserts cost the same, the various frozen desserts producers compete with each other in terms of quality. They try to make their product the most desirable in the eyes of consumerists. So, some would try to make their desserts as healthy as possible (least fat and calories) and others would try to make original flavors. The different producers would make flavors of frozen desserts that would attract consumerists. Instead of being able to choose from 6-8 flavors in a grocery store operating under the free-market system, in the consumerist system, there would be maybe 25-30 flavors to choose from. Thus the consumerists have access to the best quality frozen desserts.

As another example of quality selection let's take a look at the computer family of products. All computers would cost the same. Suppose that the central bank sets this at 600.00 Θ and the retail markup at 30%. So if someone wants a computer they would go to an electronics store and pay (600.00 Θ x 0.3) + 600.00 Θ = 780.00 Θ. Now, the computer producers compete with one another to make the best computer in the opinion of consumerists. So they would make their computers faster, with more space and with more improvements. They would also employ their research to find new ideas for making their computers better than before with fresh original ideas. The consumerists benefit from this type of competition because they have access to better computers.

Quality selection can also be applied to services. Let's examine the music teacher family. Every music teacher would be paid the same for the equivalent service he or she provides, with the compensation determined by the central bank. So if all music teachers cost the same to hire to teach music, students would be able to pick the best one to teach them. Music teachers would compete with each other, each trying to seem of the best value in the eyes of consumerists. This makes sure that the teachers that get hired are those that are best suited for the position. For example they may have gone to a better music school or have had more experience teaching. Here quality selection works once again in favor of consumerists.

Pizza producers would compete in accordance with quality selection. Assume that the central bank sets the price function of pizzas in terms of a unit of pizza; let's say at 6.00 Θ/per pizza. Then pizza makers would try to make better and better pizzas so that consumerists bought pizzas from them. This would mean that some pizzas are unbelievably huge or have a wide variety of toppings or are low in fat. Pizza makers would try to make their pizzas taste better than the other pizza makers. So the consumerists win by having access to well made pizza.

Grocery stores would also compete with each other in terms of quality rather than price. Thus they would have the most friendly cashiers and most knowledgeable clerks. Also they may be open 24hours a day so that if someone wants to buy a sandwich at 2 am (because they are working the night shift perhaps) they are able to do so. This really only requires one or two more extra cashiers for the night but the reputation that the store is open 24 hours a day will more than compensate for the cashiers wages.

In a consumerist society meat will probably be priced either in terms of kilograms per animal or meat from all animals may have the same price per kilogram. Suppose all meat cost the same per quantity. Let's say it is 10.00 Ө per kilogram. All types of meat would cost the same whether it is chicken, pork, beef or veal. In that case a consumerist would be able to buy the type of meat that they truly desire. If someone wants ribs, he is entitled to it. If he wants a steak, he is entitled to it. If someone wants stewing meat, he is entitled to it... All that really matters is that the price of the meat from the animal is more than the animal itself. If meat from one type of animal is more preferred relative to other types of meat, meat producers should try to raise a different type of livestock.

Quality selection can be applied to land too. Even though land of the same type costs the same, some land is of better quality than other land. For example, developed land; that is land with crops growing on it or some building on it, is more desired than land with only grass and weeds growing on it. The location of land also affects how desired it is with regards to quality selection. So, those who compete in terms of selling land ought to factor in the quality of their land when attempting to sell it.

Finally let's take a look at the potato chip family of goods. Assume that the central bank sets the price of all chips at 1.00 Ө/100 g and the retail markup at 30%. So in a convenience store or grocery store, a consumerist would find bags of chips with different prices; a 250 g bag of chips for 2.50 Ө + (2.50 Ө x 0.3) = 3.25 Ө and a 100 g bag for 1.00 Ө + (1.00 Ө x 0.3) = 1.30 Ө. The different chip manufacturers would compete with one another in terms of quality. That is they try to make their product most highly valued by consumerists. There are different ways they can compete. For example, some may be reduced in calories and fat while other potato chip manufacturers may make new and interesting flavors. A typical snack section in a free-market grocery store usually has maybe 6-10 different kinds of potato chips. In the consumerist system, to attain quality selection, a grocery store may have 30 – 40 different kinds of potato chips. Again, quality selection gives consumerists better and more improved products.

In the free-market system there already is quality selection in the movie industry. The price of a ticket to the cinema costs the same regardless of the quality of the movie. That is, how much money it took to film the movie, how good the actors are, how good the special effects are, etc... Movie goers see the movie they really want to watch and therefore the best one. This is an example of the concept of quality selection in the free-market system.

Furthermore there is some degree of quality selection in the employment market of the free enterprise system. Employers already have in mind how much they will pay their worker in terms of a salary or wage. They offer interviews to possible candidates to pick the most qualified one. Thus the worker of the highest quality is the one who is employed. For example, an accounting firm has a position for an accountant that pays $60,000 per year. They interview applicants and the one best suited for the job is the one that is hired and gets the job. This is another example of quality selection in the free-market system.

The concept of quality selection is directly derived from our definition of what it means to be "wealthy". Remember we defined being wealthy as having access to goods and services of the highest quality. Quality selection achieves that goal. The idea of quality selection ensures that consumerists have goods and services of the highest standard available to them. Quality selection guarantees us that we have the biggest, tastiest hamburger possible, the most entertaining video game, the best made bicycle and the best set of tires on our car. Consumerists are guaranteed to drive limousines and the fastest sports cars. They wear the warmest, most insulated coats and their gloves are the best that can possibly be made. They have the largest TV's and the fastest, top of the line computer. Their beds are the most comfortable to sleep on and their coaches are the most comfortable to sit on.

Quality selection does not apply to the laissez-faire sector. It only pertains to the GAM sectors. The laissez-faire sector functions based on the laws of supply and demand and therefore there is competition in price.

Some theorists may argue that it is very hard to create a fixed price function for a good or service. Let's compare a sports car and an economy car. In a capitalist nation these would have vastly different prices. The economy car may cost 10 000.00 $ while the sports car can cost up to 90 000.00 $. However these two probably cost a similar amount to produce. They both have about the same amount of steel, aluminum, copper wire, glass, plastic, upholstery, electronics, etc… Although the sports car probably costs more to produce than the economy car, the difference is not as great as the price tag would have you believe. If one adds up all the production costs, the economy car most likely costs about $ 4 000.00 to make while the sports car costs about $ 6 500.00 to make. In fact the majority of the price in the capitalist scenario is due to a markup. In that case, if we in our consumerist nation, price our automobiles at a higher price than their production costs then the whole concepts of price fixing and quality selection work. So, if we price the economy car and sports car at 12 000.00 $, then car dealers and manufacturers can sell both cars at a profit. Of course, for most people the sports car is of a higher quality so most people will buy the sports car relative to the economy car. However, since the economy car cost less to produce, car manufacturers would make more profit per car if they sold more economy cars.

We looked at the concept of quality selection. We gave several examples from different industries in the consumerist economic system. It can clearly be seen that quality selection works in favor of consumerists.

The Principals of Maximum Worker Utility and Merit

The principals of maximum worker utility and merit help us find the best jobs for our workers. When applied properly they promote economic efficiency and productivity. They are general principals regarding employment.

The principal of maximum worker utility states that essentially a worker does a job that A) he likes, B) he wants to do, C) he is most suited for, or a combination of these. One would not force a doctor to be a janitor because it is more productive if this educated person is a doctor and someone less educated is a janitor. One of the goals of employment is to find work for employees so that the job fits the worker and the work arrangements are such that society extracts the most productivity from workers.

Here is an example of the application of the principal of maximum worker utility using 4 people and 4 employment positions:

1) A man with a PhD in physics

2) A women with a high school education and a pharmacy technician diploma

3) A high school dropout

4) A developmentally challenged man with an IQ of 65 on a wheelchair

We have 4 positions:

1) A research and lecturing position at a university

2) A position as a helper at a pharmacy

3) A sandwich maker position at a fast food place

4) A job counting screws

The man with the PhD should work at the university. The women with the pharmacy technician diploma should work at the pharmacy. The high school dropout should work as a sandwich maker. The developmentally challenged man should sort screws. This is the most productive use of human resources because if the man with the PhD made sandwiches the high school dropout could not teach at university

When two people are competing for a position at a firm the employer must choose between the two potential employees. The one that has the most merit should be the one that is hired. This means that the candidate has a good education, is experienced and possesses other skills like being punctual, hardworking and trustworthy. This is the principal of merit. However, the principal of maximum worker utility should be observed. So one would probably not hire a man with a post-secondary education to be a cashier as there are other workers that could work well as cashiers with only, say, a high school diploma. A potential employee may have so much merit that he could work at a job where those skills and knowledge have applications.

In consumerism we should have as many people as possible contributing to society as this raises the total output. To find employment for everyone there are special anti-unemployment measures. We might make exceptions for people recovering from heart surgery and similar problems. But even a blind man can help society. For example, he can sing, play the flute or pack groceries. A person on a wheelchair can still do many things. The more people helping society, the better.

The principals of maximum worker utility and merit, theoretically, guide employment decisions. They ensure that an employment position fits an employee's skill. If properly applied, these principals ensure that we obtain the most value out of our workers in consumerism.

Unemployment, Wages and Salaries

In this section we will discuss unemployment, wages and salaries; what they are and what are their natures. As important determinants of an economy, not just the consumerist economy, it is paramount that they be understood. A full knowledge of these will help us understand how the consumerist system works. By wages and salaries we mean the way a worker is compensated for his work. By unemployment we mean the inability to find jobs for workers who desire them.

In the absence of a market system it is hard to calculate wages. A major argument against the communist system is that there is no sensible way of determining wages. However the consumerist system has an alternative non market based method for determining wages and salaries. This method is carried out in the central bank. The central bank doesn't simply determine wages; rather it creates wage functions per family of occupation. Once these functions are set they are permanently fixed. We now turn to the method the central bank has for setting wage and salary functions. The central bank has industry specific Chairmen and their deputies and 100 industry specific commissioners. We have industry specific Chairman and Commissioners since it would take too much time and work for a general set of Chairman and Commissioners to determine wage and salary functions. The industry specific Chairman sets the form of the wage function. By this we mean the criteria by which a worker will get paid. For example a teacher may have one like x/hour and a car salesman may have one such as x/hour + y/car. The industry specific Chairman, in this case the educational industry chairman, decides that the teacher gets paid by the hour and the transportation industry chairman decides that the car salesman is paid both per hour and per car sold. The education industry commissioners determine the value of x and the transportation industry commissioners determine the value of y. They put the variable to the vote amongst themselves. The 25 highest and 25 lowest votes are rejected and the middle 50 are averaged. The process ensures that the industry specific commissioners with a bias are excluded. As an example, suppose the education industry commissioners voted on the teacher wage function. One votes 3.00 þ/hour and another voted 40.00 þ/hour. In the process these votes were counted and the 25 highest and 25 lowest were rejected. Out of the remaining 50 votes an average mean of 29.50 þ/hour was obtained. Thus a teacher would work for 29.50 þ/hour in our example. The figures and numbers proceeding and following are examples and need not be as written in the real system.

The wages and salary functions are designed to maximize productivity and efficiency among workers so that workers contribute to society as much as possible. A policeman would not be paid by how many people he arrested. That would lead him to arrest too many innocent people. It would be better if the policeman were paid by the hour. A painter would not be solely by the hour as that way he would deliberately take a long time to finish painting. It would be better if he were paid by how many square meters he painted. A doctor would not be paid by how many pills he prescribed to his patients as this would result in patients taking drugs when they don't really need them. It would be better if a doctor were paid by how many patients he sees or how many hours she spends with her patients. A teacher would not be paid by how much chalk she used to write her lessons as that way she would write excessively to waste chalk. It would be better if she were paid by how many hours she teaches. Finally a cook would not be paid by how many spices he adds to his meals as that would make food that is undesirably salty or spicy. It would be better if he were paid by how many hours he works

Although the industry specific Chairmen ultimately create the format of the wage function, we can suggest some reasonable ones for the jobs listed above. Wage functions are not set for each profession but rather per *family of services*. Recall the section on consumerist taxonomy. The wage function forms could be:

Policeman-x/hr

Painter-x/m^2 painted

Doctor- x/hr + y/patient

Cook- x/hr

The values of x and y in each case are determined by the voting of the industry specific Commissioners.

Let's turn to the phenomenon of unemployment. Unemployment is the situation where there are more people looking for a job than there are jobs available. Thus there are people who do not work. Let's ask the question: "Is unemployment desirable or should we eliminate it altogether (or at least greatly reduce it)?" If everyone is employed, then the maximum amount of output can be produced given the technology level. However as less and less people are employed, less and less goods and services are produced. But a society that creates many goods and services is better off than one that produces less, economically speaking. This would suggest that the lowest possible unemployment level is most desirable.

Here is a thought experiment. Let's compare two island societies with the same amount of people, the same kind of people and the same conditions of regarding everything else. The only variable is the percentage of people unemployed. On island 1 there are 20 people and everyone has a job. 5 people reap coconuts, 5 people hunt fish, 5 people cook the coconut and fish and 5 people make houses. At the end of the day, each of the coconut finders reaped 4 coconuts, each house builder made 4 houses, each fisherman caught 4 fish and each cook cooked a combination of coconut and fish. The output is 20 coconuts, 20 fish and 20 huts. The coconuts and fish are all cooked. How they divide this output is irrelevant for this thought experiment. Now let's imagine an almost identical island. Here however 25 % of the people are unemployed. Otherwise the two islands are the same. 4 people reap coconuts, 4 catch fish, 4 build houses and 4 cook the food. Let's assume that each working islander has the same output. The difference is that 25 % of the people – the unemployed – do nothing. They bathe in the sun or try to look for a job. The output of the island economy is 16 coconuts, 16 fish and 16 houses. The output is clearly less than in the other island with 0% unemployment. If the output is equally divided per person, each person has less than on the other island. In fact any way one divides the output here the society is worse off. People have more if a greater percentage is producing more. This is an argument in favor of eliminating unemployment.

Now that we know what unemployment is and that it is better to reduce or eliminate it, we need a way of doing so. Suppose that there are more chairs to seat people than there is room around the table. How do we make these extra chairs useful? We make or obtain a bigger table. Suppose that there are more carrot seeds then there is soil to plant them in. How do we make these extra seeds useful? We obtain a larger piece of land. Suppose that there is more apple juice than can fit in a container. How do we make this extra juice useful? We get more containers. Therefore if there are more people than there are jobs for them, we create more jobs. How do we create more jobs for unemployed people?

How do we obtain a bigger table if we have a smaller one? We get it from someone who has a bigger table. How do we get a larger piece of land? We obtain it from someone who has it. How do we obtain more containers for apple juice? We get them from someone who has these containers. Therefore we create more jobs for unemployed people by getting jobs from someone who has them.

Who has a bigger table? A table maker or owner. Who has a large piece of land? The owner of a large piece of land. Who do we get containers for apple juice from? The owner or maker of containers. Therefore we would obtain more jobs for unemployed people from those who own or make jobs. But who is it that makes or owns jobs? It is the employer.

How do we get a bigger table from a table maker or owner? We give him something for which he will give us a bigger table. How do we get a larger piece of land from the owner of a large piece of land? We give him something for which he will give us this land. How do we get a large container from he who makes or owns a container? We give him something for which he will give us this container. How do we get more jobs from an employer? We give him something for which he will give us the job. In all cases we give money.

If there are many chairs what do we do to use them all? We get more tables. Therefore we need to increase the amount of table owners or makers. If there are more seeds than land what do we do to use them all? We obtain more land. Therefore we need to increase the amount of land owners and amount of land that can be sold. What do we do if there is more juice than there are containers? We get more containers and therefore we need to increase the amount of container makers or owners. If there are a lot more people than jobs what do we do to employ them all? We create more jobs. Therefore we need to increase the amount of employers.

How do we increase the amount of table makers or owners? We give them an incentive to produce more. How do we increase the amount of land owners who are willing to sell land? We give them a greater incentive to sell land. How do we increase the amount of container makers or owners? We give them an incentive to make them. Therefore to increase the amount of employers we need to give them an incentive to hire people.

What is the best incentive to give table makers to make more tables? The more tables a table maker makes the more money he earns. What is the best incentive to give to land owners to sell more land? The more land a land owner sells the more money he makes. What is the best incentive to give a container maker so that he makes more containers? The more containers he makes the more money he earns. Therefore the best incentive an employer can receive for employing people is also money. The more people an employer employs the more money he should earn.

The big question now is: "Who pays the employer for hiring people?" The person who buys the container for excess juice from the container maker is he who needs it. The person who buys the land for excess carrot seeds from the previous owner is the person planting the seeds. The person who buys the table for excess chairs from the table maker is the person who needs the place for all his chairs. Therefore it seems logical that the person who receives a job should be the one who needs it. That is the employee. To decrease or even eliminate unemployment each employee buys a job from an employer unless he is self employed. This gives an incentive for the employer to hire more employees.

In consumerism employment is maximized because workers buy *job contracts* from their employers. Essentially they purchase a job, thus having a right to work at it and receive a wage or salary that is ultimately higher than the price of the job contract. Once again these do not apply to owners or the self employed.

We mentioned previously that wage functions are applicable at the family taxon level of organization. The same holds for job contracts. A job contract is set for a family of services. We now show some examples of families that wage functions and job contracts apply to. A family wage function/job contract is the same for professions that are essentially similar; i.e. in the family "school teachers" we have "high school calculus teacher", "grade 7 science teacher", "high school French teacher" and "grade 8 gym teacher". In the family "building property cleaners" we have "janitor", "maid" and "window cleaner". In the family "fast food preparation work" we have "hamburger cook", "hot dog vendor" – unless he is self employed- "French fryer" and "taco wrapper". In the family "cashiers" we have "grocery cashier", "fast food cashier", "department store cashier" and "convenience store cashier". These are all examples of families with similar job contracts/ wage functions. There are many, many others and there are many more jobs under each family. The point here is to give an example.

Central to the consumerist employment system is the idea of job contracts. It is a contract for work between an employee and an employer under which the employee pays a certain price, the job contract price, to an employer in exchange for employment for a certain length of time. If an employee does not have enough money for a contract but still requires a job, he or she may borrow a certain amount of money from a regular bank- with certain interest or alternatively seek assistance through the employment assistance program. The job contract is bought with Ignits as it is in the accommodational sector - consumerists need not buy job contracts if they work in the governmental or laissez-faire sectors. The job contract is determined by the central bank in a manner similar to a wage function. That is through the voting of 100 industry specific commissioners and the rejecting of the top 25 and lowest 25 votes and averaging the middle 50. The only difference is that there is only one variable, the price of the job, meaning that there is no role for industry specific Chairman. Each industry in the accommodational and materialist sectors has 100 commissioners who decide the value of the job contract for each family of service. This is so there is less work to do if there was just one set of general commissioners. The job contract is based on productivity. This means that usually jobs that pay high wages cost a bit more to buy. The job contract price is fixed for a family of jobs. It cannot change.

Let's look at some examples. A fast food cashier pays 1 000.00 þ for a year contract. Her wage is 9.00 þ/hr. Both of these are determined by the central bank. There is no income tax. In this case she would need to work 112 hours in the year in order to get back the original 1 000.00 þ. Obviously the employer must employ the cahier for more than 112 hours in a year for the cashier to have any benefit.

A pharmacist makes 15.00 þ/hr and her job contract costs 2000.00 þ for half a year. She must work a minimum of 133 hours in half a year. A job contract must give at a minimum 100% return on the job cost.

A high school teacher makes 20.00 þ/ hr and her contract costs 5 000.00 þ per year. 5 000.00þ/20.00 þ/hr = 250 hours for 100 % return. She must work at least 250 hours per year.

A raspberry picker earns 2.00 þ/hr. A 6 month contract costs 600.00 þ per 6 months. The raspberry picker must work at least 300 hours in 6 months.

The percentage earned from buying a contract is called the *adjusted income percentage*. Some contracts are set for different time periods – some are for 6 months while others are for 3 years. Thus the adjusted income percentage must be set for a certain time frame. The most common types of adjusted income percentages are Adjusted Monthly Income Percentage (AMIP) and Adjusted Yearly Income Percentage (AYIP). They are equivalent except that they are expressed in different time frames. If the AMIP is 100 % then the AYIP is 1200%. This is set by the central bank although unlike the wage and salary functions, the AMIP is not fixed. The higher the AMIP is the more money a worker earns and the more willing he is to work. The AMIP that applies to a job contract is the one that was present at the time of the signing of the contract between the worker and the employer. Once a worker signs a contract with an employer, the current AMIP or AYIP is locked in and doesn't fluctuate.

The central bank sets the AMIP and AYIP as it sees fit. The Grand Chairman is in charge of setting it and he can vary it when he sees it is necessary to do so. Suppose the central bank sets the AMIP at 500 %. This means that the worker must earn 5 times the job contract cost during a month of work. An AMIP of less than 100% for a one month contract is bad because the worker will pay more in buying the contract than he will earn in final income from his wage/salary. In order to increase employment the central bank should lower the AIP. In order to help workers and stimulate the economy it should increase the AIP. The AYIP/AMIP may fluctuate.

Once the AMIP/AYIP is set and the central bank has fixed the wage function and job contract price, the minimum number of hours required from the worker can be found out. We will look at some specific examples.

Let's do some calculations. A teacher has a 5 month contract. She is paid 10.00 þ/hour. The job contract price is 500.00 þ for a 5 month contract. The AMIP is 500%

# of hours to work to attain 100 % profit = 500.00 þ hour/10.00 þ = 50 hours

500 %/ month x 5 months = 2500 % AIP

50 hours x 2500% = 1, 250 hours

Thus the teacher works 1, 250 hours in 5 months. Now we calculate her earnings. 1,250 hours x 10.00 þ/ hour = 12 500.00 þ

Thus she earns 12, 500.00 þ in 5 months. However she happened to borrow the 500.00 þ from a private bank to purchase the job contract. The interest rate was 5% simple interest- in the actual economy this could be compounded. Here we will simplify and use simple interest. Therefore she must pay back 500.00 þ x 0.05 + 500.00 þ= 525.00 þ. She is allowed to keep 12 500.00 þ - 525.00 þ = 11 975.00 þ. She doesn't have to pay income tax or property tax or unemployment insurance- these do not exist in our system.

Let's do another calculation. A cashier buys a job contract for 6 months. She earns 5.00 þ/hour and the job contact price is 500.00 þ for a 6 month contract. The AYIP is 2000 %. We assume that she doesn't borrow money to buy the job contract but simply has the money saved up.

500.00 þ hour/ 5.00 þ = 100 hours

AIP in 6 months (X) => 2000%/12 months = X/6 months

X = 1000%

She must work 100 hours to obtain 100 % profit. To get 1000% profit she must work 10 x 100 hours = 1000 hours in 6 months. Since she earns 5.00 þ/hour, she earns 1000 hours x 5.00 þ/hour or 5000.00 þ

Let's look at the case of a car salesman. His wage function is 1000.00 þ/car commission and 5.00 þ/ hour. The central bank sets the AMIP at 200%. There is a JCP in this case. It is 5000.00 þ. His contract is for 5 months. How many cars must he sell or how many hours must he work? In 5 months he makes 5 x 200% = 1000% profit on his JCP. Thus he can sell 50 cars in 5 months or 49 cars and 1000.00 þ/5.00 þ/hour = 200 hours or 48 cars and 2000.00 þ / 5.00 þ /hour = 400 hours. Either way, the car salesman earns a profit of 50 000.00þ – 5000.00 þ= 45 000.00þ.

The Adjusted Income Earnings (AIE) is the amount of money a person earns at the end of a contract minus what he pays to buy the contract. A worker is entitled to earn a percentage increase over his JCP at the end of his contract. This is the minimum the worker will receive at the termination of his contract. Workers are not paid once at the end of their contracts but every two weeks. The AIE can be more than the minimum guaranteed by the AIP but not less unless the worker decides voluntarily to work less. If our car salesman sells 20 cars and works 1000 hours he will make more than he had to pay for his job contract. At the same time his employer will also make a profit. The worker earns 1000.00 þ commission per car sold but the owner of the car dealership (the employer) earns profit from selling the car at the retail level.

The AIP need not be equivalent to that set out by the central bank as in the case of jobs paid by commission. However it should hold for jobs that are paid by the hour. The AIP is determined differently depending on whether a worker is paid by the hour or commission.

A police man's wage function is 20.00 þ /hour and his JCP is 2 000.00 þ for a 6 month contract. His AMIP is 200%

To find hours => 2 000.00 þ / 20.00þ/hour = 100 hours (for 100% profit)

100 hours x 6 months x 200%/month = 1 200 hours

Thus he works 1 200 hours in 6 months and his AIE is (1 200 hours x 20.00 þ /hour) – 2000.00þ = 22 000.00þ If he works 6 months and is paid every 2 weeks he receives 24 000.00þ /13 = 1 846.00 þ every 2 weeks. The 2 000.00 þ are sunk costs in buying the job.

Now we focus our attention on movie actors and hockey players. Simply put, these workers are employed in the laissez-faire sector. They do not have a wage function particular to them. How they are paid is determined by the laws of supply and demand. Furthermore, they are paid with Fortals not Ignits.

Finally let's look at the predicament of a janitor. His wage function is 20.00þ/hour. The JCP is 3 000.00 þ for 9 months. The AMIP is 150 % so he must work:

- 3 000.00 þ /20.00 þ /hour => 150 hours for 100% return on investment

- 150 % x 9 = 1 350 %

- 150 hours x 13.5 = 2 025 hours in 9 months

- 2 025 hours x 20.00 þ / hour = 40 500.00þ

He gets paid every two weeks, so 40 500.00þ /39/2 = 2 076.92þ

To sum things up, the janitor works 2 025 hours in 9 months and every 2 weeks he receives a paycheck for 2 076.92 þ .

Sometimes a worker may want to work for less for some reason. He or she may be studying or caring for a child or have several jobs. Thus he or she may not want to work full time but may want to instead work part time. We need to find a way to calculate the number of hours worked and the AIE of a part time worker. Here we will characterize *part time* as a percentage of full time. Full time is what we calculated before. A person with a Part Time Character (PTC) of 50% works half as much as a full time worker. Part Time Character is defined as how much work a part time worker has relative to a full time worker expressed in terms of a percentage or decimal.

We can gain insight by performing calculations. We have a job where the worker earns a wage of 15.00 þ/hour. The job contract costs 1 000.00þ for a 6 month period. The AMIP is 200%

- Hours worked for 100% profit => 1000.00 þ/15.00 þ/hour = 67 hours

- Increase => 6 months x 200 %/ month = 1200 %

- With the income adjustment => 67 hours x 12 = 800 hours

Amount of pay: 800 hours x 15.00 þ /hour = 12 000.00þ

Suppose the worker can't work 800 hours in 6 months. The worker wants to work about half as much as a full time worker. Therefore his Part Time Character is 0.5 or 50% of full time. We multiply the AMIP by 0.5 Thus 200% x 0.5 = 100 %. In 6 months the worker will earn 100% x 6 = 600% profit. To find out how many hours he works in 6 months we multiply 67 hours by 6. This equals 400 hours. The worker works for 400 hours in this setup. His pay is 400 hours x 15.00 þ/hour = 6 000.00 þ. He gets paid 6 000.00 þ /13 = 461.54 þ every two weeks. Since he had to pay 1000.00 þ for the job contract the AIE is 6000.00 þ - 1000.00þ = 5 000.00þ

Up to this point we have had to calculate the variables in an intuitive fashion. It would be helpful if we derive a formula for calculating these parameters. To calculate the number of hours worked during a contract period we use the formula:

Work Hours = PTC[JCP x hours/wage x AMIP x (n)]

Where PTC is Part Time Character with the values between 0 and 1. JCP is the price of a contract per n months. Hours/wage is the inverse of the wage function –the inverse of the number of Ignits paid for each hour of work. The AMIP is the profit made during a month of a contract. (n) is the length of the contract in months.

The AIE (Adjusted Income Earnings) is the money a worker earns from working minus the initial investment to obtain the job. It is paid in regular intervals rather than as a lump sum. The formula is:

AIE = {PTC[JCP x AMIP x (n)]} – JCP

Where PTC is Part Time Character, JCP is job contract price, AMIP is the adjusted income percentage in one month and (n) is the length of the contract in months.

We would like to know how much a worker is paid when he receives his paychecks. Usually checks are issued every two weeks but this is not fixed- it is up to the central bank to decide this variable. However we will use the 2 week length of time in our examples. To find the income earned on a regular paycheck we use the following formula:

Pay check Value = PTC[JCP x AMIP(/(52/12)(1/2)]

The variables were defined before. Let's give an example. For a PTC= 0.8, a JCP of 1000.00þ and AMIP of 200% and a contract length of 9 months, a bi-weekly paycheck will have this much value:

$$0.8\{1000.00þ \times 2 /[(52/12) \times (1/2)]\} = 738.00þ \text{ per 2 weeks}$$

The hours we have calculated that a worker is entitled to for buying a contract are simply the minimum that a worker is guaranteed for that length of time. However, if the employer wants to, he can offer the employee more than this. This can be due to any reason. Perhaps he likes the work ethic of the employee. However he cannot choose to give a worker less unless of course the worker desires herself to work less and have a part time character. Once a worker buys a job contract she owns the job. Although not very tangible, it is just as much of a possession as a house or car. Through working, one is entitled to reap the profits of this investment. There is the important caveat that the worker can't sell his job to someone else. The job must belong to the person to whom the firm sold it to.

A worker cannot be laid off. The only way a worker can lose his job is if he is fired. The reasons for being fired must be very serious. The employer cannot fire a worker simply because he doesn't like the worker. The worker, in order to get fired, must demonstrate gross incompetence or cause serious damage to the firm. The details for being fired will not be discussed here. Rather it will be the job of the human resources in the consumerist system (not to be confused with the human resource management commission) to come up with a list of the reasons one can be fired for. It suffices to say that being fired deserves just cause.

The employee does have the option of quitting their job. When this happens, he does not recover any money and this includes the JCP. It is disadvantageous to quit a job too soon after being hired since the worker could have made more money if he or she stays with the current employer.

Job contracts have their advantage. They aid employers in several ways. First they give employers money that can be invested in their firm. Secondly they ensure the employer that the employee won't quit the job too quickly. Job contracts also aid employees. They ensure the employee that he will make a handsome profit from working. Also the employee gains protection from downsizing and layoffs. A firm cannot downsize or lay off workers that own job contracts. Employees gain self esteem and self respect by being a valuable part of society. Job contracts are one of the best ways to fight unemployment.

From all this talk about job contracts it may seem that firms would hire anyone. Although job contracts do combat unemployment and give profit to the firm that sells them, this is not necessarily the case. A firm would still benefit from hiring the best employees and consequently selling job contracts to them. Given a choice between selling a job contract to a high school dropout and a university graduate the firm would do to its advantage if it sold the job contract to the university graduate assuming he is best suited for the position and there are other jobs for less skilled workers available. The consumerist system shares with the free-market system the idea that the best employees are the ones that should be hired.

We mentioned before that one of the major Communist objections to the free-market system is that workers are exploited. That is, workers are paid less than they should be, working in sweat shops for just enough to get buy. This objection disappears in consumerism. Employers cannot pay their workers what they like. They are constrained by the parameters set by the central bank and the government, namely wage functions, job contract prices and Adjusted Income Earnings. Also of note is that the idea of fixed wages relieves the problem of discrimination between sexes and between minority groups. All workers of the same profession have the same wage function regardless of their gender, ethnicity, religion or background.

Having discussed that it is advantageous to lower or eliminate unemployment we now turn to several other ideas that should work towards this end. First of all, there are none of the taxes that are pervasive in the free-market system. There is no corporate, income, sales, goods or property taxes. In fact there are no taxes other than the GCT. The absence of these taxes makes it more attractive to do business in a nation under consumerism than one under the free-market or communist orientations.

In consumerism a certain sense of stability is sought after. There are patents to ensure that inventors have rights to their new ideas. The prices of all goods and services, in the GAM sectors, are fixed. The costs of all inputs are fixed. Also all wages and salaries are fixed. This means that these values will not get out of hand due to unmanageable inflation. Also security must be ensured so that business can proceed and there is no danger from rebels or unrest from criminals and thieves.

There is a parameter that directly gives an incentive to firms to hire more employees. It is called the *employment reimbursement transfer* (ERT). In essence the government pays a firm or business a portion of an employee's wage/salary. The ERT is set in the form of a percentage. Let's say, for example, it is 1.5 %. A firm employs 22 workers who each make 2000.00 þ per week. So then each week the government pays the particular firm 22 x 2000.00 þ x 0.015 = 660.00 þ. It is clear that if a firm is paid for having workers and the more workers they have the more they will be paid then the firm will want to hire more workers. This should lower unemployment. The disadvantage of the ERT is that it increases government spending and contributes to the government debt.

A useful way to decrease the unemployment is to increase the size of the army. This is the quickest way to lower the unemployment rate. This may contribute to an increasing debt and deficit. However the main disadvantage of hiring more soldiers is the reputation that it creates in your neighbors and in the international community. Some countries may see this as a form of aggression and hostility and your relations with your neighbors may deteriorate. On the other hand this can be overcome if you make your large army seen not as a threat to world peace but as some kind of "global force of good". By this I mean that instead of using the army to invade your neighbors you use it to help disadvantaged nations when for example they are afflicted by a tsunami or earthquake.

Another parameter designed to lower unemployment is the *capital investment transfer* (CIT). In essence, the government pays a portion of the costs to set up or expand a firm. The CIT is a percentage that involves Ignits. Let's say for example that the CIT is 2%. A winery firm buys a factory for 500 000.00 þ and machines for 200 000.00 þ. The government would give this firm (500 000.00 þ + 200 000.00 þ) x 0.02 = 14 000.00 þ. A year later they buy 50 000.00 þ more worth of equipment. The government would give them 1 000.00 þ. If a firm has some of its start up or expansion costs decreased, it is more likely to start operating in our consumerist nation than in one where it has to pay for all its start up costs by itself. When a firm chooses to do business in our country, it will hire workers, thus lowering unemployment. The main disadvantage to this parameter is that it increases the deficit and may contribute to a greater debt.

The *profit reward transfer* (PRT) also lowers unemployment but in a different way. It is clear that if a firm makes a larger profit it is more inclined to locate itself in the place where it made that profit. The profit reward transfer can be conceptualized as a negative corporate tax. The government pays a firm for making a profit. The PRT is a percentage and has to do with Ignits. So let's say that the PRT is 3%. We have a tire producing firm that has a revenue of 1 000 000.00 þ and running costs of 800 000.00

112

þ. So its profit is 200 000.00 þ. In this case, on top of this profit the government would give the firm an extra (200 000.00 þ x 0.03) = 6 000.00 þ. A firm that makes money on top of profit will surely want to locate its production/business center in a consumerist nation that in a free-market nation where it has to pay a corporate tax just for the privilege of doing business in that country. Any investor/entrepreneur/company owner will clearly see the advantage of the PRT as opposed to paying a corporate tax elsewhere. Therefore more firms/business will be found in our nation. The presence of a firm brings a requirement of workers and thus the decrease of the unemployment rate. Again the disadvantage of the PRT is that it increases spending and may lead to a higher debt or deficit.

In Accommodation Based Consumerism we also have a parameter called the Interest Rate Stimulus (IRS). Essentially the government pays a portion of an investor/borrower's debts to a creditor. The IRS is set as a percentage and deals with Ignits. It can be applied on interest rates in general or certain interest rates (mortgage rate). So suppose the government sets the IRS at 0.02 % and suppose that the central bank sets the interest rate at 3.00 %. Now a firm making calculators and simple electronics borrows 1 000 000.00 þ from a creditor to start their business and expand. Now when it comes time to pay back the loan the firm would have to pay back 1 000 000.00 þ + (1 000 000.00 þ x 0.0028) = 1 002 800.00 þ and the government would pay (1 000 000.00 þ x 0.00020) = 200.00 þ. The creditor would earn a return equal to 3.00 % of the loan but the money comes from both the government and the investor. If the borrower pays less to borrow, he is more likely to invest in the economy. This stimulates the economy as the investment helps firms which hire more workers. In the long run the investment may indirectly increase the materialist output and thus the GDCP. So, ceteris paribus (that is, keeping taxes constant), this may lead to an increase in government revenue through the GCT. On the down side, the IRS directly increases the deficit and government debt. However it is probably the best, or one of the best, things the government can spend its money. In the end the stimulus the IRS provides for the Consumerist economy may be worth the government spending on this parameter.

The last parameter we have for decreasing the unemployment rate works rather indirectly. It is called the *consumerist spending reimbursement* (CSR). The main idea is to bring more firms to our consumerist nation so that they do business here and employ consumerists. If we increase consumerist spending on goods and services in the consumerist nation, the firms will make more revenue and thus more profit and will be more favorable to doing business in this nation. What the CSR does is that it pays consumerists for spending money on goods and services. It is set as a percentage and is expressed in Ignits, not Norses. Let's say it is 0.1 %. Suppose a car costs 20,000 Θ at a retail level (car dealership). For making this purchase the consumerist earns 20,000.00 þ x 0. 001 = 20 þ. So here the car dealership has 20,000 þ added to its Ignit account and the consumerist has 20,000 Θ deducted from his Norse account. However the consumerist is given 20 þ to his Ignit account from the government.

We talked about unemployment, wages and salaries as they exist in the consumerist system. In addition we have explored certain variables and parameters that are peculiar to consumerism. We surveyed the different parameters and ideas designed to lower unemployment. With this knowledge we can further explore the functioning of the accommodation based consumerist economic system.

Anti-Unemployment Measures

Unemployment is the occurrence when there isn't enough work for our workers. As a consequence, some people are without a job. We came to the conclusion that unemployment is very undesirable. In this section we will discuss several anti-unemployment measures; that is special programs designed to combat and eliminate unemployment.

We list anti-unemployment measures. The name of the measure is followed by a very brief description of it. These are designed to reduce the level of unemployment. Some of these have been discussed before while others will be talked about in detail in future sections.

- The non-existence of taxes besides the GCT- a lack of corporate, sale, property and income tax helps the economy while decreasing unemployment

- consumerist spending reimbursement (CSR)- money is given to consumerists for buying things, thus increasing spending and attracting firms

- Interest Rate Stimulus (IRS)- the government pays a portion of a firm's loan; thus increasing firm's investment and increasing employment

- profit reward transfer (PRT)- a firm earns money from the government for making a profit – a negative corporate tax- thus increasing the likelihood that the firm will do business in our nation and hire workers here

- capital investment transfer (CIT) – a firm earns money from the government for expanding operation; thus increasing the likelihood that the firm will do business in our nation and hire workers here

- employment reimbursement transfer (ERT)- the government pays a portion of a worker's wage making it more likely that a firm will hire a worker

- Increase the size of army- by hiring soldiers, the government directly decreases the unemployment rate; may have negative externalities

- The existence of purchasable Job Contracts- an employer is paid to hire more workers; giving him an incentive to hire more workers

- The work for freedom program- prison inmates are given an occupation in exchange for time off their sentence

- The recycle for pay program- consumerists are paid by the government when they bring in their recyclable items

- Employment agency – employers pay a firm to hire more workers

- Employment Assistance Program – the government pays employers to hire more workers in exchange for an interest on the price of the job

The above anti-unemployment measures can be considered ways to reduce the level of unemployment. The next two anti-unemployment measures are designed to completely eradicate unemployment:

- The command partition- the command partition employs virtually anyone that is unable to find a job in the natural or governmental partition

- The laissez-faire labor system- also hires anyone that cannot find work

The Employment Assistance Program

In the employment assistance program the government pays the employer to hire a worker. The worker then later pays the government for helping him find an employer. He pays back with a considerable interest.

This program is primarily intended for those job-seekers that can't afford to pay or don't want to pay for the job contract for employment. Recall that for jobs in the accommodational sector and the materialist sector of the natural partition, a consumerist must buy a "job contract". This entitles him to work for a job for a certain length of time and ensures him a considerable profit. It also protects him from being laid-off through downsizing. This gives the employer an incentive to hire more employees as the more workers he hires and more job contracts he sells, the more income he earns from that.

A worker interested in a particular job has two options. He can either buy the job contract from the employer directly, thus earning the right to work at that job. Alternatively, he can have help from the employment assistance program. In that way, the government buys the job contract from the employer and the money goes to the employer. Eventually, the employee has to pay the government the value of the job contract but with a considerable interest. This special interest is called the *Employment Assistance Program Interest Rate* (EAPIR). It is set by the government.

Let's do some calculations. Someone wants to be a cashier. The job contract to be a cashier costs 500.00 þ for a 6 month contract. The AMIP is 100 %. The EAPIR is 20 %. So in 6 months this cashier would make 6 x 500.00 þ =3000.00 þ. The cashier needs to pay the government with interest for helping him find a job. He pays (500.00 þ x 0.2) + 500.00 þ = 600.00 þ. He can pay in installments (every month or every 2 weeks) or as a lump sum at the end of the contract.

In the above example, several groups greatly benefited. First, the cashier obtained a job and made a considerable profit. The employer earned 500.00 þ upfront as a reward for hiring the worker. Furthermore the government made money through the EAPIR. In fact it made 100.00 þ.

The employment assistance program is a win-win-win system. It helps job seekers find a job more smoothly and efficiently. It ensures that employers are more likely to find an employee to hire and make a profit for doing so. It acts as a source of revenue for the government. Thus it functions as both an anti-unemployment measure and a source of governmental revenue.

Last point to mention is that in this discussion of the employment assistance program we have used the term "government" very vaguely. The profit from this program, i.e. the EAPIR, actually goes to all levels of government. All three levels of government receive 1/3 of the profit and at each level the distribution is based on relative population.

Thus functions the employment assistance program. It helps both the employee as well as the employer. It also helps the three levels of government by making interest-profit on job contracts.

Physical Inputs

To produce goods, an economy needs inputs. A physical input is a material item used to produce another good. Steel and plastic are required to make cars. Plastic is used to make certain toys. Glass and wood are used to make windows. Cotton and polyester are used to make clothes. Rubber is used to make shoes. Synthetics are used to make paint. In this section we will talk about the relationship physical inputs have with the economy.

Recall from the section on economic taxonomy that a physical input is one that has the title "input" in its designation taxon. We group inputs into families. Two inputs that can be used to make the same product are relatively similar and can be exchanged one for the other are grouped in the same family. This grouping of inputs into families is very important.

All physical inputs of the same family have the same *input function*. This is how much it costs to use such an input. An input function is created similarly to a price function or a wage function. The industry specific Chairman sets the form of the input function. The 100 industry specific Commissioners vote on the parameters of the input function. The top 25 and bottom 25 votes are discarded while the middle 50 votes are averaged. This system of setting prices for inputs is more efficient than if a single person were to pick the price of the input and is much less time consuming than if it were done by a single Grand Chairman and 100 Consumerist Commissioners.

Let's see some examples of input function families. Pine and oak are used to make tables and chairs so they would be in the same family. Cotton and polyester are used interchangeably to make clothing so they would be in one family. Duck feathers and goose feathers are both used to make pillow stuffing so they would be in one family. Suppose that in the "bird feathers" family, to which duck and goose feathers belong, the industry specific Chairman sets the form of the input function as x/kg. This means that the 100 industry specific Commissioners must vote on the value of x. Suppose that they vote a value of 2.50 þ for x. Therefore a kilogram of goose or duck feather would cost 2.50þ. Prices are in Ignits as inputs are not sold directly to consumerists and are therefore in the accommodational sector.

The point of making input families with inputs of the same cost is to instigate quality selection. Since all production choices cost the same, producers pick the input of the highest quality. French fry makers pick the tastier, healthier potatoes rather than the inferior ones. Cars brake down less frequently since their components are superior. The steak at a restaurant is always of the highest grade. Bridges collapse less often because what they are made of is longer lasting. In general all the products made by producers are top of the line.

Physical inputs, as we have seen, are necessary for the production of any and all goods. In our system we group the various inputs into families. Each family has a different input function. This ultimately leads to a situation where only the best inputs are utilized.

Ultra Universal Healthcare

Accommodation based consumerism prides itself with its grand health care system. A country's healthcare system is a direct reflection of the prosperity of a nation. The more universal the health care system, the better. We, in consumerism, want the highest level of healthcare possible as the country gains prestige by having a robust health care system.

In accommodation based consumerism, all consumerists, without discrimination, receive a government issued "health card". They present this card when seeking help from a member of the medical community. The health care provider then directly bills the government, either at the federal or provincial/state level. Free universal health care is provided entirely by the government through the sources of revenue the levels of government have; including the GCT, gambling profits, and profits from the socialist trade pool.

This universal health care coverage covers all hospital stays, all medication, vision care, dentistry, chiropractic, naturopathic treatment, trips to the local walk-inn clinic, psychologist and psychiatrist, blood work at the blood clinic and many other things. Everything that has to do with medicine is covered by the government; i.e. it is part of the governmental sector.

Each medical service; i.e. heart operation, the filling of a cavity, psychologist appointment, etc… has a price/ wage function set by the central bank. How much each medical practitioner is paid is determined by the members of the central bank as they vote on wage/price functions for medical services.

To a large extent, a universal health care system helps everyone regardless whether they are helped directly by it. For example, if a police officer has a broken leg, he can't serve the community. However, if we help heal his leg then we can get him back to his job so he can continue helping people. Providing medical services to one person invariably provides benefits to all other people that can now benefit from his services.

We saw that accommodation based consumerism has a very high standard health care system. All medical services, from trips to the doctor, the hospital or the eye doctor are financed by the government, either the federal or provincial. A healthy, well cared for population is a more productive one.

The Retail Mark-up

We define retail as the selling of final goods directly to consumerists. It would be impractical if all factories or farms sold directly to its customers. Problems such as those relating to transportation would result. An economy would function more smoothly if retailers bought goods from a producer and sold them to consumerists in convenient locations.

A retail outlet buys goods from a manufacturer or factory and in selling these must make a profit. This profit is called the *retail mark-up*. The retail mark-up is a percentage increase in the price of a good sold at a retail store. The price functions for families of goods and services set by the central bank only apply to manufactured goods; not the ones sold to the public. The price the public pays for a good is affected by the retail mark-up.

We have a store that sells shoes. A pair of shoes costs 80.00 Ο/pair. The retailer must pay 80.00 þ to the shoe factory to acquire these shoes (although the final price is in Norses the retailer must pay in Ignits because they are at this stage considered inputs for retail purposes). The central bank sets a retail mark-up in terms of a percentage. Let's assume that it is 20% in our economy. Therefore the shoe salesman can sell the shoes at 80.00 Ο x 0.2 + 80.00Ο = 96.00 Ο. The shoe salesman must sell the shoes at this price; no lower and no higher. The 16.00 Ο represent profit. It must cover all of the operating costs of the store such as shipping of the shoes, the wages of the shoe store employees and other costs. It is essential that when the central bank sets the retail mark-up it is high enough to cover the operating costs of the retail establishment. In this example, let's suppose that the consumerist spending reimbursement (CSR) is 4 %. So when the consumer buys the 96.00 Ο worth pair of shoes, the government reimburses him (96.00 Ο x 0.04) = 3.84 þ. The reimbursement is in Ignits while the shoes at the retail store are in Norses. This reimbursement encourages the consumerist to do more shopping and thus stimulate the economy.

Let's elicit two more examples for clarity. Take the case of a hardware store which sells paint. Paint from the factory costs 0.50 Ο /litre and comes in 4 L cans. The retail mark-up is 25%. Therefore the store must sell the cans of paint for (0.50 Ο x 4) x 0.25 + (0.50 Ο x 4) = 2.50 Ο. This should cover operating expenses like the shipping costs and wages and rent. If the CSR is 4%, then the consumerist buying the paint receives 2.50 Ο x 0.04 = 0.10 þ.

Now take the case of a car dealer. Cars from the car factory cost 10 000.00 Ο and the retail mark-up is 25 %. The car dealership can sell each car for 10 000.00 Ο x 0.25 + 10 000.00 Ο = 12 500.00 Ο. This should cover operating costs. If the CSR is 1 %, the consumerist buying the car receives 12 500.00 Ο x 0.01 = 125.00 þ.

The retail mark-up can be manipulated by the central bank. It can be lowered to decrease retail profit and increase the amount of sales or it can be raised to help retailers and decrease sales. It does not have to remain fixed but can fluctuate from time to time. Its value is determined by the Grand Chairman of the central bank.

It is possible that factories, farms and manufacturing facilities may sell directly to the public if they wish. They then don't earn the amount set in a price function but are entitled to a retail mark-up. If they didn't we would have a problem as factories would sell for a lower price than the retailer and there would be competition in price. But this cannot be. Prices must be fixed and producers must compete in quality (in the GAM sectors). Let's look at an example of this. A shoe factory makes shoes. A pair of shoes costs 80.00 Ѳ. Instead of charging this much to a shoe store which would charge a retail mark-up on this, the shoe factory has another option. They can sell directly to consumerists. The shoe factory builds a huge warehouse right next door to its factory. Let's assume that the retail mark-up is 25%. The shoe factory could charge each consumerist 80.00 Ѳ x 0.25 + 80.00 Ѳ= 100.00 Ѳ for a pair of shoes.

The question now arises: if a factory can sell its products at a higher price by selling directly to the public, why would it bother to sell at the price set by the price function to retailers? There are a few reasons. Not everyone is willing to travel all the way to a factory to buy a good. Secondly, there are also costs associated with selling the good at the factory as there are in any retail store with the exception of transportation costs. A factory selling to the public would still have to pay its utility fees, worker's wages and for space. Also, retailers order goods from a factory in bulk whereas individual consumerists buy in much smaller quantities. In the shoe case, a consumerist may buy a pair of shoes from the factory at 100.00 Ѳ, but a shoe retailer would probably order several hundred at 80.00 þ per pair.

The retail mark-up must be included in the price of a good. A price tag on a good cannot say, for example, (1.00 Ѳ + 25% retail mark-up). This may lead consumerists to believe that they are paying some kind of tax on the good. The retail mark-up is simply how much the retailer makes extra for retailing a final good. The price tag from before should say "1.25 Ѳ" not "1.00 Ѳ + 25%".

The retail markup in general only applies to firms in the materialist and accommodational sectors. In the governmental sector, the purchases are essentially done by the government so there is no need for a retail markup. In the laissez-faire sector, final sale prices, including at the retail level are determined by the forces of supply and demand. Thus the retail markup is not necessary in the laissez-faire sector.

The retail mark-up is the incentive for retailers to serve consumerists. Profit in the form of a retail mark-up ensures that consumerists will always have close access to quality goods. People with quality goods are in some ways happier people. At least, they are not worse from it.

Gross National Product

The Gross National Product (GNP) is the main way to compare the consumerist economy relative to other nations in terms of productivity/prosperity. The GNP is to the accommodational sector what the GDCP is to the materialist sector. Basically the GNP refers to the final output of goods and services in the accommodational sector.

The GNP measures the output of the accommodational sector. It is therefore expressed in Ignits. Let's talk about what is and what isn't included in the GNP. All land bought and sold is part of the GNP. This includes residential, commercial and recreational land. All accommodation is also included. This means all houses, apartments, office buildings and palaces. But it would not include the cost of building materials or construction workers salaries that were needed to construct buildings. All utilities are also included. This means the price of electricity, hot water and cable. Thus if a consumerist owes 200.00 þ to his electricity provider, this would count towards the GNP. Appliances and home accessories are included. Their value is after the retail markup. It would thus pertain to things like a refrigerator at a department store but not the price the department store had to pay to the factory to purchase the refrigerator. Also all leisure factors in. So the price of vacations and tickets to events are involved. For example a ticket to an opera concert worth 100.00 þ would be included.

The GNP does not tell us anything about the output of either the materialist, governmental or laissez-faire sectors. Thus it clearly underestimates the actual value (output) of our economy. However since all Norses eventually, at some point, become turned into Ignits, the GNP has some usefulness in categorizing the prosperity of a consumerist nation.

The main purpose of the GNP is as a statistic. It has no real effect on other aspects of the economy but tells us where we stand relative to other nations. A large GNP may indicate a prosperous economy or as we will see in the next section one with an overabundance of Ignits in circulation.

We defined the term gross national product (GNP). We gave examples of what would be counted towards the GNP. The main value of this parameter is as some abstract measure of prosperity between nations.

Anti-Inflation Measures

Inflation is defined as the steady increase in general prices from one period of time to another. Most economists agree that when it is extremely low < 2%, it shouldn't be a problem for any economy. However it is universally recognized that an economy can be virtually destroyed with a huge inflation. Such was the case in Germany in the 1920's when their currency devalued a billion or trillion percent over a span of three years.

For the most part, inflation shouldn't be much of a problem for our system since the price/wage/input functions in the GAM sectors are fixed by the central bank. There may be difficulties in the laissez-faire sector as in that sector prices are not fixed and the prices of goods/services/wages are determined by the forces of supply and demand. Nevertheless there is still some problem as the money supply in the four sectors increases due to the consumerist grant (both general and non-working) and the GCT. This is caused by the GDCP which every once in a while creates a greater money supply.

So the state of affairs is such: there are constantly more and more money, Norses, in the materialist and governmental sectors due to the GCT and working and nonworking consumerist grants. After transactions for goods and services, the money turns into Ignits in the accommodational sector. From there it either circulates indefinitely or is turned into Fortals and it circulates there indefinitely. This, of course, does not cause major problems if there isn't too much circulating money. In fact such a setup actually indicates a healthy growing economy.

The problem occurs when there are too many Ignits and Fortals circulating in the accommodational and laissez- faire sectors due to the fact that, in the accommodational sector there is pressure on fixed price functions and in the laissez-faire sector demand starts to outstrip supply causing inflation. We need some kind of mechanism or mechanisms to slow the rate of money supply growth in the accommodational sector. For the laissez-faire sector we need something to prevent hyperinflation and keep the inflation at as low a level as possible. In this section we describe six such mechanisms

There are six anti-inflationary measures in the accommodation based consumerist economic system. Although they refer to controlling inflation, these parameters actually control the money supply. They are 1) the accommodational markdown, 2) the Ignit/Fortal exchange rate mechanism, 3) the consumerist central bank stock, 4) the speculative central bank stock, 5) the consumerist governmental bond and 6) the speculative governmental bond. They will be discussed in detail in later sections but for now let's examine each of them briefly in turn.

The first is the accommodational markdown. This will be discussed in the next section. The accommodational markdown is a special parameter that controls the removal of Ignits from the accommodational sector. This parameter does not affect either the governmental, laissez-faire or materialistic sectors. Essentially, a portion of the revenue from sales for certain goods and services in certain industries and classes is deducted from the seller in the accommodational sector. This money does not go to the government as revenue for social services. It is completely destroyed. That is, it is removed from bank book entries. In a way it appears as a strange sales tax but the difference is that no money goes to the government. The accommodation markdown is set by the central bank. Suppose it is set at 20%. If John sells a 1 000 000 þ piece of land to Kevin, Kevin pays John 1 000 000 þ but John only keeps 800 000 þ. The 200 000 þ (20 % of 1 000 000 þ) are taken away from the bank records. To help the economy grow, the accommodational markdown could be very small or even zero. We will discuss in future sections what goods and services could potentially be under the influence of this parameter although decisions regarding the accommodational markdown are ultimately under the control of the central bank

There are quite a few goods and services under the accommodation markdown. Those that are not are usually those affected by the retail markup. But certainly, things like land, accommodation and utilities are.

The second anti-inflation measure is called the Ignit-Fortal exchange mechanism The Ignit/Fortal exchange rate mechanism is a special program that decreases money in circulation- both Ignits and Fortals- in a quite roundabout way. Essentially it costs money to exchange Ignits to Fortals back and forth. The exchange rate mechanism refers to how much it costs to trade one Fortal for an Ignit and one Ignit for a Fortal. The key idea is that the two are not necessarily inverses. For example, it is possible that $5 \text{ þ} = 1\text{f}$ and $7\text{f} = 1 \text{ þ}$. So for every 5 Ignits one gets 1 Fortal, and for every 7 Fortals one gets 1 Ignit. Clearly, if one were to continuously exchange the two currencies back and forth, he would lose a lot of money. The Ignit-Fortal exchange mechanism is a very subtle way to decrease the money supply and take Ignits and Fortals out of circulation.

The consumerist central bank stock represents stock that the central bank sells to investors for a fixed price. Investors make a profit on these stocks based on an interest rate. The money (in Ignits) received from selling these stocks goes to a special pool called the Consumerist Anti-Inflationary Pool and is thus taken out of circulation from the accommodational sector. Investors can sell these stocks to other investors or the central bank as long as it is at the price set by the central bank. When an investor makes an interest profit or wants to sell his consumerist central bank stock to the central bank, the central bank repays him through the money still in the Consumerist Anti-Inflationary Pool. The fact that this pool is always larger than an investor's single investment ensures us that the central bank can always repay investors their gains and the value of the stock through the Consumerist Anti-Inflationary Pool. As a final consequence, investors are guaranteed to earn a profit by buying Consumerist Central Bank Stock.

The speculative central bank stock is similar to other speculative stocks and stocks in free-market capitalism in general. The central bank sells speculative central bank stock to interested investors. The money (in the form of Fortals) from selling this stock is taken out of circulation in the Laissez-faire sector. It is not spent on anything but taken out of circulation and put into the speculative anti-inflationary pool. Traders and investors trade the speculative central bank stock on a speculative stock market. The price of the stock is not fixed and can fluctuate up or down in value. Investors/traders loose or gain money depending on how they sell or buy the stock as the price of the stock goes up or down.

The consumerist governmental bond is very important in controlling the money supply- particularly in the accommodational sector. The government sells bonds to investors. It sets an interest rate and an interest repayment frequency. When the government sells a consumerist governmental bond, the revenue from the purchase is placed inside the consumerist anti-inflationary pool. When it is time to repay the investor his maturity or pay him his interest rate profit, the money in the consumerist anti-inflationary pool is used for that purpose. Usually the money in the consumerist anti-inflationary pool is much greater than what is needed to pay an investor what he is owed from his bond maturity or interest payments. In this way the government reduces the amount of Ignits circulating (in bank book entries) in the accommodational sector.

Finally, the speculative governmental bond functions to reduce the money supply (in the form of Fortals) in the Laissez-faire sector. The government sells speculative governmental bonds to investors.

However, unlike in the case with consumerist governmental bonds, the parameters regarding these bonds are not set by the government. The interest rate, repayment frequency, size of bond as well as the maturity are determined through the interaction of the government and investors. The money (in Fortals) from selling speculative governmental bonds is put into the speculative anti-inflationary pool. When it is time for the government to pay an investor his maturity and interest payments, the payments are taken directly out of the speculative anti-inflationary pool.

The last two ways to decrease the money supply and fight inflation involve governmental bonds, both consumerist and speculative. Consumerist governmental bonds decrease the amount of Ignits in circulation (in bank book entries) while speculative governmental bonds decrease the amount of Fortals in circulation (in bank book entries). Essentially, the government sells one of the two types of bonds. Instead of investing this money into infrastructure, schools, defense, health care, it puts it aside into a governmental bond pool made of both the consumerist and speculative anti-inflationary pools. The governmental bond pool contains both large sums of Fortals and Ignits. The investor is paid from the governmental bond pool every set amount of time that is dictated by the repayment frequency. When it is time to pay the whole value of the bond upon the maturity of the bond then either 1) the government subsidizes the bond repayment from the government budget. Or 2) there may still be money in the governmental bond pool from selling government bonds previously that have a maturation date a long time in the future.

The GDCP and the six anti-inflationary measures can, very generally, be used to manipulate the money supply in accommodation based consumerism with regards to 2 currencies Fortals and Ignits. If the GDCP is higher than the anti-inflationary measures than there will be a greater amount of Ignits and Fortals in the accommodational and laissez-fare sectors. However, if the six measures remove more money than the GDCP puts in, the total money supply should steadily decrease

Of the six anti-inflationary measures the AMD is least favorable. When trying to reduce the money supply it is preferable to make use of the other anti-inflationary measures first. This is due to the fact that the AMD has a negative effect on the economy more so than the other anti-inflationary measures. The AMD should be used as a last resort to combat increases in the money supply.

These are the 6 anti-inflationary measures. This is how we fight inflation and decrease the money supply. There are six main measures to combat inflation that we saw. These are the accommodational markdown, the Fortal-Ignit exchange mechanism and the Speculative/Consumerist governmental bond and stock markets. Some are under the influence of the government while others are under the influence of the central bank. They are meant to reduce and control the money supply in the accommodational as well as Laissez-faire sectors. They are designed to restrict the quantity of Fortals (f) and Ignits (þ) in two very important sectors of the accommodation based consumerist economy. With a managed inflation/money supply we can avoid many of the problems that have plagued other economies.

The Accommodational Markdown

We now come upon one of the more important parameters in the Accommodation Based Consumerist economy. This is the accommodational markdown. The accommodational markdown is a deduction of money in the form of Ignits from certain industries in the accommodational sector upon a transaction between two agents. This money is not given to the government or back to the central bank. It is completely destroyed- erased from the bank records.

The reason for the accommodational markdown (AMD) is to have something to combat the problem of the accommodational overflow calamity. This occurs when the amount of money in the accommodational sector keeps growing out of control like a pool. The logic for the presence of this calamity is this. The central bank grants Norses to consumerists. These turn into Ignits during a transaction. Ignits are used to purchase accommodational goods and services because they cannot be used to purchase materialist goods nor can they be exchanged for Norses. Thus everything turns into Ignits in the end; which circulate in the accommodational sector. The problem is not that they end up there but that they cannot leave. Since more and more Norses are granted, the amount of Ignits becomes bigger and bigger, in a sense overflowing. This makes it hard to keep the prices of goods and services fixed and to maintain the steadiness of wages and salaries. Thus the forces of inflation and the steadiness of prices rip at each other. The excess of Ignits tries to raise inflation in the same way that more money in a free- market causes the prices of goods to increase. So what are we to do? Either we let prices fluctuate or dispose of this excess of Ignits and keep prices constant. The solution is the Accommodational Markdown. During many transactions in the accommodational sector a percentage of the trade is taken out of the sector. The value of this percentage is set by the central bank.

The AMD affects the sellers much more so than the buyers. In many circumstances, which we will soon discuss, when someone sells something in the accommodational sector, a percentage of the trade is deducted from the seller and destroyed. It is taken permanently out of bank account records. This money does not go to the government as a tax but is completely eliminated. To be cynical, this could be called a "tax". However unlike a usual tax none of the money goes to the government.

Let's work through some examples, Joe works in a doughnut shop and he is paid 20 000.00 þ a year for his services. He can spend this on the accommodational sector. He finds a house costing 20 000.00 þ and wants to buy it. Paul owns the house. Joe gives Paul the 20 000.00 þ and he receives the house. Now Paul has 20 000.00 þ. However he must give a percentage of this to be taken out of the economy in accordance with the AMD. If the AMD is 20 % then Paul keeps 16 000.00 þ for his profit to spend as he sees fit. 4 000.00 þ are erased from his account. In this example we have omitted a parameter that we will discuss more fully later. This is the Real Estate Profit Percentage. This factors in if real estate agents are used to buy or sell the house in the above example.

Mike works at a car dealership. In a year he accumulates 30 000.00 þ. He wants to own land. Residential land costs 500.00 þ per square meter. He can therefore buy 60 square meters of land. Mrs. Sue owns such land. She sells 60 square meters of land to Mike and she earns 30 000.00 þ minus the AMD. If the AMD is 20 %, she earns 24 000.00þ and 6 000.00 þ are destroyed (erased from bank records). The AMD factors in cases where land is exchanged.

Pat works as a dentist. He makes 50 000.00 þ per year. He has to pay 400.00þ for electricity to his electricity provider. During payment the 400.00 þ are deducted from his bank account and the utility company takes this minus the AMD. If the AMD is 20% the utility company has 320.00 þ added to its bank account and 80.00þ are destroyed. The AMD factors in cases where utility services are provided.

An interesting question arises. Why would anyone sell a house or land or anything at a loss? In the first case Paul sold a house for 20 000.00 þ but received only 16 000.00 þ. Why would he be willing to incur such losses? The reason is that now he needs only 4 000.00 þ to buy a better house than the one he sold to Joe. So suppose he finds a job as a grocery clerk. He earns 15 000.00 þ more. (For simplicity we forget about other purchases in the accommodational sector such as utilities, appliances and vacations). With the new money he can now buy a better house and earn 24 800.00 þ assuming 20% AMD earn some more money and repeat the process. This way he can go from a better to a better house every time.

Now let's look at the case of buying and selling land. Why would Mrs. Sue want to sell land at a loss? She has 60m^2 of land worth 30 000.00 þ which Mike buys from her. She only keeps 24 000.00þ. If she only finds a job and makes more than 6 000.00 þ she can earn enough to buy more land than she originally started off with. Suppose she becomes a cashier and makes 20 000.00 þ in a year. In this case we are also assuming that all her expenditures are on land (not utilities, appliances or accommodation etc) Thus she now has 44 000.00 þ (24 000.00 þ + 20 000.00 þ) She can buy 44 000.00 þ worth of the same type of land. She buys residential land with the money. She can buy 88 square meters of residential land (44 000.00 þ /500.00 þ/m^2) She can repeat the process. She can sell the land earning 35 200.00 þ (assuming the AMD is 20%) and continue working as a cashier. The following year she would have 55 200.00 þ. With this she can buy a plot of residential land the size of 110 square meters. Mrs. Sue gradually becomes better and better off.

Let's see how the AMD operates in the other industries of the accommodational sector. Let's look at the utility industry. Let's suppose that electricity costs 10.00 þ /kWh. Alex is a doctor and earns 100 000.00 þ a year. We assume that the AMD is 20 % and he only spends his income on electricity (just to isolate the case). In a year he uses 500 kWh. Thus he must pay 500 kWh x 10.00þ /kWh = 5 000.00þ per year for electricity. The electricity provider earns 5 000.00 þ x 0.8 = 4 000.00 þ and 1 000.00 þ are destroyed. This would not affect the electric company much because it is probably operating at economies of scale and is a monopoly. This is how the AMD would apply to the utility industry.

The AMD doesn't apply to the appliance and home accessories industries. Suppose a stove costs 800.00 þ from a factory and that the retail mark up is 25 % and the accommodational markdown is 30 %. If this were the case then the retailers that are selling the stove must necessarily lose money. Now suppose a rug costs 2.00 þ/m^2 and the retail mark-up is 25 %. Now if the AMD is anything higher than 25 %, the retailer would be losing money. Yet it is sometimes necessary to set a high AMD. There is no AMD on stocks, bonds, salaries, wages, loans and investment profit. The financial, appliance and home accessories industries are the main industries to which the AMD does not apply.

Regarding the leisure industry of the accommodational sector, the AMD does apply. It applies because there is no retail mark-up to worry about. In the appliance and home accessories industries the sellers obtained all their income from the retail mark-up. Therefore any accommodational markdown greater than the retail mark-up would result in negative profit. The leisure industry is mostly a service industry. If a vacationer pays for a vacation in a Caribbean resort, those that provide the vacation package will receive what the consumerist paid minus the AMD. Suppose Kurt makes 100 000.00 þ a year as a lawyer. He is interested in a 2 week vacation to Jamaica. The all-inclusive package costs 5 000.00 þ.This is how much Kurt pays. If the AMD is 20 %, the vacation company earns 0.8 x 5 000.00 þ = 4 000.00 þ. The 1 000 þ is simply destroyed (deducted from the bank accounts). Here's one more example. Joanne makes 15 000.00 þ as a waitress per year and loves a local rock group (let's assume that she only spends on tickets). Tickets cost 100.00 þ. She pays this to get in. The rock group earns (assuming 20% AMD) 80.00 þ from every ticket sold. This is how the AMD affects the leisure industry.

So which industries in the accommodational sector does the AMD apply to? As a principle, it does *not* apply to those that are affected by the retail mark-up. We have mentioned the appliance, home accessory and financial industries. We can add to this the "alcohol and tobacco" industry. The AMD does not apply to inputs to products, i.e. cotton for a t-shirt.

A very important point about the AMD is this. It necessarily shrinks the economy, lowering the GNP. Therefore when the economy is just developing it would make more sense to just leave it at 0%. An economy may be better off without it. It should only be invoked if the economy has certain growth and the accommodational overflow calamity is perceived to be a problem.

We saw the importance of the accommodational markdown. We saw how it works. Finally we saw how it applies to the consumerist economy.

The Gross Domestic Consumerist Product

We begin by talking about what the Gross Domestic Consumerist Product (GDCP) is. The official definition is: "the value of all final goods sold or in a position to be sold at the set price in the materialist sector plus the value of all final services in the materialist sector purchased by consumerists at the set price in a given period of time". The meaning of this definition will be made clear shortly.

Next we give examples of what would be counted in the GDCP. It would include a loaf of bread bought by Joe in grocery store. It would not include the cost of wheat, flour or water used to make bread or the purchase of the bread by the grocery store from a bakery. It would include the price of a car at a dealership. It would include the price of a chair at a furniture store. But not the wood or how much the furniture cost at the factory. The final good sold to the consumerists is included in the GDCP but the means of how it was produced is not.

Included in the GDCP are all products in the materialist sector which have the potential to be sold to consumerists. However they can only be counted once- not in several periods. If a convenience store does not sell 10 bags of chips, these are still counted towards the GDCP. If a car is not sold, it will nevertheless be counted towards the GDCP. It doesn't matter whether goods are actually sold. The crucial point is that they be available to consumerists. It is also crucial that they be only counted once, not every time they are not sold.

Services in the materialist sector are also counted towards the GDCP. The main distinction between the contribution of goods and services to the GDCP is that services must actually be bought by consumerists. Services such as teaching, cleaning, fixing cars or painting are included because they are final services. Non-final services like the work of a janitor, waitress, cashier, cook or baker are not included.

Final goods and services must originate from the materialist sector- not the accommodational, laissez-fare or governmental sectors. A house or a bottle of beer would not be included because they are items from the accommodational sector. Goods and services in the accommodational sector are discluded from the GDCP.

Business investments are not included because they are in the accommodational and laissez-faire sectors. Exports and imports only factor in as much as they affect the ability of consumerists to purchase goods from the materialist sector. Thus an export would not be added since consumerists can't purchase it. Imports may be added if a consumerist has the ability to purchase it. For example if a car dealership imports a car, that car would be added to the GDCP. Whether an item is added depends on the consumerist's ability to purchase it.

The time period in which the GDCP is counted is one month. Every month firms and retailers must report their contribution to the GDCP to the central bank. This is called the Individual Consumerist Product. In a way this is similar to reporting one's taxes every year in the free-market system. The important difference is that the firms and individuals do not actually give any money to the central bank. They just mention how much they contributed to the economy. As was mentioned, goods that were not sold but had the potential to be so, can only be reported for one period. Let's do a simple example. John's convenience store sold 10 bags of chips, 5 bottles of pop and 3 boxes of cookies. He had in stock 2 more boxes of cookies but couldn't sell them. This example is very simplified but it will serve its purposes. The chips cost 1.00 Θ each bag. A bottle of pop costs 2.00 Θ and a box of cookies cost 3.00 Θ.

There is a retail mark-up of 50 %. Let's see what John's convenience store's Individual Consumerist Product is:

10 x 1.00 ☉ + 10 x (1.00 ☉ x 0.5) = 15.00 ☉

5 x 2.00 ☉ + 5 x (2.00 ☉ x 0.5) = 15.00 ☉

3 x 3.00 ☉+ 3 x (3.00 ☉ x 0.5) = 13.50 ☉

2 x 3.00 ☉ + 2 x (3.00 ☉ x 0.5) = 9.00 ☉

Total= 52.50 ☉

Thus John must fill out a form stating exactly all his transactions (with records and receipts) and tell the central bank that he contributed 52.50 ☉ to the GDCP. Once again, he doesn't actually give any money to the central bank. All other firms that contribute to the GDCP do something similar to what John did. If the central bank thinks he stated that he contributed more than he actually did, he can be audited. That is, he has to meet with a representative from the central bank to talk about his statement.

That is how the central bank arrives at a particular month's GDCP. With this figure the central bank grants money to consumerists and to the government. The central bank does not tax to earn money so as to redistribute it. It grants the equivalent of the GDCP to the government and the consumerists. For example let's suppose the GDCP for the month of January was 1 000 000 000.00 ☉. The government sets a tax called the Grand Consumerist Tax. Let's suppose that it is 30%. Therefore the central bank will grant the government 300 000 000.00 ☉ to spend on social services. This is all there is in terms of taxes in consumerism. We will give more detail on this tax later on in the section on taxes.

Now we have 700 000 000.00 ☉ to give to consumerists. The population is 15 000 000 people. The non-institutionalized population is 10 000 000. Of these 9 000 000 work and 1 000 000 are unemployed or not in the labor force and are non-institutionalized. If everyone was working the 700 000 000 ☉ would be divided equally between the 10 000 000 people. However those that do not work must receive a smaller percentage of the money so that they will have a reason to work. The government sets the Non-Working Consumerist Grant Reduction. This is how much money the unemployed and those not in the labor force are granted by the central bank relative to working consumerists. Let's say it is 20%. To find how much the working consumerist and non-working non-institutionalized consumerists are granted we must calculate the amount:

X = 700 000 000.00 ☉ / [9 000 000 + 0.2(1 000 000)]

X = 76.09 ☉

Therefore the 9 000 000 working non-institutionalized consumerists would receive 76.09 ☉. The 1 000 000 non-working non-institutionalized consumerists would receive 0.2 x 76.09 ☉ = 15.22 ☉. These grants seem small but our population in this example is exceptionally large.

The difference between a working and non-working consumerist is defined by the government. If a worker only works an hour a month, this shouldn't qualify him as a "working consumerist." The definition would probably be based on how many hours he contributes to society a week as well as how much revenue (in Ignits or Fortals) he earns if he makes money through commission. The distinction between a working and non-working consumerist is determined by the government using a parameter called the Working Grant Threshold (WGT). It is how much a consumerist must contribute to society in hours worked or Ignits earned in order to be designated a working consumerist. So suppose that the government sets the WGT at 50.00 þ per week or 35 hours worked a week. A consumerist who earns 45.00 þ per week would earn the non-working consumerist grant and a worker who earns 89.00 þ would earn the general consumerist grant. A consumerist who works 43 hours a week would earn the general consumerist grant while one who worked 32 would earn the non working consumerist grant.

We need a formula for determining the consumerist grant. To determine the General Consumerist Grant (that is received by working non-institutionalized consumerists). We use:

$$GCG = [GDCP - GCT]/[WC + NWCGR(NWC)]$$

Where GCG is the General Consumerist Grant. GDCP is the Gross Domestic Consumerist Product. GCT is the Grand Consumerist Tax. WC is the number of working non-institutionalized consumerists. NWCGR is the Non-Working Consumerist Grant Reduction in decimal form; NWC is the number of not working, in the labor force non-institutionalized consumerists.

The formula for the Non Working Consumerist Grant (the amount of money the non-working consumerists are granted by the central bank) is:

$$NWCG = GCG \times NWCGR$$

Where NWCG stands for Non Working Consumerist Grant. The other two variables have been defined above.

Now the consumerists can buy whatever they want with the Norses in the materialist sector and they can spend as much of it as they desire as long as they still have it. Rather than being granted once a month, the grants are made every two weeks or twice a month. Thus in our calculations above we simply divide the GCG by two to determine how much working consumerists receive from the central bank bi-monthly. The NWCG also needs to be divided by two to come up with the value the non-working consumerists are granted from the central bank twice a month. Every two weeks almost every consumerist is granted some money to spend as see fit. The reason for the grant stems from the beginning of this treaty. It benefits the consumerists.

Although the two types of consumerist grants are given once every two weeks, not all consumerists are given their grant on the same day. If this was the case there would be a sudden rush to buy things the day the grant was given and consumerists would be fighting each other to buy various goods and services. Rather, the government enacts a *Consumerist Grant Distribution Schedule*. If we divide a 2 week period into 14 days, some people would be given their grant, either General or Non-Working, on day 1, others on day 2, others on day 3… and so on. People would be given their grant on different days of a 2 week cycle. One way to accomplish this is to differentiate people based on the first letter of their last name. So, people whose last name begins with A or B would be given their grants on day 1, people with last names beginning in C or D would be given their grant on day 2, people with last names beginning in E would be given their grant on day 3 and so on.

The money the consumerists are granted cannot be used in the accommodational or laissez-fare sectors. That requires other currencies and to obtain those currencies consumerists must somehow contribute to society. More about this will be mentioned later on.

The process of calculating the GDCP is repeated every month. Therefore the central bank is able to grant money to consumerists about every half a month. Every month the consumerists have money to spend on materialist goods and services. Each month they should earn more money as the process of granting money greatly stimulates the economy.

We have mentioned that the government receives money. How much it earns and how it spends it will be discussed in other sections.

A good question is how does the GDCP increase? The best and most productive way is if the actual output increases. That is, firms sell more goods and consumerists take advantage of more services. The GDCP can also increase if the retail markup increases. However that way consumerists have to pay more for the goods they buy. Another way to make the GDCP larger is to shift the consumerist quatrotomy and make more industries and families of goods and services part of the materialist sector.

We have defined and talked about the GDCP and the Individual Consumerist Product. We mentioned how consumerists and the government are granted money from the central bank based on the GDCP. These are some of the fundamental concepts of the entire system.

The Central Bank

The central bank is one of the cornerstones of the accommodation based consumerist economic system. It has tremendous power and influence. Many jurisdictions are directly under the control of the central bank.

The central bank is an institution with many purposes that works with the government but is separate from it. It is designed to aid the economy. Strictly speaking it is not a for-profit institution.

The central bank is a body of economists called central bankers. There are two types of central bankers- prime central bankers and industry specific central bankers. Thus there are hospitality industry central bankers, apparel central bankers, transportation industry central bankers. Each type has 102 members. For the prime central bankers, one is called the Grand Chairman. There is a Deputy Grand Chairman. The other 100 members are called Consumerist Commissioners. For hospitality industry central bankers we will have a hospitality industry chairman, a hospitality industry deputy chairman and 100 hospitality industry commissioners. The same reasoning applies for the other industry specific central bankers. They are all appointed by the government (president, king, prime minister, finance minister); they are not elected. Each member is appointed for 15 years although this is not fixed; i.e. the length of being a member may be 10 or 20 years. The Grand Chairman, Deputy Grand Chairman and the Consumerist Commissioners have different jobs.

Certain parameters of consumerism are under the jurisdiction of the central bank. They are:

- Accommodational Markdown

- Retail Mark-Up

- Price Functions

- Wages and Salary Functions

- Consumerist Universal Stock Price

- Real Estate Profit Percentage

- Adjusted Revenue Price Duration

- Rental Equivalence Duration

- Input Price Functions

- Delivery Price Functions

- Injury Severance Payment

- Interest Rate

- Job Contract Price

- Adjusted Monthly Income Percentage

- Adjusted Yearly Income Percentage

- Adjusted Income Earnings

- Consumerist Trade Pool

- Nominal Exchange Rate

- Supply of Norses

- Work Schedule

- Industry Patent Period

- General Consumerist Grant

- Consumerist General Bond Interest Rate

- Consumerist Profit Bond Interest Rate

- Consumerist General Bond Interest Repayment Frequency

- Consumerist Profit Bond Interest Repayment Frequency

- Non-Working Consumerist Grant

- Rental Repayment Value

Some of the above parameters are under the control of the Grand Chairman, others under the control of the Consumerist Commissioners and others both groups have a voice in determining. Yet for others, the industry specific central bankers play a roll. The following are directly under the control of the Grand Chairman:

- Accommodational Markdown

- Retail Mark-up

- Real Estate Profit Percentage

- Adjusted Revenue Price Duration

- Interest Rate

- Adjusted Monthly Income Percentage

- Adjusted Yearly Income Percentage

- Nominal Exchange Rate

- Rental Equivalence Duration

- Consumerist General Bond Interest Rate

- Consumerist Profit Bond Interest Rate

- Consumerist General Bond Interest Repayment Frequency

- Consumerist Profit Bond Interest Repayment Frequency

- Rental Repayment Value

For some parameters the Consumerist Commissioners and the Grand Chairman interact. They are:

- Delivery Price

- Adjusted Income Earnings

- Supply of Norses

- Work Schedule

- General Consumerist Grant

- Non-Working Consumerist Grant

For other parameters only the Consumerist Commissioners have influence. These are:

- Consumerist Universal Stock Price

- Industry Patent Period

- Injury Severance Payment

For still other parameters, both the industry specific Chairman and the industry specific commissioners have influence. They are:

- Price Functions

- Wage/Salary Functions

- Input Functions

Lastly, only the industry specific commissioners have affect on:

- Job Contract Price

We have already mentioned the Retail Mark-up and the Accommodational Markdown. They are both set by the Grand Chairman. The Grand Chairman has the power to adjust either the Retail Mark-up or the Accommodational Markdown, which are set as a percentage, when he sees fit. Every once in a while, the Grand Chairman announces a new Retail Mark-up or a new Accommodational Markdown. All industries in the sectors to which these changes apply must comply with the proclamation.

The Grand Chairman has power over the Real Estate Profit Percentage. He or she simply states the percentage of the transaction a real estate firm will earn in the process of a sale. The Grand

Chairman can change this whenever he wants to. Whatever the Grand Chairman sets this parameter at, all individuals must comply with it in the transactions that this parameter applies to.

The Grand Chairman has control over the Adjusted Revenue Price Duration. He or she simply dictates the price of buying or selling a firm based on the length of time it takes the firm to make a certain amount of revenue. The Grand Chairman can also change this whenever he wants to. When the Grand Chairman sets the parameter, all firms that the parameter pertains to must abide with it.

Also under the Grand Chairman's control is the Yearly Vacation Duration Period. He sets the amount of paid time off a worker is entitled to in days. This can be altered at any time and all firms and individuals must comply with this parameter.

The Yearly Sick Leave Exemption Period is dictated by the Grand Chairman. The Chairman can influence and change the number of days a worker is allowed to miss from work due to sickness. All workers and employers must abide with this proclamation.

The Interest Rate is under the direct influence of the Grand Chairman. He has the power to change the cost of borrowing and lending a set amount of Ignits. Changes to the Interest Rate can be made at any time and the Interest Rate applies to the whole economy.

The Consumerist General Bond Interest Rate is also under the direct influence of the Grand Chairman. He has the power to change the cost of borrowing and lending money, in Ignits, through general consumerist bonds. Changes to this can be made at any time and this applies to all consumerist bonds.

The Consumerist Profit Bond Interest Rate is under the control of the Grand Chairman. The Grand Chairman can dictate this variable that is important in the payments of consumerist profit bonds

The Consumerist General Bond Interest Repayment Frequency can be manipulated by the Grand Chairman. He sets how often an investor is paid interest on the general consumerist bonds he holds. This can be changed at any time.

The Consumerist Profit Bond Interest Repayment Frequency is under the control of the Grand Chairman. He can decide how frequently an investor is paid his interest on the consumerist profit bonds he holds. This can also be manipulated at any time by the chairman under his discretion.

The Rental Equivalence Duration is set by the Grand Chairman. He determines how long it will take a person to pay the price of the accommodation that he rents. He has the discretion to manipulate this variable every so often to adjust the economy, either to help renters or to help landlords.

Similar to the Rental Equivalence Duration is the Rental Repayment Value. Whereas the Rental Equivalence Duration deals with accommodation, the Rental Repayment Value deals with all goods and services other than accommodation. The Grand Chairman determines how much it will cost to borrow and lend a certain good or service. This is set as a percentage. If this parameter is high, this helps those that lend the good or service. On the other hand if this is low, this would favor those who borrow.

The Adjusted Monthly and Yearly Income Percentage are under the control of the Grand Chairman. He sets how much more a worker will earn from buying his job. This can be changed at any time and applies to all of the economy.

For all of the above jurisdictions, the Grand Chairman has supreme control. He can change any of them at any time. He does so through press releases. All the entities to which these parameters apply must use the Chairman's edicts. There is veto power however. If the minister of finance or head of state disagrees with any of the Grand Chairman's policies, they can veto them. At that point if ¾ of the Commissioners (75) overrule the veto, the Grand Chairman's declaration still holds. However if they do not the Grand Chairman must change the policies so that they are not vetoed by the head of state or the minister of finance.

Most of the time, the Deputy Grand Chairman doesn't do anything. His function is to replace the Grand Chairman in case of an emergency. If the Grand Chairman becomes ill or something tragic happens to him, the Deputy Grand Chairman takes his post and becomes the Grand Chairman until the original Chairman comes back or a new central bank is appointed by the government.

For the following parameters both the industry specific Chairman and the industry specific Commissioners have a say: Prices, Wages and Salaries and Prices of Inputs. These are expressed as functions. The industry specific Chairman sets the form of the function while the industry specific Commissioners determine the monetary variable of the function. One such function could be a price function for the family of milk products. All things in the same family (taxon) and their substitutes have the same price/wage/input function. The industry specific Chairman, in this case the hospitality industry chairman, may decide to set the price in terms of price per 100 ml. Then, the price function might look like, x/100 ml. The hospitality industry commissioners vote on the value of x. The top 25 and bottom 25 votes are discarded and the middle 50 are averaged. This ensures that there won't any ridiculous votes lie 500 million ☉ /100 ml or 0.01 ☉/100 ml. This is the democratic method of determining prices. It applies similarly to wages and salaries as well as to input price functions. The form of the function can be more complicated (this is up to the industry specific Chairman). The price functions are defined so that the consumerists will buy the products of the highest quality since prices for similar goods are the same.

The central bank works closely with the patent office to give prices to new goods and services that are completely original or have no known substitutes. After someone is granted a patent for inventing a completely new family of products he is given a price function for his product by the central bank and he gains a monopoly on the production of his product for some time.

The wage functions and input functions are set by the central bank also by the democratic process described above. Wage functions are designed so that the worker is more productive and efficient; i.e. a janitor is paid by the hour (this would be determined by the industry specific chairman). He could be paid 10.00 ₱/hour (this would be determined by the industry specific commissioners)

The following is a demonstration of the democratic method of price/wage/salary/input function determination. To make things simple, we have 20 Commissioners in this example and this is how they voted on the price of a light bulb family of products:

1) 5.00 ☉

2) 4.00 ☉

3) 0.01 ☉   x

4) 200.00 ☉ x

5) 7.00 ☉   x

6) 2.00 Θ

7) 1.00 Θ x

8) 1.50 Θ

9) 0.50 Θ x

10) 8.00 Θ x

11) 9.00 Θ x

12) 3.00 Θ

13) 2.00 Θ

14) 1.00 Θ x

15) 3.00 Θ

16) 4.00 Θ

17) 5.00 Θ x

18) 2.00 Θ

19) 1.00 Θ x

20) 4.00 Θ

The votes with an (x) are discarded and the middle 10 are averaged to give us a price of 3.05Θ.

When deciding on these functions, the central bank's mandate is this: "To form a coherent system of prices for goods, services, wages, salaries and inputs by setting functions that are fair. Fair meaning that which is acceptable to both consumerists and producers". The finance minister and head of state also have veto power over price/wage/input functions. If either of these thinks that resulting function is unfair, they may veto a function forcing the commissioners to re vote their function. The consumerists also have veto power. If a considerable portion of the population signs a petition against a price/wage/input function, the function is vetoed and the commissioners must vote again. Also, as mentioned previously, producers can appeal a price function if they can demonstrate to the central bank, using business documents, that it is unprofitable to do business under the current price/wage/input function.

Why exactly do we have various types of central bankers, each particular to a different industry? The reasoning is that there are a lot of goods, services, wages, inputs to price even if we price things at the family taxon level. Having industry specific central bankers speeds up the process of finding prices for families of goods, services and wages.

The Consumerist Universal Stock Price is solely in the hands of the 100 Consumerist Commissioners. The reason that the Chairman has no influence is that there is no function to form. It is understood that the Consumerist Commissioners are voting on the price of a single stock. The cost to an investor, that is the price for one unit of stock, is determined by the democratic method of voting, discarding votes and averaging the remainder as described above. It is determined by the voting of

Commissioners. The major difference between this and the above functions is that once set, the Universal Stock Price can never be changed or vetoed. Extreme havoc would result if the Consumerist Universal Stock Price were allowed to change.

The Industry Patent Period is also set democratically (i.e. through voting) by the Consumerist Commissioners. They determine how long a firm or person can hold a patent in a particular industry.

The delivery price is set democratically by both the Consumerist Commissioners and the Grand Chairman. This concerns the cost of delivering certain goods over a certain distance. The form of the function is set by the Grand Chairman and the variables are determined by the Consumerist Commissioners by voting.

The Injury Severance Payment is determined by the Consumerist Commissioners. They use the democratic method to determine how much money a worker is entitled to receive in case of a debilitating injury. This is in the form of a function that takes into account his income and the extent of his injury; i.e. how career ending it is.

The Job Contract Price is set by the Industry specific Commissioners. Through the democratic method, the industry specific Commissioners find a price for all families of jobs.

The Adjusted Income Earnings are determined by both the Grand Chairman and the consumerist Commissioners. This is determined by the value of the Adjusted Monthly Income Percentage and the Job Contract Price. The Work Schedule is also derived by the interplay of other variables.

The supply of Norses is set by both the Consumerist Commissioners and the Grand Chairman. They must simply ensure that the amount of Norses granted each month is exactly equal to the Gross Domestic Consumerist Product.

The General Consumerist Grant and the Non-Working Consumerist Grant are also set by both groups of prime central bankers. The central bank functions in granting money (Norses). After the value of the GDCP is compiled each month from individual consumerist producers the central bank grants a sum of Norses to the government to spend on social services, based on the tax rate. What's left goes to the consumerists. Those that work earn more than those that are unemployed. Those working receive the General Consumerist Grant while the non-working or those below a certain threshold, receive the Non-Working Consumerist Grant. This money the consumerists can spend on goods and services in the materialist sector.

These are the powers and responsibilities of the central bank. It is indeed a powerful entity. Almost everything that happens in the economy is in some way influenced by the central bank.

The Consumerist Trade Market

In the Consumerist market we analyze how the consumerist economy works. The Consumerist market explains at the microeconomic level the functioning of the accommodation based consumerist economic system. By studying it we gain valuable insight. Note that this discussion does not apply to the laissez-faire sector where economic decisions are based on the law of supply and demand.

We construct quality-demand graphs. Quality is plotted on the y-axis. Output is plotted on the x-axis. We define quality as a rating of superiority in make, usefulness or consumerist satisfaction. The higher the quality rating the more valued is the good or service; i.e. the more people would prefer it to other substitutes. Quality is a relative term. When a good or service is chosen over another by a consumerist, we say it is of better quality. Output refers to how much of a product or service is produced, used or made available to consumerists.

In quality-demand graphs we look at the production of a family of goods or services. Recall from our discussion on economic taxonomy the following taxonomic hierarchy:

- Economy
- Sector
- Industry
- Class
- Category
- Family
- Service/Product
- Designation

Therefore we study not just potatoes but all root vegetables which could include carrots. Wines of all makes and from all places are studied regardless of their alcohol content. We look not just at strawberries but all berries including raspberries, blueberries and gooseberries. Likewise for all families of goods and services.

How do we go about constructing quality-output graphs (we use this term interchangeably with "quality-demand" graphs and "consumerist demand graphs")? We poll a set number of consumerists regarding a particular family of goods or services that we are interested in. We ask them to pick three goods or services out of that family. If they wish they may pick the same product/service more than once. Usually the higher the number of people we poll the better the graph.

We make a quality demand graph for automobiles. We give the consumerists 5 choices to choose from:

1) A 1980 Foreign Economy Car
2) A 1990 Domestic Economy Car
3) A new Foreign Compact Car
4) A new European Sports Car
5) A new limousine

They were given 3 choices. Here is how the votes came in:

1) 1980 Foreign Economy Car -   1
2) 1990 Domestic Economy Car -   2
3) New Foreign Compact Car-   2
4) New European Sports Car-   5
5) New limousine-   5

Now we graph the results. Let the number represent the different choices for automobiles instead of writing the name of the automobile

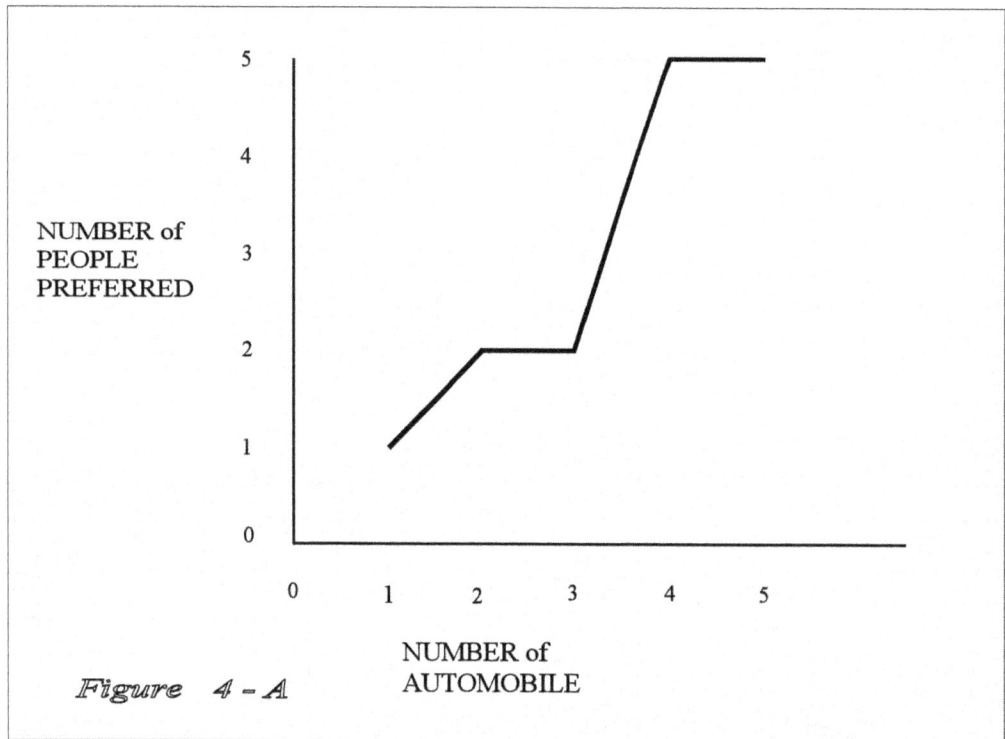

Figure 4-A

The above is a quality demand curve. What the above graph means is that more people will buy a limousine or a European Sports Car rather than a 1980 Foreign Compact Car, Foreign Economy Car or Domestic Economy Car since the price is the same for each.

Let's repeat the procedure for another family of goods- root vegetables. Again we have 5 consumerists and they have to make 3 choices. Their choices are:

1) Golden Potatoes
2) Yams
3) White Flesh Potatoes
4) Carrots
5) Onions
6) Radishes

Technically a potato is not a root but it is easier to classify it with these others because the part of the potato we eat grows underground. There are many more root vegetables than in the above list. We omit them for simplicity as we are only interested in constructing consumerist demand tables and graphs. If we had more people to poll we would add to our list.

This is how the votes came in:

1) Golden Potatoes- 2
2) Yams- 1
3) White Flesh Potatoes-2
4) Carrots- 4
5) Beets- 1
6) Onions- 3
7) Radishes- 2

If we now make a graph with the root vegetables on the y-axis in the order we arranged them our graph would look something like this:

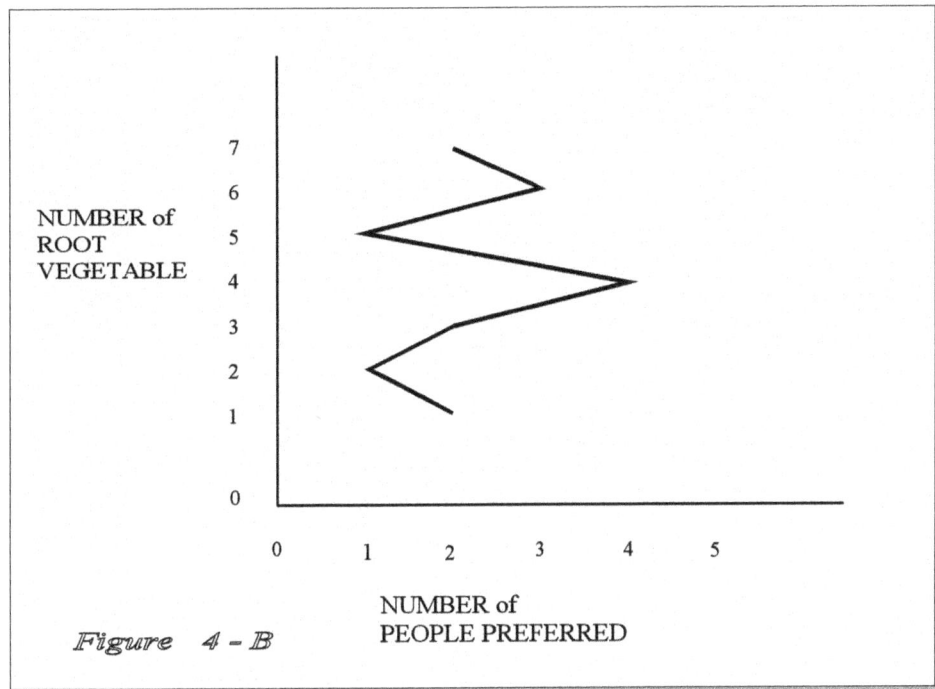

Figure 4-B

This graph looks different than the one for automobiles and is confusing. Instead of a number corresponding directly to a good or service arbitrarily, in this case to vegetables, in our new quality demand graphs, the number will correspond to a "quality rating"; the higher the better.

To revisit our previous root vegetable demand table we have the following:

1) Beets- 1 vote
2) Yams- 1 votes
3) Radishes- 2 votes
4) White Flesh Potatoes – 2 votes
5) Golden Potatoes- 2 votes
6) Onions- 3 votes
7) Carrots- 4 votes

The consumerist demand graph now looks like the following:

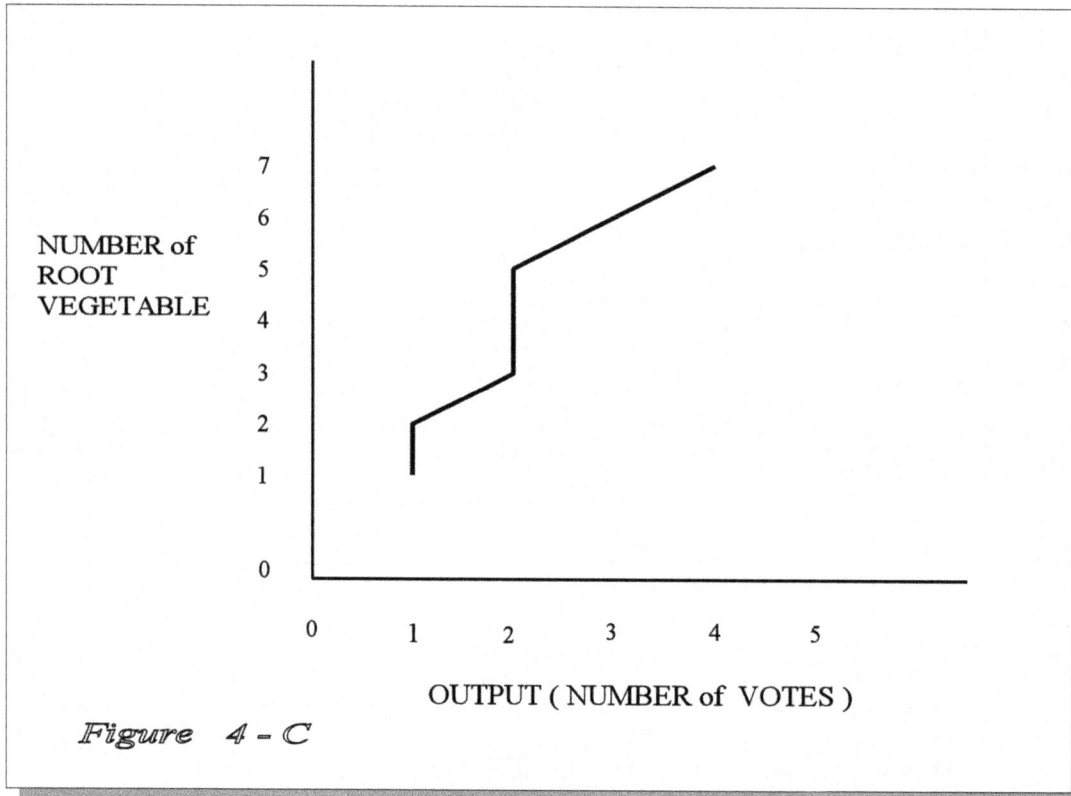

Figure 4-C

How about if we add another product to our consumerist demand table; let's say celery root. Let's also add more consumerists. Our new table could look like this:

- Beets   1
- Yam   1
- White Flesh Potatoes 2
- Radish 2
- Golden Potatoes 2
- Onions 3
- Celery root 3
- Carrots 4

If we compare these two tables we see that the only differences are that celery root received 3 votes. Everything is the same as before. How does our consumerist demand graph change? Notice that celery root has 3 votes –the same as onion but less than carrots. What we do is give it a quality rating of 6.5. Our new graph looks like this. (We label each point: A- Carrots, B- Celery Root, C- Onions, D- Golden Potatoes, E- Radishes, F- White Flesh Potatoes, G- Yams, H-Beets)

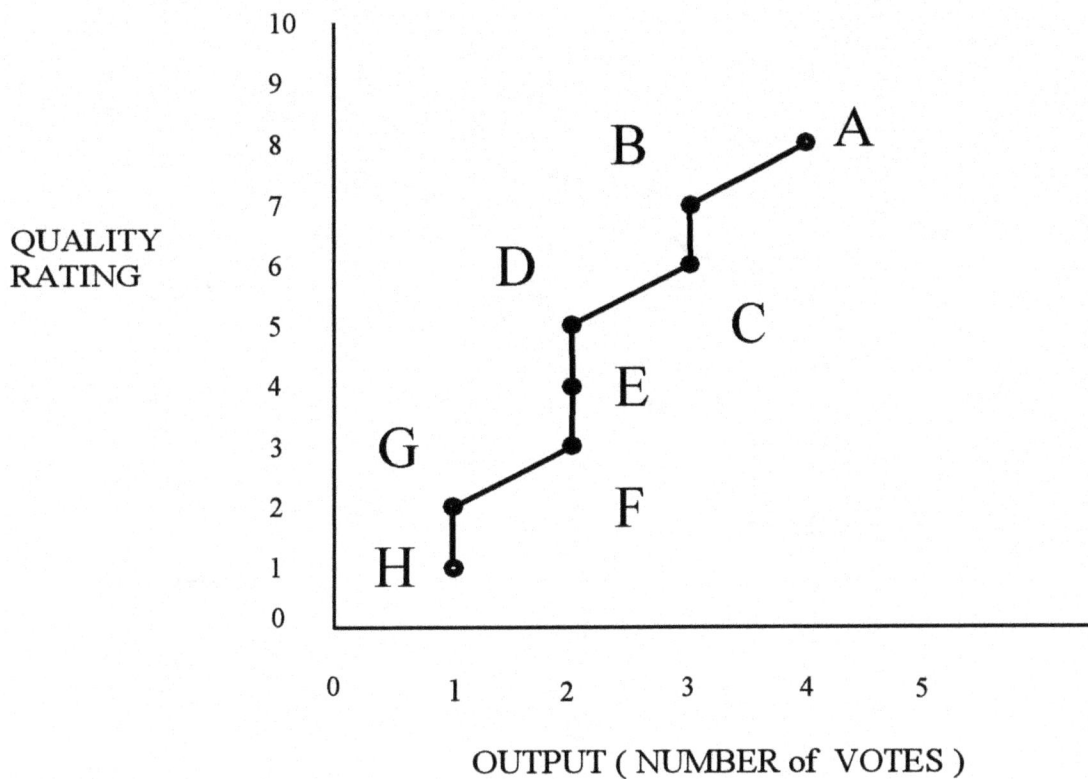

Figure 4-D

We would use the same procedure for any additional new product or service we add into our analysis. We simply give it a quality rating in between those products it has a greater or lesser output (vote) than.

Let's look back at our root vegetables analysis. This time there are 10 consumerists who each have 3 votes. This is how they could respond to a poll:

- Yam   2 votes
- Beets   2 votes
- Radish   3 votes
- Golden Potatoes   3 votes
- White Flesh Potatoes-   3 votes
- Celery root   4 votes
- Carrots   7 votes
- Onions   8 votes

A demand graph can drastically change the more people are polled or if different people are polled. The demand graph would look like this: We label each point: A- Onions, B- Carrots, C- Celery Root, D-White flesh potatoes, E- Golden Potatoes, F- Radishes, G- Beets, H-Yams)

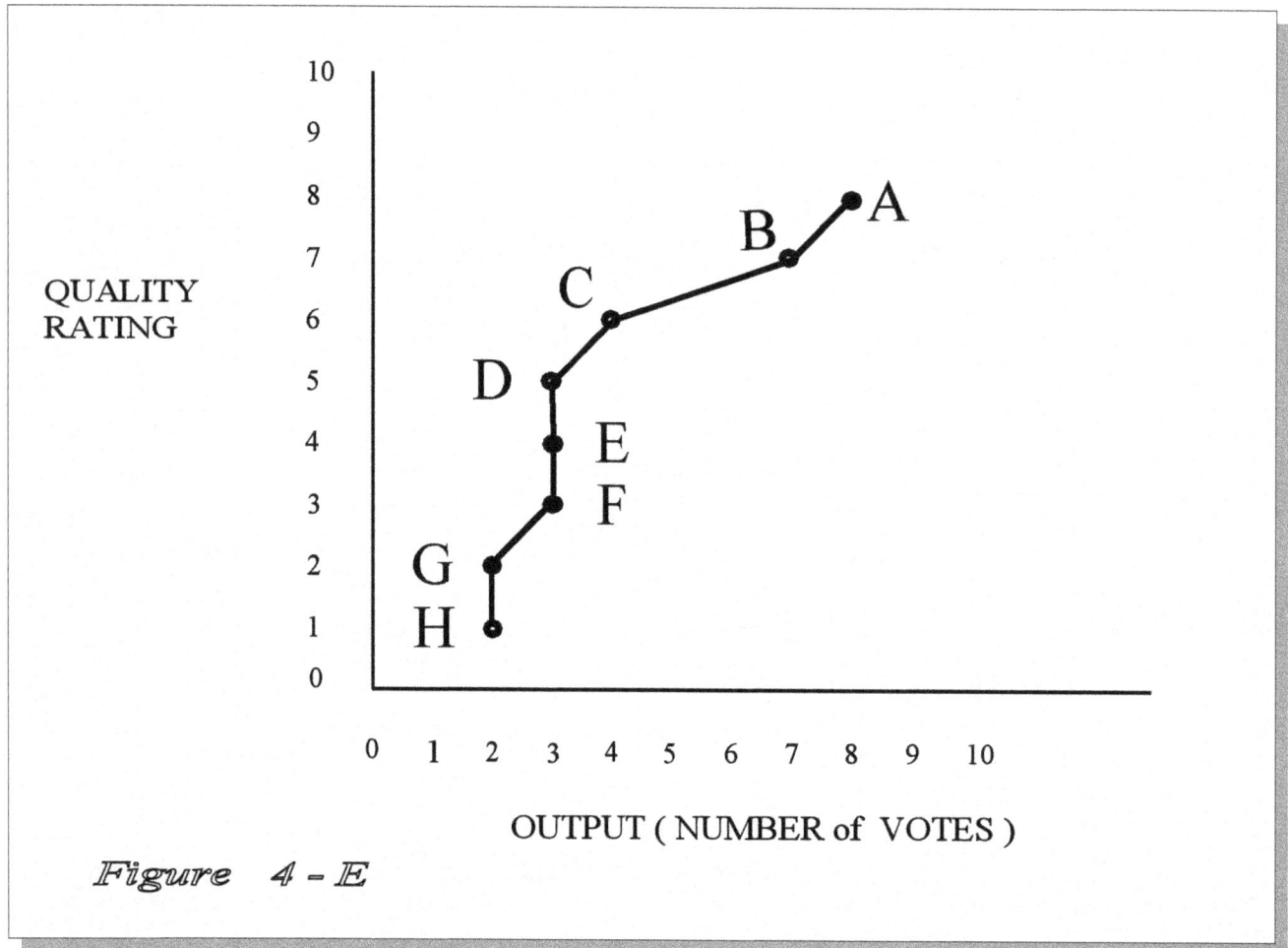

Figure 4-E

These two graphs and tables are very different even though the same root vegetables are being analyzed. However if a large number of people are polled, say 1000, than the graph and tables would be more accurate.

Now let's analyze consumerist supply tables and graphs. Let's take our first root vegetables demand table. Here each vote equals one kilogram

- Onions- 3 kg
- Golden Potatoes- 2 kg
- White Flesh Potatoes- 2 kg
- Radishes- 2 kg
- Yams- 1 kg
- Beets- 1 kg

A farmer grows root vegetables in order to make a profit; i.e. to spend on the accommodational and laissez-faire sectors. All root vegetables in our example are 0.35 Ө /kg regardless of which vegetable. It would make the most sense if our farmer grows the root vegetables that are desired. 4 kg of carrots are demanded but just 1 kg of beets is demanded. If the farmer grew 4 kg of carrots he would sell them all. If he grows 1 kg of beets he would also sell them all. How about if he plants 6 kg of carrots and 0.5 kg of beets? He would have too many carrots and the possibility of selling 0.5 kg more of beets. It would make the most sense if the farmer planted root vegetables in the exact same ratio as they are demanded. That is, carrots, onions, golden potatoes in a 4:3:2 ratio. So it seems that the supply curve coincides with the demand curve. The producer will make the most money when he makes goods or offers services in the way that they are demanded.

Let's go back to our automobile graph from the beginning.

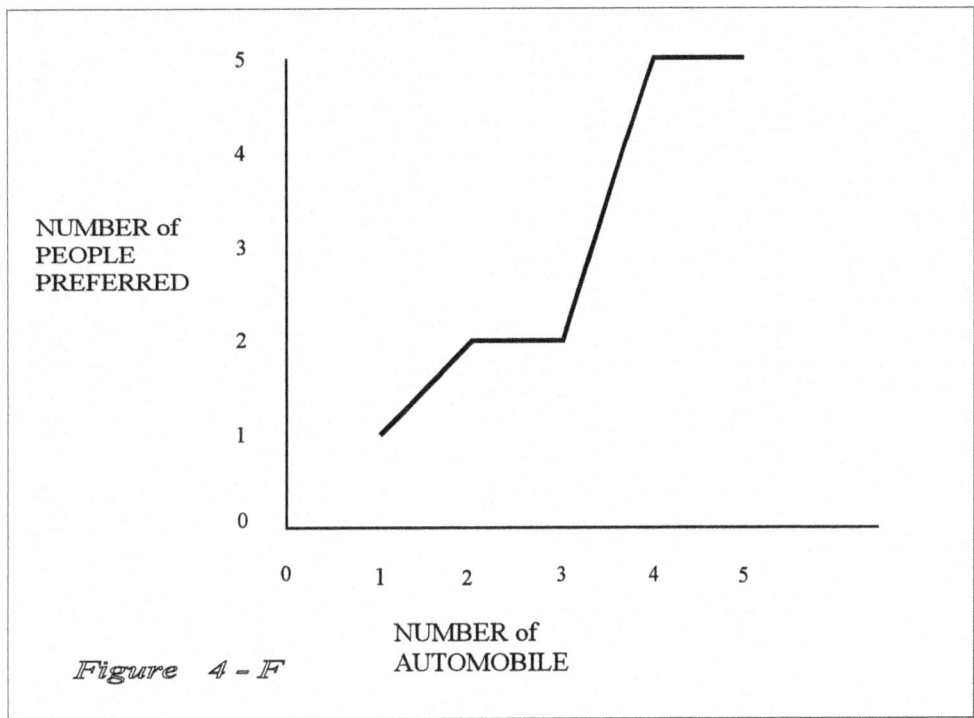

Figure 4-F

Figure 4-F

145

In this case producers will produce more limousines than European Sports Cars, more European Sports Cars than Foreign Compact Cars and more Foreign Compact Cars than Domestic Economy Cars. All automobiles have the same price. Since more consumerists prefer limousines than Foreign Compact Cars, more limousines will be sold than Foreign Compact Cars. Thus producers have an incentive to produce limousines over Foreign Compact Cars. Therefore the shape of the consumerist supply curve should have the same shape as the consumerist demand curve.

We construct a graph for wine. There are four wines to choose from: a South American wine, a Californian wine, a French wine and an Australian wine. We poll 1000 people. Each person has 3 choices and each choice represents a litre of wine. The results of the poll are:

- South American-   1500 L

- Californian-   750 L

- French-   500 L

- Australian-   250 L

The graph looks like this: (We label each point: A- South American, B- Californian. C- French, D- Australian)

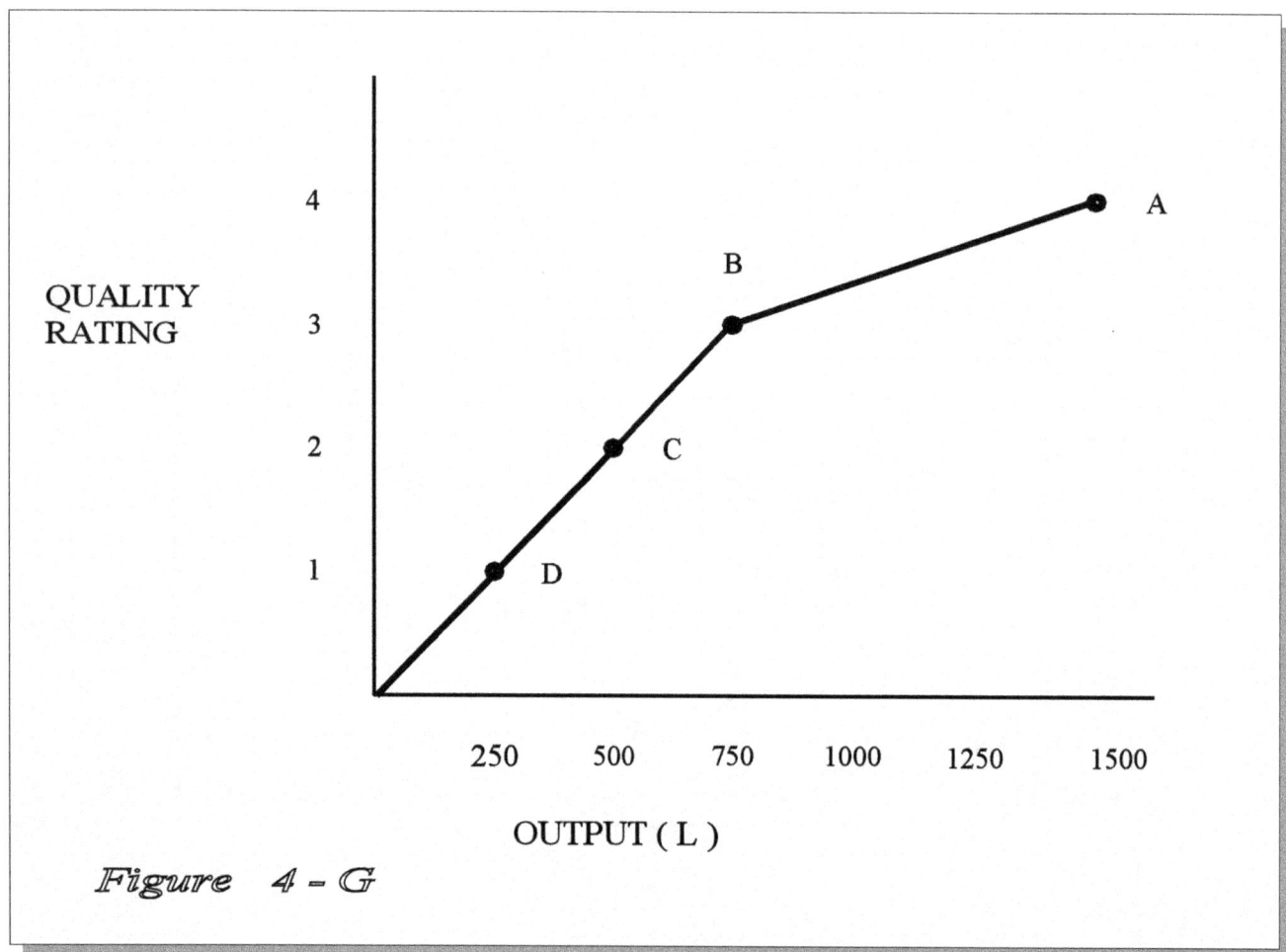

Figure 4-G

Now we find out how much each wine maker is able to bring to the market. The supply table looks like this:

- South American   1000 L

- French   1000 L

- Californian   1000 L

- Australian   1000 L

The consumerist supply curve would then look like this (The points are: A- South American, B- French, C- Californian, D- Australian)

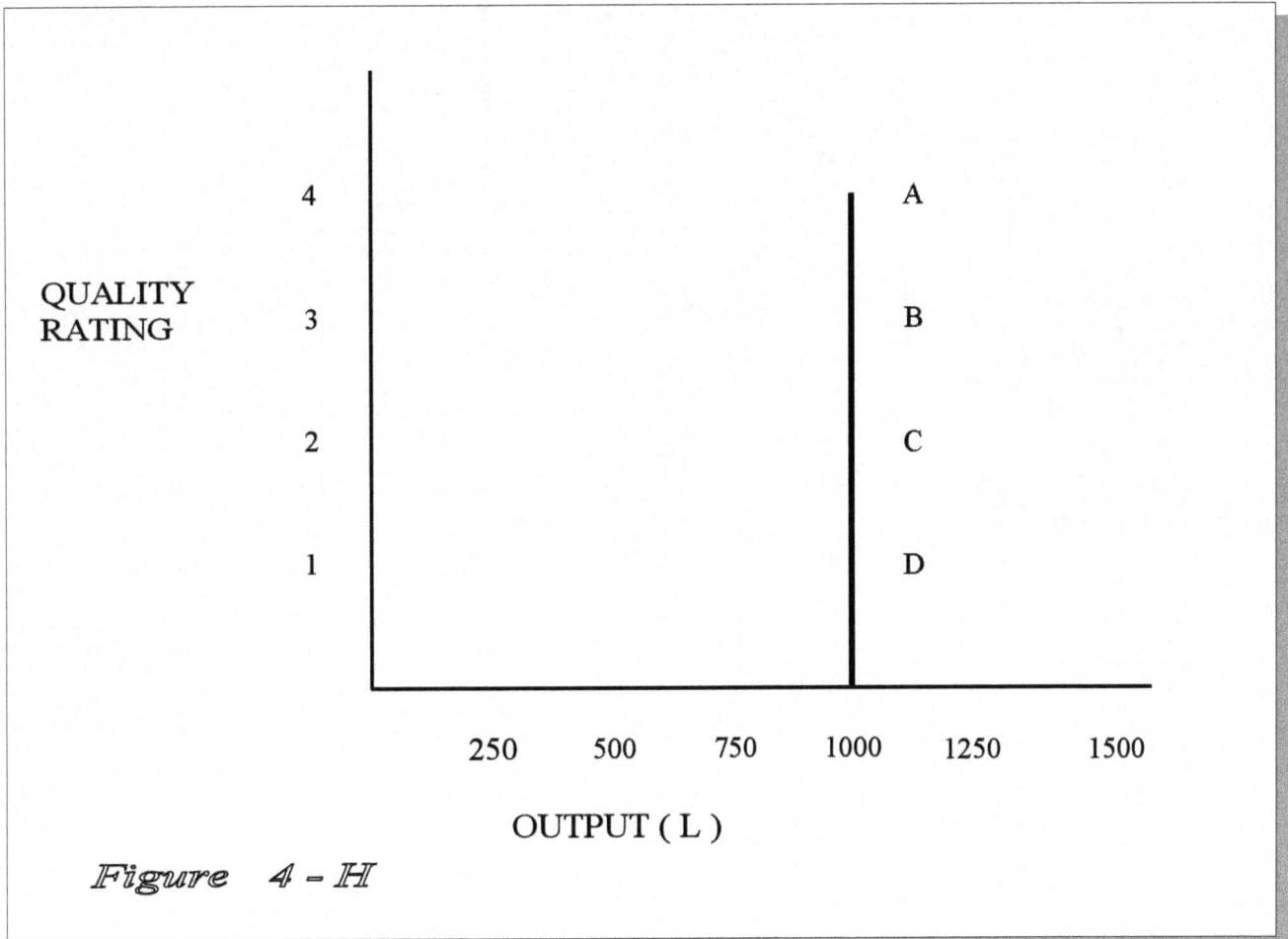

Figure 4-H

If we put both the supply and demand curves together we get: (The labeled points are: A- South American, B- Californian, C- French, D- Australian)

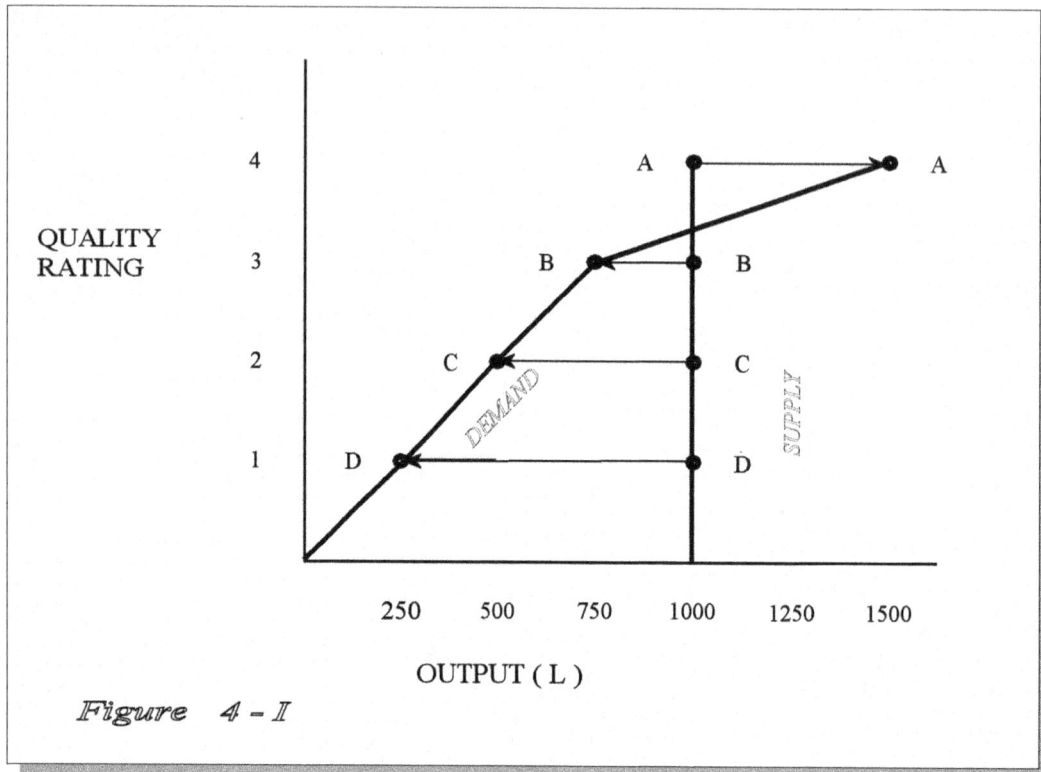

Figure 4-1

The supply curve shifts to fall on the demand curve. If this is so then the Consumerist market is said to be at its optimal.

Here is an imaginary graph:

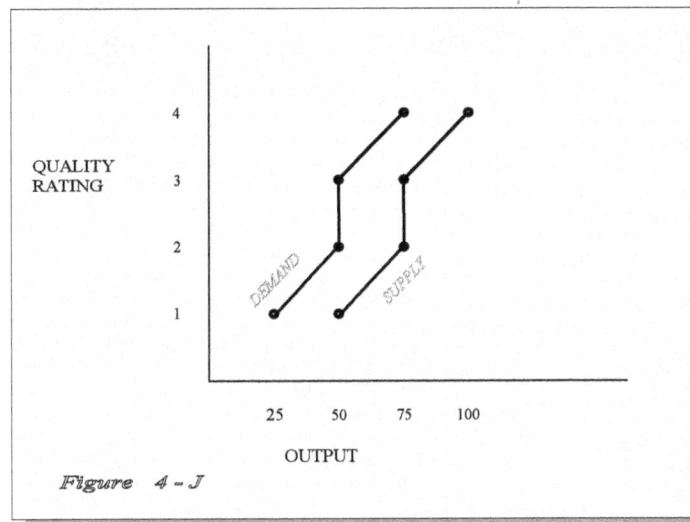

Figure 4-J

When for a given product the supply curve is to the right of the demand curve, the market is said to be in surplus for that good. Likewise if the demand curve is to the right of the supply curve there is a shortage. Both situations fix themselves as both curves try to coincide with one another,

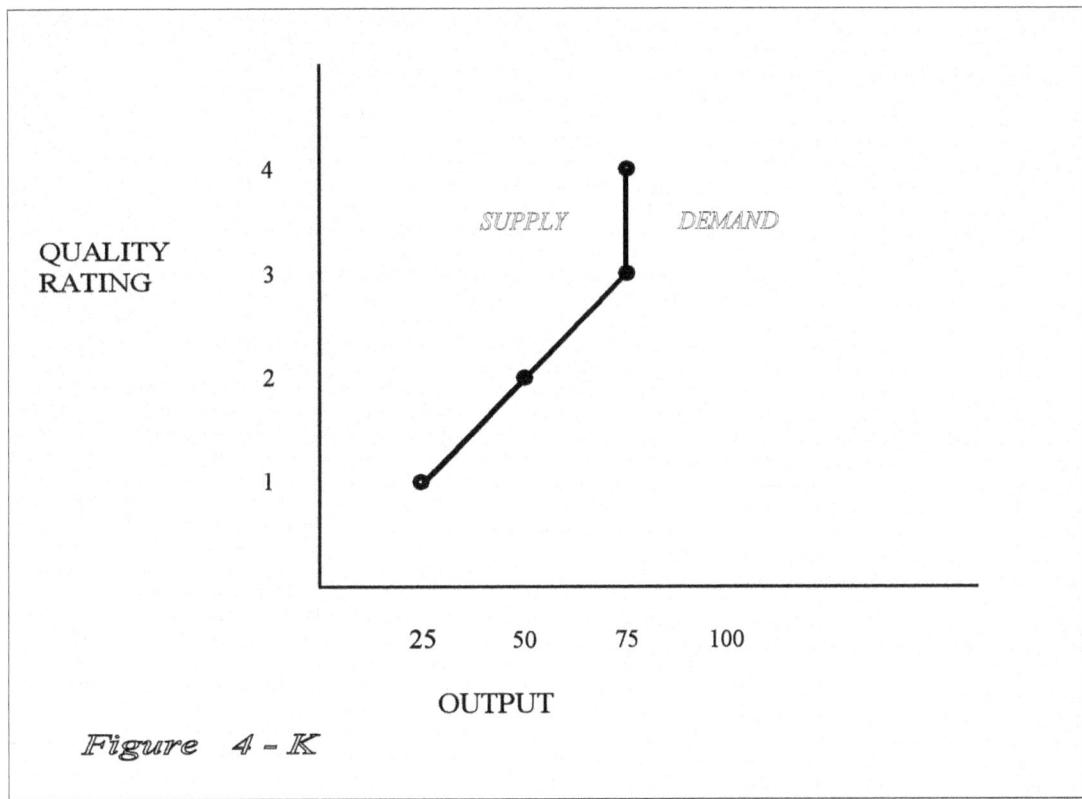

Figure 4-K

The most interesting and informative demand graphs are those where the goods or services are given a quality rating from 1 to 10. The products or services in a market are given a quality rating based on how much of them are demanded.

Assume that there are 30 000 consumerists. We are interested in a limited time frame. Let's say it is a month and this is how often the central bank grants money to consumerists. The price of wine is 0.50 þ /litre. We omit the retail mark-up for the time being. 100 000 litres of wine are bought in the market. The demand schedule is:

- Australian-   40 000 L

- Californian-   30 000 L

- South American-   20 000 L

- French-   10 000 L

The consumerist demand curve looks like this: We label the points: A- Australian, B- Californian, C- South American- D- French.

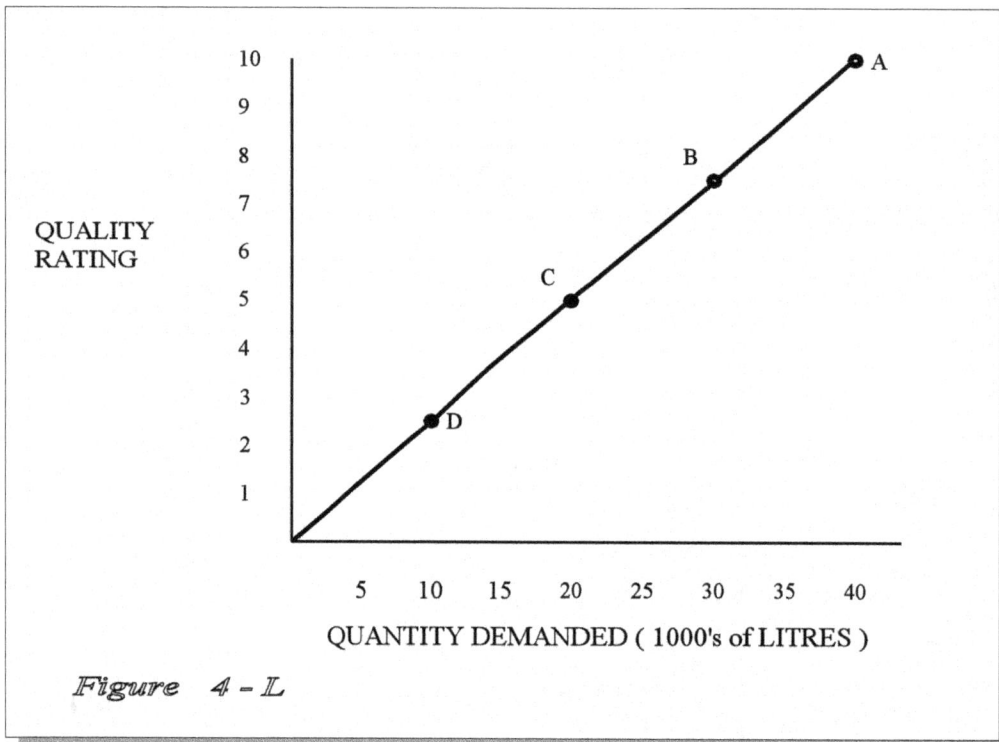

Figure 4-L

French wine has a quality rating of 2.5. South American wine has a quality rating of 5. Californian wine has a quality rating of 7.5 and Australian wine has a quality rating of 10. We will soon see how these quality ratings were calculated.

What could change this graph? There are four main causes. They are:

1) The introduction of a newer and better product of a particular family in this case wine. An example is the introduction of Polish wine.

2) A change of taste. People may prefer South American to Australian wine

3) The number of consumerists who want to buy wine changes or there is a change in how much wine existing consumerists buy.

4) There is an increase in income (or there is a decrease) If consumerists are granted more (or less) money they can buy more (or less) wine.

Let's analyze the effects of these adjustments to our wine market (as an example). First let's see what happens when there is another new product. Suppose that there is a new wine on the market- Polish wine. Everything else is the same (ceteris paribus). All other factors are kept constant. *Ceteris Paribus* is a Latin expression meaning "all things remaining equal."

So our new consumerist demand schedule looks like this. There are 100 000 L of wine bought and wine costs 0.50 þ /litre regardless of type. We ignore the retail mark-up

- Polish wine-   40 000 L

- Australian wine-   30 000 L

- Californian wine-   15 000 L

- South American wine 10 000 L

- French wine-   5 000 L

Our new graph is: (The labeled points are; A- Polish, B- Australian, C- Californian, D-South American, E- French)

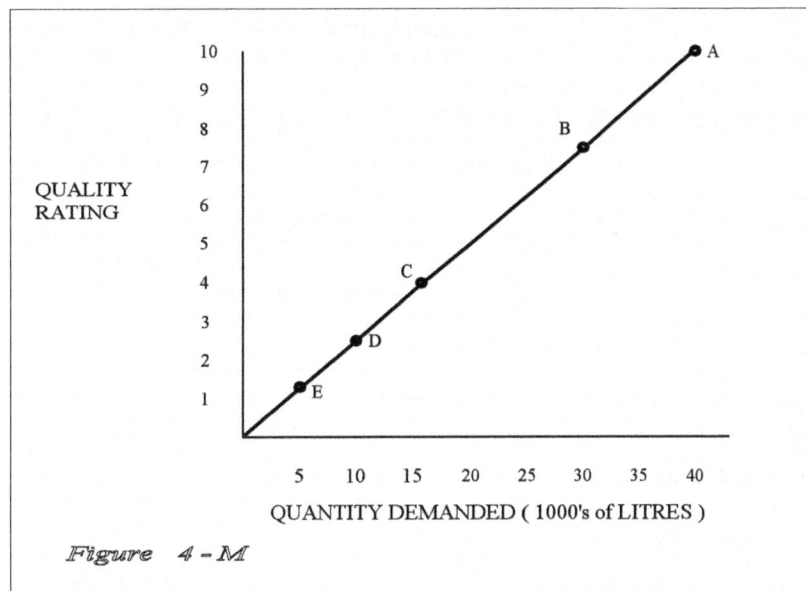

Figure 4-M

To determine quality ratings we do the following. We set the family leader's quality rating equal to 10. Polish wine automatically receives a quality rating of 10 as it is demanded the most. We use a formula that uses ratios to determine the quality ratings of the other wines. The formula has the form

151

$10/A = x/B$

Where A is equal to the family leader's demand. B is equal to the demand of the wine being sought and x is the particular wine's quality rating. Let's do the calculations for the four other types of wines. We know Polish wine has a quality rating of 10.

Australian wine- $10/40\ 000 = x/30\ 000$

$x = 7.5$

Therefore Australian wine has a quality rating of 7.5

Californian wine- $10/40\ 000 = x/15\ 000$

$x = 3.75$

South American wine- $10/40\ 000 = x/10\ 000$

$x = 2.5$

French wine- $10/40\ 000 = x/5\ 000$

$x = 1.25$

So to summarize, Polish wine has a quality rating of 10. Australian wine has a quality rating of 7.5. Californian wine has a quality rating of 3.75. South American wine has a quality rating of 2.5. French wine has a quality rating of 1.25. This is shown in the graph we drew above.

Let's analyze what happens when people change their tastes. They for some reason like the taste of one wine over another. This may be caused by aggressive advertising or by a study that indicates that one type of wine is better for one's health than another. We will stay with our original four wines.

A new consumerist demand schedule could look like this (still 100 000 L of wine is bought and the price is 0.50 þ/L)

- South American   50 000 L

- Australian   25 000 L

- French   20 000 L

- Californian   5 000 L

We now determine the quality ratings

South American   10 (it is the family leader)

Australian $10/50\ 000 = x/25\ 000$

$X = 5$

French $10/50\ 000 = x/20\ 000$

$X = 4$

Californian   10/50 000 = x/5 000

X = 1

Our graph looks like this

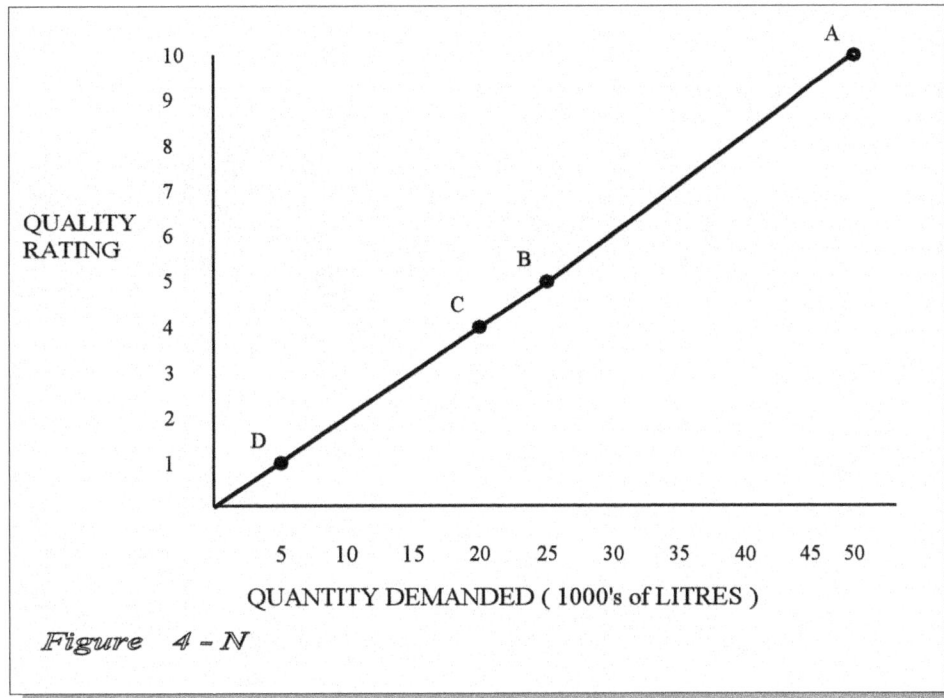

Figure 4-N

We could label points corresponding to the wines. Let A represent South American wine, B represent Australian wine, C French wine, and let D represent Californian wine. It appears that our graph is a straight line.

Now we will see what happens when there are more consumerists in the market than before. This could happen if more people immigrate to our society. This would naturally increase the number of litres of wine bought. Instead of 100 000 L of wine bought, 200 000 L of wine are bought. The price of wine is 0.50þ /L. We will use the same few types of wines. Everything else is ceteris paribus. Our new consumerist demand schedule could look like this:

- South American wine   90 000 L

- Californian wine   60 000 L

- Australian wine   40 000 L

- French wine   10 000 L

Our quality ratings are:

South American wine-   10

Californian wine   10/90 000 = x/60 000

X = 6.7

Australian wine   10/90 000 = x/40 000

X = 4.4

French wine   10/90 000 = x/10 000

X = 1.1

Our graph is

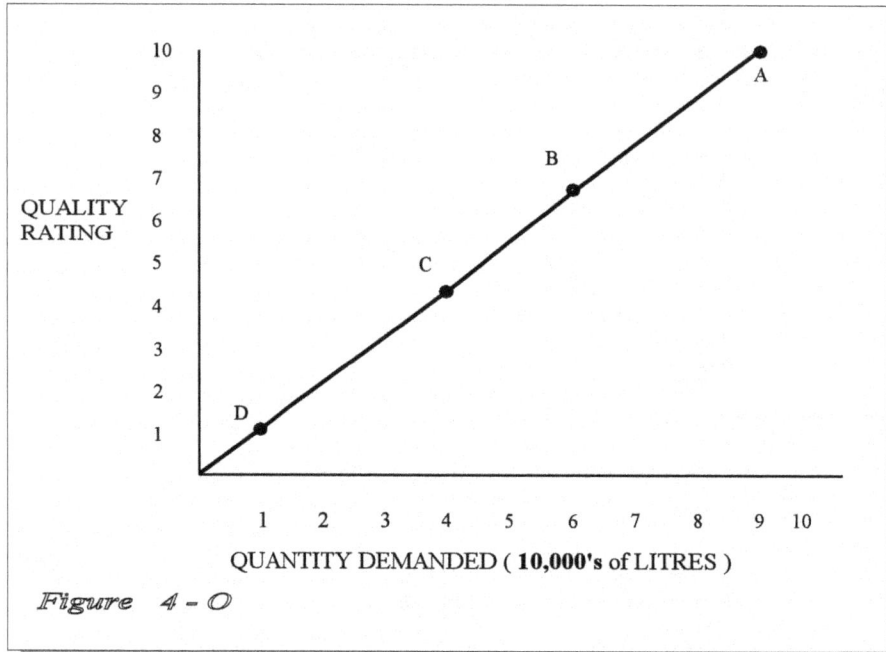

Figure 4-0

Where: A stands for South American wine

              B stands for Californian wine

              C stands for Australian wine

              D stands for French wine

Now let's see what happens when consumerist's income increases. This occurs when there is growth in the materialist sector or there is a cut in taxes or there is a birth in the household. With a higher income consumerists are able to buy more. Almost the same thing happens in this case as when there are more consumerists because the net effect is more wine bought.

Now let's analyze the supply of goods and services. Suppose we have four makers of wine and that one maker of wine cannot make another type of wine. So we have an Australian wine maker, a French wine maker, a Californian wine maker and a South American wine maker.

Each wine maker wants to make money. This is his incentive for working. The more money he earns the more he can spend on the accommodational and laissez-faire sectors; i.e. he can buy land, a house or pay bills. It is also true that each producer wants to make as much money as possible. If a producer makes less wine than is demanded he can increase his profit by making more of that type of wine. If a producer makes more wine than is demanded than he has extra wine on his hands. When a wine maker makes as much wine as is demanded than we have a situation we will call equilibrium.

Let's analyze a particular consumerist supply schedule

- French wine   50 000 L

- Australian wine   50 000 L

- Californian wine   50 000 L

- South American wine 50 000 L

We can superimpose both the demand and supply curves on one graph as follows:

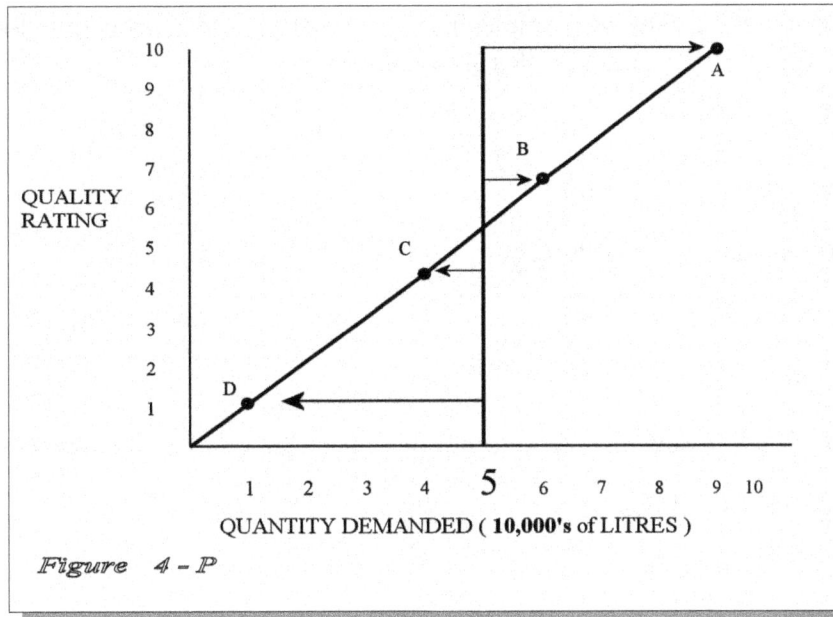

Figure 4-P

The point of intersection does not have any real significance. The quality ratings are the same as for the demand schedule. If a product is in greater supply then it does not necessarily have a greater quality rating. Quality ratings are determined by the demand schedule. The supply curve has a tendency to coincide exactly with the demand curve. In this condition consumerists are buying all they want and suppliers are selling all they have.

If there is a shortage for a product then either

1) Producers will make more of it, or

2) It will be imported from another country

If there is a surplus than either:

1) Producers will make less of the product

2) The product will be exported to another country

It is a good thing if the supply curve is a bit more to the right than the demand curve. This indicates an expanding economy. Both the demand and the supply curves slope in the same direction.

Let's go back to our automobile example. The consumerist demand schedule looks like this. (Each car costs 1000.00 ⊙) 10 000 automobiles are demanded.

- Limousine-   5 000

- European Sports Car-   3 000

- Foreign Compact Car-   1 000

- Domestic Economy Car-   500

- Foreign Economy Car-   500

A retail mark-up of 20% means that the automobiles cost 1200.00 ⊙ at the dealership.

The quality ratings are as follows:

A) Limousine-

   10

B) European Sports Car $10/5\ 000 = x/3000$

   $X = 6$

C) Foreign Compact Car $10/5\ 000 = x/1\ 000$

   $X = 2$

D) Domestic Economy Car $10/5\ 000 = x/500$

   $X = 1$

E) Foreign Economy Car $10/5\ 000 = x/500$

   $X = 1$

The demand curve looks like this:

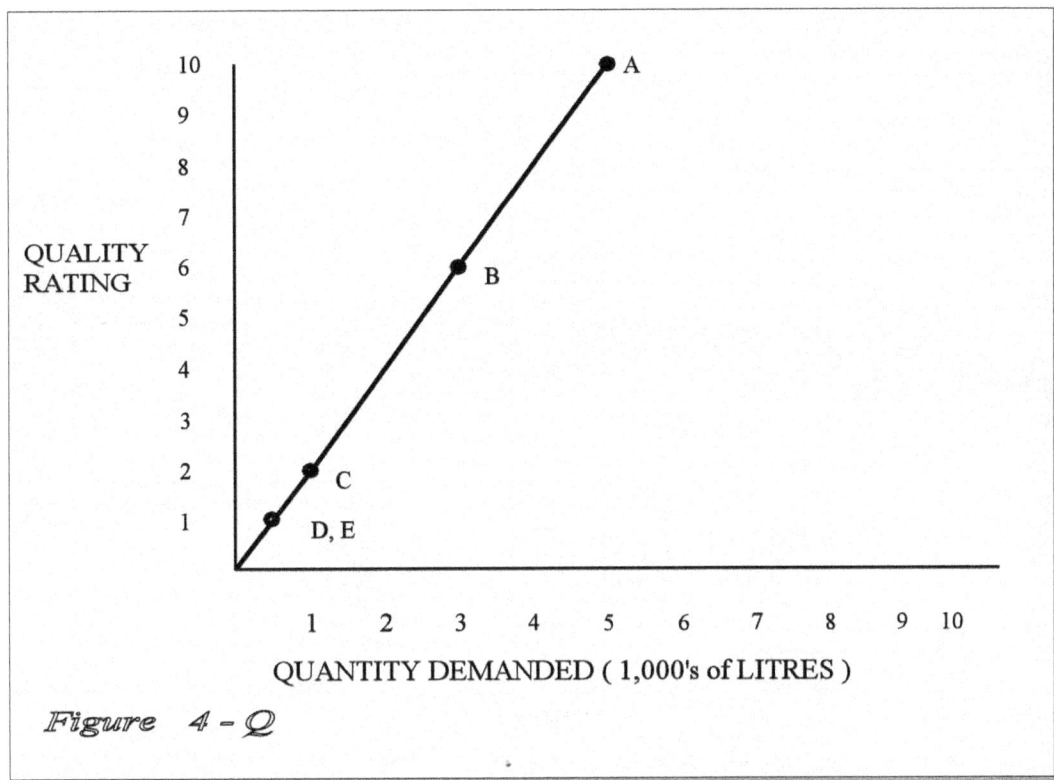

Figure 4-Q

The consumerist supply schedule looks like this:

A) Limousine-   5000

B) European Sports Car-   4000

C) Foreign Compact Car-   1000

D) Domestic Economy Car-   2000

E) Foreign Economy Car-   250

Each automobile sells for 1 000.00 Θ. It is sold to car dealerships who make a 20% profit (retail mark-up) of 200.00 þ /car. The cars the dealership buys depend on the cars consumerists buy from the dealership. The same quality ratings used for demand curves are used for supply curves; i.e. we do not calculate new ratings based on how much of a good is sold or produced. For example, if a product has a quality rating of 4 calculated by how much it was demanded, it will have a quality rating of 4 on its supply curve regardless of how much it was supplied. The supply curve looks like this. In general it is not a straight line.

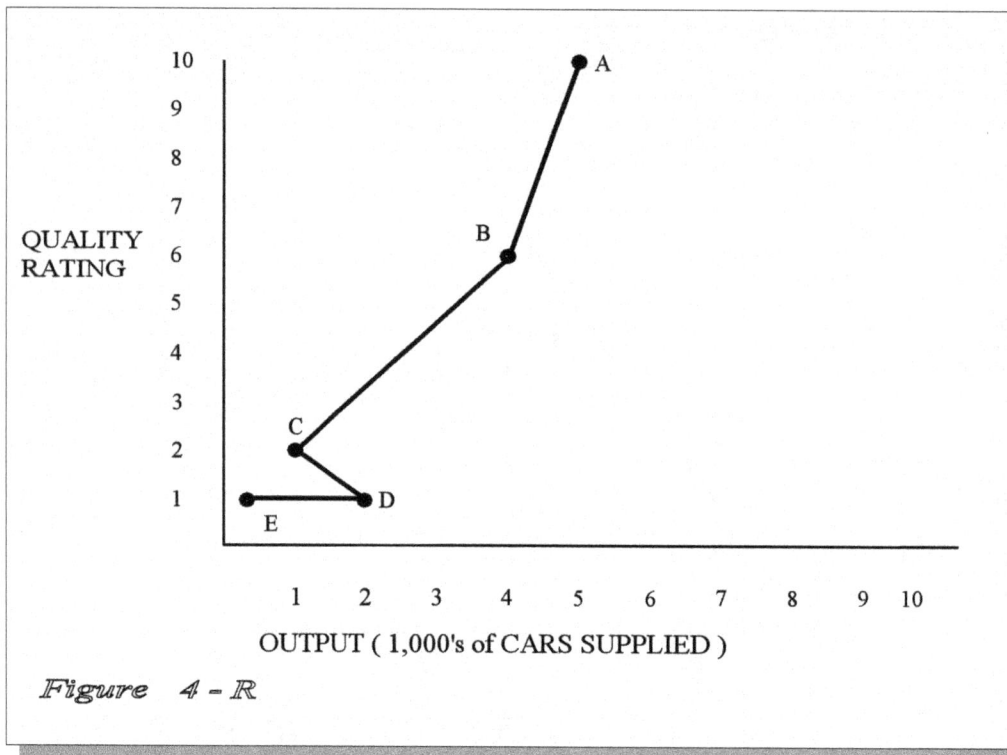

Figure 4-R

We now put the two together:

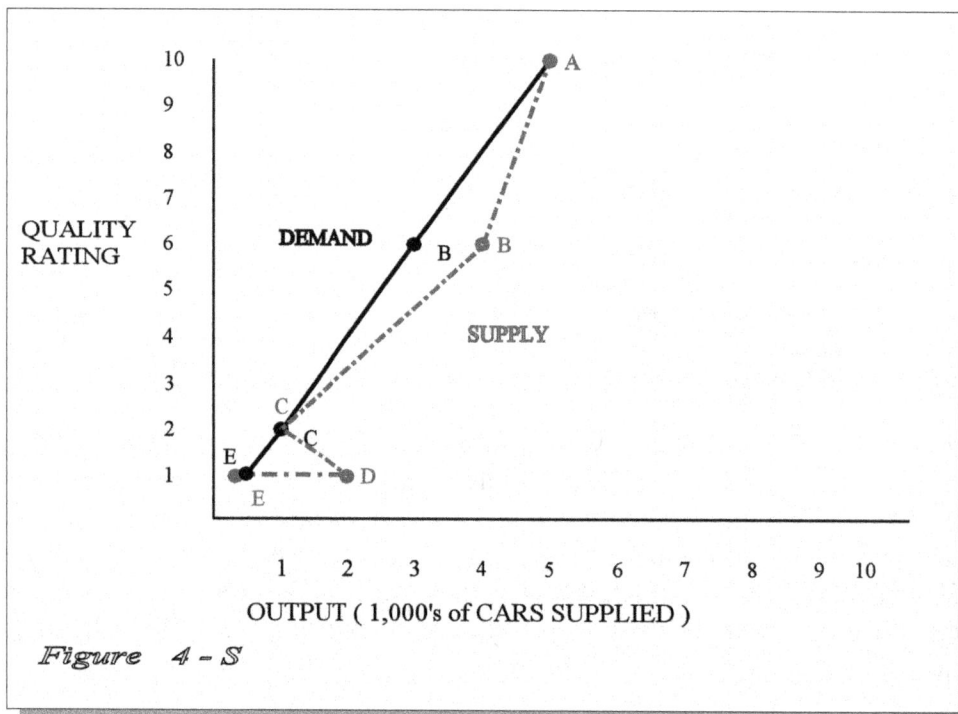

Figure 4-S

Here A represents limousines, B represents European Sports Cars, C represents Foreign Compact Cars, D represents Domestic Economy Cars and E represents Foreign Economy Cars. In the above graph, 5000 limousines were purchased and 5000 were demanded so they are in equilibrium. The same is for Foreign Compact Cars; 1000 were made and 1000 were demanded. Thus Foreign Compact Cars are also in equilibrium. In the case of Foreign Economy Cars only 250 were made but 500 were supposed to be bought. 250 Foreign Economy Cars could have been bought/sold. The makers of Foreign Economy Cars step up their production of Foreign Economy Cars or else car dealers import Foreign Economy Cars from a foreign country. From the curves we can see that the number of European Sports Cars and Domestic Economy Cars made and sold to car dealers is higher than the amount bought. Although this would lead to a surplus of both European Sports Cars and Domestic Economy Cars at a car dealership, this actually spurs on the economy. The reason being that for every Domestic Economy Car and European Sports Car at a car dealership (it is directly available to consumerists) the equivalent of their value (number of automobiles x price) is counted towards the GDCP which is tabulated by the central bank and given to consumerists. As more consumerists have more income they will be able to buy more automobiles. The economy is driven by surplus.

Now let's analyze the consumerist supply curve and schedule. There are 3 main factors that affect quantity supplied.

1) Technology- if a firm creates a machine for making its products more efficiently it can produce more of that product.

2) Number of sellers- if a firm makes the same product as another, the original can't sell or produce as much

3) Invention or innovation- if a firm makes a product which is more preferable than any others in its family, it will sell more of this product and other firms will produce and sell less of theirs

Suppose that in our example the Foreign Compact Car makers find a robot for every part of the manufacturing process. This saves money otherwise spent on human workers. The firm now earns more money on each automobile (1000þ - manufacturing costs) and makes more automobiles for the same cost. A schedule could look like this

	Original	After technological change
Limousine	5 000	5 000
European Sports Car-	4 000	4 000
Foreign Compact Car-	1 000	3 000
Domestic Economy Car-	2 000	2 000
Foreign Economy Car-	250	250

The only difference (ceteris paribus) here is that Foreign Compact Car has made technology that makes its production more efficient; i.e. replacing human laborers with robots. The curve is:

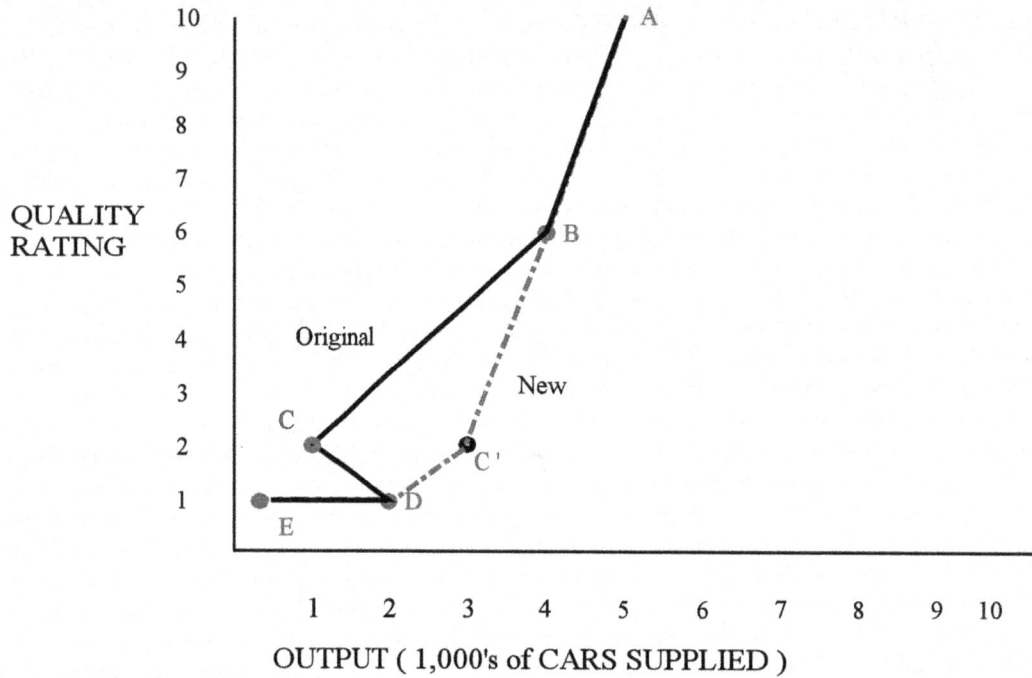

Figure 4-T

Let's see what happens to our graph and schedule when the numbers of sellers increases.

Suppose another company starts making limousines

	Original	With a new limousine company
Limousine	5 000	10 000
European Sports Car-	4 000	4 000
Foreign Compact Car-	1 000	1 000
Domestic Economy Car-	2 000	2 000
Foreign Economy Car-	250	250

In this case there are now more limousines made.

A graph of both schedules looks like this

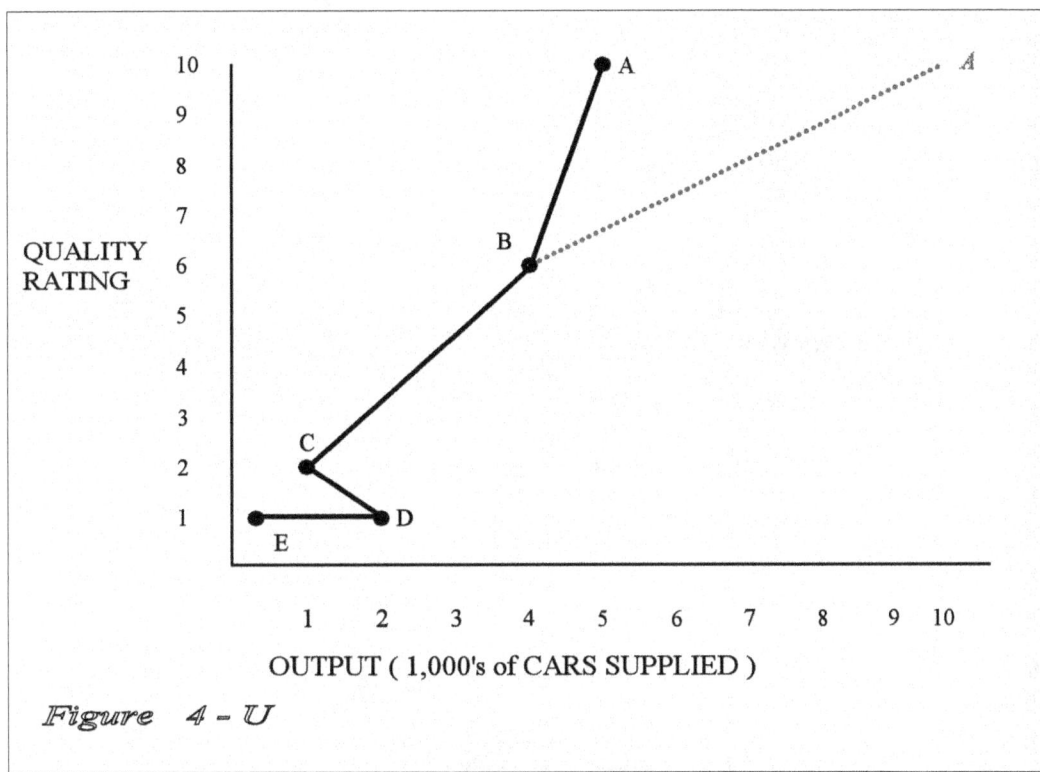

Figure 4-U

Another factor that can change our consumerist supply schedule or graph is (ceteris paribus) if a new firm produces an original invention that improves the products in a family. For example a firm invents a flying automobile. We first need to give it a quality rating. We go back to the demand schedule. Originally the demand schedule looked like this. There were 10 000 cars demanded.

Limousine	5000
European Sports Car	3 000
Foreign Compact Car	1 000
Domestic Economy Car	500
Foreign Economy Car	500

The quality ratings were:

Limousine	10
European Sports Car	6
Foreign Compact Car	2
Domestic Economy Car	1
Foreign Economy Car	1

With the addition of a new product (flying car) the schedule could look like this:

Flying car-   5000
Limousine   3000
European Sports Car   1 000
Foreign Compact Car   500
Domestic Economy Car   400
Foreign Economy Car   100

The new quality ratings would then be:

Flying car   10

Limousine $10/5000 = x/3000$
$X = 6$

European Sports Car $10/5000 = x/1000$
$X = 2$

Foreign Compact Car $10/5000 = x/500$
$X = 1$

Domestic Economy Car $10/5000 = x/400$
$X = 0.8$

Foreign Economy Car $10/5000 = x/100$
$X = 0.2$

Our flying car has a quality rating of 10. More people buy it and less of the other automobiles.

Now let's see a consumerist supply schedule

			Quality rating
A-	Flying car-	6 000	10
B-	Limousine	5 000	6
C-	European Sports Car	4 000	2
D-	Foreign Compact Car	1 000	1
E-	Domestic Economy Car	2 000	0.8
F-	Foreign Economy Car	250	0.2

Our new consumerist supply graph is:

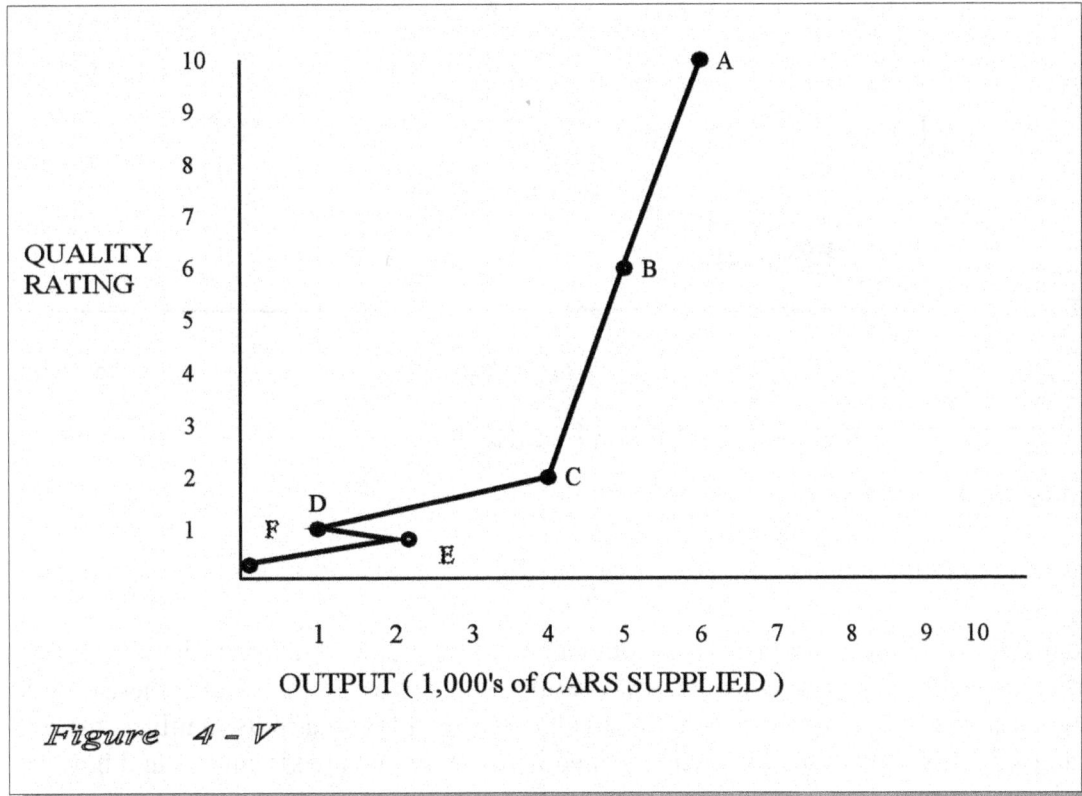

Figure 4-V

Now let's put both the supply and demand curves together:

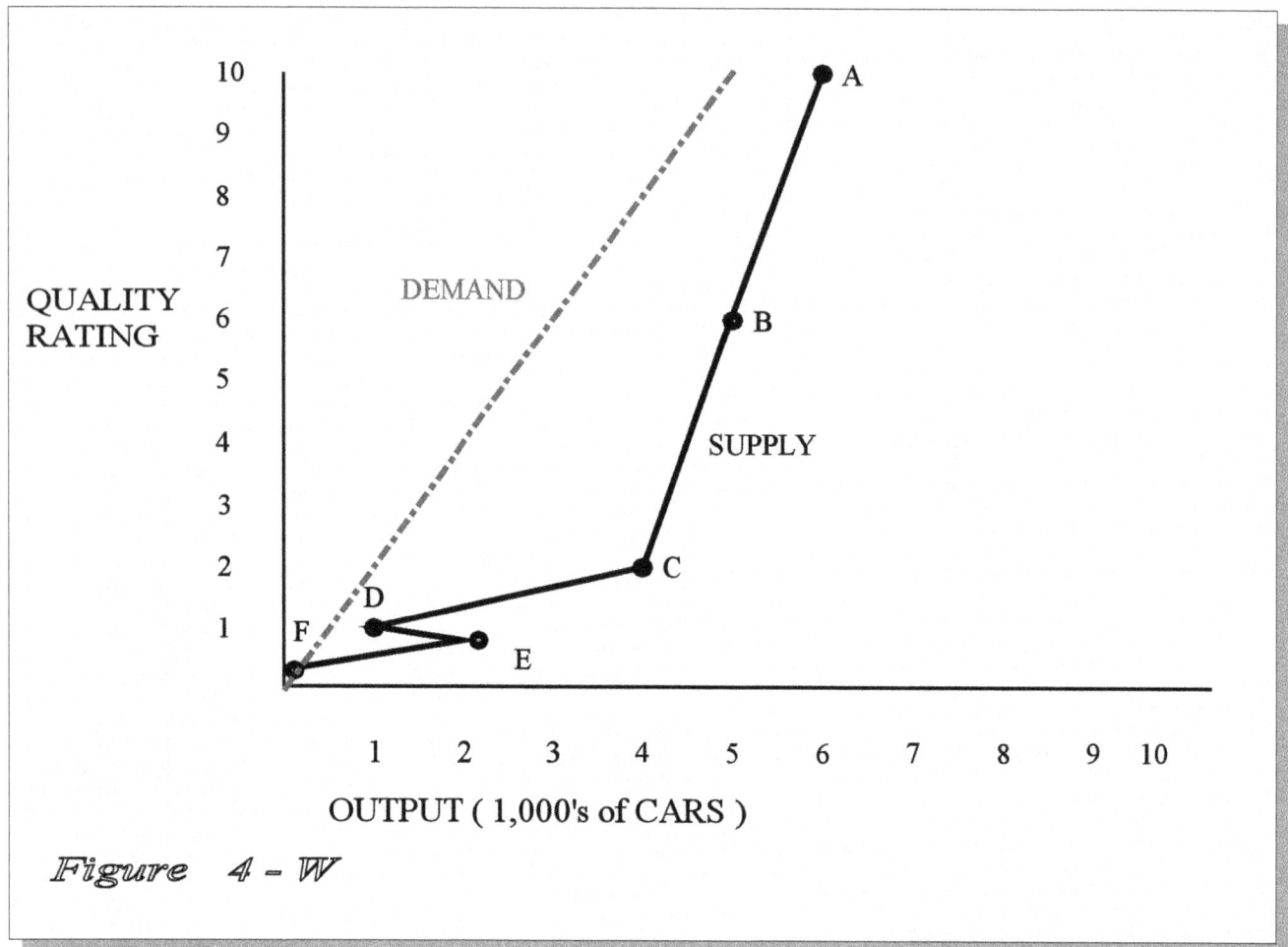

Figure 4-W

We mentioned almost everything we could about these graphs. Our analysis of the Consumerist Trade market is over. The general conclusion we get from the analysis of the Consumerist Trade market is that the good of the highest quality rating, that is the one most favored in its family, is the one bought, produced and sold most. With the knowledge gained here we will be able to understand how everything else works in this system.

Interest Rates

Interest rates are the profit earned from lending money. They are also the cost incurred from borrowing money. People who lend money want to earn interest for lending their money. People who want to borrow money must pay interest on what they borrow.

Interest rates are determined by the central bank. The Grand Chairman sets the interest rate. He does so once a week and without the input of the Consumerist Commissioners. Thus the interest rate is not fixed but can fluctuate freely. Whatever the Grand Chairman sets the interest rate at, all private banks and lending institutions must charge the same interest rate. The central bank is in charge of setting the interest rate that all private banks charge their clients for borrowing money.

The interest rate does not apply to all money. It only applies to Ignits and Fortals. No one can borrow Norses from the private bank, the reason being that it will distort the GDCP. For the same reason there cannot exist credit cards (in the materialist sector). A lender can borrow Ignits to buy things in the accommodational sector but cannot borrow Norses to buy things in the materialist sector. A person can borrow money to purchase a firm or finance a mortgage. However this same person cannot borrow to purchase a car or a desk. There is a schism between the sectors in terms of borrowing and lending.

Interest rates have a strong impact on the economy. High interest rates are good for lending and bad for borrowing. Low interest rates are bad for lenders and good for borrowers. The central bank through the Grand Chairman can manipulate the economy by adjusting the interest rate.

The interest rate at the time of borrowing/lending is the one that is in place until the debt is repaid even if the interest rate goes up or down during that time. Interest rates are compounded continuously. For example a shoe factory borrows 1000.00þ at 5%. The shoe company must pay the principle plus the interest in 3 years. This is given by the equation:

$$A = A_o e^{rt}$$

Thus in our example:

$$A = 1000.00 \text{ þ } e^{(0.05)3}$$

$$A = 1000.00 \text{ þ } e^{(0.15)} = 1\ 161.83\text{þ}$$

The shoe factory must pay this amount even though the central bank may decrease the interest rate to 4.5 % the next day.

To increase investment, stimulate the economy and lower the unemployment, the government can set an Interest Rate Stimulus (IRS). Thus the government pays a portion of the loan giving the effect that the interest rate is actually a bit lower than that set by the central bank. So suppose that the government sets the IRS at 0.5 % in the above example.

The government would pay:

$$A = 1000.00 \text{ þ } e^{(0.005)3}$$

$$A = 1000.00 \text{ þ } e^{(0.015)} = 1\,015.11 \text{ þ.}$$

$$1\,015.11\text{þ} - 1000.00 \text{ þ} = 15.11\text{þ}$$

The creditor earns $1\,161.83$ þ

And the shoe factory pays $(1\,161.83 \text{ þ} - 15.11 \text{ þ}) = 1146.72$ þ

It doesn't matter whether the interest rate is higher or lower than the accommodational markdown. The things that interest rates apply to are different than what the accommodational markdown applies to. Whereas the interest rate raises the supply of Ignits in the accommodational sector, the accommodational markdown serves to lower it.

Interest rates are the mechanism by which lenders and borrowers come together to exchange money. The interest rate is set by the Grand Chairman of the central bank. Unlike some of the other parameters set by the central bank, interest rates have the potential to fluctuate.

Surplus, Shortage and International Trade

It is appropriate to discuss shortages and surpluses; how they arise and how to be rid of them. We begin with a definition. A surplus occurs when there is more of a good than there are people who want to buy the good. The result is that goods are not sold. In contrast a shortage occurs when there is less of a good than there are people who want to buy the good. The result is that not enough of a good is available.

The traditional free-market response to surpluses is to lower the price of the good. The traditional free-market response to a shortage is to raise the price of the good. The consumerist response to these situations is different. In most cases a surplus is remedied by the exportation of the good to a country that wants to buy the good. The remedy to a shortage is to import more of the good from countries that are willing to sell the good. Through international trade consumerist nations eliminate their surpluses and shortages.

Price is not the only factor when considering international trade. We should not import things we do not need regardless of the price. If there is too much bread and we cannot eat any more bread then there is no point in importing more. Inuit would not import snow and people in the dessert would not import sand regardless of the price of these items. We also shouldn't export things that are needed by people regardless of price. If a person walking the dessert only has a canteen of water, he would be wise not to sell it. If he sells it for a lot of money he would die of thirst and be unable to spend his money. Also, a person travelling the Arctic would not sell his clothes. Even if he sold them for a lot of money, he would freeze to death along with his money. Necessity is just as important as price when considering whether or not to buy or sell.

We must now make a distinction between 3 types of surpluses/shortages. We will call one International, one Domestic and the third Absolute. An international surplus or shortage can be elevated simply by exporting and importing the good in question. An example is oil. If there are not enough we simply import it. Domestic shortages and surpluses cannot be gotten rid of by international trade. An example of a domestic shortage is parking space. The third surplus/shortage will be discussed at the end. We will first deal with international shortages/surpluses.

We now introduce the concept of the *consumerist trade pool*. The consumerist trade pool is a trading fund operated by the central bank where excess profits from exporting and importing are used to subsidize the importing and exporting of other goods. There are four possible scenarios. We deal with each of them in turn.

In the first case there are 1000 too many chairs in the economy. For the purpose of this section let's assume that the retail mark-up is 25%. The price of a chair from the factory is 20.00 þ. If the chair were sold to a retailer it would cost a consumerist $20.00 \ \Theta + 0.25 \times 20.00 \ \Theta = 25.00 \ \Theta$. A quality market graph could look like this where sofas (D) have a rating of 2, stools (C) have a rating of 3, chairs (B) have a rating of 5 and rocking chairs (A) have a rating of 10.

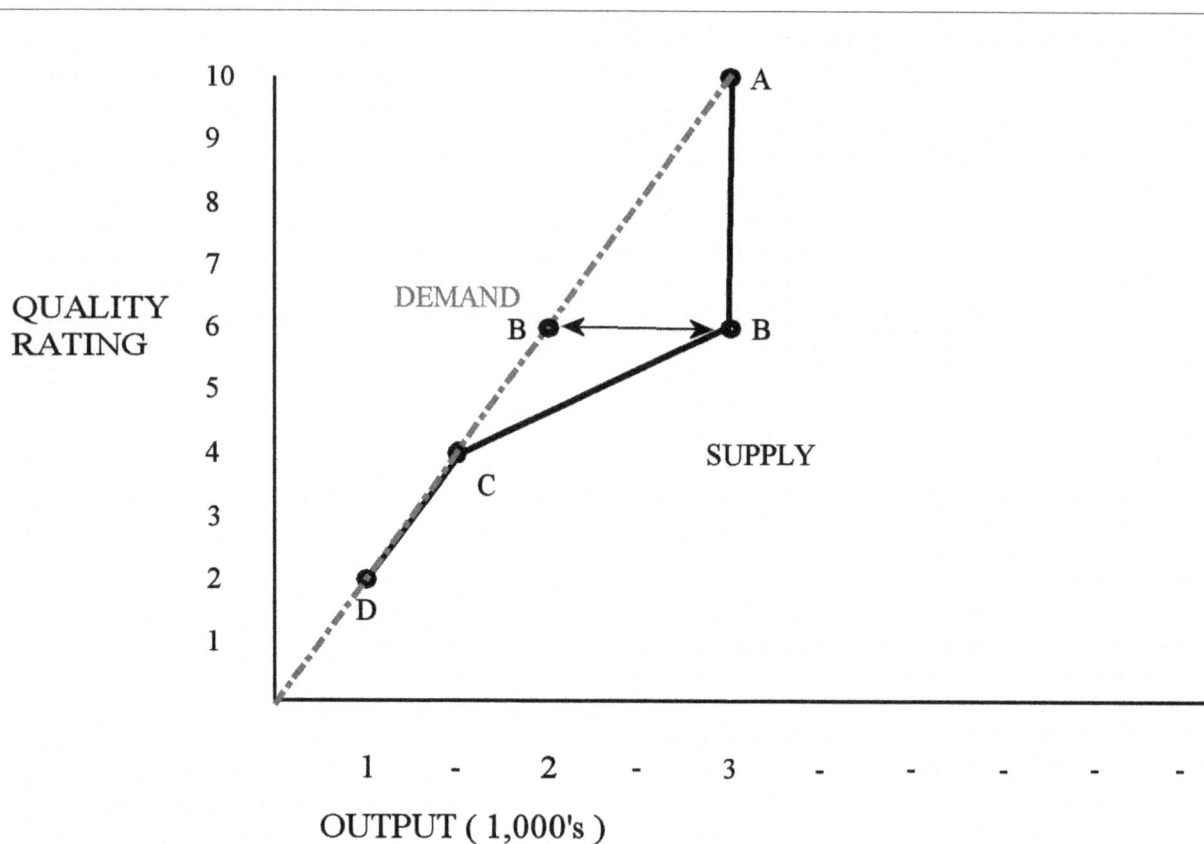

Figure 5-A

Since there are 1000 excess chairs, they should be exported. We assume that the exchange rate is 1$ = 1þ. We will deal with exchange rates in detail later on. Keep in mind that 1.00 Θ = 1.00 þ but that they cannot be exchanged directly for one another. The international market equilibrium price for a chair is 30.00 $ and the factory exports the 1000 chairs to a foreign country, let's say the U.S. We will use the U.S. as our trading partner throughout this section. During exporting the chair factory earns 30.00 þ per chair since 1$ =1 þ in this example. The chair factory earns profit in Ignits not in Norses. The chair factory's international trade profit is (30.00 þ– 20.00 þ) x 1000 = 10 000.00 þ. However the chair factory does not keep this extra profit. Rather it earns as much as it would earn if it sold those chairs to retailers in the consumerist nation at 20.00 þ per chair. They would earn 20.00 þ x 1000 = 20 000.00 þ. The 10 000 þ from the international trade goes to the trade pool. The reason that this factory must not earn a higher profit from exporting is that it would then choose to export rather than sell internally. This is how the consumerist trade pool factors in when a firm is exporting to a nation where the price of the good in the foreign nation is higher than in ours.

We now move onto a different case. Unless the consumerist nation has a natural source of oil, it is likely that the nation will require to import oil. Suppose that the nation needs 1000 L of oil. The price of oil in the consumerist nation is 0.50Θ /L and since the retail mark-up is 25%, the gas station charges 0.50 Θ + 0.25(0.50 Θ) = 0.625 Θ /L. A quality market graph might look like this:

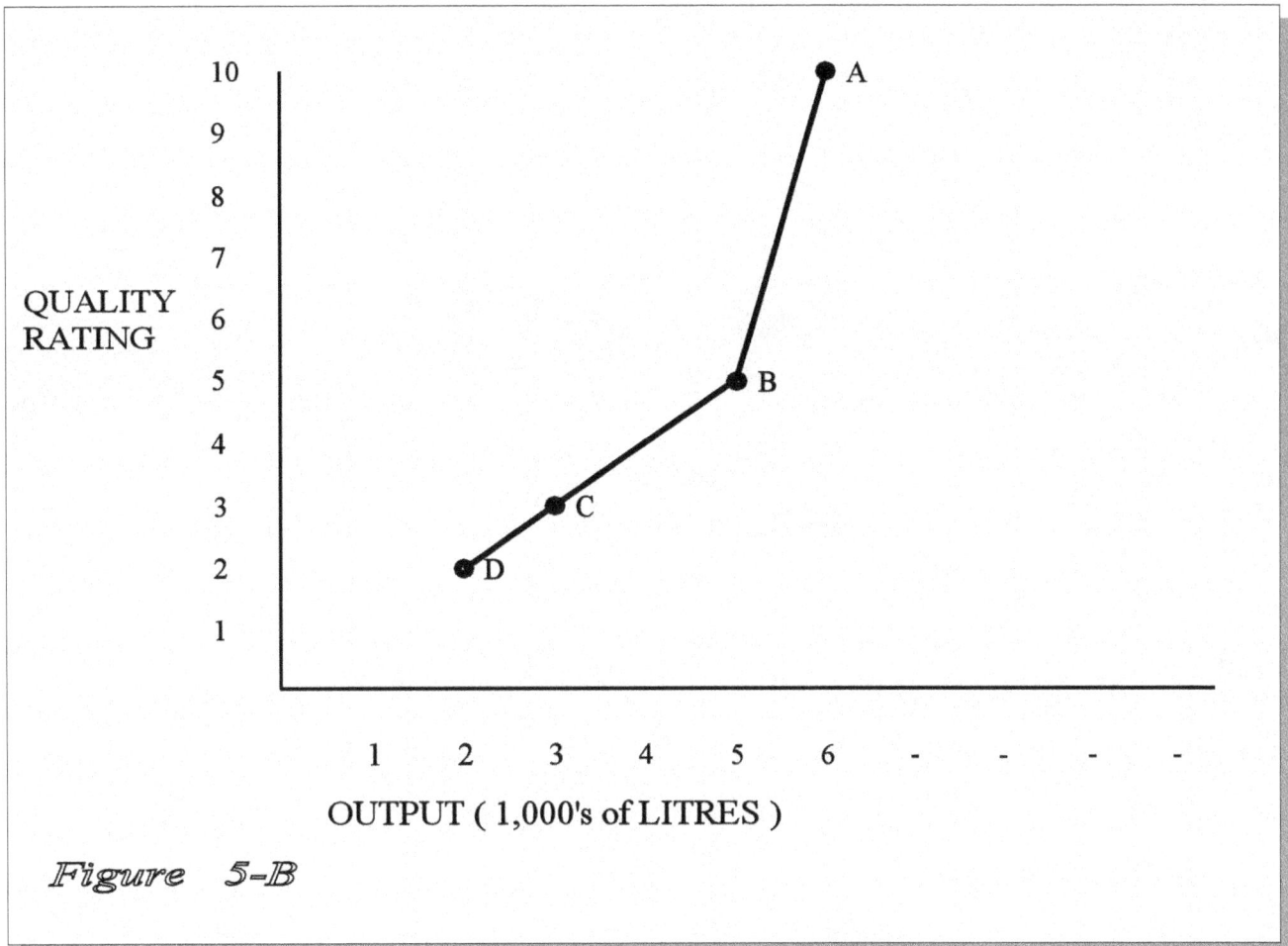

Figure 5-B

Where oil (A) has a quality rating of 10, propane (B) has a quality rating of 5, natural gas (C) has a quality rating of 3 and kerosene (D) has a quality rating of 2.

The international price of oil is $0.30 per litre and the consumerist nation imports the 1000 L of oil. Since in our example 1$ = 1þ our nation pays 0.30 þ per litre thus paying the foreign nation a total of 1000 L x 0.30þ /L = 300.00 þ. The oil is directly imported by gas retailers which bear the cost of transportation. During the trade they create 1000 L x 0.625 þ /L = 625.00 þ. The gas retailers earn 125.00 þ (625.00 þ - 500.00þ). Actually they make a bit less than this due to transportation, advertising and other costs. The trade pool profits 500.00 þ– 300.00þ = 200.00þ. This helps to offset the subsidies in cases we will see next.

Let's move onto another case. Here exporting takes place when the international market equilibrium price (say the price in the U.S.) is higher than the consumerist price. Suppose we have too much ketchup. We have an excess of 5000 bottles. The consumerist price is 2.00 þ and the product at the retail level costs 2.50 Θ. A quality market graph might look like this. Where D stands for mustard, C stands for ketchup, B stands for relish and A stands for mayonnaise.

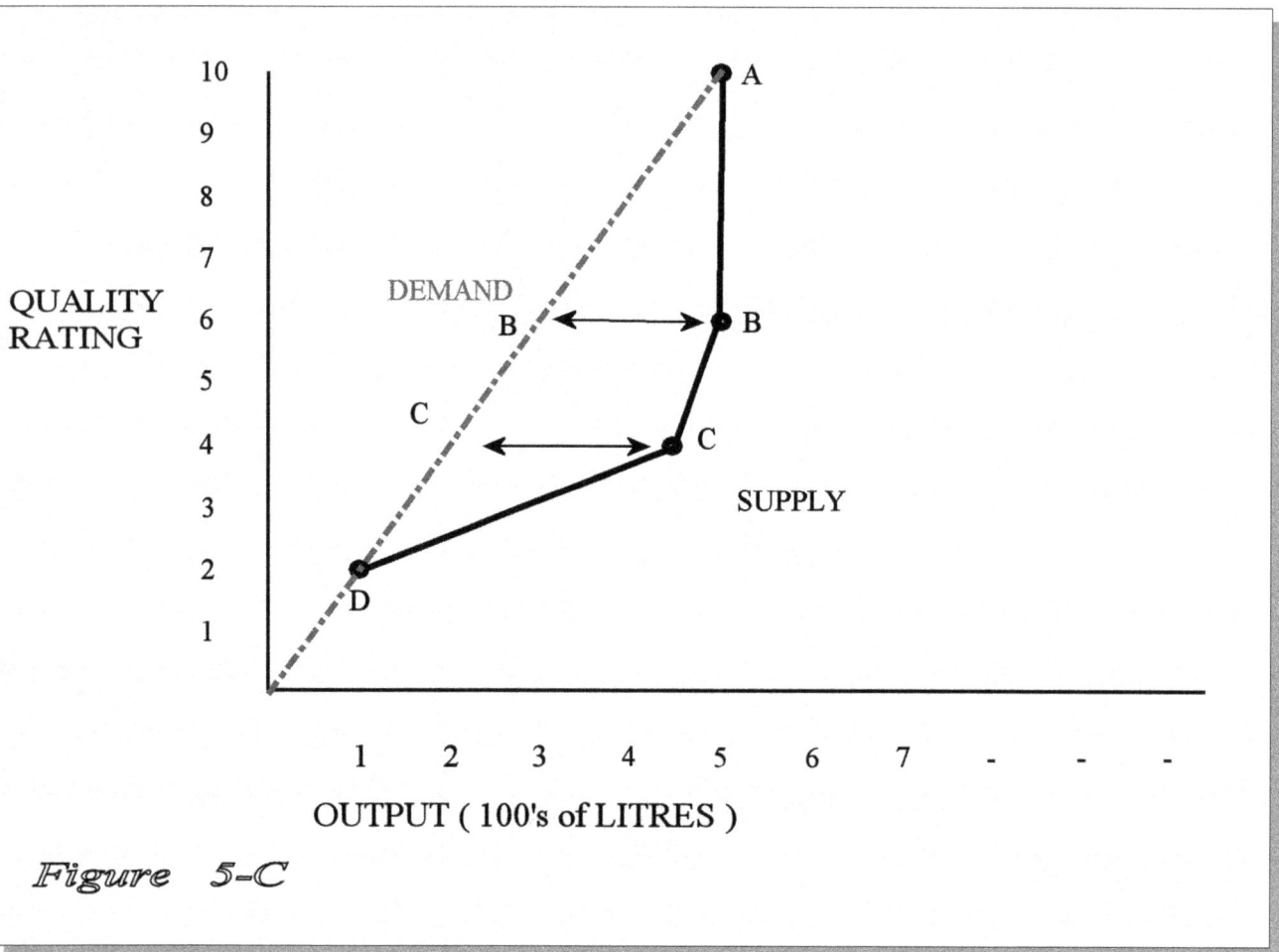

Figure 5-C

The international market price is $1.50. The trade is subsidized. The trade pool gives each bottle an extra 0.50 þ. So the trade deficit in the trade pool is 5000 x 0.50 þ = 2 500.00 þ. The domestic ketchup makers and exporters earn 2.00 þ x 5000 = 10 000.00 þ. This is one case where the trade pool has to subsidize.

Another case involves imports. Suppose that we have few automobiles and we need another 50 cars. The consumerist factory price is 10 000.00 þ and the retail price is 12 500.00 Θ per car. The international market equilibrium price is $20 000.00 per car. A quality market graph might look like this:

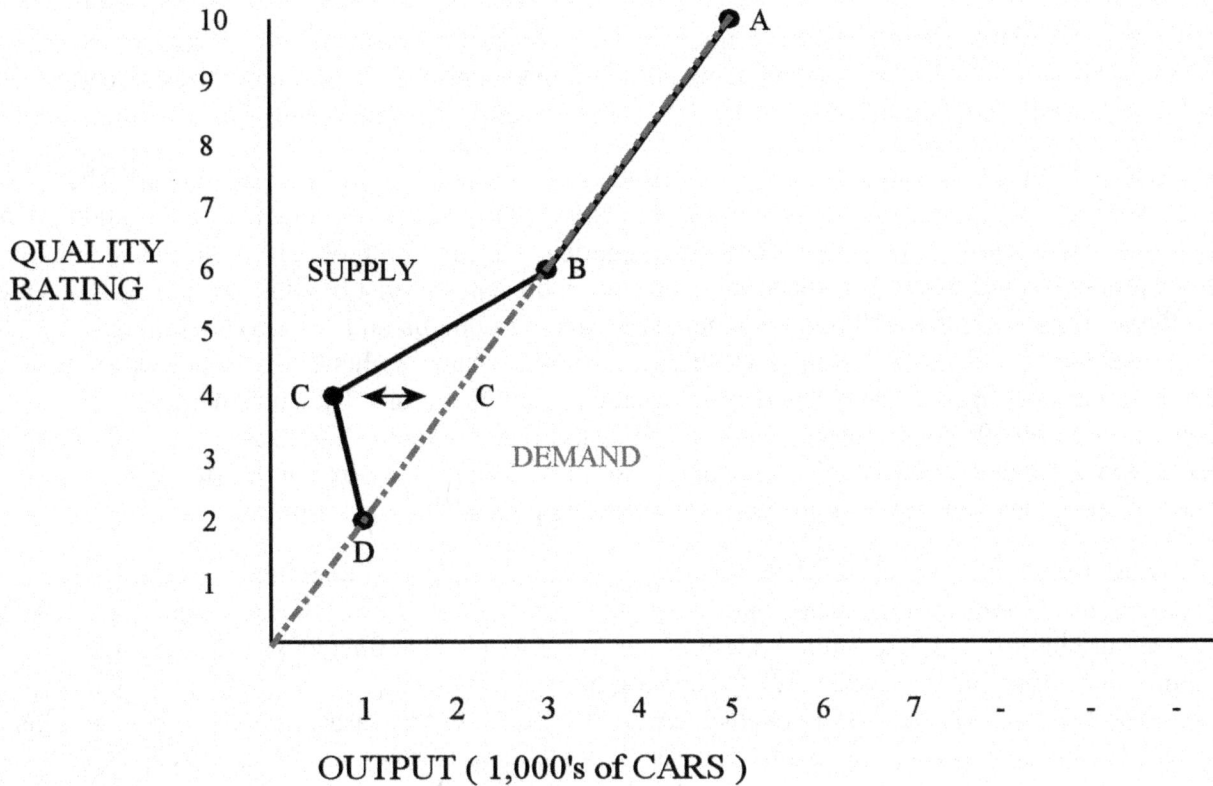

Figure 5-D

Where A is limousines, B is S.U.V.'s, C is minivans and D is sports cars. Here the trade pool pays a subsidy of $10 000.00 = 10 000.00 þ per car and the retailers are the importers so the retail profit is 50 x (12 500.00þ – 10 000.00þ) = 50 x 2 500 = 125 000.00 þ. Although retailers make a profit the trade pool is decreased.

The trade pool is designed to balance the profits from the first and second cases and the losses from the third and fourth cases. We calculate the trade pool balance from the above examples:

Case 1	+ 10 000.00 þ
Case 2	+ 200.00 þ
Case 3	- 2 500.00 þ
Case 4	-500 000.00 þ
Balance=	-492 300.00 þ

The trade pool has a negative balance. This is not a good thing. The central bank should manipulate the things that are exported and imported in order to achieve a favorable trade pool balance. More on this later.

The consumerist economy thrives on trade. It would be to the consumerist's advantage that the goods of the highest quality are bought. If the products are made cheaply in other countries and are imported to the consumerist nation then we would have a scenario like case 3. This hurts the trade pool.

Suppose that the U.S. is making a car, car A, and the final price of the car is $5 000.00. The exchange rate is $1 = 1þ. In our country the price of cars is 8 000.00 þ from the factory and 10 000.00 ʘ at the dealer. In this case the car dealer will buy the American car for $5000.00 and sell it for 10 000.00 ʘ. At the moment of purchase of Norses are deducted from the consumerist buying the car and Ignits are added to the retailer. Thus of the 10 000.00 þ the dealer keeps 2 000.00þ and 3 000þ (8000.00 þ– 5000.00þ) goes to the trade pool to subsidize other trades. As we can see, this is a win-win-win-win situation for several groups. First the Americans managed to sell their cars. The consumerist retailer made a profit of 2 000.00þ. The consumerists have the choice of buying an American car in addition to the ones already available. Finally the trade pool increased by 3000.00þ, allowing the subsidization of other trades. This is one way in which the consumerist trade pool assists open trade.

Now let's examine a situation where the exporting country has a product that is costly. Let's use cars as an example. Once again the factory price is 8 000.00 þ and the price at the car dealership is 10 000.00 ʘ. We are importing goods from the U.S. Their cars cost $15 000.00 and $1 = 1. Here, the importation of cars must be subsidized. The trade pool must pay 15 000.00 þ – 8 000.00 þ= 7 000.00 þ per car to import the cars. The car retailer sells them for 10 000.00 ʘ and earns 2 000.00 þ per car. This is a loose-win-win-win situation. The main looser is the trade pool. It is not very wise to keep subsidizing everything. The consumerists win because they have the opportunity to buy an American car. The car dealership gains 2 000.00þ for every car they sell. The Americans earn $15 000.00 per car. Some trades would not be possible without the existence of the consumerist trade pool.

Ideally the trade pool should be balanced. However the situation may occur where there may be more trade expenditures than income (i.e. more subsidizing than profit). It is the central bank's duty to make sure that the trade pool is positive most of the time or that trades involved give the least difference between subsidies and earnings. To do this it has the right to restrict certain subsidies if it deems that they are too expensive. Thus the economy does not have 100% complete free trade although it strives for it. The balance of the trade pool is the foremost concern.

We will now talk about exchange rates. A real exchange rate is the relative price of foreign goods in terms of domestic goods. A nominal exchange rate is the price of foreign currency in terms of domestic currency. Norses (ʘ) cannot be exchanged for any other type of currency; not $; not þ; not £. They can only be used by consumerists to purchase goods and services in the materialist sector. However Ignits can be traded for any other foreign currency.

Let's look directly at exchange rates. Suppose a chair in a consumerist factory costs 20.00 þ. The same chair in the U.S. costs $40.00. We drop the supposition that $1 = 1þ. The real exchange rate is now $40.00/20.00 þ= $2/1þ. Although this is the real exchange rate, the nominal exchange rate can be a lot different. Suppose that the nominal exchange rate is (again) $1 = 1 þ and we are selling 20 chairs. The U.S. must pay $800.00 and we earn 400.00 þ The U.S. pays us $800.00 x 1 þ/$1 = 800.00 þ. The 800.00 þ - 400.00 þ = 400.00 þ is kept by the trading pool.

Now suppose that the nominal exchange rate is $3/1þ. We are again selling 20 chairs to the U.S. The U.S. must pay $800.00 and we earn 400.00 þ. The U.S. pays us $800.00 x 1 þ/$3 = 267/00 þ. The 400.00 þ - 267.00 þ = 133.00 þ must be given to the trade pool.

We have seen what happens when, during exporting, the nominal exchange rate is higher and lower than the real exchange rate. Now let's see what happens during importing. We will use chairs as our product and our trading partner will once again be the U.S. The price of a chair in a factory is 20.00 þ and 25.00 Ѳ at the retail level. It is $40.00 in the U.S. The real exchange rate is again $2.00/1.00 þ The retailer imports 20 chairs when the nominal exchange rate is $1.00/1.00 þ The retailer has to pay 400.00 þ for the chairs and the U.S. manufacturer receives $800.00 The retailer must pay $800.00 x 1.00 þ/$1.00 = 800.00 þ. The 400.00 þ (800.00 þ– 400.00 þ) is subsidized by the trading pool. The retailer earns (25.00 þ x 20) - 400.00 þ= 100.00 þ on the trade. Only one more scenario follows.

Again an importer imports 20 chairs from the U.S. The prices are the same as above but the nominal exchange rate is $3.00/1.00 þ. The retailer has to pay 400.00 þ and the manufacturer must receive $800.00. The retailer must pay $800.00 x 1.00þ /$3.00 = 266.00 þ. The retailer pays 400.00 þ and (400.00 þ– 266.00 þ) = 133.00 þ are gained by the trade pool. Thus appear all possible scenarios.

The next question is this. How is the (nominal) exchange rate determined? The closer the exchange rate is to the real, the less is the need for a trade pool. It is hard to apply a fixed exchange rate because the prices of foreign goods are constantly fluctuating. In some countries the exchange rate is fluctuating. In others it is fixed. Still in others it is pegged to some other currency. In accommodation based consumerism the nominal exchange rate is dictated by the central bank and it is usually calculated. The nominal exchange rate is calculated using real exchange rates of imports or exports and their weights in the process of trade on world markets. Finally all of this is averaged to arrive at a nominal exchange rate. An example follows.

Quantity	Product	U.S. Price	Consumerist Nation Price
200	Chairs	$1.00/Chair	0.50 þ /chair
300	Automobiles	$1000.00/car	1000.00 þ/car
400 L	Oil	$0.50/litre	1.00 þ /litre
500	Hamburgers	$2.00/burger	5.00 þ /burger
100	Pillows	$3.00/pillow	4.00 þ/pillow
800	Windows	$10.00/window	5.00 þ/window
1000	Books	$8.00/book	10.00 þ/ book
500	Jars of Pickles	$1.00/pickle jar	2.00 þ / pickle jar

Real Exchange Rates

- Chairs $2/þ

- Automobiles $1/þ

- Oil $0.5/þ

- Hamburgers $0.4/þ

- Pillows $0.75/þ

- Windows $2/þ

- Books $0.8/þ

- Pickle Jars $0.5/þ

Nominal exchange rate=

# of units = 200 + 300 + 400 + 500 + 100 + 800 +1000 + 500 = 3 800 units

Units x real exchange rate = (200 x $2/þ) + (300 x $1/þ) + (400 x $0.5/þ) + (500 x $0.4/þ) + (100 x $0.75/þ) + (800 x $2/þ) + (1000 x $0.8/þ) + (500 x $0.5/þ) = 3 825 $/þ

Nominal exchange rate = (3 825$/þ)/(3 800) = $1.0066/þ

This exchange rate is not definitely the one that gives the most positive balance, but one that will give the smallest differences between subsidies and profits for the trade pool.

Now that we know how to calculate the nominal exchange rate, let's observe some generalizations

1) During importing, a nominal exchange rate higher than the real exchange rate means that there will be a positive trade pool balance

2) During importing, a nominal exchange rate lower than the real exchange rate means there will be a negative trade pool balance

3) During exporting, a nominal exchange rate higher than the real exchange rate means that there will be a negative trade pool balance

4) During exporting, a nominal exchange rate lower than the real exchange rate means that there will be a positive trade pool balance

5) Whether the exchange rate is high or low is indifferent to the exporter and importer

The exchange rate must be adjusted to ensure a favorable trade balance. During cases when there is more importing than there is exporting, the central bank strives for a low foreign nominal exchange rate. During times when exports exceed imports, the central bank strives for a high foreign nominal exchange rate. The central bank has no effect on real exchange rates. Therefore it must manipulate the nominal exchange rate by restricting the trade of certain goods.

There is another type of exportation in accommodation based consumerism. There exists something called *exportation companies*. These can be run either privately or through the government. That is they exist in all three partitions- the governmental, the natural and the command partitions. The purpose of these companies is to buy products from consumerists and firms in consumerism and sell them to other countries or give them as gifts.

We have previously discussed Type 1 trade. This involves the consumerist trade pool. Now we can discuss Type 2 trade. This involves exportation companies. To preserve quality selection (in 3 of the

174

4 sectors), we must not allow consumerists to compete for goods and services in terms of price so as to make sure that only the highest quality goods are bought. However, we still have the option of selling lower quality goods to foreign countries as this does not interfere with quality selection. This is where exportation firms enter into the arena. What they do is that they buy lower quality good from consumerists or producers in consumerisms and sell them to another country or perhaps even give them as gifts to improve international relations. Whether they are sold or given to another country, the other country will be more than happy to receive these goods.

This is how Type 2 trade functions: An exporting company buys a good from someone in consumerism for less than the fixed price of the good and sells it to another nation for the price set by the bank. Whatever the difference is, this the exporting company gets in terms of profit. How much the consumerist or producer sells his good for depends on the interaction of exporting firms and producers/consumerists. The main stipulation is that the agreed upon price must definitely be lower than that fixed by the bank. The consumerist trade pool is involved. Usually this is a win-win-win situation. The consumerist/producer got money for something that he didn't want more of anymore. The foreign nation received a good they can use in their economy. Finally, the exportation firm made a profit.

Let's work out a concrete example. The central bank sets the price of a car at 10 000.00þ. Our exporting company is called ACEBS and we our exporting to Nicaragua. We are making the assumption that the Nicaraguans are using the same currency. A consumerist, Bob, has a 5 year old car but he doesn't need it anymore as he is planning to buy a limousine with the money he saved up. He sells his car to ACEBS for 8 000.00 þ. The firm ACEBS sells the car to someone in Nicaragua for 12 000.00 þ. The trade pool earns 2 000.00 þ (12 000.00 þ – 10 000.00þ) while ACEBS earns 2 000.00 þ (10 000.00 þ- 8 000.00þ). Bob earns 8 000.00 þ. All parties benefit and this is a win-win-win-win situation. Bob got money for a car he did not need. ACEBS made a profit from exporting vs. buying the used car from Bob. The Nicaraguans now have a car to drive in. We did not value that car that much, but they probably would. Lastly, the consumerist trade pool made a profit from the trade that allows it to subsidize other trades.

There is another situation where the price of the car in Nicaragua is lower than our fixed price, perhaps 7 000.00 þ. Assuming all other variables are the same, this is a loose-win-win-win situation. The Nicaraguans, firm ACEBS and Bob all make a profit while the consumerist trade pool must lose some money.

The exportation firm can exist in either the natural, governmental or command partitions. It primarily involves Ignits. However the consumerists can still get rid of goods they no longer need by selling goods to the exportation firm that are in the materialist sector and involve Norses. For example, a consumerist can sell that old suit that he doesn't need to the exportation firm. He must sell it, however, for less than the price set by the central bank. He would like to sell it for as close to the fixed price as possible. So if the suit cost 100.00 Ө, he can sell it for 90.00 þ to the exportation company. Upon selling the suit to another country, with the help of the consumerist trade pool, the exportation firm will earn 10.00 þ

We will now discuss domestic shortages and surpluses. The free-market response to a shortage is to raise the price of the good. If there is a surplus one would lower the price. In consumerist domestic shortages we expand the operation. In consumerist domestic surpluses we decrease the scope of the operation or get rid of it entirely. Let's look at some examples.

First we will look at domestic shortages. Suppose that we have a university parking lot and that there are more students needing to park than there is space for them to do so. Instead of raising prices, we buy the land around the parking lot and turn it into a parking lot. Since there are already students willing to use the parking lot we have a "profit vacuum" That is, we are sure to make a profit. Our only constraint however is that the price of the nearby land is less than the profit from renting the parking space to students. A diagram that follows on the next page illustrates the idea.

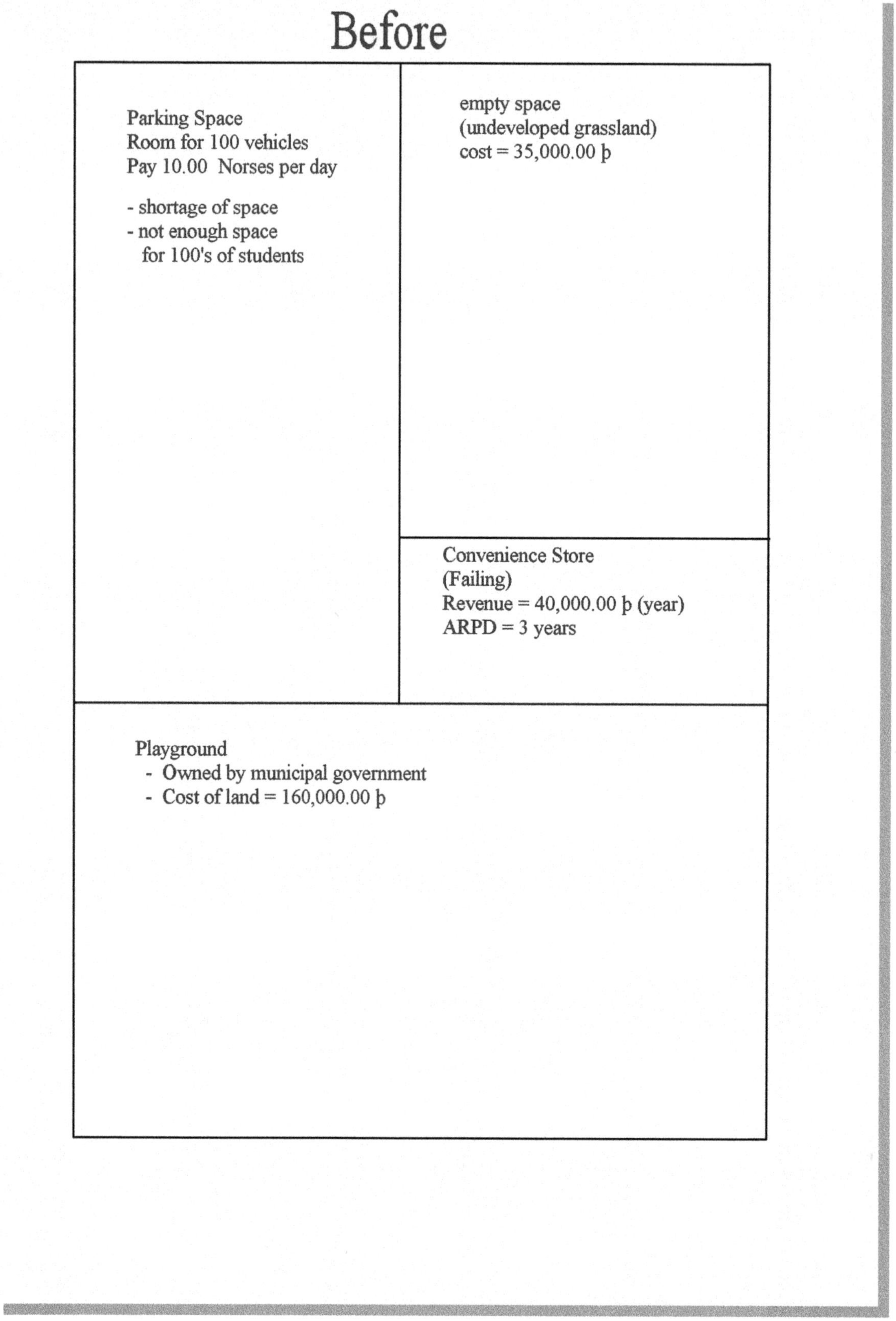

Before

Parking Space
Room for 100 vehicles
Pay 10.00 Norses per day

- shortage of space
- not enough space
  for 100's of students

empty space
(undeveloped grassland)
cost = 35,000.00 þ

Convenience Store
(Failing)
Revenue = 40,000.00 þ (year)
ARPD = 3 years

Playground
- Owned by municipal government
- Cost of land = 160,000.00 þ

Figure 5-E

After

Parking Space
(After buying surrounding land)

950 Students pay 10.00 Norses/day
Total maintenance per day = 15.00 þ
Result = no shortage

Figure 5-F

Calculations: in one year => 950 x 10.00 þ x 365 = 3 467 500.00 þ

Costs: Maintenance per year=> 15.00 þ x 365 = 5 475.00 þ

Land Purchases: 35 000.00 þ + 160 000.00 þ + (3 x 40 000.00 þ) = 315 000.00 þ

Balance = 3 467 500.00 þ – 315 000.00 þ – 5 475.00 þ = + 3 147 025.00 þ/year

Now let's look at another example; let's say a lemonade stand. Suppose someone selling lemonade experiences a shortage of lemonade. Instead of raising the price, the owner should buy more lemons and make more juice. For our third example we will examine a chair shortage in a school classroom. The sensible thing to do is to take chairs from a classroom that has too many of them. The consumerist response to shortages has the advantage that it doesn't discriminate in favor of the prosperous but rather it tries to give as many people as possible a particular good. By raising prices the effect is that only a select group, the prosperous group, receives a good while the others still need it. Try this thought experiment. There are 10 people starving for food. 1 of them is extremely rich and the other nine are not. There is not enough food to go around. Due to the shortage in this free-market example the price of food goes up. Now only the rich one can eat. The shortage is alleviated but there are still 9 desperately hungry people with nothing to eat since they cannot afford the food. Wouldn't the sensible thing to do be to increase the production of food, raise more cows, and grow more apples etc. (without raising prices)? That way every one has enough to eat.

Now we look at domestic consumerist surpluses. If we have a factory that makes widgets and nobody at all wants to buy them then such a factory shouldn't even exist. The factory should bankrupt and close down. Suppose a pop company comes up with a soft drink that just tastes awful. If people don't want the drink the pop company should halt production and try to come up with something more flavorful. Lastly, let's look at a fashion company that makes ugly clothes. Instead of lowering the price of the clothes and making some people look very unfashionable, they should change the clothes they sell or fire their fashion designers. These would be the best responses to a consumerist domestic surplus.

There is also a third type of shortage called an absolute shortage which cannot be dealt with by importing or rising prices or expanding the operation. Here there is a limited amount of a good and there can only be less of it. Examples of this type of shortage include food in a submarine, air in outer space and perishables in a winter cabin.

The counterpart of absolute shortage is absolute surplus. Here one cannot get rid of the surplus by exporting, price lowering or decreasing the scope of the enterprise. Examples of this include pollution and garbage accumulation.

This is a good time to discuss a major problem that could arise with regards to free trade. It is absolutely mandatory that Norses not be exchanged directly for Ignits. If they are, the incentive for work is lost as consumerists trade the Norses they were granted by the central bank for Ignits they could then use to improve their accommodational standing. A problem arises when the following happens. A consumerist purchases a limousine with Norses, drives it to another country, sells it, trades it for Ignits and now has Ignits for spending. This is known as the *export-smuggling calamity*. It must be guarded against. We have made it illegal to trade Norses for a foreign currency. If this were not the case, a clever consumerist would trade Norses for dollars and dollars for Ignits. So to stop the calamity we need controls at the borders so that consumerists don't cross the border with something valuable just to sell it. This would not include things like food, clothes, shoes, blankets or presents. It would concern things like TV's, stereos, watches and jewelry. Some things it would be completely illegal to smuggle while other things must be noted by the officer in charge of border crossings. It may be required that some travelers pay a deposit upon leaving the country. Upon returning if they come back with everything they brought over the border, their deposit is given back. Further discussion on this calamity is not required here as it is for the most part a matter for law.

We have examined the three types of shortages and surpluses. We have found the solution to the more common two using mathematics as our tool. Now we know how the trade and exchange of goods and money happens in accommodation based consumerism.

Volunteers

Volunteers are people who donate their free time to various causes. They offer their services for what they think is a worthy cause. What sets them apart from regular workers is that they do not want money for their time and effort.

Volunteers work in many areas of the economy. Some work in hospitals, some work at retirement homes while still others work to build playgrounds in the local park. Their contributions are wonderful and accommodation based consumerism wholly encourages their activities. The more volunteers the better.

Volunteers are clearly very useful. Our economy is better for their contributions. Their contributions in terms of time and effort make a consumerist society a more pleasant one for the lives that they touch.

Those that volunteer increase the output of society in general. Whatever service they provide or good they produce the more society gains. If a volunteer spends time at a hospital, the doctors and nurses benefit. But so do the patients and their families. And what is more, the volunteers gain a profound satisfaction for the work that they do.

We saw what volunteers are. We saw how they function. Clearly they make accommodation based consumerism better.

Population

People are one of the most important resources in a society. We need to have a coherent policy as to the size and fluctuation of a population. There are essentially 3 possibilities. 1) To decrease the size of the existing population, 2) To let the population stay roughly the same size and 3) To increase the size of the existing population. What is the wisest policy- a society with a large population or a society with a small population?

The consumerist grant depends on the population and how much of it is employed. If the GDCP, the GCT and the amount of employed people stay the same and the population increases, then each consumerist is granted less Norses to spend on the materialist sector. Conversely, if the GDCP, the GCT and the amount of employed people stay the same and the population decreases, then each consumerist is granted more Norses to spend on the materialist sector. These are the ways in which a change in the size of a population (ceteris paribus) affects the amount of Norses that are granted to consumerists.

There are two ways for the population to increase- through an increase in the number of immigrants and an increase in the number of births. In this case there is a decrease in the General as well as the Non-Working consumerist grants. We will call the sum of the general and non-working consumerist grants, the "GDCP per capita", even though it doesn't apply to those that are institutionalized. For those households where a birth occurs there is an increase in the amount of Norses granted to the whole house hold even though each member of the house hold earns less Norses. This is because all non-institutionalized members of society are issued Norses including new-borns. The new born would be granted the non-working consumerist grant as he is without a job. Consequently, the house hold into which the child was born has a higher amount of Norses collectively. They can use the money (Norses) issued to the newborn to buy materialist goods and services. The same cannot be said of a single new immigrant. Although the GDCP grant decreases (assuming the same GDCP) only a new household becomes created in the society. This becomes different if a family immigrated to someone who is already a citizen. In this case the household is also granted more Norses collectively. It is clear that there are incentives to procreating as well as to bringing over relatives if one is an immigrant.

What happens when the population decreases or stays the same? Suppose that a population decreases. The amount of workers would decrease and so would the amount of entrepreneurs. Clearly, the GDCP would decrease. With less consumerists, the GDCP is divided among less people. Now suppose that the population stays the same. New births and new immigrants have to balance deaths and emigrants. As the GDCP increases so would the GDCP per capita. However the GDCP would increase less for a population that stayed the same size than for one where the population grew due to an increase in workers and entrepreneurs.

What conclusion can we draw from the above for a society with a decreasing population? There is a decreasing GDCP. Also the GDCP increases less quickly in a society where the population stays the same than in one where there is a growing population. However in a society where the population is growing (assuming that most of the people are used to contribute to society) there is an increasing GDCP. On the other hand, in a steady or decreasing population there is an increase in the GDCP per capita. Yet it is not impossible for an increase in the GDCP per capita in the increasing population case if the GDCP grows faster than the population for a particular level of GDCP per capita. Thus the best choice is to have an increasing population, as long as the GDCP is increasing as well.

The population should steadily increase. However it should increase such that the GDCP per capita also increases from period to period. Although the government cannot influence deaths and births directly it can influence migration. The government should be in charge of controlling the population since the population size is a matter of public policy. From an economic point of view, however the government must only allow as many immigrants such that the GDCP per capita is increasing. Also which immigrants to let in should be at least partially based on the skills and education that the immigrants have. Thus it makes the most sense to allow immigrants to our country who are well educated in a trade or have advanced degrees. It appears that it is better to allow into our country a doctor who specializes in open heart surgery or a chemical engineer than a potential immigrant that was on social assistance in his original country. The movement of people across borders is in the hands of the government.

Here is an observation. All animals strive to multiply. Nature prohibits their populations from exploding. When there is plenty of food and there are good living conditions, rabbits will increase the size of their population. When the amount of food is limited and the living conditions are poor, rabbit populations decrease. Here is another observation. The population of bacteria increases if the bacteria have good growing conditions and plenty of food and space. Their populations decrease as food and space become limited. From these observations it appears that we should increase the population as long as the GDCP per capita is increasing for the last several periods. When the GDCP per capita repeatedly decreases for a few periods, the government should take measures to decrease the rate of immigration. The government's decision to allow more or less immigrants depends on the magnitude of the increase or decrease of the GDCP per capita.

Let's do some calculations. In January (period 1) suppose the population is 10 000 people of which 9 000 are working. The non-working grant reduction (NWGR) is 20%. The GDCP is 4 000 000.00 Θ. We assume a GCT of 10%. Thus the GDCP per capita is:

(4 000 000.00 Θ – 400 000 Θ)/10 000 = 360.00 Θ

(4 000 000.00 Θ – 400 000.00 Θ)/(9 000 + (0.2 x 1000)) = 391.30 Θ

391.30 Θ x 0.2 = 78.26 Θ

The GDCP per capita in period 1 is 360.00 Θ. The general consumerist grant is 391.30 Θ and the non-working consumerist grant is 78.26 Θ

In our calculations 1 month is equal to 1 period. We are now in February. There were 500 deaths and 1 500 births. Our population is 10 000 - 500 + 1 500 = 1100. The GDCP is 4 500 000.00 Θ. The GCT is still 10% The NWGR is still 20%. There are 7 500 workers and 3 500 people are unemployed. Actually the "unemployed" are working for the command partition.

The GDCP per capita is

(4 500 000.00 Θ – 450 000.00 Θ)/11 000 = 368.18 Θ

(4 500 000.00 Θ – 450 000.00 Θ)/(7500 + (0.2 x 3 500)) = 489.02 Θ

489.02 Θ x 0.2 = 97.80 Θ

The GDCP per capita increases by (368 Θ– 360 Θ) = 8 Θ in one month. Also the general consumerist grant increases by (489 Θ – 391 Θ) = 98 Θ and the non-working consumerist grant rose by (97.8 Θ – 78.28 Θ) = 19.52 Θ

The government opts to allow new immigrants in March. 1800 new immigrants enter our country and 200 emigrants leave. There are 800 births and 500 deaths. Thus our population is now 11 000 – 500 – 200 + 1800 + 800 = 12900. The GDCP increases sharply to 6 000 000.00 Θ. The GCT is still 10% and the NWGR is 20%. There are 8 000 workers. The GDCP per capita is

(6 000 000.00 Θ– 600 000.00 Θ)/12 900 = 418.60 Θ

(6 000 000.00 Θ – 600 000.00 Θ)/(8 000 + (0.2 x 4 900)) = 601.34 Θ

601.34 Θ x 0.2 = 120.27 Θ

In one month the GDCP per capita grew by (418.60 Θ – 368.18 Θ) = 50.42 Θ. The general consumerist grant rose by (601.34 Θ– 489.02 Θ) = 112.32 Θ. The non working consumerist grant rose by (120.27 Θ -97.80 Θ) = 22.47 Θ

In April the government realizes how prosperous the economy is and how dramatically the grant to each consumerist is increasing. They do two things. First they raise the Grand Consumerist Tax to 25 % and allow 2000 new immigrants in. At the same time 200 emigrants leave the country. There are 200 births and 100 deaths. Thus our population is now, 12 900 + 2000 + 200 -100 – 200 = 14 800. The GDCP increases but not as sharply as before to 6 800 000.00 Θ. The amount of workers is 9 500 and the NWGR is 20%. The GDCP per capita is

(6 800 000.00 Θ – 1 700 000.00 Θ)/14 800 = 344.60 Θ

(6 800 000.00 Θ – 1 700 000.00 Θ)/(9 500 + (0.2 x 5 300)) = 482.95 Θ

482.95 Θ x 0.2 = 96.59 Θ

This is a tremendous decrease in the GDCP per capita (344.60 Θ – 418.60 Θ) = 74.00 Θ

The general consumerist grant drops by (482.95 Θ – 601.34 Θ) = 118.39 Θ. The Non-Working consumerist grant drops by (96.59 Θ – 120.27 Θ) = 23.68 Θ

The government needs to do some changes in May. First, it lowers the GCT to 5% and then it closes its borders to new immigrants. In May there are 500 deaths, 1500 births and 200 emigrants. The population in May is 14 800 – 200 -500 + 1500 = 15600. The GDCP grew to 7 500 000.00 Θ. The NWGR is 20%. There are 7 300 workers. The GDCP per capita is equal to

(7 500 000.00 Θ– 375 000.00 Θ)/15 600 = 456.73 Θ

(7 500 000.00 Θ– 375 000.00 Θ)/(7 300 + (0.2 x 8 300)) = 795.20 Θ

795.20 Θ x 0.2 = 159.04 Θ

This is a tremendous increase in the 3 parameters. The GDCP per capita rose by (456.73 Θ– 344.60 Θ) = 112.13 Θ. The general consumerist grant rose by (795.20 Θ – 482.95 Θ) = 312.25 Θ. The non-working consumerist grant rose by (159.04 Θ– 96.59 Θ) = 62.45 Θ

In June the government could perhaps slightly increase the tax and let some (very few) immigrants in. However we have seen all that can happen in these possible circumstances. Therefore we will end our calculations with those of May's.

We have seen that it is best to have a society with a growing population. We have witnessed that it is essential for both the GDCP and the GDCP per capita to grow in a thriving economy. Finally we have seen how the government can manipulate the number of immigrants it allows in in order to achieve these ends.

The Consumerist Stock Market

The consumerist system has its own stock market. In general, a stock is a claim of partial ownership of a firm. The purpose of this stock market is to allow firms to raise money to start and expand their operations. The consumerist and free-market stock markets are drastically different.

The consumerist stock market is not really a "market" in the free enterprise sense. It is more of a great exposition. In a giant multi-storied building, investors and firm representatives come together to buy and sell shares. Each firm has its own kiosk where it presents investors with the firm's business plan and answers any questions the investors may have about the firm.

The most important feature of the consumerist stock market is this. All shares, regardless of the company or firm that issues them and regardless of the number of shares issued, cost the same amount per share. This price is set by the central bank. It is called the *Consumerist Universal Stock Price* (CUSP). The consumerist stock market falls under the accommodational sector. We will assume for the purpose of this section that the CUSP is 10.00 þ, although this need not be. Investors do not make money by buying and selling stock as they would in a free-enterprise stock market system or the speculative stock market (which we will discuss shortly). Investors earn dividends on their stock which are paid on a per month basis. Shares represent a right to a firm's profit. The greater the percentage of shares of a company an investor has, the more dividends he earns. The firm's profit in this case is not total profit but *post-reinvestment profit*. That is the profit a firm has left over after re-investing back in itself. It is = (price of goods x quantity sold) – running cost – money used to build another outlet or buy more things that will improve the functioning of the firm (such as machinery). Whatever is left over goes to the investor. If an investor has 25 % of a firm's shares and the firm makes 1500.00 þ and reinvests 500.00 þ, then the investor earns (this month) 0.25 x (1 500.00 þ– 500.00 þ) = 250.00 þ. The firm has a right to issue an amount of shares once a month but it must announce that it is doing so.

Firms must be careful about how many shares they issue. If a convenience store issues 10 million shares, few investors would buy the shares because the investor will not earn enough money to cover the cost of buying the shares. If someone buys 10 % of the convenience store shares, he would have 1 million shares and since in our example shares cost 10.00þ, he would have to pay 10 million þ. Even if the convenience store earns 1 million þ post re-investment profit, the investor would only have 10% of the profit = 100 000.00þ per month. In this example it would take the investor 100 months to earn any profit. Investors are not likely to invest in firms that do not have much potential to flourish.

Let's see an example. A firm that wants to start a car factory and make cars is more likely to sell a large amount of stock. It must convince investors, using its business plan, that the firm knows what it is doing and has good plans. A car factory is more likely to earn profit than other firms like a lawn mowing service. Let's suppose that a firm needs to buy inputs for its factory. It issues 10 000 000 shares. Each is worth 10.00 þ. Thus the company has 100 000 000 þ to start production. Within a year it makes a lot of profit. It earns 10 000 000.00 þ profit and reinvests 5 000 000.00 þ into research and building another plant. The 5 000 000.00 þ leftover is divided up by the investors. Someone who bought 100 shares for 1 000.00 þ will have 0.001 % of the profits which is 50.00þ. The shareholder will earn what he invested in 20 months. Assuming the firm does not issue more shares, it will take less than 20 months to see a considerable return on investment because the firm is continuously reinvesting in itself, making it possible for even greater profit.

The owners of a firm face tradeoffs. Owning a firm is a kind of juggling act. Three important variables are the number of shares issued and how much money to reinvest and how much money to give to investors. The more shares a firm issues, the more money it has for starting and expanding if it sells all of its shares. However if it issues too much, the stock will be more diluted and the less dividends an investor will earn per share owned. The other variable to juggle is what to do with the profit. The more that is reinvested, the more the firm can earn in the future; i.e. two stores will earn more money than one, but the investors will earn less and less investors will want to own stock. However if more profits are given to investors as dividends, the more shares they will buy because each share has a greater return. But then the firm will not be able to expand as quickly as if it reinvested all of the profit back in itself.

Let's talk about "risky stock". This is stock that comes from a company that doesn't have a certain future, i.e. an oil drilling company. This type of company would issue fewer shares. Each investor would earn a higher percentage of profit the risky firm made. Suppose an oil drilling company formed. It issues 100 shares. If someone bought 80 of the shares or 80% he would receive 80% of the profit of the company. Thus if the company found oil and earned a million Ignits (post re-investment) the investor would earn 800 000.00 þ. However this is not usually the case as most drilling companies do not make much profit (hence the name "risky firm"). Therefore they would issue very few shares and the investors who find the profit making firm in the stock market are the ones that thrive.

It was said that dividends are paid based on post-reinvestment profit. But what if a firm does not have much profit? What if it loses money? Investors ought to be well advised not to invest in such a firm. A good investor does research first. If the firm wants to sell more shares it ought to remedy its financial situation first. If an investor has shares of a firm that is losing money, he doesn't receive any dividends. However he may want to hold onto such shares if in the future the firm does end up making a considerable profit.

The consumerist stock market system works as long as the price of a share traded is unchanged from that set by the central bank. The free-enterprise stock market can easily collapse if everyone starts panicking and starts selling shares at lower and lower prices. This collapse is impossible in the consumerist stock market as prices are frozen permanently. If they are frozen they cannot crash.

In the free-enterprise stock system the big crime is inside trading. The consumerist counterpart is overpricing or under-pricing. That is selling or buying stock at a price higher or lower than the consumerist universal stock price. Investors caught in this felony must be prosecuted as this ruins the system.

Although stocks can be bought directly from firms, they can also be bought from traders (as long as it is at the consumerist universal stock price). Investors who do not want a stock can sell it to another trader at the universal stock price. Also investors who want a stock can buy one from another investor at the universal stock price. If investors like the idea of trading stocks for fluctuating prices; that is buying at one price and selling at another- they are more than welcome to do so in the speculative stock market that we will discuss shortly. That stock market was specially created for those kinds of investors.

Stocks have another function besides being traded and raising funds for firms. The owner of 50 % of the stock of the firm is the owner of the firm. Owners of stock can vote for the leader of a corporation called the Supreme Firm Director based on how much stock they have. This will be discussed later.

The most wonderful thing about this consumerist stock market is that it is impossible to lose any money. In fact an investor is guaranteed to make money. Before a firm issues stock, it must purchase bankruptcy insurance. This is a form of insurance where the insurance firm will pay the bankrupting firm all its bankruptcy expenses. One of these bankruptcy expenses is stock dissolution. This means that if a firm bankrupts, it must buy all the stock it issued to investors. So if an investor bought 800 shares for 10.00 þ, he will be reimbursed the 8000.00 þ. However he probably made some dividend profit. Therefore he must have made some money. This applies to everyone. If a firm issues 100 000 shares worth 10.00 þ per share and bankrupts, it must buy back these stocks with whatever money they have left. If they do not have enough then the bankruptcy insurance firm helps in stock dissolution.

There is a special type of consumerist stock that is important to talk about. It is called *Consumerist Central Bank Stock*. It is actually a special anti-inflationary measure. That is, it is an instrument used to control the money supply. In order to remove money (particularly Ignits) from the economy, the central bank sells Consumerist Central Bank Stock to investors. When it does so, it takes money in the form of Ignits out of circulation (from bank entries). The money taken out of circulation is placed in the *Consumerist Anti-Inflationary Pool*. It is not spent by the central bank, the government or any other entity for any purpose.

There are two very important parameters regarding Consumerist Central Bank Stocks. One is the Consumerist Central Bank Stock Price. This is how much it costs to buy one unit of this stock. There is also the Consumerist Central Bank Stock Interest (CCBSI). This is how much profit one earns from owning Consumerist Central Bank Stock. Both parameters are set by the central bank. Whereas the Consumerist Central Bank Stock Price is fixed, the Consumerist Central Bank Stock Interest can fluctuate depending on the wishes of the central bank.

Let's discuss an example. John, an investor, buys 1000.00 þ worth of Consumerist Central Bank Stock from the central bank indirectly but through his local bank directly. The Consumerist Central Bank Interest is 0.5 %. Every month John owns this stock he earns 0.005 x 1000.00 þ = 5.00 þ. He will continue to make this amount as long as he owns the stock. Actually, he will earn more as the 5.00þ profit he earns is reinvested. Thus in month #2, he will earn 1005.00 þ x 0.005 = 5.025 þ. At any time John can sell back this stock to the central bank. John can also sell these stocks to another interested investor under the stipulation that they are sold at the fixed price. If an investor wants to sell (or buy) stocks at fluctuating prices, he is entitled to do so in the speculative stock market. Clearly, an investor is guaranteed to make money on Consumerist Central Bank Stock since there is a positive interest rate, there are no barriers to reselling the stock to the central bank and the central bank can never possibly bankrupt.

The money (in Ignits) that the central bank receives from this stock is held in the Consumerist Anti-Inflationary Pool. It is kept there so that there is less money in the accommodational sector being exchanged by consumerists. When the investor wants to sell back his stock, the central bank uses the money in the Consumerist Anti-Inflationary Pool. Also the profit of owning the stock also comes out of the Consumerist Anti-Inflationary Pool. Here's an example: Suppose Kevin buys 5000.00 þ worth of Consumerist Central Bank Stock and the CCBSI is 0.1 %. 30 other investors also invested. In total they invested 1 000 000.00 þ. Thus the value of the Consumerist Anti-Inflationary Pool is 1 005 000.00 þ. Kevin keeps his stock for one month and then sells his stock back to the central bank. At that time the central bank gives Kevin 5000.00 þ + (5000.00 þ x 0.001) = 5005.00 þ. This is deducted from the Consumerist Anti-Inflationary Pool, leaving the pool with 1 005 000.00 þ – 5005.00 þ = 999995.00.þ

There is a possible situation where the amount of money in the form of stocks owned by a particular investor is large compared to the money in the pool. Like in the previous example, we have Kevin who bought 5000.00 þ worth of consumerist central bank stock with a CCBSI of 0.1%. He wants to sell back the stock to the central bank after one month. The central bank should pay him 5005.00 þ. However, in the extreme example where he is the only investor owning Consumerist Central Bank stock some of what he is entitled to after selling his stocks back to the central bank must come from the government. In this case, since Kevin is the only investor in this type of stock, the consumerist anti-inflationary pool is 5000.00 þ, that is, the value of the stock. After a month, after which point Kevin desires to sell his stock, he receives 5005.00 þ. 5000.00 þ comes from the consumerist anti-inflationary pool and 5.00 þ comes from the government. However, this is an extreme example as the consumerist anti-inflationary pool will most of the time be much larger than the gains from interest profit.

We have seen how the consumerist stock market works. We saw the operation of two different types of consumerist stocks. We have seen the advantages of the consumerist stock market and we have noted its important points. With a functioning stock market, the consumerist economy can prosper.

The Speculative Stock Market

The speculative stock market is an alternative to the Consumerist Stock Market. It is a little bit different than that system. The main difference is that the price of stocks can fluctuate up or down. The speculative stock market exists in the laissez-faire sector of accommodation based consumerism and Fortals are involved.

The company issuing stock has to insure its stock in case it bankrupts. If the company bankrupts the bankruptcy firm buys back the stock at the issuing price. If a firm bankrupts investors do not lose everything. The bankruptcy insurance firm buys back the value of the stock at the original issue price. Thus the issue price of a stock is very important.

One can still lose money on the speculative stock market. If one buys a stock at 50 f and sells it for 30 f he will have lost 20 f in the process. However, if the price of the stock goes below the original issuing price one can still hold to the stock in case, 1) the price of the stock goes up or 2) the firm bankrupts. If a stock trades at 10 f and a firm issued these stocks at 20 f and the firm bankrupts, investors receive 20 f per stock.

Prices of a speculative stock can go up or down and people can lose or make money but there is protection from total crash if a firm issuing stock bankrupts. Investors are guaranteed to receive a payout equal to the original stock price. This is guaranteed by the bankruptcy insurance system. Upon bankruptcy, the stock issuing firm buys back the stock the investors bought at the original price. If they can't, the bankruptcy insurance agency steps in and pays the investors the original value of the stock.

The good thing about the bankruptcy insurance firm is that it takes some of the risk of investing off the hands of the investors. The result is that it is less risky to invest in companies. Therefore more investors are willing to invest, thus boosting the economy. More investors are likely to invest in the speculative stock market of accommodation based consumerism than a stock market in a free-market nation because the majority of the risk is in the hands of the bankruptcy insurance firm rather than the investors themselves.

A stock is a claim of partial ownership in a firm. Like in the consumerist stock market, the more shares one owns, the more of that firm the investor has. If one has more than 50 % of the stock of a firm he is considered the owner of that firm.

A firm has choice as to what type of stock to issue. A firm can only issue consumerist stock or speculative stock but not both. This would cause problems in terms of the issue of partial ownership of the firm. For example if one investor has over 50 % of speculative stock and another has over 50% of consumerist stock, who owns the firm? Furthermore, there are other issues regarding bankruptcy.

In our system there is also something called a speculative mutual fund. A mutual fund is an institution that sells shares to consumerists and uses that money to purchase a portfolio of various stocks and bonds. The size and value of the mutual fund can be anything. It is determined by the interaction of consumerists and investment firm. Like in other cases, the investing company selling mutual fund shares has to buy bankruptcy insurance for their financial product. In case the mutual stock issued losses its value due to firms bankrupting, the bankruptcy insurance firm steps in to buy the worthless mutual fund shares. The upside to this is that it decreases the risk associated with investment, thus encouraging investors to invest and benefiting our economy as a whole.

The speculative stock market has a built in anti-inflationary measure. It is called *speculative central bank stock*. These are special stocks the central bank issues so as to decrease the money supply (in Fortals) in the laissez-faire sector. This idea is similar to that of the Consumerist Central Bank Stock we discussed previously. However there are some important differences.

The central bank sells Speculative Central Bank Stocks to interested investors at an official offering price. There is no built in interest-earning or dividend system with these stocks. Rather, investors make money through pure speculation. The price of the Speculative Central Bank Stock is in no way fixed like the Consumerist Central Bank Stock. It is completely free to fluctuate. Money is made by anticipating whether the Speculative Central Bank Stock will go up or down in price.

The money (in Fortals) that is exchanged for Speculative Central Bank Stock is placed into the Speculative Anti-Inflationary Pool. This money is removed from circulation (in terms of bank book entries) and the money supply in the laissez-faire sector is decreased. That is, there are less Fortals being exchanged for laissez-faire sector goods and services. The money in the Speculative Anti-Inflationary Pool is not spent on anything at all. It is just there to be removed from circulation in the Laissez-faire sector.

Let's look at a particular example. Joseph buys 1000.00 ₤ worth of speculative central bank stock from the central bank (through a private bank). This goes into the Speculative Anti-Inflationary Pool. The stock is traded on a stock market and it goes up in value to 1050.00 ₤. Joseph sells this to another investor, Chris at that price. Now Joseph has made a profit of 1050.00₤ – 1000.00 ₤ = 50.00 ₤. This is clearly good for Joseph. Now, a week later the value of the stock goes down to 1030.00 ₤. Chris sells this to Curtis. Chris has lost 1030.00 ₤– 1050.00 ₤ = 20.00 ₤. Chris has lost money on the stock market. It is clear that through speculation, investors can make money or lose money on the speculative stock market where speculative central bank stocks are involved.

Essentially, it can be considered that the money (in Fortals) in the speculative anti-inflationary pool is kept there indefinitely. Unlike the case regarding consumerist central bank stocks, there is no need for the central bank to buy back the speculative central bank stocks. The more of these stocks are sold, the more the laissez-faire money supply is decreased. The stocks themselves circulate among investors in the speculative stock market.

There is really no need for the central bank to take bankruptcy insurance. The central bank cannot bankrupt. The central bank is not really a firm like the other firms in consumerism.

We have seen how the speculative stock market is designed to work. We examined the role of Speculative Central Bank Stocks. The speculative stock market is contrasted against the consumerist stock market. In some regards it is similar to the stock market in the free-market system. However the guarantee, through the bankruptcy insurance bailout mechanism, makes it in some ways better than that system. Another important advantage is that there is less risk on the shoulders of investors.

The Consumerist Bond Market

In general, a bond is a certificate of indebtness. The consumerist bond market has two purposes. First it is an alternative market for loanable funds. It is designed to provide firms or the government with additional money to expand, start up or provide services. As a corollary, it benefits investors. It is part of the accommodational sector. Secondly, it has an anti-inflationary measure designed to take money out of circulation in the accommodational sector.

In accommodation based consumerism there are four basic types of consumerist bonds. There is a consumerist general bond, there is a consumerist profit bond, there is consumerist government bond and then there are consumerist savings bonds. We will discuss all four but first we will take a look at consumerist general bonds. A consumerist general bond is a promise to pay back a certain amount of money (Ignits) after a length of time called a maturity. In the meantime the consumerist general bond holder receives interest on his bond. There is a bond market in the free-enterprise economy. However there also exists one in the accommodational based consumerist economy. Let's see how it works and how it differs from that of the free-market system.

In a free-enterprise bond market a company receiving money sells a certificate of indebtness where the company promises to pay back the bond holder what he lent with interest. At the date of maturity, the company must pay back the bond holder. With bonds in the free-market economy there is a credit risk where the company may not be able to repay the bond holder everything. In the free enterprise system higher interests are paid to riskier investments and to bonds with longer dates of maturity.

Now let's turn to the consumerist general bond market. The interest paid on a consumerist general bond is determined by the central bank. The central bank sets an interest rate (per unit of time) called the Consumerist General Bond Interest Rate (CGeBIR). For example it could be 10% per year. Then a consumerist general bond with a 6 month maturity will give 5 % interest. A consumerist general bond with a maturity of 30 years will have an interest repayment rate of 300%. This interest rate could also be set in terms of days. For example it could be 0.01% per day. Then a two year maturity bond will give an interest of 7.3%

Another important variable is how often a consumerist general bond holder receives his interest profit. This is called the Consumerist General Bond Interest Repayment Frequency (CGeBIRF). This is set by the central bank. Let's suppose that it is one month. Then for a consumerist general bond with a maturity of 1 year, the bond holder receives interest earnings every month.

Let's look at an example. Joe buys 50.00 þ worth of general bonds from a telephone company. The CGeBIRF is 2 months. The date of maturity is 5 years. The central bank sets the yearly bond interest rate at 40%/year. Thus Joe's bond would give him 40% x 5 = 200 %. Since he invested 50.00þ, he would make 50.00 þ x 200 % = 100.00þ. Since there are 30 two month periods in five years, Joe will receive 100.00þ /30 = 3.33þ every two months. At the end he will also get back the 50.00þ that he invested.

What about firms that are risky; i.e. have a high credit risk? In the free-market system, such firms are likely to default and thus must pay higher interests on their bonds. But in the consumerist general bond market all firms have the same interest for a certain amount of time for their bonds. So what happens when a firm defaults on its general bond? The answer lies with the fact that every firm must purchase bankruptcy insurance in order to issue consumerist general bonds. We will discuss the details of the concept of bankruptcy insurance later on. We will say that if a firm is unable to pay its interest and the amount lent for any reason (i.e. bankruptcy) the bankruptcy insurance company does so for the firm. Suppose a firm, ABC, issues a consumerist general bond for 1000.00 þ and with a maturity of 5 years. The interest rate is set at 25% and the CGeBIRF is set at 6 months. These are set by the Central Bank. Suppose firm ABC defaults on its bond repayment. Then the bankruptcy insurance company that the firm ABC bought insurance from would have to pay the investors 1000.00 þ + 1000.00 þ x 0.25 x 5 = 2 250.00 þ

As for the parameters of the consumerist general bond market, the consumerist general bond interest rate (CGeBIR) and the CGeBIRF, these are not fixed. They can be manipulated by the central bank. The Grand Chairman can at any time decrease or increase (change) either the CGeBIR or the CGeBIRF. As soon as he announces it, all firms must follow these instructions.

What about trading bonds? Consumerist general bonds can be traded among investors on one condition. That is that the price of the general bond does not fluctuate. Suppose firm ABC issues a 1000.00 þ bond with a CGeBIR of 25 % and a CGeBIRF of 2 months. This general bond can be sold to another investor for 1000.00þ.

So far we have given lengths of maturity as arbitrary examples. The length of maturity of a consumerist general bond is not determined by the central bank. The length of maturity can be any size. It can be a few days or many decades. The length of maturity of a consumerist general bond is determined by the interaction of investors and firms.

The same reasoning applies to the value of the consumerist general bond. The bond can be from 0.01þ to millions of Ignits. The central bank, to give flexibility, does not impose a particular size to the consumerist general bond. Here also, the size of the bond is determined by the interaction of investors and firms.

Now let's take a look at consumerist profit bonds. A consumerist profit bond works quite differently from a consumerist general bond. Suppose Joe buys a consumerist profit bond from company ABC worth 1000.00 þ. Company ABC has a revenue of 50 000.00 þ and running costs of 30 000.00 þ. It reinvests 10 000.00 þ back in itself, leaving a post-reinvestment profit of 10 000.00 þ. The central bank sets a parameter called the *Consumerist profit bond interest rate* (CPBIR). Let's say it is 25 %. To calculate the return on investment of this profit bond we divide the value of the profit bond by the firm's revenue and multiply by the CPBIR. This value is then multiplied by the firm's post reinvestment profit. This value is paid to the investor. To determine how often the investor is paid we use the same parameter as the CGeBIRF. For simplicity this can be called the BIRF.

Let's do the calculations for Joe's investment in company ABC. The formula we will use, as mentioned above, is the following:

(PBI/FR x CPBIR) x FPRIP = Payment to investor per period.

Here PBI stands for Profit Bond Investment, which is in our case 1000.00 þ. FR stands for firm revenue, which in our case is 50 000.00 þ. FPRIP stands for firm's post reinvestment profit, 10 000.00 þ.

(1000.00 þ/50 000.00 þ) x 25% x 10 000.00 þ = 50.00 þ.

The central bank can raise the CPBIR if it wants investors to earn a higher investment profit and thus encourage investment in profit bonds. Or else, it can lower this parameter to help the firm that issued the profit bond.

There is another type of consumerist bond. It is called the Consumerist Governmental Bond. Unlike the other two bonds described above which are issued by firms to increase revenue to promote their business, the consumerist governmental bond is designed for the purpose of taking money out of circulation in the accommodational sector. What the government does is that it sells consumerist governmental bonds to consumerists in exchange for Ignits. One might assume that the government would use this money for government services. This is not the case. The government does not spend this money at all. It just takes it out of circulation (in bank entries).

The government sets an interest rate and repayment frequency for consumerist governmental bonds. These function quite similarly to consumerist general bonds. The interest rate for consumerist governmental bonds is called the Consumerist Governmental Bond Interest Rate (CGoBIR) and the repayment frequency is called the Consumerist Governmental Bond Interest Repayment Frequency (CGoBIRF). Officially they are under the influence of the federal government.

When the government sells a certain amount of consumerist governmental bonds it keeps them set aside in a "Consumerist Anti-Inflationary Pool". The government uses the money to pay the interest payments on these bonds. When it is time to pay the maturity of a consumerist governmental bond, the government uses the revenue in its budget to pay the value of the bond. The size of the bond and the length of maturity are determined by the interaction of consumerists and the government.

Here's an example. A consumerist, John, buys a 10, 000 þ consumerist governmental bond with a maturity of ten years. The CGoBIR is 1% per year and the CGoBIRF is one year. So, since the maturity is ten years, John will make 0.01 x 10, 000 þ x 10 = 1000 þ in total for his investment. Since the CGoBIRF is one year and there are ten one year periods in ten years, John will receive 100 þ every year for 10 years and after 10 years he will receive the original 10 000 þ investment. From the standpoint of the government, the original 10 000 þ are saved in the consumerist anti-inflationary pool. Every year the government takes 100 þ from this pool and uses it to pay John's interest payments. After 10 years, when the maturity is due, the government still has 10 000 þ – 1000 þ = 9000 þ. To pay the full value of the maturity, the government takes money out of its operating budget. Thus the government transfers 1000 þ to John after 10 years in addition to the 9000 þ still left in the consumerist anti-inflationary pool. Although the government usually functions using Norses, it can directly convert 1 þ = 1 ☉ for the purpose of this parameter.

Usually the consumerist anti-inflationary pool will be quite large as many, many individuals will want to buy consumerist governmental bonds. The government can set goals as to how many consumerist governmental bonds to sell and it can encourage more people to buy these bonds by increasing the interest rate i.e. CGoBIR.

The goal of selling this type of bond is to lower the amount of Ignits circulating in the accommodational sector in the form of bank book entries. After some thought, one can see that after the length of maturity is over, the government has actually increased the amount of Ignits in circulation. However, what is actually happening is that the government is continuously selling bonds so that amount of bonds sold is greater than that has to be repaid. Here's an example. Suppose John bought 10000 þ worth of bonds with a maturity of ten years. Before the ten years are over, however, the government sells 15000 þ worth of bonds to two other individuals. Thus, when it comes to repay John's

10000 þ maturity, there is still a lot of money left in the consumerist anti-inflationary pool. The government can continue this indefinitely, always increasing the governmental bond pool to lower the Ignit money supply. If, by chance the government does want to pay back all bond holders in full, this would come from the consumerist anti-inflationary pool and the government operating budget.

One final bond or rather type of bond is the Consumerist Savings Bond. There are three categories of Consumerist Savings Bonds. They are Federal Consumerist Savings Bonds, Provincial Consumerist Savings Bonds and Municipal Consumerist Savings Bonds. The main purpose of these special bonds is to raise additional revenue for the 3 levels of government when the levels of government are short in revenue and need a source of income to finance social services. The basic idea is that the government exchanges a certain quantity of a particular variety of Consumerist Savings Bond in exchange for Ignits which it then uses to pay for social services. Every once in a while the particular government makes interest payments to bond holders and at the end of the maturity the government pays the total value of the bond. There are two important parameters regarding the 3 types of Consumerist Savings Bonds. They are the Consumerist Savings Bond Interest Rate (3 types- federal, provincial, municipal), CSBIR and the Consumerist Savings Bond Interest Repayment Frequency (3 types – federal, provincial, municipal), CSBIRF.

The size of the bond or the length can be anything the investor wishes it to be. So if an investor wants a Federal Consumerist Saving Bond worth 5 000.00 þ and a maturity of 10 years, he can purchase such from the private bank. Also there is no bankruptcy insurance involved in the issuing of the three kinds of consumerist saving bonds. The government can't default on a bond.

These are the workings of the consumerist bond markets. The consumerist profit bond market, the consumerist government bond market, the consumerist savings bond market and the consumerist general bond market differ on several major points from the free enterprise bond market. With a strong bond market comes a strong economy

The Speculative Bond Market

The consumerist bond market has a counterpart. It is the speculative bond market. The speculative general bond market and the speculative profit bond market help firms earn money for expansion while also helping investors. The speculative government bond market has an anti-inflationary measure designed to control the amount of money. Whereas the consumerist bond market is in the accommodational sector, the speculative bond market is in the laissez-faire sector. Thus Fortals are involved.

Unlike in the consumerist bond market, the speculative bond market has three basic types of bonds. They are the speculative general bond, the speculative governmental bond and the speculative profit bond. We already discussed the consumerist bond market counterparts of the three types of speculative bonds and indeed the three types are somewhat similar. First we will talk about the speculative general bond. A speculative general bond is a promise to pay back a certain amount of money (Fortals) after a length of time called a maturity. In the meantime the speculative general bond holder receives interest on his bond.

The speculative general bond market is similar in some respects to the consumerist general bond market although in other ways it differs. The interest paid on a general bond is determined by the interaction of consumerists and those selling bonds rather than through a central bank. Together they arrive at an interest rate (per unit of time). For instance it could be 2% per month. So a speculative general bond with a 12 month maturity will give 24 % interest. A speculative general bond with a maturity of 10 years will have an interest repayment rate of 240%.

How frequently a speculative general bond holder is given his interest profit is also a crucial variable. We call this the Speculative General Bond Interest Repayment Frequency (SGeBIRF). This is not set by the central bank but through the interaction of consumerists and bond sellers in a speculative general bond market. For our purposes, let's assume that it is two months. This means that for a speculative general bond with a maturity of 6 months, the bond holder obtains interest earnings every two months. Then for a speculative general bond with a maturity of 1 year, the bond holder receives interest earnings every two months.

Let's look at a numerical example. Peter buys 100.00 ₤ worth of speculative general bonds from a telephone company. The SGeBIRF is set at 1 month. The date of maturity is set at 2 years. The yearly bond interest rate is 50%/year as determined by the action of buyers and sellers of bonds. Thus Peter's bond would give him 50% x 2 = 100 %. Since he invested 100.00 ₤, he would make 100.00 ₤ x 100 % = 100.00 ₤. Since there are 24 one month periods in two years, Peter will receive 100.00₤ /24 = 3.33 ₤ every two months. At the end he will also get back the 100.00₤ that he invested.

Speculative general bonds, like consumerist general bonds, can be issued by firms that have a high credit risk. To circumvent this problem we do something similar to what we did for consumerist general bonds. That is we introduce the bankruptcy insurance firm into the equation. What do we do when a firm defaults on its speculative general bond? The solution to this problem lies with the idea that every firm must purchase bankruptcy insurance in order to issue speculative general bonds. If a firm cannot pay its interest and the amount lent for reasons like bankruptcy the bankruptcy insurance company helps the firm. Suppose a firm, let's call it ZZZ, issues a speculative general bond for 100.00 ₤ and with a maturity of 10 years. The interest rate is 10% per year and the SGeBIRF is 12months. If firm

ZZZ defaults on its bond repayment, then the bankruptcy insurance company that the firm ZZZ bought insurance from would have to pay the investors 100.00 £ + 100.00 £ x 0.25 x 5 = 2 250.00 £

What is the policy regarding trading speculative general bonds? Speculative general bonds can be traded freely among investors. The price of the general bond can freely fluctuate. If a firm, ZZZ, issues a 5000.00 £ bond with a SGeBIR of 50 % and a SGeBIRF of 4 months this speculative general bond can be sold to another investor for any amount that is agreed upon.

The central bank does not set the length of maturity of a speculative general bond. The length of maturity can be any amount. It can be a few days or many decades. The length of maturity of a speculative general bond is determined by the interaction of investors and firms. The value of a speculative general bond is also not dictated by the central bank but is rather determined by the interaction of investors and firms. So it can be anything from 1.00£ to 1 billion £.

The speculative profit bond is similar to its counterpart in the consumerist bond market but it works a little differently from a speculative general bond. Suppose Peter buys a profit bond from company ZZZ worth 5000.00 £. Company ZZZ has a revenue of 100 000.00 þ and running costs of 70 000.00 þ. It reinvests 20 000.00 þ back in itself, leaving a post-reinvestment profit of 10 000.00 þ. We assume that the exchange rate is 1£ = 1þ and 1þ = 1£. A parameter called the *Speculative profit bond interest rate* (SPBIR) is determined by the interaction of investors and firms. Let's say it is 15 %. To calculate the return on investment of this profit bond we divide the value of the profit bond by the firm's revenue and multiply by the SPBIR. This value is then multiplied by the firm's post reinvestment profit. The investor is paid this amount. The SBIRF previously set is used to determine how frequently the investor is paid.

We can do the calculations for Peter's investment in company ZZZ. We will use the following formula:

(PBI/FR x PBIR) x FPRIP = Payment to investor per period.

Here PBI represents Profit Bond Investment, which is in our case 5000.00 þ. FR stands for firm revenue, which in our case is 100 000.00 þ. FPRIP stands for firm's post reinvestment profit, 10 000.00 þ.

(5000.00 þ/100 000.00 þ) x 15% x 10 000.00 þ = 50.00 þ.

Lastly, let's talk about the Speculative Governmental Bond. It functions quite similarly to the Consumerist Governmental Bond that was discussed in the previous section. It is supposed to be a mechanism to decrease or manipulate the money supply. Whereas the consumerist governmental bond market involves Ignits, the speculative governmental bond market involves Fortals.

The government sells speculative governmental bonds in exchange for Fortals. The government does not use this money to pay for social services. Rather it takes it out of circulation to lower the money supply. The money goes to the Speculative Anti-Inflationary Pool. All the parameters, the interest rate and the repayment frequency are set by the interaction of the government and investors.

Suppose Mark buys 1000 £ worth of speculative government bonds with a maturity of 10 years. The interest rate is 1% every year and the repayment frequency is every 2 years. Thus in total Mark will earn 1000£ x 10 x 0.01 = 100 £. Every 2 years he will receive 20 £.

To pay for Mark's interest payments, the government takes money out of the Speculative Anti-Inflationary pool and the rest is subsidized through the government transfers from the government budget. So if Mark is to be paid his original 1000 ₣ investment plus a cumulative series of payments worth 100 ₣, he is entitled to 1100 ₣. The government pays the 1000 ₣ it has put away in the Speculative Anti-Inflationary pool and the government pays 100 ₣. Since the government functions with Norses, it has to first exchange Norses to Ignits. These are at par, i.e. 1Θ = 1 þ. Then it has to convert Ignits to Fortals using the Ignit – Fortal exchange mechanism. So if 1₣ = 4 þ, the government has to give 400 Θ = 400 þ to give Mark the 100 ₣ he is owed through this speculative government bond transaction.

Like in the consumerist governmental bond market, in this market the eventual money supply ought to be greater than at the beginning. However, the government is consistently selling speculative governmental bonds so that the Speculative Anti-Inflationary pool is always positive. So, in our above example, before Mark's maturity expires and he must be repaid 1000 ₣, the government could sell 2000 ₣ worth of bonds with a maturity in the future.

These are the workings of the speculative bond markets. The speculative profit bond market, the speculative governmental bond market and the speculative general bond market differ on several major points from the free enterprise bond market and the consumerist bond markets although there are parallels. A strong bond market helps ensure a strong economy.

Taxes

Taxes are a payment to the government as a result of different situations and transactions. In order for the government to operate, providing services that can only be provided publicly, it needs revenue. There is a dramatic difference between the tax system of the free-enterprise economy and that of the consumerist economy.

Above a certain income, people under the free-enterprise system pay income tax. This income tax is designed so that the more one works, the more money he or she must pay to the government. Some people who earn a considerable amount of money can pay as much as 50% (or even more) of their income to the government.

There is also a property tax in capitalism. The people who own property have to pay the municipal government this tax. This tax pays for such things as schools, parks and waste pick-up. Even for a relatively modest amount of property, this tax can amount to tens of thousands of dollars per year.

Under the free-enterprise system we have sales tax. Many jurisdictions make people pay additional money for every good or service they buy. In some places this tax is small while in others it is over 20%. Usually it is around 15%.

Corporations have to pay corporate tax. This shrinks their profits. Money that could be reinvested back into the company goes to the government.

There are various other taxes on almost any good or service that the government decides to levy a tax on. These include alcohol, gasoline and cigarettes. There are also many other forms of luxury tax.

One of the greatest advantages of the accommodation based consumerist economic system is that none of the taxes mentioned above exist. The government has a different way to raise funds.

Each month all final goods and services in the materialist sector are counted. They are counted whether they are sold to consumerists or have the potential to be so. A restaurant adds up all the meals they sold and multiplies this by their price. As for all retail stores, grocery stores, convenience stores, department stores, car dealerships etc. the amount of goods they have in stock is multiplied by their price. The value of all services purchased (mechanics, teachers, gardeners, taxi cab drivers) is added up. This calculation does not include intermediate services or goods like cashiers, cooks, janitors or flour, wheat, plastic, steal or coal. Once all of these are added up, the central bank has a value of the GDCP.

The government sets a tax called the GCT in terms of a percentage. The central bank grants the government a portion of the GDCP equal to the GCT. Thus no consumerist actually pays tax out of his own pocket.

How is the GCT determined? There are 3 levels of government; federal, state/provincial and municipal. Each of the 3 levels of government votes on the tax, with each level having exactly one third of the total representation. If there are several governments in a level (state or municipal) each has a weight for voting proportional to its population.

Thus if a province has twice as many people as another and there are only 2 provinces, one province will have a voting of 22% and the other 11%. An example illustrates this.

As an example, there is one federal government. There are four states. They have populations in the ratio 1:1:2:3 There are 6 municipalities with populations in the ratio1:2:3:3:4:4. They vote on the GCT as such

	Vote	Weight
Federal	25%	33%
State 1	40%	33%/7
State 2	10 %	33%/7
State 3	30 %	33% x 2/7
State 4	20 %	33% x 3/7
Municipality 1	20 %	33%/17
Municipality 2	30 %	33% x 2/17
Municipality 3	30 %	33 % x 3/17
Municipality 4	20 %	33 % x 3/17
Municipality 5	25 %	33 % x 4/17
Municipality 6	35 %	33% x 4/17

The GCT is (8.25 + 1.88 + 0.47 + 2.83 + 2.83 + 0.39 + 1.16 + 1.75 + 1.16 + 1.94 + 2.72) = 25.38 %. Thus the GCT is 25.38%

The GCT is divided similarly to how it is determined through voting. The federal government receives 33% of it and each of the state and municipal governments receive their share based on their ratio of populations. Now let's see the revenue. We will assume that the GDCP is 100 000.00 ☉

	Weight	Revenue
Federal	33%	8 375.00 ☉
State 1	33 %/7	1 196.00 ☉
State 2	33%/7	1 196.00 ☉2
State 3	33 % x 2/7	2 393.00 ☉
State 3	33% x 3/7	3 529.00 ☉
Municipality 1	33 % x 1/17	492.00 ☉
Municipality 2	33 % x 2/17	985.00 ☉
Municipality 3	33% x 3/17	1 478.00 ☉
Municipality 4	33% x 3/17	1 478.00 ☉

| Municipality 5 | 33% x 4/17 | 1 976.00 ʘ |
| Municipality 6 | 33 % x 4/17 | 1 976.00 ʘ |

For the vote weights of the municipal and state/province governments it may be simpler to use percentage weights as opposed to ratios. In our example the state/provinces had populations in the ratios of 1:1:2:3. These are equivalent to weights (respectively) of 14%, 14%, 28%, 42%. Thus each state has a vote weight corresponding to the percent of the whole population that is contained in that state.

Besides the GCT, the government has no right to additional taxes. If a government votes a tax that is too high, it will probably not survive the next election. Thus the citizens have veto power over the government's (tax) voting powers.

It is possible that one level of government may transfer some of its tax revenue to another level of government. For example, if the federal government made 1 000 000 000.00 ʘ and a municipal government earned only 50 000.00 ʘ, then the federal government can transfer some of its revenue to the municipal government. So the federal government transfers 500 000.00 ʘ to the municipal level government.

It is quite important to the workings of the system that there is only one tax- the GCT. This ensures that other groups are not discouraged from contributing to the economy. For example the lack of a corporate tax encourages more firms to do business in our nation and the lack of an income tax leads a worker to be more efficient as what he earns he can keep to spend as see fit. It is strongly discouraged to invent original taxes (property, income, sales, and luxury) even if it is to relieve the tax burden of the GCT. The GCT must be the only tax.

The taxes may change from month to month. Every month when the GDCP is determined, the governments come together and vote on the GCT. They do so every month.

There are several other sources of revenue that a government has. It can sell land to consumerists. It can sell licenses or permits. It can issue savings bonds. The command partition can make a profit. It can make profit through the work for freedom program. It can also make profit through the recycling-for-pay program. There may be profits from gambling and casinos/lotteries.

We have seen how the tax system works in consumerism. We saw the differences between the free-enterprise and consumerist tax systems. We witnessed how the GCT is calculated. The consumerist tax system is an integral part of the system.

The Welfare System and the Socialist Labor Pool

The welfare system can be defined as the system that takes care of those who are temporarily unable to provide for themselves. It is there so that the poorest do not live in abject misery and poverty. It is one of the government's duties to help the poorest of society at least as long as they can't help themselves.

In a free-market system the poor and those who do not have a job are assisted by the government. The government gives them a welfare check which they exchange for goods and services. However two problems arise from such a setup. First, people who still work may still be able to get a welfare check. There is welfare fraud. The second problem is that many unemployed lose their motivation for finding a job. Our welfare system must be able to help out the poor and avoid these problems.

In consumerism no one should have to worry about materialist things. Things like food, transportation, clothing and entertainment are provided to consumerists when the central bank grants Norses to them as part of the general and the non-working consumerist grants. Consumerists can exchange this money (Norses) for materialist goods and services. Governmental services like healthcare, sanitation and defense are provided by the three levels of government through the GCT and other sources. Many goods and services are within the easy reach of most consumerists.

The accommodational and laissez-faire sectors are the incentives for a consumerist's contribution to society. He who works harder receives a better house and a bigger property. But what if a consumerist is unemployed? He should not have to live on the street.

This is how the consumerist welfare system works. The government provides a decent sized apartment or condominium for the welfare recipient. It also provides him with running water, heat and electricity and some appliances and an additional check in Ignits and Fortals that the welfare recipient can exchange for goods and services in the accommodational and laissez- faire sectors. The government provides minimal living space and access to utilities to the welfare recipient in addition to money (£, þ) to do what they will.

The government issues welfare checks and provides housing. However, as soon as the welfare recipient finds a job, he will have to repay part of the cost of the apartment and appliances and all of the utilities that he took advantage of as well as the unemployment check. He will also have to pay with compound interest. The reasoning for this is this. If the welfare recipient knows that he is continuously getting into debt by living in a welfare apartment, he will have more of an incentive to look for a job. The longer the recipient spends in his welfare apartment, the bigger his welfare debt grows. The government actually makes money on the welfare system.

Suppose that in addition to the accommodation and appliances provided by the government, the welfare recipient receives 500 þ and 500£ every month. This is to spend on goods and services in the accommodational and laissez faire sectors. To discourage fraud and encourage finding work in partitions other than the command partition, we have two parameters: Auxiliary Reimbursement Deduction (ARD) is how much less a welfare recipient receives per month for being in the socialist labor pool. This is expressed as a percentage. So in our example if it is set at 1%, every month the auxiliary worker will receive 1% less than he did last month. The higher this parameter is, the more welfare recipients are encouraged to find a job in the natural or governmental partitions.

Another parameter is the Unemployment Assistance Repayment (UAR). This is how much money a worker has to repay the government when he finds a job in a partition other than the command partition. It is expressed as a percentage and set by the government. Like the ARD it is designed to discourage fraud. If a worker has to pay back for the assistance the government provided he is less likely to want to be on welfare. Let's suppose it is 20%. If an auxiliary worker receives 500 þ and 500£ every month, he will have to repay 20 % of this when he leaves the socialist labor pool. Here, if we want to support a welfare recipient's well being we would keep this parameter low, maybe even zero. However if we want to discourage people from being on welfare, we would make this value higher. Furthermore, people who go on welfare go find another job and then return to welfare have their welfare payments as they were when they were on welfare previously.

A natural question comes up. If the welfare recipient receives free living space and his utility bills are paid for and the longer he stays there the greater his welfare debt becomes, why wouldn't he just chose to live there indefinitely. The answer is that his living arrangements are very minimal; i.e. he will probably live in some kind of small apartment, and with several bedrooms. He may want to do better. He may want to own a house of his own one day. He will not want to live on welfare forever then and will start looking for a job. The quicker he does so the less he will have to pay back the government for providing him welfare and the sooner he can move onto bigger and better things.

There appears to be another problem. If everyone is granted Norses by the central bank for the materialist sector, why worry about the accommodational sector? Some people may see a positive trade off of not working and living in an apartment because the most important things are in the materialist sector (food, clothes, entertainment). The way out of this is that the non-working consumerists are granted much less Norses than their working counterparts. The government sets this. It is called the Non Working Grant Reduction. If this is 20% and each working consumerist is granted 1000.00 Θ per month, the non-working consumerist is granted only 200.00 Θ per month.

Back to the two problems we found in the free-enterprise system. People are unlikely to commit fraud as they will eventually have to pay the government back for what it provided them. Second we saw two ways to increase the motivation to find work. First, welfare recipients become indebted the longer they are on welfare. Secondly, consumerists on welfare receive drastically less Norses from the central bank to spend on the materialist sector than those that work.

People on welfare do not receive their welfare check for doing nothing. All unemployed, whether able or disabled- with a few exceptions- become part of the Socialist Labor Pool. The Socialist Labor Pool is a part of the Command partition and it is run by the Human Resource Management Commission. Whereas other measures reduced unemployment, the socialist labor pool completely eradicates unemployment. As stated in another section, this concept is similar to Chinese State Capitalism.

Both able bodied and disabled people can be made to contribute in the socialist labor pool. Whereas we find a suitable job for a skilled worker, we also try to find employment for a disabled or developmentally challenged individual. For example, these people can be made to sort screws, lick envelopes or push shopping carts.

When a worker loses his job he can apply for extra-work transfer payments (similar to welfare). The individual fills out a form similar to an application or resume describing what he or she is good at, his education and experience. Jobs that match skills, knowledge or experience are assigned to that person. For example a person with martial arts training could be hired in an HRMC run martial arts training school while a developmentally disabled person could be put in an HRMC run grocery store packing shopping bags with groceries or pushing shopping carts. The Human Resource Management Commission is like a big hiring company that matches (currently unemployed) workers to jobs using the principle discussed before to find the most suitable jobs for people. For a person working in the socialist labor pool, the experience he receives is great on a resume after he leaves the socialist labor pool. Interestingly, workers in the socialist labor pool do not need to buy jobs.

We saw the nature of the consumerist welfare system. We saw how it operates. We found the solutions to the problems that appear in the free-enterprise welfare system while still helping those with limited income.

The Laissez-Faire Labor System

The laissez-faire labor system is designed to eliminate unemployment. It is a program created to put people to work that would otherwise be unemployed. It minimizes the cost of people on social assistance like "welfare".

Before we go into the details of this system let us show the logic of this program using dollars as our example. We have a welfare rate of 10.00 $/hour. We recognize that many of our major manufacturing firms have outsourced their production to other third world nations like Bangladesh, Pakistan or Cambodia. Over there, the minimum wage is, for example, 2.00 $/hour. We want those factories back so we provide an even lower minimum wage of 1.00$/hour. So these major companies come back to our country. These companies pay our workers 1.00$/hour and we subsidize this payment by 9.00$/hour. So instead of ideal workers doing nothing at all besides sleeping in and watching TV and getting paid 10.00$/hour from the government, the government only pays 9.00$/hour and the workers are doing something productive. In both cases the workers are paid 10.00$/hour. Clearly this is better. But there is another benefit. Suppose a textile (clothing) company re-outsourced back into our nation. This company needs cotton and polyester thus giving business to our cotton and polyester manufacturers. The company needs machines to make clothing. This gives business to our manufacturers that make these machines. The company also needs to build a factory in our nation. This gives business to construction workers and contractors, and those that make building equipment like cement trucks.

Using the logic that was described above, the laissez-faire labor system strives to provide jobs for our workers that would otherwise be transferred to less well-off countries where workers are paid less. To accomplish this we completely redefine the notion of "minimum wage". The government sets aside several industries that participate in the laissez-faire labor system. For these industries there is no minimum wage. The manufacturing firm can pay their workers as little as it wants to. The workers working at these jobs are paid the equivalent of the extra-work transfer. The government pays these workers the equivalent of the extra-work transfer minus the wage given by the manufacturing firm. So, for example suppose the extra work transfer is 7.00 þ/hour + 3.00£ /hour and a company producing spoons pays 1.50þ /hour. In this case, the government pays each worker 7.00 þ/hour – 1.50þ /hour (+3.00 £/hour) = 5.50þ /hour + 3.00£ /hour. Clearly this is better than if the government had to pay the total of the extra-work transfer directly to the worker.

Whenever we bring back a factory or manufacturing firm to our country, there are economic side-effects. If we entice a car manufacturing firm to come back to our country from say, Guatemala or Thailand, we are helping our economy in many other ways too. That car factory needs steel, glass, plastic and rubber. Our firms that produce steel, glass, plastic and rubber will have someone to sell their inputs to. A car factory needs a building to produce its cars. This represents jobs for construction workers and companies that make building supplies and equipment. Furthermore, the workers as well as the executives need food and accommodation. This also provides business to our firms.

The workers in the laissez-faire labor system should be entitled to union representation. The workers pay a small amount from their wages so as to be represented by a union. The union fights for the rights of the workers. They ensure that workers have proper working conditions and safe working standards. That is they ensure that the worker is not exploited and treated unfairly. One thing they can't interfere with, though, is the wages the firms pay to their workers. In fact it is counterproductive to do so. Ultimately, the workers are paid the equivalent of the extra-work transfer. How much the government pays for that depends on the wages the firms in the laissez-faire labor system give their workers.

Thus would work the laissez-faire labor system. It allows us to re outsource firms from other countries while giving work to others in different industries. This system functions also to eliminate what is left of unemployment in our system.

Minimum Wage

The concept of minimum wage is important in the free-enterprise system. Essentially the government sets a minimum wage a business can pay its employees in exchange for their services. Its necessity is evident when one considers that if a factory paid its workers a low wage, it may be impossible for the workers to earn enough to buy clothes or even food.

Countries with high minimum wages usually have high standards of living. Yet if the firms in a free-market system could pay their workers lower wages they would hire more workers. Under low minimum wage there is higher employment. There is a trade-off. Governments that set higher minimum wages have people that are well off but less are employed than if the minimum wage was lower.

Usually the minimum wage increases as time goes by. As minimum wage increases some firms raise the prices of their products to compensate for the loss they incur having to pay their employees more. Although this phenomenon is usually restricted to companies that give low wages it nevertheless contributes to an inflationary spiral.

With regards to accommodation based consumerism, the concept of minimum wage does not apply to the GAM sectors. Actually under accommodation based consumerism, minimum wage totally does not exist with the exception of the laissez-faire sector. All wages in the governmental, materialist and accommodational sectors are set by the central bank. They may be changed by veto; i.e. if a finance minister or head of state vetoes it or a considerable portion of the population signs a petition against a particular wage function.

In the laissez-faire sector, however, there must be a minimum wage. This is because prices and wages are set by the interaction of consumerists and producers. We must make sure that there is a limit as to how little income a worker in the laissez-faire sector earns. This minimum wage is dictated by the government and is expressed in Fortals, the currency of the laissez-faire sector.

The minimum wage in the laissez-faire sector must be equal to the extra work payments made to workers that are unemployed. However this minimum wage is not necessarily what a firm in the laissez-faire sector pays. The value of the minimum wage, which is equivalent to the extra work transfer payment, is paid jointly by the government and a firm in the laissez-faire sector. This has been discussed before when we talked about the laissez-faire labor system.

Minimum wage, as we have discussed, is not necessary in the GAM sectors of accommodation based consumerism. It is important for the laissez faire sector for the reasons we discussed.

The Accommodation Award

In many, if not most, of the leading economic superpowers there is a substantial portion of people who are homeless. These people either have no job or have a very low paying one and struggle for food, clothing and most of all, shelter. One just needs to walk down the busy streets of major cities like New York, Chicago, Toronto or Los Angeles to see people in desperate need of a place to live. The problem is even worse in third world nations. In consumerism, one homeless person is one too many. In a consumerist nation, everyone should have access to a shelter.

In major cities under capitalism the remedy is to provide emergency shelters for the homeless. Usually a well-meaning charity or the government will provide a bed for people who would otherwise freeze outside, especially in the winter. The problem is that the number of people who are homeless usually far exceeds the number of special beds in shelters. As a result, some people freeze and hope that their coat will keep them warm.

In consumerism, absolutely everyone is entitled to a place to live. First of all, we assume that most of those who work for the government sector/partition and accommodational sector of the natural partition, where wages are fixed by the central bank, all are able to buy a decent form of accommodation. The way that wages and price functions for accommodation are set (by the central bank) assures us of this with quite certainty.

Now, what about those people who don't have a job through either the accommodational sector or natural partition or government sectors? Remember that whoever is still "unemployed" is guaranteed a job through either the command partition or the laissez-fare labor system. All a homeless person has to do is sign up for work through either of these anti-unemployment systems and they are guaranteed a form of accommodation. Even if they don't work they are still entitled to shelter although they will not be receiving much in the form of the extra-work transfer in terms of money.

The accommodation that previously homeless people receive should be "minimal but not abysmal". That means it must be of sufficient quality but not so prestigious that other workers in the other sectors, will have worse accommodation. That means that the previously-homeless should not have to live in shacks, one bed-room apartments or trailers. Yet they shouldn't either live in a luxurious mansion or 6 bedroom houses. Perhaps something like a condominium, a small bungalow or 3 bed-room apartment will be sufficient. The previously-homeless also receives utilities (hot water, electricity) and several appliances (fridge, oven, and microwave).

All those individuals eligible for the accommodation award are under the constraints of a parameter called the *accommodation award repayment percentage* (AARP). Essentially this means that a previously-homeless will have to pay a portion of the accommodation award that he was provided. The AARP could be 100 %, 0% or something in between. If it is 100 %, the individual must repay the value of the accommodation, the utilities and the appliances after he finds a job in either the governmental or accommodational sectors. If it is 0%, the individual doesn't pay anything, in the end, for what the government provided for the previously-homeless person. If it is for example, 70 %, the individual pays back 70% of the value of the accommodation award he was given. For example if someone got a condominium worth 1000 þ per month. 2000 þ worth of appliances and 400 þ worth of utilities per month and he lived there for 5 months he would have to pay the government 0.7(1000þ x 5 + 2000þ + 400þ x 5) = 3500þ. The higher the AARP, the more it discourages people from taking advantage of the accommodation award. The lower the AARP, the more it helps people in need- those that were previously homeless. The main purpose of the AARP is to overcome fraud.

When the previously-homeless do decide to do work in the command partition or laissez-fare labor system, they will then be able to receive the extra-work transfer. This may offset the cost of the AARP, perhaps even neutralizing it. For example suppose that the extra-work transfer is 10þ /hr (we ignore gains in Fortals for this example). If a previously-homeless person now gets a job in the command partition building houses and works 400 hours in 5 months, he can use this to offset his AARP payments. In the end he will still have (10þ/hr x 400 hours) – 3500þ = 500.þ So he will have 500þ left to buy things like a trip to a vacation destination or wine.

It is possible (although very unlikely) that individuals working for either the accomodational or governmental sectors could apply for the accommodational award if they are having a hard time making ends meet. They will be able to pay for their accommodation through their wages they receive in the accommodational or governmental sectors. For example, suppose a janitor makes 2500þ/month. He applies for accommodational award where the AARP is 60%. Over the time frame of a month the accommodation (including utilities and appliances) add up to 2000 þ. The janitor must pay 0.6 x 2000 þ = 1200þ a month to the government for being able to live there. This leaves him with 2500 þ – 1200 þ = 1300 þ a month to spend on things in the accommodational sector like vacations or entertainment.

This is how the accommodational award works. It is designed to give accommodation as well as utilities and several appliances to those that have a hard time affording them. It ensures that no one in our consumerist society is homeless.

The Employment Agency

The employment agency is a crucial type of firm in the accommodation based consumerist economic system. Its main role is to find workers for other businesses. Whenever a firm needs workers but is simply unable to find them on its own, it can hire workers through the employment agency.

If a firm has a shortage of workers, it turns to the employment agency. In exchange for a payment, the employment agency tries to find the best workers for the firm. At the same time, people without work approach the employment agency so that it can help them find work. The job-seekers do not have to pay the employment agency for the service of helping find work. The employment agency makes money when firms looking for workers ask their help.

One of the reasons that a firm may have for not being able to find workers is that their wages/salaries are just too low. In the free-market system this would be remedied by increasing the wage. In consumerism what we do is introduce the existence of an employment agency. Although a firm may have a hard time finding workers with its current salary, there is, with quite certainty, a lot of people- for example those on welfare- that would definitely take the job if they only knew about it. The concept of the employment agency accomplishes in consumerism what wage manipulation achieves in the free-market system.

We mentioned earlier that for most jobs the employing firm makes money by selling jobs to workers. They can find these workers on their own or enlist the help of an employment agency. To hire workers that would otherwise be unavailable, the firm pays the employment agency. How much it costs to hire a worker is not set by the central bank. The employment agency actually functions in the laissez-faire sector. This is because there really isn't any quality selection involved in this case. It makes the most sense for employment agencies to compete for money as opposed to anything to do with quality.

The employment agency operates both in the natural partition and command partition. However it does not operate in the governmental partition. Thus profit-maximizing firms in the natural partition compete with each other to give firms the best workers for the best price and as many of them as possible. Meanwhile, firms in the command partition ensure that there are employment agencies to begin with and also that they provide worker-seeking firms with high quality workers for a good price and an adequate amount of them.

This is how the employment agency functions in accommodation based consumerism. Its existence is necessary to ensure that worker-seeking firms have access to workers without having to manipulate wage functions set by the central bank. Employment agencies help maximize employment for those that seek it.

Bankruptcy

It is important to know the circumstances regarding a bankruptcy. By bankruptcy we mean the stoppage of production and functioning of a firm. Examples of firm bankruptcies include the following. A doughnut shop stops selling doughnuts and coffee and no longer services its customers. A farm no longer raises or sells its livestock or crops. A music teacher no longer teaches students at her facilities. A construction company no longer uses cement and trucks to put up buildings. A real estate company no longer engages in helping people find homes.

When a firm is losing money during operations, it may be better for it to close down and declare bankruptcy. When a firm bankrupts it ceases to exist. It must sell off all its assets. The bankrupting firm has four primary obligators. They are stockholders, bond holders, workers and creditors. When a firm bankrupts and sells its assets it must pay its obligators in this order: workers, stockholders, bondholders and finally creditors.

Before a firm can sell bonds or stocks or issue job contacts, it must buy bankruptcy insurance. This insurance helps pay off the obligators if there is not enough money after the firm has sold off its assets. The central bank does not set the *Bankruptcy Insurance Premium Rate.* This is how much a firm must pay an insurance company each month to protect it in the case of a bankruptcy. It is determined by the interaction of the bankruptcy insurance firm and the firm wishing to buy bankruptcy insurance.

Let's take the case of a convenience store, Bob's convenience. We examine how it bankrupts. The bankruptcy of other firms is similar to this case. The store has 3 workers. They buy job contracts for 500.00 þ and the Adjusted Yearly Income Percentage is 2000 %. They are given contracts for one year. The convenience store issues 100 stocks. The consumerist universal stock price is 10.00 þ per share. They issue 1000.00 þ worth of bonds with a maturity of one year at an interest rate of 10% per year compounded yearly. The convenience store borrows 5000.00 þ from a private bank.

Bob must take out bankruptcy insurance in case his business fails. This is based on the total of his obligations to A) stockholders, B) bondholders and C) workers. He does not need to take insurance against his other creditors like the bank. The bankruptcy insurance premium rate is 0.5% per month. So Bob has to pay:

Workers-   3 x 500.00 þ x 2000% = 30 000.00 þ

Stockholders- 1000 x 10.00 þ = 10 000.00 þ

Bondholders- 1000.00 þ + (10% x 1000.00 þ) = 1 100.00 þ

Total-   41 100.00 þ

So he pays 41 100 þ x 0.005 = 205.50 þ to the bankruptcy insurance firm every month,

The convenience store is in a bad neighborhood. It is surrounded by 2 big grocery stores and other stores which compete with it. Sales are low and Bob decides to close his business.

Bob files for bankruptcy. He must first sell off all his assets. After selling all the inventory of goods in his store, the building and the land the building was on he accumulates 30 000.00 þ. Since the bankruptcy insurance does not cover bank creditors or those who lent money to the firm, the money made from selling assets is first used to pay these creditors. Bob pays the creditors (bank) which lent him 5 000.00 þ at 10 % interest (5 500.00 þ). So he still has 30 000.00 þ – 5 500.00 þ = 24 500.00 þ left over from selling his assets. He owes the other 3 obligators 41 100.00 þ. Since he doesn't have enough, the bankruptcy insurance firm helps him. The bankruptcy insurance firm pays 41 100.00 þ - 24 500.00 þ = 16 600.00 þ. Now that all debts are settled, the bankruptcy process is complete.

It may be possible that a bankrupting firm may have a bigger debt to its creditors (the bank, lenders) than it has assets. Although this is very unlikely as s firm that is bankrupting will probably have accrued some revenue and can sell its building and land for the same price that it bought it for. However if this happens the debt will either A) be forgiven or B) the owner will take on the debt for the future to pay back.

Usually bankruptcy is unfortunate for the firm bankrupting. However, it may be beneficial for society as resources are transferred to another project. Suppose a firm that sells CD's bankrupts and the workers that worked there and lost their job find another job at an online firm. This is clearly beneficial from the standpoint of society.

Clearly the owner of a bankrupting firm is worried when his firm bankrupts. However, neither the workers, stock holders nor bond holders are particularly upset as the bankruptcy insurance firm pays either the value of their contract (how much they would earn if they worked the duration of their job contract) or the value of their bonds and stocks.

It may seem to some that the existence of bankruptcy insurance may cause those managing companies to want to bankrupt. However, this makes as much sense as saying that those who desire life insurance want to die or that those who desire car driver's insurance want to get into an accident. A firm that bankrupts must first pay its obligators from what it can accrue from selling all assets. Only then does the bankruptcy insurance firm play a role.

We analyzed the concept of bankruptcy as it applies to the consumerist system. We took the example of Bob's convenience. We looked at the payment of debts to obligators. This section explained what happens during a bankruptcy.

Inflation and Deflation

Inflation is the constant rise in prices, whether of products, services, inputs or wages. Deflation is the constant decline in prices whether of products, services, inputs or wages. Here we take a look at them.

It is usually believed that when inflation is quite low (1% to 4%), it is not a problem. In fact an equal inflation- when the prices of everything rise all at once – is considered neutral. Deflations are usually much rarer than inflations but when they are small they are also not much of a problem.

There are some problems with inflation. One is called "shoe leather cost". This has to do with the constant trips to the bank an individual has to make. Inflations are bad for the creditor and good for the borrower. Inflations are also a key component of the wage-price spiral that hampers the economy.

A hyper inflation can almost destroy an economy. In Germany in the 1920's the value of the Mark was inflated from 1 Mark per Dollar to 10 trillion Marks per Dollar in the span of 3 years. If an economy is experiencing hyperinflation, we know it is falling apart.

Another problem of inflation that is often overlooked is that it is an integral component of the free-enterprise business cycle. See figure 6. When there is a boom, eventually the demand outstrips the supply and prices rise. There is an inflation. At point (X) the bank raises interest rates to stop the inflation and the economy heads towards a recession. If we eliminate the possibility of inflations the central bank has no need of raising the interest rate and we thus put a stumbling block in any business cycle and possibly eliminate it altogether.

In consumerism there is no inflation or deflation in the GAM sectors. It is not possible as the prices of all goods are fixed with the exception of the laissez-faire sector. There may be one time increases in prices at the retail level due to manipulations with the retail mark-up; but this is not inflation because it is a onetime adjustment. The central bank doesn't just print money and issue money at random as it does in the free-market economy. Rather, the central bank only issues an amount of Norses equal to the production of the materialist sector.

One problem is that this money eventually turns into Ignits when there is a transaction and it ends up in the accommodational sector. To combat the possibility of excess money, there are six anti-inflationary measures – for example the accommodational markdown-which suck the Ignits out of the accommodational sector and take them out of circulation in bank book entries. Yet there is no inflation or deflation as prices are fixed in the GAM sectors.

It is completely illegal for anyone to manipulate either the price of goods, services or wages (with the exception of the laissez-faire sector). Doing so would hurt the economy.

We have talked about inflation and deflation; what they are and how they function. We have seen why these two phenomena do not exist in our system. We have seen how their absence benefits our economy.

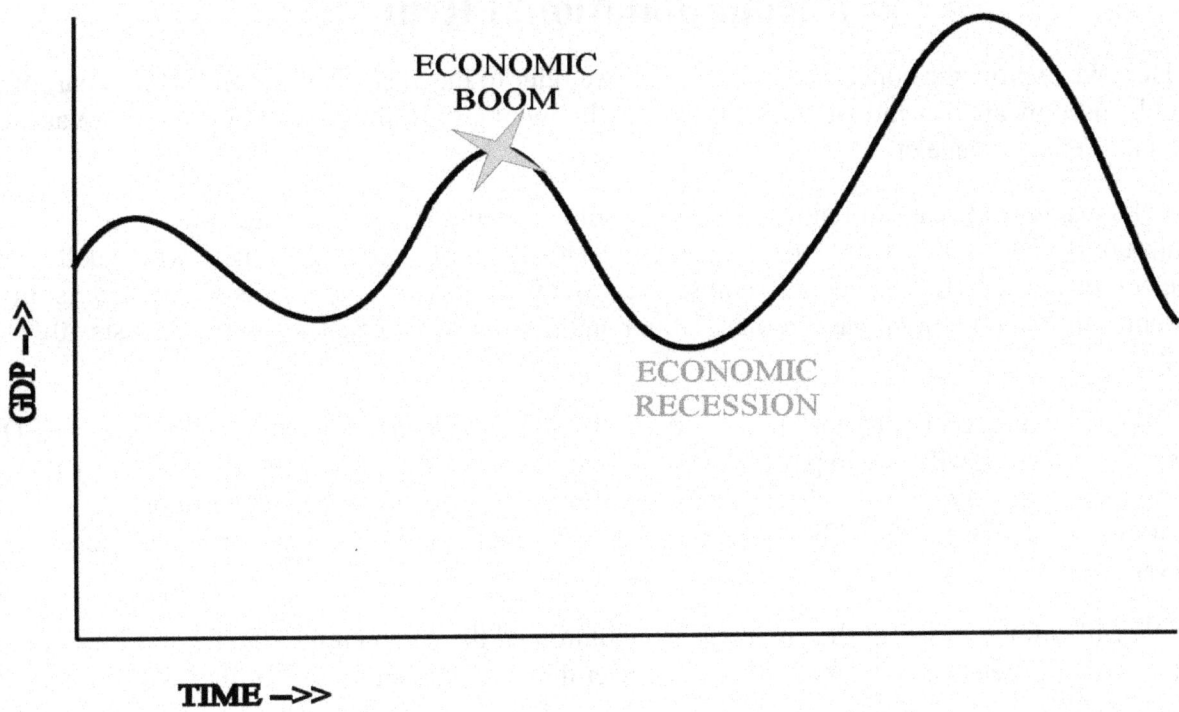

ECONOMIC
BOOM

GDP -->

ECONOMIC
RECESSION

TIME -->>

Figure 6

Figure 6 - The free-market Business Cycle

Accommodational Rent

Here we explore the concept of rent. By rent we refer to the idea where a building or a part of it is able to be used by another individual without actually owning it. Buildings can be rented for various reasons; i.e. shelter, storage etc.

Let's examine the case of renting a condominium. Suppose that the price function of a condominium is x1000.00 þ+ y2000.00 þ+ z100.00 þ. This is a simple function. These will usually be a lot more complicated. Here x represents rooms, y represents floors and z represents square meters. In our example, our condominium has 3 rooms, 1 floor and 50 square meters. Thus to buy it costs 10 000.00 þ

Now we introduce a new concept into our discussion- *The Rental Equivalence Duration* (RED). This means how long it will take to pay for the total cost of the building being rented. It is set by the central bank and can vary. Suppose that the RED is 5 years. Thus each year the renter of our condominium would have to pay 2000.00 þ or 167.00 þ per month to the land owner to rent the condominium.

We will call the owner of the property the landlord and the person renting it, the tenant. The higher the RED the better it is for the tenant. The lower the RED the better it is for the landlord.

Suppose that a tenant does not want an entire property but only a portion of it. He pays only the percentage of the RED of the building that he rents as his rent to the land lord. Take the case of an apartment. The entire apartment complex costs 1 500 000.00 þ. Land owner Betty owns it. There are 50 apartment suites. Joe is a tenant in one of them. The RED is set by the central bank at 2 years. Thus every month, Joe must pay = 1 500 000.00 þ/ (50 x 2 x 12) = 1 250.00 þ. If the accommodational markdown is 20%, Betty keeps 875.00þ from what Joe gave her.

Let's give one more final example. Suppose Mike's firm wants to rent a space to start their firm. They find one where the land lord had to pay 100 000.00 þ for. The RED is 6 years. Each month Mike's firm must pay = 100 000.00 þ/(6 x 12) = 1389.00 þ. The landlord receives, assuming 30% accommodational markdown, 972.22þ

We have discussed the concept of rent. We learned about the RED and how it affects rent payments. With all this information, it is possible for people to rent and use property.

Rent of Goods and Services

We have discussed the renting of accommodation in the last section. Now we turn to the topic of renting other goods and services. By this we mean the use of a product or service without having complete ownership of it. For example someone may want to rent a DVD from a movie store and watch it once or twice without fully owning the DVD.

It is important that certain items be allowed to be rented. Sometimes a consumerist may want to use a good or enjoy a service without fully owning the good or having total control over the service. He may want to enjoy a good but not need to own it outright. He would rather pay a smaller price for renting the good than pay the full price for the good in question.

To allow for the renting of certain goods and services we must allow for the idea of rent in our system. So we introduce the Rental Repayment Value (RRV). This indicates how much of the original product or service the renter has to pay in order to use the product or service once. It is determined by the Grand Chairman of the Central Bank. So if the RRV is 3% and a car costs 10 000.00 Θ, the person renting the car must pay 300.00 Θ to use the car. The car renting firms will compete with each other in quality. That is they will compete, among other things, in how long the renter can keep the car before he has to return it. This competition ensures that renters have access to the best services.

As another example, imagine that a DVD costs 30.00 Θ to own. At a movie rental store they would rent the movie to movie watchers. If the RRV is again 3 %, then the renter has to pay 0.90 Θ to rent the DVD. Again the different DVD outlets would compete in quality. They would offer longer and longer rental periods. So consumerists pick the DVD outlet that provided the best service for example, the longest length for keeping the movie before having to return it.

There are many examples where it makes perfect sense to rent the item or service as opposed to owning it outright. Someone may want to rent a limousine for his wedding or graduation rather than owning one. Someone may want to rent a tuxedo for an important event without buying it outright. There are also other examples.

We discussed the idea of rent of goods and services in the accommodation based consumerist system. We introduced the Rental Repayment Value. We gave some examples of how the idea of rent would work. Renting would provide consumerists access to goods and services without having to own that good or service outright.

Incentives

It is true that in order for people to do something, they usually need incentives to carry out such action. But just what are incentives and what is their nature? We need to motivate workers to produce goods and services, to produce a lot of them and to produce the best ones possible. But what will motivate them?

What follows is an illustration of the *principle of motivation*. In order to get a dog to sit one would give him a treat. In order to get a fussy child to finish his dinner of spinach or broccoli one would give him dessert- ice cream for example- as a reward. In order to get a student to study hard, teachers would give him an A for a good performance on an exam and an F for a bad performance. To encourage a horse to pull a carriage, one would whip him to make him go faster.

But will a dog do a trick if there is no promise of a treat? Yes- if doing the trick was in some way important to him. Will a child finish a dinner of broccoli even if there is no dessert? Yes- if he realizes that he needs broccoli to be healthy. Will a student study hard even if he doesn't earn an A for doing so? Yes- if he realizes the value of being educated. Will a horse pull a carriage even if it isn't whipped? Yes- if it realizes that the owner must arrive somewhere on time.

Then why do we need a motivation, such as a treat, an A, a bowl of ice cream, if we do things we are rewarded for, for our own good? What role does the dog treat, the ice cream, the A, play to all those to whom it is given? They are all a reward- something we like to receive and would like more of. The reward is clearly seen for what it is. It is something that keeps us going when we lose sight of the benefit of what we are working at. It is something we work for.

Why does a student need an A to work hard if studying hard favors him by making him more educated? It motivates him to study hard; it keeps him going. He is rewarded with something he likes in exchange for something that is subtly good for him. Why does a dog need a doggy biscuit to encourage him to sit and to do tricks? He is rewarded with something he likes, what makes him happy, what he wants in exchange for doing tricks. Why does a child need ice cream for eating dinner he doesn't like? To encourage him to eat it. In all these cases the reward is something the individual being rewarded likes or wants. The principal of motivation states that in order for an individual to do work, there must be a reward or the acquisition of something the individual likes. If this principal is violated, the economic system will not work as no one will want to work.

We have analyzed the concept of an incentive. We came across the principal of motivation and saw that it is important. In the coming sections we will see how incentives apply to productivity, efficiency and progress.

Incentives for Productivity

Agents in consumerism need an incentive to be productive. By productivity we mean contributing to society. Workers need a motive to work and firms need a motive to operate and expand.

In the free-market, people are led as if by an invisible hand to contribute to society when in fact they are actually trying to contribute only to their own well being. In consumerism there are two invisible hands. The left hand operates as the more people produce, the greater is the output of the economy. As the population remains the same size, each person receives more materialist money. The right hand operates as the more people produce, work, labor and invest the more accommodational money they earn. This whole concept is a lot like a horse pulling a person in a carriage. When the horse advances it moves forward but at the same time it drags the carriage along with the person forward.

There are two types of incentives. We will call them noble incentive and individualistic incentive. By adding to the GDCP, a firm in the materialist sector increases how much money each consumerist is granted by the central bank. Suppose a car dealership puts on the market 200 cars which sell for 15 000.00 Θ. Thus it contributes 3 000 000.00 Θ to the materialist sector. This helps society as each consumerist will now be better off, receiving a larger consumerist grant, either general or non-working. With this money these consumerists can buy goods and services in the materialist sector. This is the concept of the noble incentive for motivation or the left-hand that guides the consumerist society.

Another incentive for productivity is the profit motive (in the accommodational and laissez-faire sectors). All the profits that a firm earns are used to pay the employees and to cover the costs of doing business. What is left goes to the owners and bondholders. The money earned by workers are Ignits. With this money he who has it can buy anything in the accommodational sector of the economy- but he can't spend it on the materialist sector. This means that he can use it to buy more land, a new house or mansion, household accessories, alcohol, vacations or use it to pay his bills. The more a firm sells, the higher its profit and the greater is its accommodational prosperity. On the downside it is possible for a firm to bankrupt if no one wants to buy its products or use its services. This is the concept of individualistic incentive or the right hand that guides the consumerist system.

We have seen the need for incentives for productivity. We saw that there are two types of incentives in our system. Together they give a reason for our society to produce goods and services.

Incentives for Efficiency

It is important that an economy be efficient. An efficient economy runs more smoothly. By efficiency we mean using inputs to the fullest advantage.

The incentive for efficiency in the consumerist system is profit. All inputs that a firm needs have the same price function regardless of their quality. It follows that a firm will employ those inputs that make it most efficient. When it does so, it lowers production costs and it will make more profit for every good or service the firm sells. However it still strives to produce goods and services with inputs of the highest quality as all inputs in the same family have identical price functions.

A firm will hire the hardest working clerks, the most competent cashiers and the most knowledgeable accountants. A firm will hire the best employees depending on the business the firm is in. This is due to the fact that all workers in the same family (taxon) have the same wage function. This is an example of the principal of merit.

All other inputs also have the same input function within the same family. Thus those workers with the highest quality are obtained. A car factory will buy the best capital, in this case car making machines. An ice cream provider will also buy the best capital. Here the most professional ice cream machines. Offices will also maximize efficiency since their capital input has a fixed price function. They will employ the newest, high tech computers and internet services.

Another input is land. It also has a price function. Thus firms will get the best land onto which to place their factories, offices and firms.

A firm can also maximize efficiency by manipulating the number of employees it has. This is called downsizing. By limiting staff to the minimum that is essential, a firm can maximize profit. However a firm can also earn profit by selling jobs to employees. A firm cannot downsize or lay off workers that it sold jobs to. Workers are protected from being laid off due to the fact that they own job contracts that give them the right to work at a job for a certain length of time. There is a juggling act to find the right number of employees.

Efficiency is important. Fixed functions for families of inputs and land help insure that a firm runs efficiently. An efficient firm is better able to compete in a world market.

Incentives for Economic Progress

It is essential that there is economic progress in a thriving economy. By economic progress we mean mainly the creation of inventions and innovations. This includes 1) New products, 2) a greater variety of products, 3) new services and 4) better ways of doing things,

How do we encourage invention and innovation? We already described quality selection. Under this type of paradigm firms compete to make their goods and services most desirable to consumerists. Those goods and services of the best quality are those that "survive" the market and are sold.

We can encourage invention and innovation through patents. A patent is a right to exclusive production by the inventor of the product for a set amount of time. How long should a patent be? Should it be granted per profit or for a fixed number of years?

If the patent length was determined by profit, the patent would last as long as the firm making the invention makes a certain amount of profit. The problem with this is that clever accountants can warp financial records so as to under-report the actual profit the firm makes and prolong the patent period. This is not a favorable way to determine the length of a patent.

With a single patent period, a patent period for a fixed number of years would apply to the whole economy. The problem with this is that firms with the potential to make a good but who are unable to cover their costs during the patent period will not start up. On the other hand, those firms who make more money than their set up costs during the patent period have an unnecessary monopoly and there isn't any competition.

A different option exists for consumerism. In consumerism the patent period is different for each industry. The pharmaceutical industry will have one, the electronic industry will have one and the software industry will also have one, etc. The logic behind this is that the ideal patent length (the one that maximizes profit and limits monopoly periods) is similar for goods in a certain industry. Therefore each industry has its own patent period in terms of years. These are set by the government.

Also to help investors there should be rewards. Even though no money is made, the thrill of winning a reward and being recognized as the best in one's profession is an incentive for economic progress. Thus the government and industries should come up with as many rewards as possible. Almost every industry should have its specific reward. A reward is a great motivator even if it is not money. Examples include the Stanley Cup, the World Cup and an Olympic gold medal. These awards push athletes to new levels of excellence. It is logical that similar economic awards should push investors to new levels of excellence.

It is optimal that every industry has its own patent period. This helps investors to invent and innovate, with rewards for economic success in various industries of the economy. Investors and producers are challenged to make goods and services that help us all.

Simple Two Person Economy/Production Possibilities

We can visualize a simple two person economy to help us understand production possibilities. Often a two person economy is used as an example to explain the dynamics of trade between to agents in an economic system. This example, a two person economy, is common today in economic discussions to illustrate the mechanics of an economic system, and is often used to teach various economic systems in universities and colleges. Although this analysis is very basic and doesn't reflect how a complete consumerist system would function, it is nevertheless helpful for us to get a certain understanding of some economic concepts; i.e. efficient trade and allocation of inputs for production of goods as well as comparative advantage.

We start with the assumption that there are two individuals in our society; an egg farmer and a pig farmer. Each can produce a certain amount of eggs and pork. The amount of eggs and pork that the egg farmer can produce is different from that which the pig farmer can produce. In one hour the egg farmer can produce 1 kg of eggs or 1 kg of pork. The pig farmer can produce 8 kg of pork or 2 kg of eggs in the same amount of time. We assume that they work 6 hours per day.

The following table shows the hypothetical output of both types of farmers:

	Amount produced in 1 hour (in kg)		Amount produced in 6 hours (in kg)	
	Eggs	Pork	Eggs	Pork
Egg farmer	1	1	6	6
Pig farmer	2	8	12	48

The following are called production possibility frontiers. They graphically illustrate how much the egg farmer and pig farmer can produce and the tradeoffs they encounter if they chose a particular amount of good to produce.

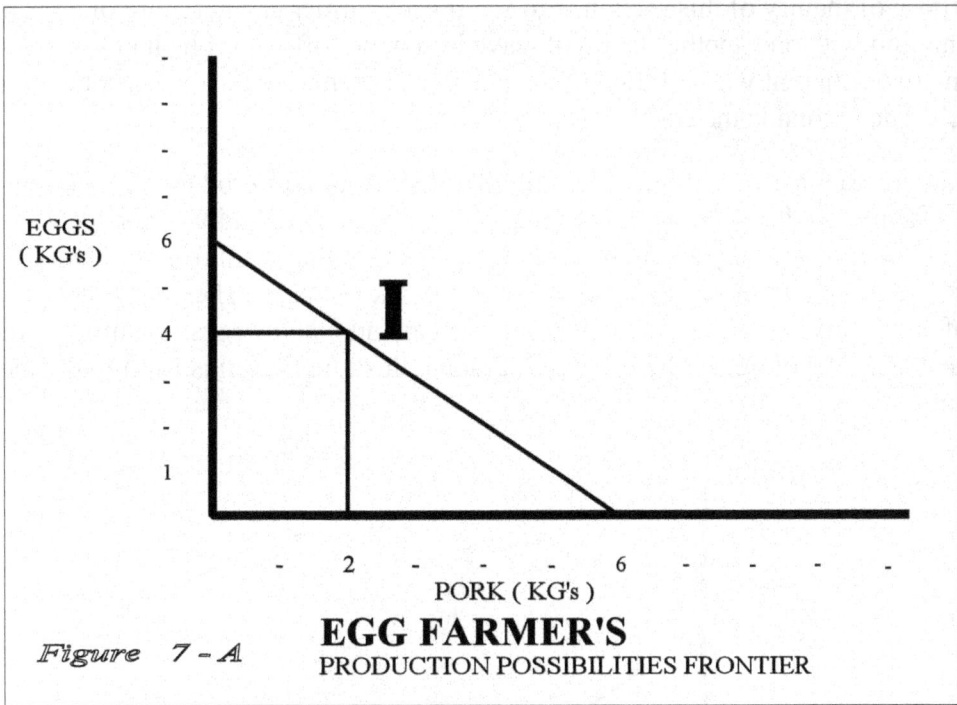

Figure 7-A

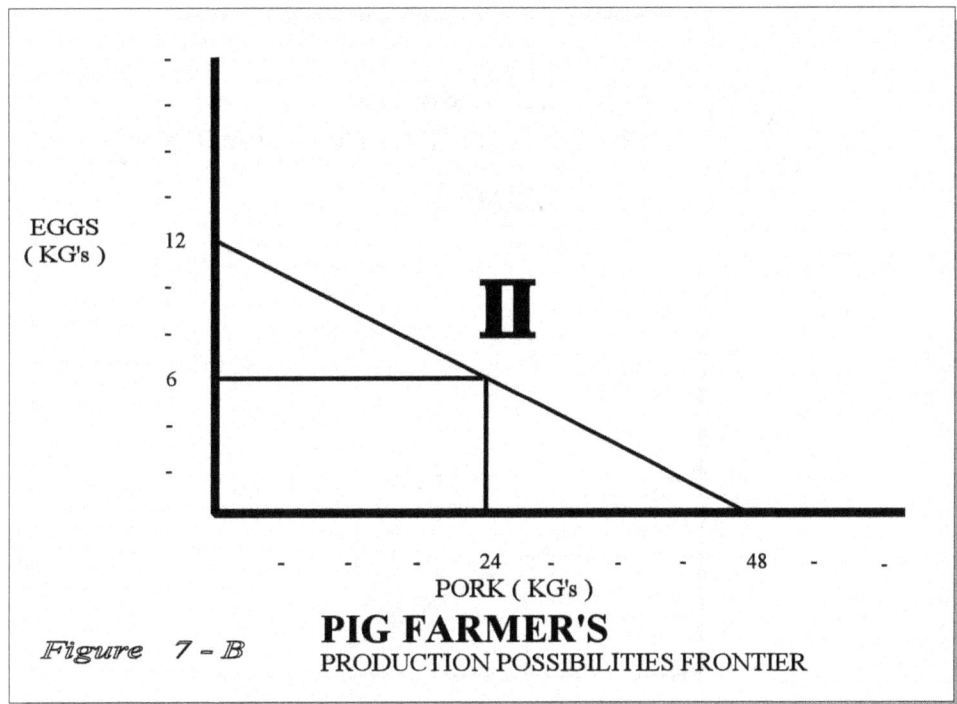

Figure 7-B

Note in the above that the pig and egg farmer can produce any amount of eggs and pork that is on the frontier. For example, the egg farmer can produce 4 kg of eggs and 2 kg of pork as given by "I". Similarly the pig farmer can produce 24 kg of pork and 6 kg of eggs as given by "II".

The purpose of inquiry of this section is to see if each farmer can get more of eggs and pork by somehow exchanging with one another that will leave him better off than if he had to subsist on his own. We will examine two different ways of doing this. For lack of better terms, one method is the free-market approach. The second is the consumerist approach.

Let's examine the free-market method. Initially, the egg farmer produces 3 kg of eggs and 3 kg of pork. The pig farmer produces 24 kg of pork and 6 kg of eggs. Both individuals decide to specialize at what they can produce more easily and trade with each other. So the egg farmer produces 6 kg of eggs and no pork while the pig farmer makes 32 kg of pork and 4 kg of eggs. The pig farmer gives 6 kg of pork for 3 kg of eggs. Now the egg farmer has 6 kg of meat and 3 kg of eggs. Meanwhile the pig farmer has 26 kg of meat and 7 kg of eggs. The following graphs illustrate the gains from trade under the free-market approach.

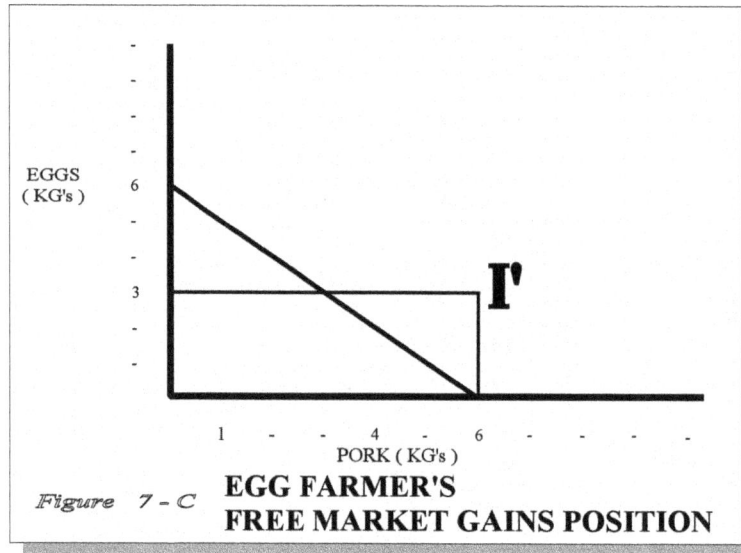

Figure 7-C

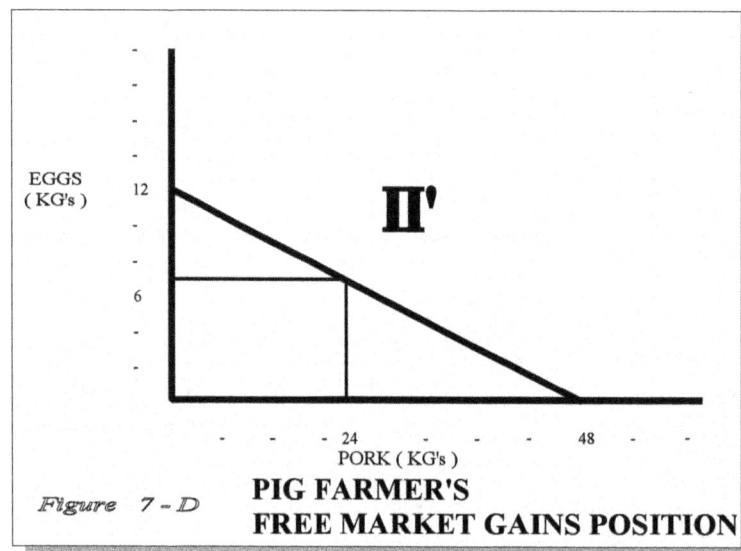

Figure 7-D

224

Now let's see how this problem resolves itself under the consumerist paradigm. We set two goals: 1) the total output of the entire economy must be as large as possible. And 2) both individuals, the pig and egg farmers, should have a total of goods that is beyond the production possibilities frontier.

First of all we need to ask, what is worth more: a kg of eggs or a kg of pork or are they equivalent? That is, is 1 kg of eggs worth as much as 1 kg of pork? To answer this we find a very special important number that we will soon see is very useful. To calculate it, we find the ratios of the ability to produce eggs and pork for each farmer. Next we add them both and divide by 2. So let's proceed. The egg farmer can produce eggs and pork in a 1:1 ratio. That is, the opportunity cost of producing eggs and pork are equal. The pig farmer produces pork and eggs in an 8:2 ratio or 4:1. Now we add: 1/1 + 4/1 = 5/1. Dividing by 2 we get a figure of 2.5. We can think of this value of 2.5 as the most efficient value of pork in terms of eggs. Thus we can say that 1 kg of eggs is worth 2.5 kg of pork.

Now that we know that 1 kg of eggs is worth 2.5 times as 1 kg of pork, let's find a way to produce pork and eggs among the two farmers such that the output is greatest. The egg farmer can produce 1 kg of eggs for every 1 kg of pork. But since 1 kg of eggs is worth 2.5 times as 1 kg of pork, it makes sense for him to produce the maximum of 6 eggs. Now what does the pig farmer produce? Since the pig farmer can produce 8 kg of pork for every 2 kg of eggs, it makes sense for him to dedicate his time to producing just pork even though eggs are worth more. Thus in our analysis the output that is most efficient for both farmers collectively is one where the egg farmer just makes eggs (6 kg) and the pig farmer just makes pork (48 kg).

Now we want to create a trade where both the pig farmer and egg farmer have more eggs and pork than they could produce on their own. The special number, 2.5 is the ideal ratio for which the farmer should trade eggs in terms of pork that will maximize both of their gains from trade. So the egg farmer has 6 kg of eggs and the pig farmer has 48 kg of pork. Unless each of them just wants to eat one type of food, they will begin to trade with each other, exchanging 1 kg of eggs for 2.5 kg of pork. The following is a list of the various combinations that could result from trade between the farmers.

Egg farmer			Pig farmer	
Eggs	Pork		Eggs	Pork
6	0		0	48
5	2.5		1	45.5
4	5		2	43
3	7.5		3	40.5
2	10		4	38
1	12.5		5	35.5
0	15		6	33

Now each of the above combinations will result in a situation where both farmers have a combination of goods beyond the production possibilities frontier. Of course, how many eggs or pork is traded depends entirely on how much each farmer wants to trade. Suppose the egg farmer likes eggs a lot. He might want to keep 4 kg and trade 2 kg. He trades 2 kg of eggs for 5 kg of pork. Otherwise the egg farmer might want both so he trades 4 kg and keeps 2 kg. He is left with 2 kg of eggs and 10 kg of pork. This means that the pig farmer has 4 kg of eggs and 38 kg of pork. Let's draw production possibility curves to see what is happening:

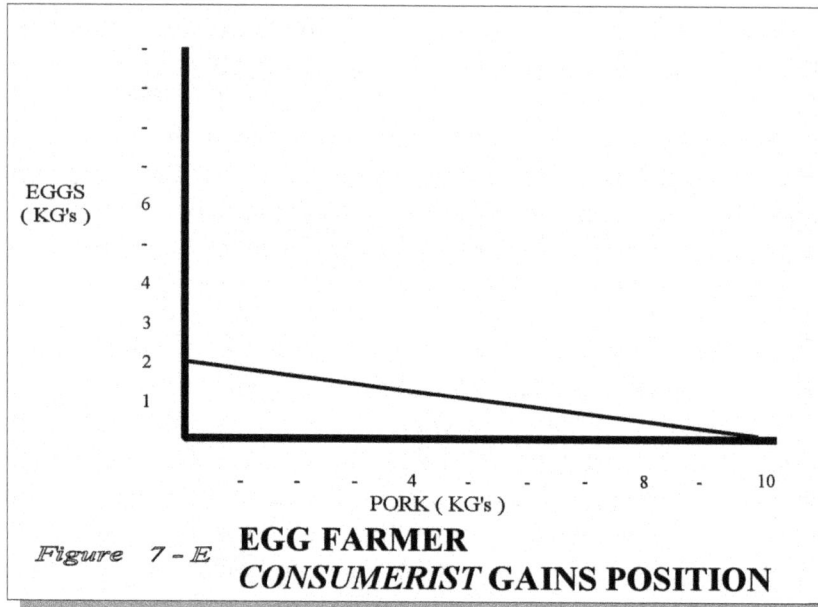

Figure 7 - E **EGG FARMER**
CONSUMERIST **GAINS POSITION**

Figure 7-E

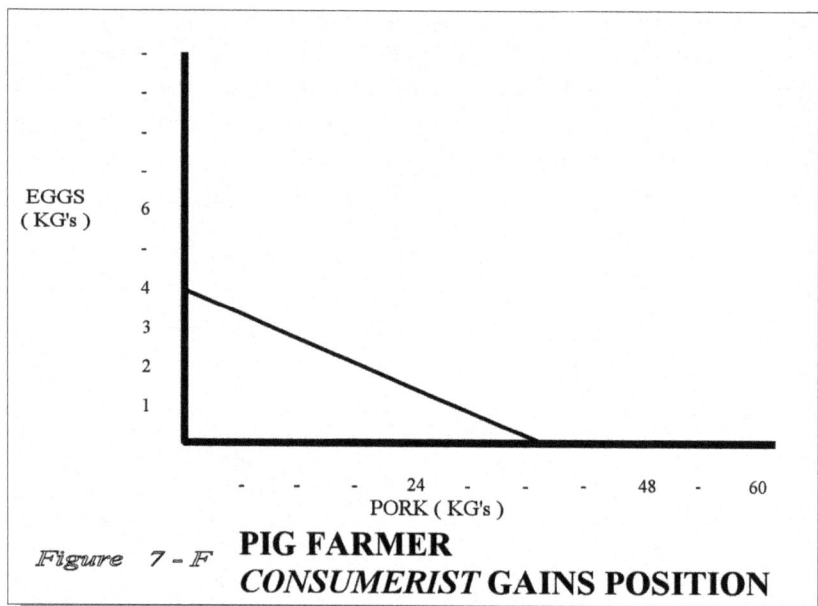

Figure 7 - F **PIG FARMER**
CONSUMERIST **GAINS POSITION**

Figure 7-F

Now we can compare both types of solutions; the free-market and the consumerist. In the free-market system the egg farmer made 6 kg of eggs while the pig farmer made 32 kg of pork and 4 kg of eggs.

226

To see the output, we add everything:

6 kg of eggs

+ 4 kg of eggs

+ 32 kg of pork

= 10 kg of eggs and 32 kg of pork

In consumerism, 6 kg of eggs and 48 kg of pork are produced. The free-market approach produces more eggs but less pork. The consumerism approach produces more pork and fewer eggs. Which output is better? If we value 1 egg as 2.5 pork, then

Free-market: $(10 \times 2.5) + 32 = 57$

Consumerist: $(6 \times 2.5) + 48 = 63$

We have seen that in the consumerist approach both farmers benefit; they gain more goods then they could individually. Let's compare the consumption of the egg and pig farmer in the free-market paradigm versus the consumerist paradigm

Free-market:

Egg farmer-	6 kg of pork
	3 kg of eggs
Pig farmer-	26 kg of pork
	7 kg of eggs

Consumerist:

Egg farmer-	7.5 kg of pork
	3 kg of eggs
Pig farmer-	40.5 kg of pork
	3 kg of eggs

The egg farmer is better off in consumerism; in both approaches they have 3 kg of eggs, but in consumerism the egg farmer has 1.5 kg more of pork. As for the pork farmer, he has 14.5 kg more of pork but 4 kg fewer eggs.

How is it possible that both farmers are able to get a higher combination of eggs and pork after trading than if they were left to themselves? The answer is a concept known as "comparative advantage". This means that it is easier for the egg farmer to produce just eggs since the opportunity cost for 1 kg of eggs is just 1 kg of pork. However, the pork farmer on the other hand, has an opportunity cost for producing pork equal to 0.25. Thus it makes sense for the egg farmer to specialize in egg production and the pig farmer to specialize in pork production.

We examined a simple 2 person economy consisting of an egg farmer and a pig farmer. We took a look at their production possibility graphs. We came to the understanding that if both produce products in which they have a comparative advantage and trade eggs for pork at a specially calculated exchange rate, then they can accumulate a larger number of eggs and pork for each of them than they could by themselves.

The Work for Freedom Program

The work for freedom program is a special economic arrangement whereby prison inmates can work in exchange for time off their sentences. A prisoner is able to contribute to society by increasing the output of goods while being rewarded with slightly less prison time. This program is beneficial not only for the prisoner but also for the government and certain profit maximizing firms.

In the work for freedom program a judge or a panel of judges creates a special parameter called the *work/freedom incentive ratio*. Essentially this sets how much time off a sentence an inmate receives in exchange for work. For example, if it is 1hr W/2hr F, for every 1 hour of work an inmate performs, he receives 2 hr off their sentence. So if a shoplifter receives a sentence of 6 weeks or 42 days = 1008 hours, for every hour of work he does, he has 2 hours less of time to serve. If in week one he works 40 hours, he has to spend 80 hours less in the remaining 5 weeks.

When a person is convicted in court the judge gives him a sentence and offers him the opportunity to work in the work for freedom program. If he agrees, the inmate together with his lawyer, the judge (or panel of judges) and the prosecution determine what kind of work will be done. Finally the judge or panel of judges set the work/freedom incentive ratio.

Clearly the jobs the inmate can do are quite limited. Generally speaking, the inmate can't do anything that will help him escape or that is dangerous and can aid in the making of weapons. Some suggestions include adhering stamps to envelops, checking the address on letters, ensuring that the labels on packages are properly attached, putting letters into envelopes, counting papers and other jobs that are similar.

In this program, a firm in the natural partition approaches the judicial committee in charge of the program and asks them to find inmate workers for their positions. They pay a payment that goes directly to the government to pay for social services. In exchange this committee assigns workers to that occupation. The inmates work not for money but for a reduced prison sentence. For example, a telemarketing company goes to this committee looking for people to fill letters into envelopes. Instead of giving this work to someone with a commerce degree it is more economical to give it to a prison inmate while the university graduate does more demanding work in line with the principal of maximum worker utility. The judicial committee assigns workers to this position and gives them a proper work/freedom incentive ratio. The firm pays, for example, 2.00þ /hour for the service of the inmate. This goes to the government as revenue. The worker, that is the inmate, in the meantime, works to have a shorter sentence. If the work/freedom incentive ratio is 1 hr W/ 3hr F the worker will get three hours off his sentence for every 1 hour that he works.

The prisons in a consumerist nation will have a special section set aside for inmates to do productive work through the work for freedom program. This is similar to having a factory inside the prison where inmates can do things like weighing letters on a scale or making sure that there is a stamp on every envelope they inspect. In that case there must be special correction officers whose job it is, besides making sure the inmates are safe, to ensure that the inmates are doing their job and doing it properly.

There may be problems when inmates deliberately try to sabotage the work they are doing. In that case they get three warnings and after each warning the inmate is penalized. Suppose the work for freedom incentive ratio is 1W/1F and for every hour of work the inmate does, he has one hour deducted off his sentence. If he is caught sabotaging for example putting labels on jars improperly, he is penalized by having his work for freedom incentive ratio increased to say 2W/1F. Now he has to work 2 hours for every hour of freedom he earns. The second time the inmate causes problems he has the work for freedom incentive ratio increased even further and he receives more time on his sentence. So now that parameter becomes 2.5W/1F and he has 3 weeks added to his sentence. The third time the inmate causes problems he is simply expelled from the program all together. In addition, his sentence is severely prolonged. If it was originally 52 weeks it now becomes 104 weeks.

What about the cases where people have life sentences? If such inmates do a lot of work it may be possible for them to have their sentences slightly reduced or enhance their likelihood of being let out on parole. However in this case the work for freedom incentive ratio should be steeper than for other inmates. Now, if these inmates cause problems they will be penalized by being removed from the program, losing their ability for parole and if the problems reoccur two or three times, they may be moved to solitary confinement.

On the other hand if inmates are consistently doing a great job for a very long time, they may be entitled to a "raise". This raise is not in terms of money but with regards to a decreased work for freedom ratio incentive. Suppose a shoplifter is sentenced to prison for 150 weeks and the judge along with the attorneys present determine the work for freedom ratio at 1W/2F. If, for 50 weeks the inmate does an exemplary job at say, putting letters into envelopes, he may have his work for freedom ratio incentive improved to 1W/3F. Now he earns three hours of freedom for every hour of work.

Clearly it is better from the standpoint of society as a whole if inmates are doing something productive rather than simply wasting time in a cell staring at the wall. Any time more goods or services are produced, it is better for society. It is also evident that the inmates benefit because they serve a shorter sentence. The firms that participate in this program clearly benefit as they get very cheap labor- much below what they would normally pay if the wage for these jobs was dictated by a central bank or a market. Also, the government benefits since the money firms pay for this work goes directly to three levels of government as revenue. Thus this program is a win-win-win-win proposition.

In essence, that is how the work for freedom program works. Clearly, it is good for several individuals or entities. Through this program, the inmate, the government, participating firms and society as a whole gain.

The Recycle-For-Pay Program

The recycle for pay program is a setup where things that would otherwise be considered waste are exchanged for money. Things like cardboard, plastic, glass, paper, etc are exchanged for money.

In the recycle-for-pay program the government, whether federal, provincial or municipal assigns a monetary value for things that are normally considered waste. A consumerist takes the item to a special store run by the government. We will call such a store simply, "recycling store". The government pays the individual a certain amount of money for the items. Afterwards the government sells the item to an input receiving firm for profit.

Initially, the government sets a special parameter called the *recycle for pay percentage*. (RFPP) This dictates how much a consumerist is paid when selling his useless things. Suppose that an aluminum making factory makes usable aluminum for 1.50 þ per kilogram and that they pay 1.00 þ per kilogram for raw materials. Let's suppose that the RFPP is 50%. In that case for every kilogram of aluminum that a consumerist brings to a recycling store, he will receive 50 % of the basic value of the raw aluminum. In this case it is 0.50 þ.The other 0.50 þ goes to the government to pay for social services.

The RFPP can be universal or it can be specific to an item for recycling. There could be RFPP's for paper, RFPP's for glass and RFPP's for plastic. Alternatively, there can be one RFPP for everything.

Suppose that a paper mill buys raw material for creating paper for 2.00 þ and sells it later as paper to other firms. If the RFPP is 40%, the consumerist who brings various forms of paper to a government recycling store would get 0.80 þ for every kilogram of useless paper he brings in. The government receives 1.20 for every kilogram of paper brought in.

Many things other than obvious "waste" can be bought by the government through this program. The government can buy (and set RFPP's for) things like the rubber from bicycle tires or wheels, the steel from old utensils and the cotton and polyester from t-shirts.

What the recycle for pay program accomplishes is that it gives value to things that in other economic systems would be considered "garbage". Our landfills should be considerably smaller than those in other economic systems. The problem we will have won't be what to do with useless garbage, but how does one protect one's garbage so that one can get paid for selling it.

It is true that people in free-market economies already recycle to some degree. However they don't have any real monetary incentive to do so. Furthermore, the range of things that can be "recycled" is far greater in consumerism than in other systems. Many of the things that go directly to the landfill- for example, apple cores, banana peels, and tea bags can be purchased by recycling stores. The government buys these things and sells them to companies that make compost – for soil, for example. If we have too much soil from compost we can export this to other nations where they would be grateful to buy it from us.

There will probably still be people who do not have the initiative to take their garbage to a recycling store, even if they gain money for doing so. We have to make use of waste management trucks and waste management workers in this case. They pick up the garbage on the edge of the driveway; whether it is paper, pop cans, and plastic or apple cores. At that point the government sells the recyclable and garbage material to various firms where they transform it to useful inputs- paper, steel, aluminum, soil, etc... The RFPP in this case is 0%. The government makes all the profit for selling recyclables to input processing firms and uses this to pay for social services. Its costs are the waste management workers and equipment used to collect the garbage and bring it to recycling stores.

Clearly, the recycle for pay program succeeds in four areas. We already mentioned that it decreases the amount of garbage that goes into our landfills. It also acts as a source of revenue for the three levels of government. It decreases the amount of spending by the government on waste management so that the government can spend that money on things like defense, education and health care. Of course some money will still have to be spent on waste management but considerably less than if the recycle for pay program wasn't in place. Finally, it works as an anti-unemployment measure. If an individual has a hard time finding employment, he can start collecting pop cans or cardboard.

These are the ways the recycle-for-pay program works. It helps our economy in various ways. Both the government, the unemployed as well as the environment benefit from the recycle for pay program.

The Consumerist Money Supply

Here we look at the money supply in the consumerist economy. Recall firstly that there is no cash in circulation. That is there are no coins or paper bills. Also there are three kinds of currency, Ignits, Fortals and Norses. We analyze how these three circulate throughout the economic system.

In our system there are four sectors; the materialist, the governmental, the laissez-faire and the accommodational. Generally speaking, Norses (Θ) are used in the materialist and governmental sectors whereas Ignits ($\þ$) are used in the accommodational and governmental sectors and Fortals are used in the laissez-faire sector. It is important to note that always Norses and Ignits are equal to each other in monetary value; i.e.$1\þ =1\Theta$

The circulation of money in the consumerist economic system is something like the circulation of water through a human being. Initially water is consumed by drinking. It then circulates through the body in the form of blood, plasma fluid, and other liquids. It is then expelled from the body either as urine or sweat. Something similar happens in accommodation based consumerism.

Norses are created when there is an output in the materialist sector. All firms report their productivity or potential productivity to the central bank about once a month. They report what they sold or could potentially have sold. Firms report how many services they provided. Other firms, like car dealerships or apparel providers mention how many goods they sold and how much inventory was potentially available to be sold in that time period but not directly purchased. The sum of all this output is called the Gross Domestic Consumerist Product (GDCP).

When the central bank receives a record of the GDCP, they must grant the equivalent of it three ways. Some of it goes to the General Consumerist Grant, some to the Non-Working Consumerist Grant and some of it s taxed. This is how Norses are created. The supply of Norses in one month is exactly equal to the output or potential output of the materialist sector (GDCP). The Norses granted need not be done so every month. Perhaps if they were granted biweekly things would be smoother.

Now when the consumerists are granted Norses, they can spend it on goods and services in the materialist sector regardless of whether they were given the General or Non-Working grants. Upon the transaction, Norses are deducted from the consumerists and Ignits are added to the producer. This is how Ignits are created.

When the government (whether federal, provincial/state, or municipal) spends the Norses they were granted from the central bank, some of the Norses are deducted from their account and Ignits are added to the producing firm. For example, if the provincial government provides a knee operation for a consumerist the government gives 400 Θ to the doctor or hospital. The 400 Θ are deducted from the provincial government's account and 400 $\þ$ are added to the doctor's account. This is another way that Ignits are created.

Unless they are saved for the future, all Norses that are spent eventually end up in the accommodational sector as Ignits. While there they circulate between firms and consumerists (households) who earn Ignits from providing inputs to firms, i.e. labour. The supply of Ignits is called the Gross National Product (GNP).

The Gross National Product will constantly be rising as Norses from the GDCP are turned into Ignits. When an economy is starting out this is a good thing. However, it may be possible to slow down the increase of the GNP. Thus we introduce the accommodational markdown. In several industries of the accommodational sector, a portion of the sales are deducted and destroyed. They are permanently taken out of circulation.

Now we analyze changes in the supply of money on the economy.

If GDCP ↑, then (ceteris paribus), GCT ↑, NWCG ↑, GCG ↑, GNP ↑

If GDCP ↓, then (ceteris paribus), GCT ↓, NWCG ↓, GCG ↓, GNP ↓

If GCT ↑, then (ceteris paribus), GCG ↓, NWCG ↓

If GCT↓, then (ceteris paribus), GCG ↑, NWCG ↑

If Accommodational Markdown ↑ (ceteris paribus) GNP ↓

If Accommodational Markdown ↓ (ceteris paribus) GNP ↑

If population ↑, (ceteris paribus), GDCP?, GNP? GCT?, NWCG ↓, GCG ↓

If population ↓, (ceteris paribus), GDCP?, GNP? GCT ?, NWCG ↑, GCG ↑

If Retail Markup ↑, (ceteris paribus), GDCP ↑, GCT ↑, NWCG ↑, GCG ↑, GNP ↑

The accommodational markdown can be manipulated to control the money supply in the accommodational sector. If the accommodational markdown is equivalent to the GDCP the money supply is said to be "balanced". That is, the net effect is that the money entering the economy through the materialist and governmental sectors is coming from the accommodational sector and laissez- fare sectors. If this is the case then the flow of money among the various sectors is essentially circular.

The money supply in the Consumerist economy looks like this:

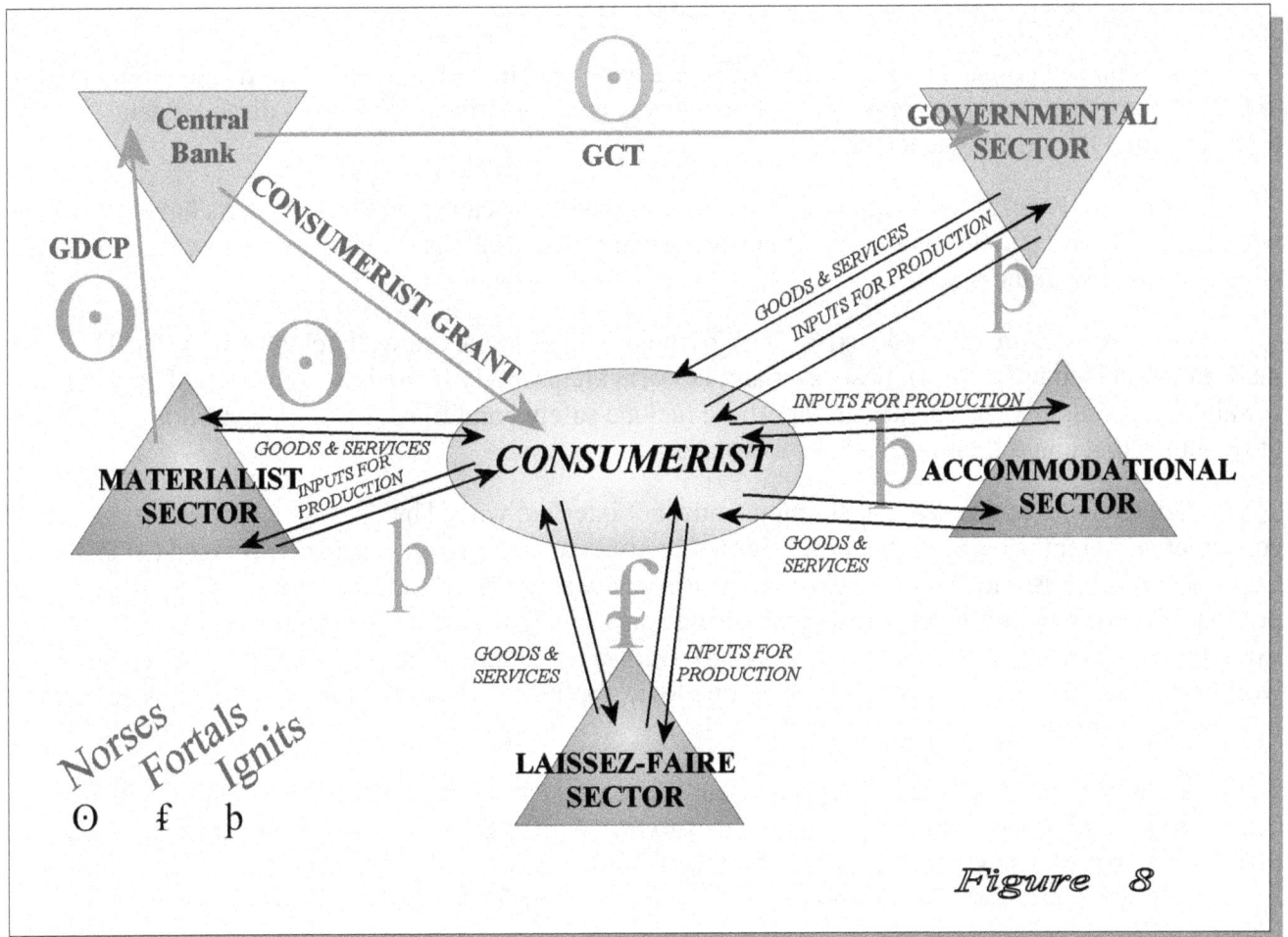

Figure 8

Unions

A union is an organization within a firm that fights for the rights of workers. Its main objective is to help the workers, going to great lengths to do so and causing strikes if there is a disagreement between it and the firm's management.

There are benefits to having unions in an economy. They can ensure that workers have better working conditions and they can ensure that workers are given full rights. They make sure that workers have a positive working place.

In consumerism unions do exist. Their purpose is to promote the well being of workers. Their main function is to guarantee that workers and laborers are properly treated by employers. There are certain things that unions can bargain for. These include safety conditions, working conditions and many other things that could improve the lives of workers.

There is one critical thing that unions must not interfere with. That is wages. The entire consumerist system is based on the proposition that prices and wages are permanently fixed (in the GAM sectors). Consumerism may collapse if prices and wages fluctuate. However if a significant portion of the population signs a petition against a wage function, that wage function will be re-examined (the central bank will vote on it again). But wages cannot arbitrarily increase just because workers think they deserve a pay hike. The same logic applies to job contract prices and adjusted yearly income percentages.

Unions work for workers. They represent them. As such, it may be necessary that for some occupations, workers will have to pay union dues to their union. So a portion of a worker's paycheck may have a special deduction that goes to the union. However, we will not go into the details of union dues and how much unions charge workers for being members. This is more of a political question rather than a purely economic one.

Unions can represent workers better collectively than if each worker in a firm had to represent himself individually. Unions give all the workers that they are fighting for a "common voice". Thus a worker is better able to get a demand from his company if the workers form a union than if the worker had to argue alone. This idea of "common representation" is the greatest value of the existence of unions.

Unions are important because of the service they provide for workers. They function to protect the working class. The only matter that they should not interfere with is wages.

Insurance

Many types of insurance are essential in an economy. By insurance we are referring to payments to a firm in case of a calamity. During a calamity the insurance firm provides assistance. The different types of insurance include life insurance, house insurance, car insurance, fire insurance, bankruptcy insurance and others. An insurance company, a car insurance company for example, receives payments from an interested consumer. If there is a car accident, the car insurance company pays for its repair. Insurance companies are in the laissez-fare sector and thus operate with Fortals.

The central bank does not set the Insurance Premium Rate. This parameter is set by firms in the laissez-fare sector and it is different for different types of calamities. Thus there is a "life" Insurance Premium Rate, a "house" Insurance Premium Rate and a "car" Insurance Premium Rate. This is how much a person being insured must pay the insurance company each month (or fixed amount of time) for coverage. Insurance companies of the same type compete not in quality but price. That is they fight with each other to provide the best coverage possible at the most competitive price. Since all insurance company coverage's of the same type cost differently, consumers pick the best one. Life insurance companies compete with each other in how much coverage and benefit a consumerist receives for belonging to its company plan as well as monthly payments. Car insurance companies compete on how responsive their service is and on how inclusive their firm is about its membership as well the insurance payments.

Insurance Premium Rates are obtained through by the interaction of consumerists and insurance providing firms. Life insurance could be 25.00 f/ 100 000.00f. Car insurance could be 200.00 f/car/month. Fire insurance could be 150.00f /house/month.

The different insurance providing firms can work either in the natural partition or in the command partition. In both cases firms compete with each other. However if the organizers of the command partition, i.e. the Human Resource Management Commission, want to set a goal for a certain insurance premium it can do so. Thus if insurance company ABC sets it car insurance premium at 5 % and a command partition firm sets this at 2 %, more people will want to buy insurance from the command partition firm. To be competitive firm ABC needs to lower its premium to around 2 % or else the command partition firm will have the majority of the market.

Bankruptcy insurance needs special mention. If a firm wants to sell shares or bonds or wants to hire workers it must purchase bankruptcy insurance. A bankruptcy insurance company helps pay stockholders, bond holders and workers what they are entitled to in case a firm bankrupts. The interaction of firms and bankruptcy insurance agencies set a bankruptcy Insurance Premium Rate in terms of a percentage per given time- usually a month. Let's suppose that it is 0.25%/ month. So if a firm sells 1 000 000 shares costing 10.00 þ, they have to pay 10.00 þ x 1 000 000 x 0.0025 = 25 000.00 þ/ month to the bankruptcy firm. If a firm sells job contracts and at the end of their job contract workers are entitled to 800 000.00 þ, the bankruptcy firm must receive 2 000.00 þ per month. In case of a bankruptcy however, the bankruptcy firm must pay the stockholders the value of the stock they own which has become worthless as a result of the bankruptcy. It must also pay the workers who lost their jobs as a result of the bankruptcy. In the case of stock, the bankruptcy firm only pays those stock holders who actually bought their stock. For example if Joe is an entrepreneur and issues 1 000 000 stocks and keeps 500 000 of them he doesn't receive anything for them if he bankrupts. The bankruptcy firm does not pay him the value of his 500 000 shares. It does pay the other half that were bought by investors at the universal stock price.

More "risky" firms have to pay more for being insured. What the idea of bankruptcy insurance accomplishes is that the default risk is in the hands of the insurance company not investors.

Since the insurance firms are in the laissez-fare sector, they operate with Fortals. However for things like insuring bankruptcies and houses, they must pay those who bought insurance packages in Ignits. To satisfy this, we avoid the Ignit-Fortal exchange rate and use the idea that $1 ƒ = 1 þ$. The reciprocal is the same.

Insurance companies are vital to an economy that faces risks. The various insurance companies compete with one another as the premium rates are not fixed by the central bank. The bankruptcy insurance firm is necessary to protect workers, shareholders and bond holders in the event a firm bankrupts.

Savings, Debt and the Materialist Overdraft

By savings we mean spending less money than earning. Thus there is more to spend in the future. By debt we mean spending more money than earning. Thus there is less money to spend in the future. Savings can be either in the form of Norses, Fortals or Ignits. There can also be debt in terms of Ignits, Fortals; and Norses. If one spends more Norses than are granted to him by the central bank they are still entitled for the *materialist overdraft*. It is also possible that a consumerist may have to make monthly payments for goods and services he purchased.

Normally, all consumerists are granted either the General Consumerist Grant or the Non Working Consumerist Grant. However in some emergencies, the consumer may be a little short on essential things like food or beverage items. To help him out we introduce the materialist overdraft. Basically, the consumerist can have some extra Norses granted to him. How much he is granted is based on the *materialist overdraft limit*. This is how much of the Consumerist grant he is given as set by percentage. This is given to him from the government. It should usually be below 5 % of the grant given to the consumerist. The next month, the consumerist must pay back the value of the materialist draft with a high percentage. This is called the *materialist overdraft interest*.

Let's see an example. Joseph received the General Consumerist Grant of 1000.00 ☉. The materialist overdraft limit is 5%. The materialist overdraft interest is 50 %. So, this month Joseph is given an extra 50.00 ☉ to help him out. For simplicity, let's suppose the General Consumerist Grant is also 1000.00 ☉ next month. However, instead of getting that, Joseph receives 1000.00 ☉ – 50.00 ☉ - (50.00 ☉ x 0.5) = 925.00 ☉. The government receives 75.00 ☉. It uses it to pay for social services. Clearly this idea of the materialist overdraft is good for two entities. Joseph has money he needed for very essential things. The government has an extra source of revenue.

It is quite possible that someone would get into a debt of Ignits. A businessman may borrow Ignits from the (private) bank in order to expand his business. A consumerist may buy a house using a mortgage. In both cases the people own property (house, new retail outlet) but still owe money to a bank that gave them the money to finance their purchase.

People can spend less Norses than they are granted. This is neither terribly good nor terribly bad. It simply represents a future purchase. A consumer may save the money he is granted for some time so that in a few months he can buy himself a car. An advantage of saving Norses is that not all people rush to buy popular products.

It is possible that a consumerist may buy something he does not have the Norses to pay for. For example, someone, Joe, earns 1000.00 ☉ every month as part of the general consumerist grant. Let's suppose that a car, a sports car, costs 8 000.00 ☉. Even though he doesn't have the money, he can pay in monthly installments. So he pays 400.00 every month for 20 months (there is no interest).

Consumerists can also spend less Ignits than they earn. Once again this represents future purchases. A consumerist who works as a cashier earns 500.00 þ/month. In three months she – if she saves- can afford that dream cruise to the Caribbean for 1200.00 þ. The problem with savings in general is that producers earn less money than they would if consumerists spent everything, For some industries this means lost business; i.e. restaurants, mechanics, music teachers.

Saving and debt are also possible with regards the laissez-faire sector. One can borrow Fortals and be in debt for the future. This may be due, for example, to an investment. Also one can save their Fortals for the future. Then they have more money (Fortals) to spend in the future.

Consumerists are able to get into debt and to save for the future. The economy is not tremendously hurt by these actions. Saving and being in debt are common experiences for anyone in the consumerist system.

A Basic Demonstration of the Accommodation Based Consumerist
Economic System on a Small Island

We need to know how our system works on a larger scope. Here we very basically demonstrate how our system works on a simple level- that is, on an island.

We make several assumptions that are not necessarily found in the grand system but are made here for simplicity.

1) The land is limited

2) The population is only 9 people

3) People sell what they make

4) Producers and thus workers require no inputs for their operations

5) The people can produce their products very quickly; i.e. a hut can be built in a day

6) The ratio of accommodational to materialist prices is imbalanced

7) The operation of the central bank is simplified

8) There is no laissez-fare sector

9) There is no command partition- everything involves the natural or governmental partition

Let's begin our analysis. We have 9 adults. To keep track of them we give them names. Their names are: John, Sue, Peter, Joanne, Sam, Kate, Nick, Lou-Anne and George.

The islanders are under a democracy. They elect John to be president. He is also the chief of the central bank. Thus he sets prices for all families of goods and services that can be produced.

The islanders also chose for themselves how they contribute to the island economy. We assume that everyone wants to work and that there are no idle islanders. Sue collects coconuts. Peter catches fish. Joanne picks berries. Sam makes clothes. Kate makes blankets. Nick, Lou and George all make living quarters such as huts, teepees and cabins.

John divides the primitive economy into accommodational, governmental and materialist sectors. Nick, Lou and George who work in making products for accommodation- huts, teepees, etc. - comprise the accommodational sector. All the others except John work in the materialist sector. John, the president and head of the central bank, works in the governmental sector.

John, as head of the central bank, puts price functions on everything that is produced. These prices are permanently fixed. They are expressed in terms of two currencies, Norse (Θ) and Ignits ($\þ$). Although $1\Theta = 1\þ$, these cannot be exchanged for each other. The prices of materialist goods are expressed in Norses while accommodational ones are expressed in Ignits. The price functions of products and services made on the island in the materialist sector are the following: The price of a fish is

2.00 ☉ per fish. The price of a tree fruit (i.e. a coconut) is 0.50 ☉ per fruit. Berries are worth 2.00 ☉/kg. A shirt is worth 5.00 ☉ per shirt. The price of a blanket is 2.50 ☉ /blanket.

The price functions for accommodational goods are as such:

5.00 þ /hut

7.00 þ/teepee

8.00 þ /lodge

10.00 þ/ cabin

15.00 þ /bungalow

20.00 þ /house

At the end of the day, the things produced that day are counted. Only materialist rather than accommodational things are counted. This means we count how much coconuts, fish, berries, clothes and blankets are made but not any of the buildings.

During the day the islanders were busy contributing to the island society. At the end of the day, Peter caught 5 fish, Sue collected 20 coconuts, Joanne picked 5 kg of berries, Sam made 2 shirts and Kate made 4 blankets.

If everyone only kept what they made then no one would be too happy. Peter would be sick of fish and cold at night while Sam would be clothed but hungry. To overcome this we don't simply divide all products evenly. In that case everyone would have an equal amount of everything. Joanne would have as many blankets as Lou-Anne even though she still might be cold. Similarly, Sue might have the same amount of berries as Peter even though she doesn't like them. This situation would result in barter. Those who have a lot of what they don't want will give those things to those who want them in exchange for what they want more of. Thus if Peter likes coconuts and hates blankets, he would exchange the blankets for coconuts.

However, on this island the islanders do something different. They take the consumerist approach. Recall that John, the head of the central bank, put a price on everything. At the end of each day he calculates the island's GDCP. This is an important concept that is much different from the notion of the GDP in the free-market system.

The GDCP in our island example is calculated thus:

Coconuts-   20 x 0.50 ☉ /coconut = 10.00 ☉

Fish-   5 x 2.00 ☉ /fish = 10.00 ☉

Berries-   5 kg x 2.00 ☉/kg = 10.00 ☉

Clothes-   2 shirts x 5.00 ☉/shirt = 10.00 ☉

Blankets   4 blanket x 2.50 ☉/blanket = 10.00 ☉

We have used these figures because they give simple numbers. The total of the GDCP is 50.00 ☉

At this stage, John grants the equivalent of the GDCP per capita- the consumerist grant- to the islanders. Since all are working, they all receive the same amount. However, John sets a tax- the only one in accommodation based consumerism- the Grand Consumerist Tax, which is a percentage of the GDCP. John sets it at 5%. The central bank grants 5 % of the GDCP (5.00 Θ) to the government. On a bigger island the government could spend these 5.00 Θ on services or products normally provided by the government.

It must be mentioned that no cash or coins are granted in this process. All the granting is carried out in the bank account each islander has in the central bank. This bank account, operated by John, is very simple. It simply reads the islanders name and how many Norses and Ignits he has is written next to his name.

After subtracting the tax, the central bank grants the equivalent of the GDCP on a per capita basis to all islanders. There are 45.00 Θ. There are 9 people so all islanders are granted 5.00 Θ. The money that is granted is not taken from anywhere; it is simply granted by the central bank to each islander. John writes 5.00 Θ next to each islander's name.

Now with the 5.00 Θ all islanders can spend the money on any of the materialist sector goods and services that were produced. The price of a good is the same as that use to calculate the GDCP. When an islander buys a good from the materialist sector, the price of that good is deducted from his bank account. The equivalent amount of Ignits is added to the seller's bank account. Here is an example: Suppose George wants to buy a fish from Peter. A fish costs 2.00 Θ. Upon the transaction, George receives a fish from Peter and 2.00 Θ are deducted from George's Norse bank account, leaving 3.00 Θ to his name. At the same time John writes that Peter earned 2.00 þ, thus writing 2.00 þ next to Peter's name in his bank account records.

One of the curiosities of this setup is that if an islander wants to buy something from himself then he has to sell the product to himself. If Peter wanted to buy one of the 5 fishes he caught he would have to pay himself 2.00 Θ (he would receive 2.00 þ at the same time).

John earns 5.00 Θ from the tax for keeping track of all transactions. This is automatically turned into 5.00 þ as he works. He can spend this on the accommodational sector.

Let's assume that all of the islanders who work in the materialist sector sell what they produce. All these workers now have money that they can spend on the accommodational sector of the economy. People are hungry and buy all of Peter's fish. He earns 10.00 þ. People are cold so they buy all of Kate's blankets. She earns 10.00 þ. Not everyone likes coconuts so Sue only sells 6.00 þ worth of coconuts. Not everyone likes Sam's shirts and he only sells 8.00 þ worth. People like Joanne's berries but she only sold 9.00 þ worth. Evidently, someone or a few people did not spend all of the money that they were granted. They can save this for the next day when more goods will be produced.

Now the workers in the materialist and governmental sectors must purchase goods (types of accommodation) from the workers in the accommodational sector. Let's summarize how many Ignits the workers from the materialist and governmental sectors posses:

John- 5.00 þ

Peter- 10.00 þ

Kate- 10.00 þ

Sue-   6.00 þ

Sam-   8.00 þ

Joanne-9.00 þ

To summarize, the different accommodational structures cost:

5.00 þ/hut

7.00 þ /teepee

8.00þ /lodge

10.00þ /cabin

15.00 þ/bungalow

20.00þ / house

On our island John and Sue buy a hut costing 5.00 þ each hut, Sam and Joanne each buy a lodge costing 8.00 þ per each lodge. Peter and Kate buy a cabin worth 10.00 þ each cabin.

Nick, Lou-Anne and George are the builders. Nick builds the 2 huts earning 10.00 þ. Lou- Anne builds the two lodges earning 16.00 þ George builds the cabins earning 20.00 þ.

Right now, assessing the economy, Sue and John have a hut, Sam and Joanne have a lodge, and Peter and Kate have a cabin. While,

Nick has 10.00 þ

Lou-Anne has 16.00 þ

George has 20.00 þ

Now all we need is to provide accommodation to those who provide accommodation. If things kept going the way they are going we fall into a problem called the accommodational overflow calamity. Things could collapse into the following: Recall that we have three workers in the accommodational sector- Nick, Lou-Anne and George. Nick has 10.00 þ, Lou-Anne has 16.00 þand George has 20.00 þ. They all need accommodation. So Nick buys a cabin from George for 10.00 þ, Lou–Anne buys a bungalow from Nick and George buys a house from Lou-Anne. Then George has a house, Lou-Anne has a bungalow and Nick has a cabin. Yet George now has 10.00 þ, Nick has 15.00 þ and Lou-Anne has 20.00 þ. Now everyone has accommodation but those that provide accommodation could still buy more accommodation. George could buy from Nick another cabin, Nick could buy from Lou-Anne a bungalow for 15.00 þ. Lou-Anne could buy a house from George for 20.00 þ. So now George has a house and a cabin, Nick has a cabin and a bungalow. Lou-Anne has a bungalow and a house. Yet they would also have:

George-   20.00 þ

Nick-   10.00 þ

Lou-Anne-   15.00 þ

As we can see, the workers in the accommodational sector get more and more accommodation as money is just exchanged back and forth between them. To overcome this, the central bank could introduce the accommodational markdown. Basically for each transaction in the accommodational sector a percentage is deducted from the revenue of the seller. It is not kept by anyone but simply destroyed; put out of circulation.

So let's retrace our steps to the point where the workers in the materialist sector and governmental sectors purchase accommodation. Sue and John have a hut. Sam and Joanne have a lodge. Peter and Kate have a cabin.

John sets the accommodational markdown at 50%. This may seem like a lot but usually the higher the accommodational markdown the more offset the accommodational overflow calamity is.

Nick would receive 0.5 x 10.00þ = 5.00 þ

Lou-Anne would receive 0.5 x 16.00 þ = 8.00 þ

George would receive 0.5 x 20.00 þ = 10.00 þ

So now Nick, Lou-Anne and George buy accommodation. Nick could buy a hut for 5.00 þ. He buys it from Lou-Anne who receives 0.5 x 5.00 þ = 2.50 þ Lou-Anne could buy a lodge for 8.00þ. She buys it from George who receives 0.5 x 8.00 þ = 4.00 þ. George could buy a cabin for 10.00 þ. He buys it from Nick who receives 0.5 x 10.00 þ = 5.00 þ

Now Nick has a hut, Lou-Anne has a lodge and George has a cabin. In terms of money, Nick has 5.00 þ, George has 4.00 þ and Lou-Anne has 2.50 þ

At this point Nick could buy another hut for 5.00 þ. However, neither George nor Lou-Anne can buy anything because the cheapest thing (a hut) costs more money than they have. Suppose that Nick buys a second hut from Lou-Anne. Now Lou-Anne has 5.00 þ. She buys a hut for 5.00 þ from Nick who receives 2.50 þ (50% of 5.00þ). Now none of the three accommodational sector workers can afford anything.

This concludes our examination of a small island society. We discussed the major points that are necessary for an understanding of our system. With a concrete example such as this, the system should seem a bit clearer.

Perfect Competition

Perfect competition is a type of market condition. It occurs when there are many sellers, the product is practically the same and there are no barriers to a firm's entry. Although a perfectly competitive market exists in the consumerist economy it is a little bit different than its counterpart in the free-market economy.

We talk about wheat. We assume that wheat is not a final product but an input used to make bread and other baked goods. It is easy to produce large quantities of wheat if the growing conditions are adequate.

Supply and demand rule the free-market. In a free-enterprise perfectly competitive market, the price per bushel of wheat and the quantity of bushels sold are determined by the interaction of wheat makers and wheat buyers. Individual wheat buyers and wheat makers have little to say about how much wheat is produced or the price at which it is sold.

Now let's turn to the consumerist perfectly competitive market. The price per bushel is set by the central bank and the quantity bought is determined by the desires of the consumerists. Let's say the central bank sets the price of wheat at 0.50 þ per bushel. The wheat is in the same family as oat and barley- the grain family. Therefore oat and barley also cost 0.50 þ per bushel. Wheat, oat and barley producing firms compete with each other. This is reasonable to assume as the cost to grow a square meter of wheat is comparable to that of growing a square meter of oat or barley. Since wheat and other grains are inputs, they are in the accommodational sector and their price is in Ignits.

How much a wheat producing firm sells depends on how much a baker buys, how much a mill processes and how much wheat made baked goods consumerists buy. When a baker buys wheat (supposing it is already ground) he must chose among various wheat producing firms. His choice is subtle since all wheat is more or less the same. He would pick based on proximity to his bakery- which should minimize transportation costs. If he finds the flour from one firm to be contaminated and dirty at one time, afterwards he might choose a different wheat firm. He may be loyal to a particular brand. He may associate a particular brand with superior or inferior quality. We discuss brands more fully in another section.

In a perfectly competitive consumerist market prices per quantity are fixed (assuming they are in the accommodational sector). The quantity purchased is ultimately dependent on the desires of the consumerists. These are the major differences between the free-enterprise and consumerist perfectly competitive markets.

Monopolies

One of the major problems of the free-enterprise economy is the existence of monopolies. Although a lot of resources have been implemented to reduce the existence of monopolies, their presence is one of the main arguments against the free-enterprise system.

By monopoly we mean a firm that is the only one that produces the same type of good or service or a close substitute to it. In the free-enterprise system, a monopoly can charge any price that it wants to for its goods or services. However in a monopoly not all the gains from trade are realized. We say there is "dead weight loss".

There are several important problems that a monopoly has. It has market power and thus charges prices that are too high. The gains from trade are not extracted since the price a monopoly charges exceeds the marginal cost of production. There is market failure due to deadweight loss. The monopolist is unable to obtain the maximum profit possible. Finally the monopolist makes more money than he would if the market were competitive. All this hurts the consumerists.

In accommodation based consumerism these problems disappear. The price function for the good or service that a monopolist can charge is set by the central bank. All inputs are fixed by the central bank. Furthermore, monopolies cannot exist in the laissez-faire sector. They exist in the GAM sectors.

Here's an example for a monopolist of hydro-electricity. The central bank sets his price function at 0.10 þ /kWh. If one of his customers uses 1000 kWh the customer would have to pay 100.00 þ. The monopolist of hydro would receive-assuming an accommodational markdown of 25% = only, 75.00þ. The monopolist cannot charge any more than the price function set by the central bank. In this setup, all the problems of monopoly that exist in a free-market economy completely disappear.

Another alternative possibility to combat the problem of existence of monopolies with excessive market power is to ensure that monopoly markets are under the control of command partition firms. So firms like for example cable companies and electricity providers will be operated by the command partition.

As we saw, the free-market system can have monopolists. They are a major problem. In consumerism these problems do not exist.

Oligopolies

Here we investigate the nature of an oligopoly. By oligopoly we mean a market in which there are a few firms that sell products that are quite similar. Examples of oligopoly markets include markets for automobiles and television sets.

In the free-market system there are two models of oligopolies – the Bertrand model and the Carnot model. In the Bertrand model, firms compete with each other in terms of prices. In the Carnot model, firms compete with each other in terms of quantity supplied to markets. We will not go too deeply into these models. They are well known and taught in most economic courses.

In the accommodation based consumerist economy, oligopolies can be seen in light of the Consumerist model. In this model the oligopolies compete in terms of quality of their products while the prices of the products remain fixed. This is a form of quality selection. The idea is that firms compete and the most successful ones in terms of quality flourish while the rest stagnate.

We show the Consumerist model in the market for batteries. We have five battery producing firms. Let's call the firms – firm 1, firm 2, firm 3, firm 4 and firm 5. We are discussing the family of batteries to which AA size batteries belong. The central bank set the price of the batteries at 1.00 ʘ each.

How will the battery firms compete under the Consumerist model? Firm 1 makes batteries that last 800 hours. In response firm 2 makes batteries that last 900 hours. Firm 3's batteries last 950 hours. Firm 4's batteries last 1000 hours. Firm 5 makes their batteries rechargeable so that they can be recharged after 500 hours. Firm 1 makes their batteries also rechargeable. Their batteries can be recharged after 600 hours. Firm 3 makes batteries that last 1500 hours. Firm 4 makes their batteries with an automatic tester that tells the consumerist how much electricity is still left in the battery. Thus they compete.

But where will this end? –It doesn't! It is only limited by the current state of technology. As new inventions, innovations and ways of doing things are created, batteries will keep on getting better and better and better…

Here's another example from the family where personal computers belong. We have four computer making firms. Let's call them – firm 1, firm 2, firm 3 and firm 4. The central bank sets the price of a computer at 800.00 ʘ. Firm 1 makes their computers function at 2.5 GHz. Firm 2 makes their computers function at 3.00 GHz while firm 3 makes their computers work at 4.00 GHz. Firm 4 makes their computers function at 4.00 GHz but they have the most advanced sound card. Firm 1 makes their computers function at 4.10 GHz and these computers have the most advanced video card. Thus they compete.

This competition, like the one for batteries, also doesn't really end. It is limited by the current state of technology.

In the oligopoly market in the consumerist system, firms compete under the Consumerist model. Firms making similar things produce more exciting products while the price of the products remains fixed. The Consumerist model ensures constant unabated progress limited only by technology.

General Microeconomic Functions of Business in the Natural Partition

In order to provide our consumerists with goods and services, we must have a way of doing so. This method must be both efficient and productive and produce goods and services of the highest quality (those most desired by our consumerists). The idea of a *firm* is a good one as it adheres to the above guidelines. A firm can be defined as "an organization that transforms inputs into goods and services that people want."

There are two types of firms in the natural partition of our system. They differ in who "owns" the firm. A firm owned by one person is called a "sole propertiorship" and a firm owned by many is called a "corporation". These two terms are similar in meaning to their free-market counterparts and finding different names would only lead to confusion.

Let's discuss the nature of the owner. The owner is he who knows the art of money making. The art of money making involves obtaining more money than before. Someone who is skilled at ending up with more money than he had before has the art of money making. A pharmacist knows the art of selling drugs. A doctor knows the art of medicine. However they both also know the art of money making as they are usually rich. A musician plays music for the love of playing music and for making money. However he must love music because there are other professions with equally high pay. A surgeon performs surgery out of the pleasure of saving lives and making money. However he must love saving lives or else he would have found another equally high paying career.

Now the owner makes money for the sole purpose and satisfaction of making money. He has the soul of a money lover. He praises prosperity and is always looking to make money and spending as little of it as possible.

We need to ask how is a man with the love of money found? How do we get owners? How do owners come about?

There are three ways an owner can become one:

A) He can buy a firm

B) He can buy the firm from someone else

C) He can buy enough stock to own the firm

For path A, a would-be owner can obtain enough money from banks, stocks and bonds or personal savings to set up a firm. For path B, a would-be owner can obtain enough money from personal savings, banks, bonds and stocks to purchase a firm from another owner. For path C, a would-be owner can obtain enough money from banks and personal savings to purchase >50% of a firm's stock.

A firm must have an incentive to produce. One of the best incentives offered by an economy is profit. The company that can make its products more efficiently will sell more of them. The company that makes its products of best quality (the most desired by consumerists) will make profit. This profit is in terms of Ignits (þ).

Let's focus on the sole propertiorship. The essence of a sole propertiorship is that it has one owner. This owner has supreme command of the firm.

It is the owner who makes money when the firm is productive and efficient. All other workers do specific jobs and are paid by the owner for doing so. The wages and salaries of workers are prescribed by the central bank. The owner is one of the few people in the accommodation sector of the economy who makes independent profit; that is profit not dictated by the central bank (the others are bond and stock holders). He makes or loses money based on the performance of his firm. This point is necessary to encourage more firms to spring up. It is the job of the owner to run the company.

This treatise does not explain exactly how an owner must manage his firm because doing so would make the management of the firm inflexible. Running a firm is an art and there is not a single correct way to run a business.

The owner of a sole propertiorship tries to make his firm earn a profit (in Ignits or Fortals). He does this by picking what the firm will do and how it will do it. He manipulates inputs (capital, labour, land and technology). He is in charge of recruiting or hiring other workers. He decides exactly how his firm is to be run. He is, however, guided by the principal of specialization.

The worker who does a particular job which he excels at either through passion, experience or knowledge, will do the job more efficiently and productively than any other worker. A 33 year old man finished a 4 year residency training program in internal surgery. Before doing so he graduated from medical school where he studied for 5 years. A hospital would be wise to hire him to their surgery unit rather than a medical graduate who had a 3 year residency in ophthalmology. However it would be wise to hire the ophthalmologist to the correct unit. By doing so, the two doctors would help more patients than if their placements were reversed. Knowing what you do, you do it well. This is the principal of specialization.

There are several things that an owner has no control over in the consumerist system. These are the pay of the workers, the price of the inputs and the price of the finished goods (in the accommodational sector). The owner has control over these things in the laissez-faire sector, however.

Now let's look at a corporation. The owner of a corporation is the individual or group that has 50% or more of the shares of the firm. The share holders congregate and vote to pick a grand owner. This person makes all the decisions for the corporate firm that an owner of a sole propertiorship would do. He is called the *Supreme Firm Director*. The share holders vote him in according to the proportion of shares they own. The more shares one has, the more influential he is in the firm. The person with more than 50% of the shares could vote anyone in as supreme firm director (including themselves). At anytime whatsoever the share holders can vote the supreme firm director out- provided the share holders vote that way. Therefore the supreme firm director answers to the shareholders and cannot make foolish managerial and administrative decisions for fear of losing his or her job.

We should mention something about stocks and owners. Suppose that there are 3 groups who own stock of company ABC. Company ABC issues 1000 shares. Group A owns 550 of them, group B owns 300 and group C owns 150 of them. Since group A has >50% of the shares, they can pick the Supreme Firm Director. They pick Bob. One of Bob's first tasks is to issue 1000 more shares. When they are issued group A has priority in buying them. Afterwards groups B and C can buy shares. These groups can buy as many shares until they own the same percentage of firm ABC as before or they may buy less. So if group A had 550/1000 x 100% = 55%, they can buy the equivalent of 55% of the new stocks (or less). The same applies to firms B and C. What is not bought can be bought by other investors.

Generally speaking, firms in the natural partition try their best to earn a high profit (in line with the stipulations discussed in this treatise regarding the GAM sectors). To do so they must sell as many goods as possible and provide as many services as possible. Firms in the natural partition that have a positive, high profit are those that survive the market. It is as if, consumerists vote on which natural partition firms thrive every time that they purchase a good or service at that particular firm.

In a corporation there may be minor firm directors for more specific areas of operation. These may include advertising, hiring, transport, input purchasing, customer relations, etc. The Supreme Firm Director still has jurisdiction over everything. This is similar to a military hierarchy where we have a Supreme Commander who answers to the people (citizens, as we are assuming a democracy). Under him we have field marshals and generals. Then we have corporals and captains. The whole setup is necessary so that the Supreme Firm Director does not need to worry about very particular things-like which window to clean (this is the janitor's job). The whole setup of the firm is also guided by the principal of specialization. Whatever the firm does, it strives to assign tasks to workers as to maximize productivity and efficiency.

The Supreme Firm Director makes the important decisions within the corporation. He is always trying to please the share holders, increasing their profits. Some of his jurisdiction includes the issuing of bonds and stocks. He is responsible for decisions regarding the construction of new buildings and infrastructure. He has control over employees and capital. He decides what and how a firm produces. He can't control input prices, wages and product prices, stock prices and the price of his final goods and services (assuming we are dealing with the accommodational sector).

We saw how the two types of firms, the sole propertiorship and the corporation, operate. We explored the nature of the owner. We examined the role of the Supreme Firm Director, noting his responsibilities and limitations.

General Microeconomic Functions of Business in the Command Partition

We have previously described how businesses are organized in the natural partition. Now we describe how they are set up in the command partition. Although there are some parallels in the way businesses are organized in the two partitions, there are, however, some key differences.

In both partitions, businesses are arranged into firms. However, who owns these firms and how they are organized differs. Firms in the command partition are run by the *Human Resource Management Commission* and there is a role for a "supreme firm director" when we are dealing with corporations under the command partition.

The Human Resource Management Commission is the highest level in the Command Partition. At the highest level it determines what firms are to be created in the command partition. It decides whether to setup a doughnut shop, a car dealership or car factory, an apartment building, a bookstore, a shoe factory, a gas station, a supermarket, etc. Now if the whole economy were organized this way there would be problems regarding allocation of resources. For example, the firm would produce things that no one needs and not produce things that are needed. However we are dealing with a very small population of the economy. That is, those in the socialist labor pool. These are people that are unemployed and would not being doing much anyways. Perhaps this is 3% or 5 % of the work force.

The human resource commission can decide to build things that are normally in a state of shortage in the natural partition. For example, if a study comes out through the census or another source that there is a severe apartment rental shortage, the human resource management commission can have several apartment buildings built.

In order for a firm in the command partition to start up, it needs a source of capital to build infrastructure, equipment, and all items to begin producing. It gets this money in one of two ways. Either it borrows money from a private bank or sells bonds. Alternatively, it could receive direct funding from a level of government as the profits from a command partition firm go to the government eventually anyway to pay for social services.

After the human resource commission creates a firm to produce goods or provide services, it hires workers for the firm. It would do so so as to hire as many people as possible. The people that are hired are from the socialist labor pool. The human resource commission tries to find a job for all in the socialist labor pool, by trying to match a worker's skill set, education, experience, abilities, etc with the jobs the human resource commission creates by producing firms. The jobs that are created do not have to be purchased like they are in the natural partition since the purpose of selling jobs is to give an incentive for employers to hire more workers. This is not necessary in the command partition. Workers working in the command partition receive a special payment and this they have to partially repay so that paradoxically, they are discouraged from being in the command partition and they move to the natural partition.

The human resource commission would try to create as many firms as possible so that it has placements for auxiliary workers. Firms are run by someone from the human resource management commission and sometimes several firms that are not competing with each other may have the same person running them. This person is analogous to the Supreme Firm Director that we discussed in the section of running businesses in the natural partition. This Supreme Firm Director hires minor firm directors for more specific duties and below these are even more specific duties. This in some ways resembles a military hierarchy. Those in the human resource department of the firm have the responsibility of hiring as many workers for the more specific duties while in some sense keeping the firm profit maximizing. Note that the human resource department and the human resource management commission are two entirely different entities. The first are the employees of a firm who employ workers for a particular firm. The latter are the institution that work in the command partition trying to create as many profit seeking firms as possible. To fill positions requiring skills like marketing and money management, the supreme firm director should hire university or college educated graduates who know how to handle the position but are currently unemployed.

For the case of a fast food restaurant, we would have someone from the human resource management commission act as the owner or supreme firm director of several outlets. He would hire a human resource agent that would oversee hiring for several outlets. It would be this person's duty to hire cashiers, bakers, waitresses and sandwich makers. The more workers employed the better as long as 1) the firm still makes a profit and 2) the workers know what they are doing.

The command partition extends into services. We could have workers (level 1 workers) assigned to a specific section of street and it would be their duty to make sure it is clean and garbage free. Then there would be other workers (level 2 workers) ensuring that these workers are doing their job properly and another level (level 3 workers) making sure these level 2 workers do their job well. This paradigm of several levels of workers extends throughout the command partition.

In general the command partition works like this: The human resource management commission creates many firms whether services or good producing that lie in the materialist, accommodational and laissez-faire sectors. These firms are run by a member of the human resource commission known as the supreme firm director (similar to the setup in the natural partition). He hires a human resource agent who hires workers for all other positions, maximizing employment and profit.

One major question we need to discuss is "how is the Human Resource Management Commission created?" It is created similarly to the central bank where there are 102 members. We will not limit the human resource management commission to a particular number of people. It could be 500 or several thousand members.

This is the general organizational framework of businesses in the command partition. As we saw, firms in this partition try to maximize profit while hiring as many workers as possible. Although there are many, many firms in this partition, they are organized along similar lines.

The Functioning of a Car Factory

Here we examine how a car factory operates. By car factory we mean a firm that takes inputs, labor, steel, machines and glass and uses these to produce automobiles. These automobiles are not sold directly to the public but to car dealerships.

Our car factory's name will be Super Plus Ultimate Motors. Our owner's (entrepreneur's) name is John Smith. In order to start his company he issues shares at the consumerist stock market. The central bank has set the Consumerist Universal Stock Price at 10.00 þ per share. He issues 2 000 000 shares and keeps 1 000 000 for himself. Thus he earns 10 000 000.00 þ. In order to issue shares he must buy bankruptcy insurance. In case his firm bankrupts and he is unable to pay back the stock owners how much they own of their stock, the bankruptcy insurance firm pays them their value of the stock they have. This is so that stock investing is risk free. So if a company bankrupts each stock owner is paid 10.00 þ x the number of stock he owns (except for John who didn't buy any). In exchange for this protection, the bankruptcy insurance company collects a premium from the firm. The car company found a premium that is set at 0.25% per month of the money covered. So every month John's firm must pay 1 000 000.00 þ x 0.0025 = 25 000þ to the bankruptcy insurance firm.

Now that he has some money, he can start building his company. We assume that he does not have to build the factory from scratch. He simply buys the land and factory building from a previous owner. The land and building cost 6 000 000.00 þ. The accommodational markdown in our case is 30%. So the previous owner of the factory and land keeps 4 200 000.00 þ. John decides to make 6 different types of cars: a limousine, an SUV, a minivan, an economy car, another economy car and a poor quality car. They all cost the same to sell- 12 000.00 þ.

The government sets the capital investment transfer (CIT) at 0.1%. Since John paid 6 000 000.00 þ for the land and building, the government would give him 6 000 000.00 þ x 0.001 =   6000.00 þ.

John has to hire workers and purchase equipment to make his cars. His sunk costs are 850 000.00 þ. They include car assembly machines, computers and equipment. As for workers, he hires 1000 of them. They each earn 12.00 þ per hour and their JCP is 600.00 þ. The AYIP is 5000 %. These values are set by the central bank. They have contracts lasting one year.

Let's calculate how many hours they will work a year:

600.00þ hr/12.00 þ x 50 = 2 500 hours per year or 48 hours a week.

From selling his job contracts, John earns 1000 x 600.00þ = 600 000.00þ. Each worker is paid every two weeks (48 hours x 2 x 12.00 þ/hour = 1 152.00þ). In total this would cost 1000 workers x 2 500 hrs/year x 12.00þ /hour = 30 000 000.00 þ.

To encourage Super Plus Ultimate Motors to hire more workers, the central bank sets the Employment Reimbursement Transfer (ERT) at 0.1%. So the government would give Super Plus Ultimate Motors 30 000 000.00 x 0.01 = 30 000.00 þ.

In case the firm bankrupts, John must purchase bankruptcy insurance on these wages. The monthly bankruptcy insurance premium is 0.25%. So John must pay 30 000 000.00 þ x 0.0025 = 75 000.00 þ/month to his bankruptcy insurance company.

Now John can make cars. Below is a list of the variable costs associated with making each type of car (this includes costs of production like steel, plastic, electricity, rubber, paint)

A) Limousine-   3 000.00 þ

B) S.U.V.   2 500.00 þ

C) Minivan-   2 000.00 þ

D) 1st economy car-1000.00 þ

E) 2nd economy car-1 100.00 þ

F) Poor quality car- 500.00 þ

Initially the car factory makes 100 of each car in 1 month and ships them to car dealers (we don't worry about shipping costs as they are paid by the car dealership)

Let's see the profit:

Limousine-   100 x (12 000.00 þ– 3 000.00 þ) = 900 000.00 þ

S.U.V.   100 x (12 000.00 þ – 2 500.00 þ) = 950 000.00 þ

Minivan-   100 x (12 000.00 þ– 2 000.00 þ) = 1 000 000.00 þ

1st economy car-   100 x (12 000.00 þ– 1 000.00 þ) = 1 100 000.00 þ

2nd economy car-   100 x (12 000.00 þ – 1 100.00 þ) = 1 090 000.00 þ

Poor Quality Car-   100 x (12 000.00 þ– 500.00 þ) = 1 150 000.00 þ

For a total profit of 6 190 000.00 þ. To encourage the firm to stay in our country and do business here, the government sets the Profit Reward Transfer (PRT) at 0.05 %. Thus the government pays the firm 6 190 000.00 þ x 0.0005 = 3 095.00 þ.

However in month 2 the demand for these cars is a lot different. Instead of 100 cars from each kind, the demand for each car is now the following:

Limousine-   250 cars

S.U.V. -   180 cars

Minivan -   100 cars

1st economy car 65 cars

2nd economy car 68 cars

Poor quality car 12 cars

Let's calculate the profit:

Limousine-   250 x (12 000.00þ – 3 000.00þ) = 2 250 000.00 þ

S.U.V.   180 x (12 000.00þ – 2 500.00þ) = 1 710 000.00 þ

Minivan   100 x (12 000.00þ – 2 000.00þ = 1 000 000.00 þ

1st economy car 65 x (12 000.00 þ– 1 000.00þ) = 715 000.00 þ

2nd economy car 68 x (12 000.00þ – 1 100.00þ) = 741 200.00 þ

Poor quality car   12 x (12 000.00þ– 500.00þ) = 138 000.00 þ

The total profit is 6 554 000.00 þ. With a PRT of 0.05%, the government pays the firm 3277.00þ.

In this way Super Plus Ultimate Motors continues to make cars, the kind being made being dictated by the consumerists. If Super Plus Ultimate Motors thinks that they can make the highest profit per car selling the poor quality car, then consumerists will simply buy better cars (from a different car firm). Super Plus Ultimate Motors is not stuck just selling limousines and S.U.V.'s. They can add fantastic features to their cars (like DVD players, air conditioning, new safety features, more leg room, etc.) Suppose that they add some of these features to their "poor quality" car and its variable production costs rise from 500.00 þ per car to 800.00 þ per car. If consumerists see this new "poor quality" car as a contender to the limousine, then Super Plus Ultimate Motors will make more of them and sell more of them.

The car factory does not report its earnings to the central bank- its contribution to the GDCP- as it is not directly involved in the materialist sector final goods sale. However the car dealership that buys cars from Super Plus Ultimate Motors would have to do this.

Let's find out how our firm did in a year. Let's compare their profits and costs. In a year they sold the following amounts of cars to dealerships:

Limousine-   15 000

S.U.V. -   12 000

Minivan-   10 000

1st economy car 750

2nd economy car 780

Poor Quality Car 100

So the yearly profits would be:

Limousine   15 000 x (12 000.00 þ – 3 000.00 þ) = 135 000 000.00 þ

S.U.V.   12 000 x (12 000.00 þ – 2 500.00 þ) = 114 000 000.00 þ

Minivan   10 000 x (12 000.00 þ– 2 000.00 þ) = 100 000 000.00 þ

1st economy car 750 x (12 000.00 þ – 1 000.00 þ) = 8 250 000.00 þ

2nd economy car 780 x (12 000.00 þ – 1 100.00 þ) = 8 502 000.00 þ

Poor quality car 100 x (12 000.00 þ– 500.00 þ) = 1 150 000.00 þ

= 366 902 000.00 þ

With a PRT of 0.05% the government would give Super Plus Ultimate Motors, 366 902 000.00 þ x 0.0005 = 183 451.00 þ

The company earned 600 000.00 þ from selling job contracts.

Let's summarize the costs:

Land + factory cost 6 000 000.00 þ. We calculated the reimbursement from the government, assuming CIT = 0.1%, to be 6 000.00 þ

Wages = 2 500 hours/year x 1000 workers x 12.00 þ/hour = 30 000 000.00 þ

Sunk costs are 850 000.00 þ

The bankruptcy insurance firm must be paid 25 000.00 þ/month for 12 months for stock + 75 000.00 þ/month for 12 months for wages. This is a total of 300 000.00 þ + 900 000.00 þ = 1 200 000.00 þ

So the firm made:

366 902 000.00 þ

+ 600 000.00 þ

+ 183 451.00 þ

+ 6 000.00 þ

-30 000 000.00 þ

-850 000.00 þ

-1 200 000.00 þ

- 6 000 000.00 þ

= 329 641 451.00 þ

John reinvests 29 641 451.00 þ back into the factory. As for the share holders, they earn 300 000 000.00 þ/ 2 000 000 = 150 þ. This turns out to be a good investment. For investing 10.00 þ in a share, an investor earns 150.00 þ per year for every share bought. This is a profit of (150 – 10)/10 = 1 400 % per year.

Each month the investor earns 150.00 þ/12 = 12.50 þ. This is definitely a good investment. As for John he owns 1 000 000 of the original 2 000 000 shares issued. He pockets 150 000 000.00þ

We saw how a car factory would operate under a consumerist system. We took the case of Super Plus Ultimate Motors and analyzed how they would go about making cars. We compared the losses they incurred with their profits to see how they would stand up in an economy.

The Functioning of a Wheat Farm

Here we will investigate the operation of a wheat producing firm. That is, a firm whose objective is to convert agricultural land and seeds into wheat.

Our farm is run by farmer Bob. Bob has come across 10 000.00 þ. He wants to become a farmer; a wheat farmer. We will follow the farm for 1 year. First he needs agricultural land. Agricultural land costs 5.00 þ per square meter. Farmer Bob wants 10 square kilometers of land. He needs to pay 50 000.00 þ for this. He is forced to borrow from a private bank. He borrows 40 000.00 þ at 5% interest (simply compounded yearly). So now he owns land. The Interest Rate Stimulus (IRS) is set at 0.5 %

Next he needs machines, storage facilities, seed and farming equipment. This costs him another 15 000.00 þ. The government sets the Capital Investment Transfer (CIT) at 0.1%. Thus farmer Bob earns from the government, (40 000.00 þ + 15 000.00 þ) x 0.001 = 55 þ

However he also needs workers. He needs 50 farm hands (people who will collect the wheat, plant the seeds, move it, package it, sort it and get it ready for transportation). All these jobs belong to the same family- the same wage function applies to all of them as they are all similar enough. The family that they belong to is the "farm technicians" family. The central bank sets the wage function at 5.00 þ/hour. The job contract is 2 000.00 þ. The contract lasts for 1 year. The Adjusted Yearly Income Percentage is 1200%. To calculate the number of hours a worker works during the time of the contract we use the formula:

=PTC[JCP(n) x hr/w x AYIP]

=1[2000.00 þ x 1 hour /5.00þ x 12] = 4 800 hours

Each worker would work 4800 hours in a year. Each worker would work 312 days a year (assuming he works 6 days a week, including holidays). It is assumed that each week he would work the same amount of hours. Every day the worker works 4800hours/312 = 15.33 hours or 15 hours and 20 minutes.

Farmer Bob sells jobs to 50 farming technicians. He picks the most qualified people to work for him; i.e. those with some kind of experience in farming or those that are hard working. Farmer Bob thus sells 50 job contracts. Each is worth 2 000.00 þ. Thus he earns 50 x 2 000.00 þ = 100 000.00 þ for his business.

The government sets the Employment Reimbursement Transfer (ERT) at 0.1%. We know that the 50 workers would work 4 800 hours in a year for 5.00 þ/hour. So each year the government gives farmer Bob 50 x 4 800 hours x 5.00 þ/hour x 0.001 = 1200.00 þ.

If Bob bankrupts he must pay his workers how much they would have earned if they worked the length of the entire contract. Thus in the case he bankrupts, he may not be able to pay his workers how much they deserve. He needs to buy bankruptcy insurance. The bankruptcy insurance premium rate is 0.25% per month. Let's calculate how much he needs to pay the bankruptcy insurance firm each month. The workers could work 4800 hours during their contract. There are 50 of them and each of them is paid 5.00 þ per hour. Thus he must pay the insurance firm 0.0025 x (4800 x 50 x 5.00þ) = 3 000.00 þ/month.

In February Bob gets his field ready for plantation. In May he starts planting wheat (actually his farm hands do this). Farmer Bob organizes them so that all of them have a job at all points in time- they are always doing something and none of them is idle.

Every two weeks, each of the 50 workers earns his paycheck. Let's calculate this. A worker works 15.33 hours a day for 6 days a week. In 2 weeks, this is 12 days. The worker is paid 5.00 þ/hour. Every two weeks, each worker earns 12 x 15.33 hours x 5.00 þ/hour = 919.80 þ

During the summer the wheat grows. Each square meter of land can yield 5 bushels of wheat. The central bank sets the price of grain crops, which include oats and barley, at 100.00 þ per bushel.

Initially farmer Bob pays his worker's wages using the money he earned selling job contracts. Eventually he needs to borrow from the bank. Let's calculate how much money he has to pay his workers at the end of the year. Each worker earns 919.80 þ every two weeks. There are 26 two week periods in a year and there are 50 workers. At the end of the year, farmer Bob must pay 1 200 000.00 þ for his workers. When a worker receives his paycheck he keeps all of it. He doesn't have to pay any tax on income or give anything to unemployment insurance. It is now August. We must also calculate other costs. The other costs include water for wheat, pesticides and other variable costs. For the year they amount to 2 000.00 þ. All other costs- fixed costs- which include machines, equipment, storage space, etc, have already been counted at the beginning of the analysis.

The harvest occurs in October. All farm technicians focus on harvesting wheat. Since there are 50 of them, no extra help is needed. There are 10 000 square meters of land and each square meter yields 5 bushels of wheat. However only 9 500 square meters of land yielded good crops- the other 500 square meters didn't produce anything that grew too well. Thus 9 500 x 5 = 47 500 bushels of wheat were harvested.

The wheat is needed by bakeries and other firms that require wheat as an input. We assume, for simplicity, that wheat processing into flour is carried out in a bakery. Farmer Bob does not need to grind it nor bring it to a mill. The firm that needs wheat buys 40 000 bushels of wheat. Each bushel costs 100.00 þ per bushel. Farmer Bob earns 4 000 000.00 þ

Now what to do with the remaining 7 500 bushels of wheat? In a free-market society the farmer would destroy it so as to artificially raise the price of wheat. However farmer Bob needs not worry about the price of his wheat. He trades with the United States. In the United States let's assume that a bushel of wheat costs $125.00. The exchange rate is $0.50/þ. Farmer Bob sells 7 500 bushels of wheat to the United States and the Americans pay $125.00 x 7 500 = $ 937 500.00. This is equivalent to $937 500.00 x $1.00/0.50 þ = 1 875 000.00 þ. 750 000.00 þ go to farmer Bob and 1 125 000.00 þ go to the consumerist trade pool. Thus in the end farmer Bob earns 750 000.00 þ + 4 000 000.00 þ = 4 750 000.00 þ selling wheat.

Now it's December. Let's calculate to see how farmer Bob did financially. He earned 4 750 000.00 þ selling wheat and 100 000.00 þ selling job contracts, for a total of 4 850 000.00 þ The CIT made him 55.00 þ and the ERT made him 1200.00 þ. He started out with 10 000.00 þ. He borrowed 40 000.00 þ from the bank at 5 % interest which equals 42 000.00 þ at the end of the year. He borrowed 15 000 þ at 5% interest from the bank for storage, seeds and equipment. This amounts to 15 750.00 þ. He must pay his workers 1 200 000.00 þ. To pay them he borrowed this money from the bank at 5% interest. This equals 1 260 000.00 þ. For every situation he borrowed, the government helps out with 0.5 % of the loan (the IRS) so essentially his interest rate is really 4.5 %. The bank receives loan payments as if the interest rate were 5 %. This should help Bob with running his business. The bankruptcy insurance payments amount to 12 x 3 000.00 þ = 36 000.00 þ When farmer Bob pays all the debts we mentioned above, he still has a surplus of 3 507 505.00 þ. Let's say that the Profit Reward Transfer (PRT) is 0.001 %, Then on top of this, farmer Bob also earns 3 507.50 þ.

We saw how a firm, in particular a wheat firm, would operate. We encountered the expenses and sources of revenue that such a firm would likely have. Most firms in the agricultural part of the economy would operate similarly to our above analysis.

Functioning of a Real Estate Company

By real estate we mean property in the form of land and living quarters. By real estate company, we mean a firm that buys and sells land and accommodation. The real estate company, which operates in the accommodational sector, using Ignits, makes money after a real estate transaction between two consumerists- in this case real estate owners. A real estate agent earns a commission on every sale. In this section we discuss how a real estate firm functions.

The real estate company brings sellers and buyers in the real estate part of the economy together, trading land and living quarters. Here's an example. A consumerist has a house costing 150 000.00 þ The house has a price function: w100.00 þ + y 1000.00 þ + z 5000.00 þ + b 10 000.00 þ; where w stands for number of square feet, y stands for number of washrooms, z stands for number of bedrooms and b stands for number of floors. This house is owned by a consumerist named Matt. It is worth 150 000.00 þ because it has 3 washrooms, 4 bedrooms, 3 floors and 970 square feet of space. Matt has a job that pays 10 000.00 þ a month. He has his sights set on a house worth 200 000.00 þ. It has 5 washrooms, 6 bedrooms, 5 floors and 1 150 square feet of living space (an actual price function for housing would be a lot more complicated, factoring in such things as number of windows, size of bedrooms, size of kitchen, presence of garage, etc.)

Matt puts his original 150 000.00 þ house on sale. He hires an agent named Max from a firm called Super Plus Ultimate Real Estate Inc. to sell his house and buy him the new one. The central bank sets a Real Estate Profit Percentage. This is a percentage of the sale or purchase that the real estate firm earns during every transaction. A real estate agent has a wage function from the real estate company that he works for. Let's use examples. The central bank sets the real estate profit percentage at 0.5% of the transaction and the real estate agent's wage function at 0.3y + 7.00þ /hour. Here y represents the real estate profit percentage. Then the real estate agent makes 30% of the real estate profit percentage or 30% of 0.5% of the transaction. He also earns 7.00 þ/hour in addition to that.

Let's go back to our example with Matt. Max sells his house to another consumerist for 150 000.00 þ. This new consumerist's name is Paul. Paul pays 150 000.00 þ (assuming that he has that much) to Matt. Super Plus Ultimate Real Estate Inc. earns 0.5% x 150 000.00 þ = 750.00 þ. They pay Max 30% x 750.00 þ = 225.00 þ. He works 12 hours to sell Matt his house. He earns an additional 7.00þ /hour x 12 hours = 84.00 þ. Max earns 309.00 þ in the transaction. However Matt must lose money due to the accommodational markdown. Let's make it 25% in our example. Therefore Matt only earns 150 000.00 þ – 750.00 þ – 37 312.00 þ = 111 937.00 þ. In this example we did not factor in the property that the house was situated on. When selling a house, the land on which the house is situated is also sold. In this example we make residential land worth 1000.00 þ / square kilometer of land.

Right now Matt has 111 937.00 þ to spend. He wants to buy that 200 000.00 þ house. It is situated on a property of 2 square kilometers. The total price is 202 000.00 þ. Max buys it for Matt. For this service, Matt has to pay Super Plus Ultimate Real Estate Inc. = 0.005 x 202 000.00 þ = 1 010.00 þ. Max earns 0.3 x 1 010.00 þ = 303.00 þ. He works for 12 hours so again he earns 12 hours x 7.00 þ/hour = 84.00 þ

Max earns 387.00 þ in purchasing the house and property for Matt. This comes out of Matt's bank account. 387. 00 þ are deducted from Matt's payment to Super Plus Ultimate Real Estate Inc. which was 1 010.00 þ. 387.00 þ are added to Max's Ignit account.

There's a problem. Matt can't pay the 202 000.00 þ for his new house. He only has 111 937.00 þ – 1 010.00 þ = 110 927.00 þ. He must take out a mortgage. The mortgage rate is not set by the central bank. It involves the Laissez- Faire sector, Fortals and takes into account the Ignit-Fortal exchange mechanism since the prices of real estate are in terms of Ignits. The mortgage rate is how much a home owner must pay the bank (private) each month for the bank giving him money to purchase the house. Matt puts 110 000.00 þ towards his house and takes out a mortgage for 202 000.00 þ -110 000.00 þ = 92 000.00 þ. The mortgage rate is 5%. Since Matt makes 10 000.00 þ per month, his mortgage payments must be less than that each month. (Matt must also pay his bills, buy appliances, home accessories, and enjoy leisure) Thus he chooses a monthly mortgage of 5 000.00 þ. Every month he must pay 5 000.00 þ. He must do this for 19.32 months. We are assuming in this case that 1 ƒ = 1þ and 1þ = 1ƒ

(92 000.00 þ + [92 000.00 þ x 0.05)/5000.00 þ = 19.32

For simplicity in this example we used simple interest although it may be better to use compounded interest.

Let's look at the case of a real estate company aiding in buying and selling land. This is similar to buying and selling housing. We assume a REPP of 0.5% and a real estate wage function of $0.3y + 7.00$ þ per hour. Suppose a farmer wants to buy 500 km^2 of agricultural land. Agricultural land costs 100.00 þ/km^2. There are two farmers here, Ken and Ryan and two real estate agents Jack, hired by Ken and Phil, hired by Ryan. Ken and Jack are doing the buying and Ryan and Phil are doing the selling. Jack buys the farm land from Phil. Ken has to pay 500 km^2 x 100.00 þ/km^2 = 50 000.00 þ to Ryan in order to purchase the land. However he must also pay Jack for his services and the real estate firm which he works for. His real estate firm earns 50 000.00 þ x 0.5% = 250.00 þ and Jack earns 250.00 þ x 0.3 = 75.00 þ and assuming he works 8 hours on this transaction he would earn 75.00 þ + 7.00 þ/hour x 8 hours = 131.00 þ. Ken must pay Jack's real estate firm 250.00 þ for this service.

Assuming Phil also works 8 hours on this transaction, he too would earn 131.00 þ and his real estate firm would earn 250.00 þ. Thus 250.00 þ are deducted from Ryan's bank account. Although Ken pays 50 000.00 þ for the land, due to the accommodational markdown, Ryan only keeps 50 000.00 þ– 250.00 þ– 13 437.00 þ = 37 313.00 þ. So, only 37 313.00 þ are added to his Ignit bank account. He probably does not have enough money to buy this much land. He must buy a mortgage in the same way that Matt did. Each month Ken must pay an amount of money to the bank. This is the interest and the principal from the amount of money that the bank lent him to buy the land.

Finally we look at how the real estate company handles transactions in the business section of the building industry. We look at the purchasing of a functional business. The price of a business is expressed in the *Adjusted Revenue Price*. This is the amount of revenue a business earns in a given amount of time. It is set by the central bank in terms of time. Say the central bank sets it at 2 years. Then the cost of a business is how much revenue it had in a period of 2 years. If a firm has existed for more than 2 years, it would equal its revenue in the last 2 years. If a firm existed less, say only 6 months, it is simply the revenue collected in these 6 months multiplied by 4. This parameter ensures that firms try to be as profitable as possible since the more revenue they accrue, the more money the person or group selling the firm earns upon selling it. Revenue is used instead of profit as the basis of the parameter since if profit were used then firms that had loses in some time (negative profit) would not be able to be sold.

Suppose John wants to buy a pizzeria. The Adjusted Revenue Price (ARP) is set for 1 year. The price of the pizzeria business in question is how much revenue the firm collected in the last year. It made 45 000.00 þ. John hires Max and Super Plus Ultimate Real Estate Inc. Company. In this scenario John took out a business loan from a bank. Max buys the pizzeria from the previous owner for 45 000.00 þ.The real estate company earns 0.5% x 45 000.00 þ– 225.00 þ. Max worked 10 hours and thus earns 0.3 x 225.00 þ + 10 hours x 7.00 þ/hour = 137.50 þ. The previous owner of the pizzeria, after paying the cost of the real estate company, earned only 75% of the sale price due to an accommodational markdown of 25%

There is an important question regarding the real estate firm that we must look at. How does the real estate company make profit? It must pay its agents, advertising costs, office space, office equipment (computers, pencils, and desks). After the firm covers these costs, it makes profit.

We looked at how a real estate company would operate in the accommodation based consumerist economic system. We looked at transactions involving accommodation land and business property. We encountered several parameters that are intrinsic to the buying and selling of real estate.

Functioning of a University

A university is a place of higher education. It is a place where, after high school or college, students go to earn degrees which enable them to obtain the jobs that they desire. Here we will see how a university operates. Let's call our university "Northland University".

We have two choices. A) The university is in the governmental sector or b) the university is in the materialist sector. Whether it is in one or the other is decided by the government. If the university is in the materialist sector then the students who wish to attend it must spend the Norses the central bank granted them. If the university is in the governmental sector, the operation of the university is funded by the Grand Consumerist Tax which is deducted from the Gross Domestic Consumerist Product. We will say that it is in the governmental sector. That is, students do not pay tuition to attend. Rather the government helps to pay for the student's education. To run the university, the government uses money from the GCT and other sources of revenue.

We do not discuss how the university teaches students but how it runs its finances. We divide the operating costs into two types- fixed and variable costs. Fixed costs are sunk. The university pays them once and cannot get the money back. Let's list the fixed costs that the university pays to set up: land, buildings (lecture halls, residencies, professor's offices, and laboratories), equipment (overheads, chalk boards, desks, chairs), books, lab equipment, building accessories, paint, windows, floor, and lamps. In our example these together cost 12 000 000.00 þ

Variable costs are the costs the university incurs every month. The variable costs include: professional salaries (salaries of professors, teaching assistants, janitors and administrators), utilities (electricity, heat), improvements (new computers, new books, new microscopes). In our example these amount to 1 500 000.00 þ/month.

The university has one main source of revenue- government transfers to the university (these come from the GCT among other things). The university could also have corporate sponsors but we ignore this. Now, let's see how the university covers its costs. There are 10 000 students in Northland University. For simplicity let's assume that each student takes 5 courses at the university per year. There is a lot of disappointment in free-market economies with regards exponentially increasing tuition costs. As consumerists, students do not pay any tuition or fee per course. Essentially the government fully pays for a consumerist student's education. Thus education is free. During the 12 months the university's operation costs are 12 000 000.00þ + 12 x 1 500 000.00 þ= 30 000 000.00 þ. Therefore 30 000 000.00þ must come from the GCT and other governmental sources of revenue. The university is not run at the federal level but at the provincial/state level. Let's suppose that the provincial government earned 15 000 000 000.00 Θ. It would allocate 30 000 000.0 Θ of this to the university (Northland University) Thus with the contribution from the GCT, we have 30 000 000.00 Θ. This equals the 30 000 000.00 þ needed to run Northland University.

How is the 30 000 000.00 Θ converted into 30 000 000.00 þ needed to pay for the inputs of the university? When Norses are given to the university or any government enterprise, they are automatically converted to Ignits. When the government gives 30 000 000.00 Θ to Northland this money is, at the private bank, turned into 30 000 000.00 þ. This goes to pay the costs of running the university. During the transaction at the bank in the above case, the amount of Norses is subtracted from the people paying (i.e. the government) and the equivalent number of Ignits is added to Northland University's Ignit bank account at the private bank.

The university strives to attract as many students as possible and to provide the highest standard of education. The government, if it sees that the university is not attracting too many students may decrease the amount of money it gives the university. So suppose a university only has 100 students. In this case the government may severely cut its funding to the university. The university embarks on a policy of attracting new students; i.e. by showing prospective students how excellent their education would be at that university. That way, the government will increase its spending on that university.

A university is an important institution in a well-off society. It is funded through government transfers from the GCT and other sources of revenue. Its ultimate goal is to have a large student population, enjoying a fine educational experience.

Functioning of a Private Bank

A bank is an institution that lends money to agents while at the same time storing people's money. There are two general types of banks in accommodation based consumerism; central and private banks. Here we will talk about private banks. In the free-market economy, the private bank is an important component of the economy. The same is true for consumerism.

Each consumerist is entitled to have a bank account at a private bank. The three major types of bank accounts are Norse accounts, Fortal accounts and Ignit accounts. These can be either in the form of savings accounts, business accounts or college funds. The bank can lend Ignits to businesses and consumerists and this is main source of profit. It lends money at an interest rate set by the central bank. The person who borrows must every once in a while pay back parts of the loan or all of it. The longer he avoids paying the whole amount, the larger the interest payment will be. Here is a simple calculation. Joe borrows 1 000.00 þ from the private bank. The central bank sets the interest rate at 5% and the compounding frequency at one year. The government sets the IRS at 0.1 %. Thus in one year Joe will have to pay back 1000.00 þ x 1.05 = 1 050.00 þ. If it takes him two years to pay he will have to pay 1000.00 þ x $(1.05)^2$ = 1 102.50 þ. Joe wants to pay back this loan as soon as possible. However to help Joe the government can pay 0.1 % of what he had to pay. So if it takes Joe one a year to pay the debt and the bank receives 1 050.00 þ, the government will pay (1000 þ x 1.001) = 1 001.00 þ. 1 001.00 þ – 1000.00 þ = 1.00 þ. And Joe will pay 1 049.00 þ

A private bank cannot spring from nowhere. A private bank must be certified, registered and approved by the central bank. Although the central bank is not the same entity as a private bank, the central bank has some control over each private bank so that they are responsible to consumerists.

In a free-market bank, the bank is constrained in how much it can lend. It has to have a reserve ratio at all times. The reason for this is that if people want cash from the bank, the bank must have enough cash to pay those who want their money out. In consumerism no cash reserve ratio is required. The economy is cashless. All transactions are made in bank books. Therefore there is no limit on how much a private bank can lend to investors.

The bank cannot lend Norses in any way. This is crucial. The amount of Norses in banks must equal the GDCP. This in turn must equal how many goods and services are made in the materialist sector. Norses cannot be simply exchanged at the bank. They can only be exchanged during a transaction involving goods and services. Suppose Joe buys a hot dog. He gives Bob, the hot dog vendor, a check for 2.50 Θ. Upon receiving such a check, the private bank deducts 2.50 Θ from Joe's Norse account and adds 2.50 þ to Bob's Ignit account.

Consider transactions involving utilities. When Bob gives a 100.00 þ check to Northern Utilities for electricity, the private bank deducts 100.00 þ from Bob's Ignit account and adds the utility profit to that company. However with an accommodational markdown of 40%, Northern Utilities receives only 60.00 þ on its account. Similar transactions are possible if individuals use debit cards.

Private banks can offer mortgages to consumerists wishing to buy real estate (accommodation, land). The mortgage rate is not set by the central bank. Also the compounding frequency is not set by the central bank. These are decided by the interaction of private banks and consumerists and mortgages in general operate in the laissez-faire sector. However, the Ignit-Fortal exchange mechanism comes into play as things like accommodation and land are in the accommodational sector and use Ignits. The longer the loan is taken out for, the more the debtor must pay the bank. We don't need to do calculations about this.

In the market system there is the possibility of a bank run. A bank run occurs when depositors demand all the money they have in their bank but the bank does not have this money. The bank then goes out of business and if this happens to many banks we have a catastrophe that leads to a depression. The unique thing about consumerism is that it is impossible for there to be a bank run. The reason for this is that the bank has no cash or coins. They do not exist in our cashless society.

How does the private bank make money? There are no service fees. It earns interest on loans. With no reserve ratio, the private bank has the opportunity to make tremendous profit through lending. In exchange for this the bank manipulates bank accounts, both Ignit, Fortal and Norse.

Private banks have the ability to convert Ignits (but not Norses) into foreign currency. The exchange rate is demonstrated in another section (surplus and shortage). Basically it is just an average of real exchange rates of products exported and imported that give the highest value for the consumerist trade pool.

We have seen how a private bank functions. We have seen its advantages over its free-market counterpart. We have knowledge of how it performs in our society.

Functioning of a Grocery Store

Here we examine the functioning of a particular hypothetical grocery store, let's call it Bob's Ultimate Grocery Mart. By grocery store we mean a retail outlet that sells food items to consumerists. It is owned by a person named Bob.

Here we assume that Bob rented the location of the store and did not build the building from the ground-up. The building he rents cost his landlord 300 000.00 þ. The central bank sets the Rental Equivalence Duration at 18 years. Thus each month, Bob the owner must pay 300 000.00 þ/12/18 = 1 389.00 þ. Bob registers his business with the government. This costs him 25.00 þ. Bob borrows 20 000.00 þ from the private bank at 5% interest (simple) to set up his grocery store and get it running.

Before Bob can hire employees, buy inputs and start selling he must incur sunk costs. We already mentioned that he has a building for which he pays 1 389.00 þ a month. Other sunk costs include lights, cash registers, shelves, counters, fridges and other things that cost him 10 000.00 þ

We assume that he has 2 employees besides himself; a cashier and someone who is both a clerk and a janitor. The cashier's wage is 12.00 þ per hour. The other person's wage is 10.00 þ per hour. The JCP (Job Contract Price) for the cashier is 600.00 þ and the Adjusted Monthly Income Percentage is 400%. The JCP for the clerk is 500.00 þ and his Adjusted Monthly Income Percentage is 400%. Their contracts are for 6 months. Let's find out how many hours each must work during their employment.

Cashier => 600.00 þ hours/12.00 þ x 6 x 400 % = 1 200 hours

The cashier must work 1 200 hours in 6 months. This is equivalent to 44.4 hours per week.

The clerk =>   500.00 þ hours /10.00 þ x 6 x 400% = 1 200 hours

The clerk must work 1 200 hours in 6 months. This is equivalent to 44.4 hours per week.

Bob chooses his employees from the best applicants. They passed high school and had 4 years experience in the tasks they were hired to perform. For now Bob earns 500.00 þ + 600.00 þ = 1 100.00 þ for selling out his job contracts.

Since Bob sells job contracts he must purchase bankruptcy insurance. This is in the event that he goes out of business and is unable to pay his employees the total amount of money they would earn if they worked during the entire length of their contracts. Let's see how much Bob would have to pay his employees at the end of their contracts:

Cashier => 600.00 þ x 6 x 400% = 14 400.00 þ

Clerk => 500.00 þ x 6 x 400% = 12 000.00 þ

This amounts to a total of 26 400.00 þ. The Bankruptcy Insurance Premium is 0.5% per month. Bob has to pay 0.5% x 26 400.00 þ = 132.00 þ each month to his bankruptcy insurance firm company.

To encourage more hiring of employees, the government sets the Employment Reimbursement Transfer (ERT) at 1 %. Thus for the six months the employees are employed the government gives Bob, 26 400.00 þ x 0.01 = 264.00 þ

An actual grocery store would sell hundreds or thousands of goods. We will assume, for simplicity, that Bob is selling only 12 goods. They are milk, cheese (mozzarella), pears, apples, beef(t-bone steak), baguettes, grapes, canned tuna, honey (pasteurized, buckwheat), sausages (pepperoni), pizza (deluxe), soy milk.

We assume that the cost of delivering these goods to the store costs 0.10 þ per unit of good. Now let's examine the prices of the foods Bob sells. These price functions are set by the central bank. Milk and milk substitutes are priced at 1.50 Ө/litre. These include 2% milk, skim milk, chocolate milk and soy milk. In our store this applies to milk and soy milk- they each cost 1.50 Ө/litre. "Cheeses" are priced at 6.00 Ө/kg. Thus our mozzarella costs 6.00 Ө/kg. "Many-seeded fruits from trees" (for lack of a better term) cost 1.00 Ө/ kg. This includes pears and apples (but not grapes). Thus apples and pears cost 1.00 Ө/kg. Beef costs 3.00 Ө/kg. T-bone steak is included in this. Breads cost 1.50 Ө/ unit. This includes baguettes. "Wine fruit" costs 1.00 Ө/kg. This includes grapes. "Canned fish" costs 3.00 Ө/unit. This includes canned tuna. "Food sweeteners" cost 1.50 Ө/ kg. This includes buckwheat honey. Sausages cost 0.50 Ө/kg. This includes pepperoni. Pizzas cost 4.00 Ө/unit. This includes the deluxe pizza. The retail mark-up is 25%. Bob can charge 25 % more than the price he had to pay for these groceries from a farm or factory.

Bob orders:

- 100 L of milk

- 30 kg of cheese

- 40 kg of pears

- 40 kg of apples

- 15 kg of t-bone steak

- 30 baguettes

- 40 kg of grapes

- 50 canned tuna cans

- 35 kg of buckwheat honey

- 125 kg of pepperoni sausage

- 30 pizzas

- 100 L of soy milk

In order to obtain these goods they have to be delivered. Although it would be more efficient if similar goods were delivered together we assume here that each good is delivered independently. The delivery fee depends on how far the good must have traveled. The delivery price (DP) is the cost of delivering a certain good to a destination using the quickest route possible. This is also set by the central bank. The central bank sets it at 5.00 þ + 0.10 þ/km.

For simplicity we assume that Bob sells all the goods that he buys from food producers. Now we find out how much he has to pay in delivery cost, how much revenue he has and what are his profits.

	Delivery	Food Cost	Revenue	Profit
Milk	8.00 þ	150.00 þ	187.50 þ	29.50 þ
Mozzarella	7.00 þ	180.00 þ	225.00 þ	38.00 þ
Pears	6.00 þ	40.00 þ	50.00 þ	4.00 þ
Apples	9.00 þ	40.00 þ	50.00 þ	1.00 þ
T-bone steak	8.00 þ	45.00 þ	56.25 þ	3.25 þ
Baguettes	8.00 þ	45.00 þ	56.25 þ	3.35 þ
Grapes	8.00 þ	40.00 þ	50.00 þ	2.00 þ
Canned Tuna	7.00 þ	100.00 þ	125.00 þ	18.00 þ
Honey	9.00 þ	52.50 þ	65.63 þ	4.13 þ
Pepperoni	8.00 þ	62.50 þ	72.13 þ	1.63 þ
Pizza	8.00 þ	120.00 þ	150.00 þ	22.00 þ
Soy milk	8.00 þ	150.00 þ	187.50 þ	29.50 þ

Therefore Bob has a profit this month of 156.26 þ on the food he sold.

Now Bob has some profit- although this does not seem like much keep in mind that we are only talking about 12 goods. Actually there would be thousands of goods.

Each month Bob has to pay his workers their wages. They are paid every 2 weeks. Since the cashier earns 12.00 þ/hour and he works 44.4 hours per week he earns 1065.60 þ every 2 weeks. Since the clerk earns 10.00 þ per hour and works 44.4 hours per week, he earns 888.00 þ every 2 weeks.

Since in our example Bob sells only 12 goods, our analysis of his monthly profits is warped- he makes less profit selling goods then he needs to pay the running costs of his business. However in a real grocery store, a real owner should make a handsome profit.

The next point is crucial. Every month Bob must give a sort of report to the central bank as to how much he contributed to the Gross Domestic Consumerist Product. His contribution is the *Individual Domestic Consumerist Product*. He has to report how many goods he was able to sell. He also has to report those he didn't sell but could have. In our example the figure is the same as Bob sold all the goods he ordered. He can only report those that were put up for sale this month. He cannot count those that were ordered half a year ago. When counting he takes into account not only the price of the good he bought (from a farm) but its price after the retail mark-up. He does not deduct his shipping costs as this is not supposed to represent his profits. He multiplies the amount of goods he put into a position to sell by their post retail mark-up adjusted price. In our example he simply adds all the numbers in the column labeled "revenues". Bob's contribution to the GDCP is 1 275.29 Ө. He files this number on a form to the central bank. This money is now added to the GDCP contributions of all the other businesses.

Let's talk about another possibility. Suppose Bob wants to expand his business but does not want to deal with a private bank. The price per (consumerist) stock is set by the central bank at 10.00 þ/share. Bob issues 20 000 shares. He keeps 12 000 of them for himself and sells 8 000. He earns 80 000.00 þ for his business. Suppose Bob's grocery store makes a profit of 1 000 000.00 þ. Bob reinvests 20 000.00 þ for further expansion. In this case, the owner of a share would earn 980 000.00þ/20 000 = 49.00 þ. Of course Bob personally earns 980 000 þ x 12 000/20 000 = 588 000.00 þ

Bob needs to take out bankruptcy insurance in case he bankrupts and people are left with worthless shares. The Bankruptcy Insurance Premium is 0.5% per month. Since Bob issues 8 000 shares and each is worth 10.00 þ, he must pay 0.5% x 10.00 þ x 8 000 = 400.00 þ each month to a bankruptcy insurance firm. This is on top of the premium for job contracts he sold before.

There is yet another quick way of getting money for expansion that both help the owner as well as the economy. Bob can sell more job contracts; i.e. hire more people. Although this gives money quickly in the short run it can be quite costly in the long run. Bankruptcy insurance must be bought for these contacts.

Suppose Bob wants to sell his grocery store. The Adjusted Revenue Price Duration is 6 years. In a year, Bob has a revenue of 200 000.00 þ. Thus the price of the grocery store is 1 200 000.00 þ. He finds a buyer and then he retires.

We used a grocery store to represent an average retail firm in the consumerist economy. We saw how it would operate; how it transforms inputs into money. We encountered the problems it could run into and saw how they would be overcome.

Functioning of a Music School

Here we investigate how a school that teaches music would work. We also see another way to teach music- through private lessons. But first let's examine the firm that teaches music. The music school is in the materialist sector.

Our music school is run by a man passionate about music, named Steve, who wants to make money by teaching students music. Steve rents an office in a building complex where there are other offices. Steve's school has several rooms for different students and classes. The land lord paid 800 000.00 þ for the whole building complex. The section Steve wants to occupy is 25% of the whole. The Rental Equivalence Duration is 18 years. Steve must make monthly payments of (800 000.00 þ x 0.25)/ (12 x 18) = 926.00 þ. Steve's sunk costs are about 5 000.00 þ. This includes furnishings, pianos, guitars, a computer as well as paintings of famous people who studied music.

Steve hires 3 music teachers; 1 piano, 1 guitar and 1 violin. The wage function for a teacher of music is 20.00 þ/hour. The JCP is 700.00 þ. The AMIP is 300%. They are given contracts for 6 months. Let's calculate the minimum number of hours each worker should work: 700.00 þ hr/20.00 þ x 3 x 6 = 630.00. Thus each teacher must work at least 630 hours in 6 months. If Steve wants them to work more, they can; they still get paid depending on how many hours they actually work. Or Steve may hire other teachers and earn JCP profits.

Since he sold job contracts, Steve must take out bankruptcy insurance. The bankruptcy insurance premium is 0.5% per month. Every month he must pay his bankruptcy insurance firm= 0.005 x 3 x 3 x 700.00 þ = 31.50 þ. If Steve's firm bankrupts the bankruptcy insurance firm pays the teachers all the money they would earn if they worked the entire length of their contract.

The government gives Steve the ERT which is set at 1 %. There are 3 teachers, each earning 20.00 þ/hour and working 630 hours in 6 months. So Steve is given, 3 x 20.00 x 630 x 0.01 = 378.00 þ

To obtain all the money needed to start up his business, Steve issues consumerist general bonds. He issues 25 000.00 þ worth of them. The central bank sets the interest rate at 15 % per year. The bonds have a maturity of two years. The Consumerist General Bond Interest Repayment Frequency is 1 month. So all investors would receive 15% x 2 = 30 % x 25 000.00 þ = 7 500.00 þ. Since there are 24 one month periods in two years, the investors would receive 7 500.00 þ/24 = 312.50 þ every month. When the two years are over, Steve would also have to repay the 25 000.00 þ. How much each investor receives depends on how much of the 25 000.00 þ worth of bonds he invested in.

Steve attracts 39 students a week. Each student has a 2 hour lesson per week. A music lesson costs 28.00 Ө per hour. Thus each week Steve's business earns 39 x 2 hours x 28.00 þ/hour = 2 184.00 þ

We assume that each teacher has 13 students and that she teaches them 2 hours a week each. Let's calculate how much they will earn in their paycheck every 2 weeks:

13 x 2 hours x 20.00 þ/hour = 520.00 þ

Every month Steve must announce to the central bank his businesses' contribution to the GDCP. Since his business is a service based business, he reports how many clients he has multiplied by their payment to him. He has 39 students, 2 hours a week (in one month) and each pays 28.00 þ/hour. Thus

Steve reports that his business contributes 8 736.00 ☉. He doesn't actually transfer any of his money to the central bank. He only reports his Individual Domestic Consumerist Product contribution.

We see how he stands in terms of profits at the end of 6 months as this is when the teacher's contracts expire. First the profit. There were 39 students a week, for 26 weeks, 2 hours per student each paying 28.00 ☉/hour = 56 784.00 þ (The Norses turn into Ignits when the students purchase the lessons) Now the variable costs. The teachers make more than they could as they have more working hours than their minimum requirement by the JCP and AMIP. Let's calculate how much each makes in 6 months. There were 13 students a week, 2 hours per student for 26 weeks and the wage is 20.00 þ/ hour = 13 520.00 þ. Together this is 40 560.00 þ as there are 3 teachers.

He has to pay for utilities, heat, electricity and gas which cost 100.00 þ/month. This is 600.00 þ in 6 months. His sunk costs are 5 000.00 þ and his rent is 926.00 þ/month or 5 556.00 þ for 6 months. He pays his bankruptcy insurance firm 31.50 þ x 6 = 189.00 þ in 6 months.

Steve earns 700.00 þ per teacher from selling his contracts. Thus he earns 2 100.00 þ. From the ERT he earns 378.00 þ. In the end in 6 months he earns 7357.00 þ. This money Steve can keep or he can reinvest it back into his business. If the PRT is 1%, Steve will be given an additional 73.57 þ as a reward for doing business in a consumerist nation.

Now let's look at the job of a private music teacher. Let's say she is a piano teacher. A music lesson costs 28.00 ☉/hour. If she would work for someone else she would receive a wage of 20.00 þ/hour. Our piano teacher's name is Sue. Sue has 10 students a week for a 1 hour lesson. In a week she earns 280.00 þ. A student writes her a check for 28.00 ☉. When she takes this to her private bank, the bank deducts 28.00 ☉ from the student's Norse account and adds 28.00 þ to Sue's Ignit account.

Although Sue is self employed, she must report to the central bank with regards to her contribution to the Gross Domestic Consumerist Product. She has 10 students a week. There are about 4 weeks in a month and she earns 28.00 ☉ from each of them. Thus she reports that she makes 1 120.00 ☉.

Here is an interesting question. Why would Sue or anyone else in the part of economy based on services want to work for a firm rather than be self employed? A self employed person earns the cost of the service while in a firm one earns a wage which is smaller than the cost of the service and must pay a fee for working. The reason is that a firm is better able to attract customers than any individual can on his own.

We saw how two different types of music teaching services operate- one a music teaching institute and the other a self employed operation. We came across the costs of running the business and the sources of revenue. Many other service based operations run similarly to the way the music schools were run in this example.

Functioning of a Construction Company

We examine how a construction company works. By construction company we mean a company or firm that transforms building inputs into structures that people can live, work and conduct affairs in. A construction company can make a house, an office, a skyscraper or a school. It belongs to the accommodational sector. Here we look at two cases- the construction of a house and the construction of an apartment complex.

Let's look first at the building of a house. The construction firm must buy residential land. In this example, land costs $20.00 \text{þ} /m^2$. The house to be built is situated on a property of $900 \text{ } m^2$. Thus the firm must pay 18 000.00 þ to buy this land. It buys it from the government.

In this house building example we assume that the construction firm is well established and has the resources for the initial costs. When considering the building of the apartment complex we assume that the firm needs extra resources.

The firm has the 18 000.00 þ to buy the residential land. It writes a check directly to the municipal level government for 18 000.00 þ. The accommodational markdown is 30% so the government only receives 12 600.00 þ in its account while the firm has 18 000.00 þ deducted from its Ignit account.

It will take 25 workers, working 3 months to complete building this house from start to finish. The builders of the house all have the same wage function as their jobs are roughly the same. They earn 10.00 þ/hour. The JCP is 500.00 þ. The Adjusted Monthly Income Percentage is 300%. The workers are each entitled to work:

500 þ hours/ 10.00 þ x 3 x 3 = 450 hours or 34.6 hours per week in that 3 months.

The firm must take out bankruptcy insurance on these job contracts. If the Bankruptcy Insurance Premium is 0.5% each month the firm must pay the insurance company 0.5% of the total value of the contracts. We don't need to do any more calculations as these were done in preceding sections.

Besides workers there are other costs of building a house. These include cement, cement trucks, wood, pipes, bricks, plastic, rubber, nails, hammers and tools and anything else needed to construct a house. We assume that in the 3 months of construction, these things cost 50 000.00 þ.

The price function for the house in question is w5000.00 þ + y6000.00 þ + z8000.00 þ + a5000.00 þ + b300.00 þ. Where w represents number of floors, y represents number of washrooms, z represents number of bedrooms, a represents the number of kitchens and b represents the square feet area. The house our construction company is building has 3 floors, 4 washrooms, 3 bedrooms, 1 kitchen and 1000 square feet of space. It thus costs 368 000.00 þ.

In 3 months the firm completes the construction of the house. Instead of 34.6 hours per week. Each of the 25 workers worked 38 hours per week or 494 hours in 3 months.

Let's calculate the total costs of the firm in 3 months. 494 hours per worker x 25 workers x 10.00 þ/ hour = 123 500.00 þ. Building materials cost 50 000.00 þ and the land is 18 000.00 þ. The bankruptcy total fee is 3 months x 0.5% x 123 500.00 þ = 1 852.50 þ. So all the costs in 3 months are 193 352.50 þ.

The firm earned 25 x 500.00 þ for the job contracts = 12 500.00 þ. They sell their house including the land for 368 000.00 þ + 18 000.00 þ = 386 000.00 þ. The buyer of the house and land must pay 386 000.00 þ for it.

The Real Estate Profit Percentage is 0.5 % and the buyer has hired an agent who works 10 hours. The agent's wage function is $0.5z + 5.00$ þ/hour where z represents the Real Estate Profit Percentage. Thus the buyer must pay 386 000.00 þ to the construction company and (386 000.00 þ x 0.005 = 1 930 þ) to the real estate company. The real estate company must pay 0.5 x 1 930.00 þ + 5.00 þ/hour x 10 hours = 1 015 þ to the real estate agent.

A real estate company also helps the construction firm sell the house they made. Let's suppose that it is the same real estate company and the same agent as above. The real estate profit percentage is 0.5% and the agent works 10 hours. The construction company earns 1 930.00 þ. But there is also an accommodational markdown of 30%. So in the end the company earns (386 000.00 þ – 1 930.00 þ) x 0.7 = 268 849.00 þ. Subtracting final costs from this, the company earns 73 644.00 þ. The company need not report its transaction to the central bank since it is in the accommodational sector. We suppose that the Profit Reward Transfer is 1%. So then, in addition the firm will receive 736.44 þ to reward it for conducting business in the consumerist nation.

It is just as possible for a construction company to hire a real estate company as it is for a real estate company to hire a construction company. We have examined the former case in the above scenario of building a house. We will examine the latter in the case of building an apartment complex. We have a hypothetical real estate company called Northern Real Estate and a hypothetical construction company called Bob's construction. The real estate and construction company work together. The construction company makes money from selling suites in the apartment while the real estate company earns a percentage of the rent for helping the construction company find tenants. Let's start at the beginning. It takes a year for the apartment complex to be completed. 50 workers are needed. Each worker earns 10.00 þ/hour. The JCP is set at 600.00 þ and the contract lasts a year. The Adjusted Yearly Income Percentage is 1200%

The construction company must buy residential land from the government. Residential land costs 20.00 þ/m². They need 1500 m². This costs 30 000.00 þ. The Capital Investment Transfer (CIT) is set to be 1 %. Thus the government gives the construction company 300.00 þ to encourage growth.

There are also other costs (cement, cement trucks, wood, pipes, steal, brick, plastic, rubber, nails, glass, and tools). For a year these cost 200 000.00 þ.

Here we suppose that the construction company needs to issue consumerist profit bonds to get going. Bob issues 1 000 000.00 þ worth of profit bonds. The Profit Bond Interest Rate is 3%. He also earns 50 x 600.00 þ = 30 000.00 þ for giving his workers jobs.

He needs bankruptcy insurance to cover his job contracts and consumerist profit bonds issued. The bankruptcy insurance premium is 0.5 % per month. Bob must pay 0.05 x 1 000 000.00 þ = 50 000.00 þ for the profit bonds and 50 x 600.00 þ x 12 x 0.05 = 1800.00 þ for the job contracts. The total is 51 800.00 þ per month.

The apartment building is 8 stories high, each floor having 10 suites. The total price of the entire apartment complex is 2 500 000.00 þ. This is defined by a price function for apartments that takes into account bedrooms per suite, size of kitchen in square feet, size of washroom in square feet, size of bedroom in square feet, size of living room in square feet, size of balcony and length of hallway. Such a function is determined by the central bank but here it can be avoided and we can simply say that the apartment building costs 2 500 000.00 þ.

In our example the Rental Equivalence Duration is 20 years. Now we find out how much each tenant must pay each month for rent. This is calculated by:

2 500 000.00 þ/(20 x 12 x 8 x 10) = 130.00 þ. The construction company earns 130.00 þ x 0.7 = 91.00 þ from each tenant because of the 30% accommodational markdown.

How does the real estate company benefit? It has a sort of monopoly on all suites in the complex in exchange for giving the construction company tenants.

The construction company sells the apartment complex to a landlord. The landlord buys the apartment building for 2 500 000.00 þ. Our hypothetical Northern Real Estate is his real estate company and Jack is his agent. The Real Estate Profit Percentage is 0.5% and the agent's wage function is $z\,0.5 + 5.00$ þ/hour where z represents the Real Estate Profit Percentage. The landlord, Mike, must pay the real estate company 12 500.00 þ. The real estate agent, working 10 hours, earns 6 300.00 þ. The landlord must pay a total of 2 500 000.00 þ + 12 500.00 þ = 2 512 500.00 þ for the apartment plus the real estate transaction.

The construction company which hires the same real estate firm earns:

(2 500 000.00 þ – 12 500.00 þ) x 0.7 = 1 741 250.00 þ.

The landlord makes profit from renting suites. The construction company could have acted as a sort of landlord or property seller as in the case of a condominium. In that case the suites are owned by consumerists rather than rented.

At some point the construction company would have to pay back the bond holders the value of their bond, plus a little extra. This little extra is given by the formula:

1 000 000.00 x (0.03/ FR) x FP = payments to bond holders

Here FR stands for firm revenue and FP stands for firm profit,

A construction company operates in the way described above. It uses building materials to create space that is later sold to a landlord with the aid of a real estate company. Since almost all businesses is carried out in buildings and people need buildings to live in, the construction company is at the forefront of the economy.

Franchises

Here we take a look at franchises. By franchises we mean a business operated under a specific brand name usually the result of a chain of outlets. For example, our hypothetical Bob's Super Burgers has 70 outlets throughout the country. Someone wants to buy another outlet and start their own business while paying royalties or some kind of reimbursement to the parent company.

In this case the Adjusted Revenue Price factors in. So our hypothetical Bob's Super Burgers has 70 outlets and Bill wants to buy another outlet and make a profit. How much would it cost him to do so? To find the price of another outlet we find the Adjusted Revenue Price and take the average of the 70 outlets. So suppose the central bank the ARP at 4 years. This means that in order to buy another outlet of our hypothetical Bob's Super Burgers, Bill will have to pay how much the average of the 70 outlets made in revenue in 4 years. Some made 1 000 000 þ per year and some made 200 000 þ per year but if we add the sum of their yearly earnings and divide by 70, and then multiply by 4 we get the price that Bill must pay to purchase a franchise of our hypothetical Bob's Super Burgers.

What if a franchise has no pre-existing outlets? In that case the cost to start the outlet would be like the starting of any other store. The would-be owner would have to buy land, the building, the equipment and hire workers. After that he can start his business.

Purchasing a franchise may be a sound decision from a financial point of view. Instead of having to "start from scratch" and build a reputation from the beginning, it is easier to buy an outlet that other consumerists have already heard about and are familiar with. So setting up a franchise already brings one customers that are loyal to one brand of franchise. Also consumerists know to a very high degree what your franchise is selling whereas firms that start from the start have to advertise aggressively to let their product be known.

We examined how franchises are stated. The Adjusted Revenue Price is crucial for this. This lets franchise owners start another outlet of a franchise in our economy.

Brand Names

It would be useful to discuss the idea of brand names. Brand names are the ways that firms designate their good or service so as to differentiate it from other goods or services of the same type. Brand names help firms distinguish their product from other firms.

The idea of having brands is very important in free-market capitalism. In that system, brands ensure quality. If a company let's say Super-Tasty Cookies, makes good quality cookies, consumerists will associate those cookies with the brand; in this case Super-Tasty Cookies. Consumerists begin to expect high quality goods, for example cookies, from this company. Given a choice between cookies made by Super-Tasty Cookies and some cookies made by someone they never heard these consumerists will likely buy Super-Tasty cookies as they know what they are buying.

On the other hand, a brand has a reputation to uphold. If a Mexican restaurant sells a burrito or taco that causes people to be ill- causing them stomach problems, nausea and indigestion- consumerists will associate this restaurant with the illness it causes. Fewer people will want to go to this restaurant and people will associate the brand name with the problems it causes.

Accommodation Based Consumerism fully supports the notion of brand names. Brand names in consumerism are helpful in ensuring the quality of a good or service. Brand names ensure that a good or service is of the highest quality as the manufacturers associated with the brand have a reputation to uphold. They have an incentive to make goods and services of the highest quality.

If a firm with a particular brand name makes a high quality good that a lot of consumerists look favorably on, the brand name will be linked in the minds of consumerists with exceptional quality. Thus a consumerist will have a greater chance of buying that good and the firm earns a greater share of the market for that good.

The opposite is also true. If a particular brand name makes a very low quality good that many consumerists do not like at all, the brand name will be linked in the minds of consumerists with poor quality. This means that a consumerist will have a lower chance of purchasing that good and the firm receives a lower percentage of the market for that good.

These are the ways that having brand names is useful. Although free-market capitalism uses the idea of brand names extensively, they also have their place in accommodation based consumerism. Brand names are a signal of product quality. They ensure that the goods and services made in consumerism are of premium quality. This is in fact one of the main goals of consumerism.

The Jones' Family Budget

Here we investigate the family budget of the Jones' family. By this we mean that we analyze how the Jones family allocates their income to provide for their needs and wants. The Jones family has six members. There are Mr. Carl Jones, 44, and Mrs. Annette Jones, 43. They have three children, Bob who is 18, Amy who is 12 and John who is three months old. Carl's mom, Mary, 65, also lives with them.

Recall that there are three types of currencies in Accommodation Based Consumerism: Norses (Θ), Fortals (Ⅎ) and Ignits (þ). First let's take a look at the income of everyone in the Jones family in terms of Ignits. Carl is an engineer and makes 1000 þ a month. Annette is a pharmacist and earns 1200 þ per month. Bob works at a fast food restaurant for 40 hours per week and in a month makes 600 þ. Amy doesn't have a job but volunteers at a hospital. John who is 3 months old obviously doesn't work either. Mary doesn't work and is retired and receives 500 þ per month as Retirement Pension Allowance.

Now let's talk about income in terms of the other currency, Norses (Θ). The General Consumerist Grant (GCG) for this month was 600 Θ. The Non Working Consumerist Grant Reduction is 0.8. The Non Working Consumerist Grant is 480 Θ.

All of Carl, Annette and Bob make the General Consumerist Grant. So each month they each earn 600 Θ. Amy, John and Marry receive the Non Working Consumerist Grant and each earn 480 Θ per month.

Let's list each family member's contribution to the household income in terms of the two currencies.

	Ignits (þ)	Norses (Θ)
Carl	1000	600
Annette	1200	600
Bob	600	600
Amy	0	480
John	0	480
Mary	0	480
Family Total	2 800	3 240

Now that we know how the Jones' family earns income for their expenses, let's talk about how they spend their money. Of course the Jones family has the absolute freedom to spend their income on anything they want in either the materialist, laissez-faire or accommodational sectors. Naturally they would spend their money on the most important things first or on things that bring them the most joy in life.

First we look at the materialist sector. Instead of mentioning every single thing they buy, let's look at the category of things they spend their money on.

Each month they spend:

800 Ο on food; (bread, milk, pizza, pie, chicken, hamburgers)

2 x 350 Ο = 700 Ο on car payments

250 Ο on clothes for five family members

40 Ο on hygiene products (toothbrush, toothpaste, soap, shampoo, deodorant)

60 Ο on singing lessons for Amy

70 Ο on guitar lessons for Bob

200 Ο on electronics (CD's, computer games)

300 Ο on miscellaneous (diapers for John, batteries, detergent)

So each month the family spends 2 420 Ο on items in the materialist sector. The rest they save for the next month.

Now let's look at the accommodational sector.

Each month they spend:

700 þ on utilities (heat, gas, internet, cable, telephone, hot water)

400 þ on appliances (stove, refrigerator)

50 þ on alcohol (beer, wine)

200 þ on leisure (rock concert, opera, hockey game)

Now let's look at the laissez-fare sector: (we assume that 1 þ = 1ƒ)

150 ƒ on various forms of insurance (life, home, auto)

1200 ƒ mortgage on their house

So each month the Jones family spends 2700 þ on items in the accommodational and laissez-fare sectors. The rest they save away for the next month.

In this scenario all the family members of the Jones family pooled all of their Norse and Ignit income and worked together. Technically however, 3 month old John earns a 480 Ο grant. Although this is his money, he probably doesn't know what to do with it. So it makes sense if everyone in the household worked together.

We analyzed the Jones family budget. We compared the income against the expenses of the 6 family members with regards to the 3 currencies. This concludes the investigation.

The Predicament of Students and Minors

Here we talk about the special circumstances regarding students and minors. By students we mean individuals in college, university, high school or elementary school. Minors are people below a certain age threshold; usually 16 or 18 years of age.

First of all, all services in the government sector are provided to every student and minor regardless of their age or whether they contribute to the consumerist society. Thus all students and minors receive protection from the police, have a right to go to school and are provided medical treatment for all health problems; for example a knee operation, an appendix operation or fungal infection. Students and minors have complete access to the services provided through the governmental sector.

With regards the materialist sector, recall that there are two types of consumerist grants- the general consumerist grant and the non working consumerist grant. All consumerists, and this includes minors and students, start receiving a consumerist grant as soon as they are born. However this is usually the non working consumerist grant since they are not working. All students and minors can spend the money they receive (Norses) from the central bank in the form of the non working consumerist grant on goods and services in the materialist sector. Thus they can buy whatever they want to eat, what to wear and anything else they find interesting in the materialist sector. Alternatively they can pool their consumerist grant with their family and work together as a household. Now, it may be the case that some university or college students may find a part time job on top of their studies. If they work above the Consumerist Grant Threshold, they are entitled to the General Consumerist Grant. In that case, they may be able to buy more goods and services in the materialist sector.

Both the Accommodational sector and Laissez-faire sector serve as a reward for contributing to the materialist sector as well as for contributing to the laissez-faire and accommodational sectors. Usually students and minors will be living with their parents/family so they do not need to worry about accommodation and things like paying utility bills. In fact when someone is still a minor or student, his parents pay for many of the things in the accommodational and laissez-faire sectors. Thus students and minors living with their family need not really worry about paying for goods and services in either the accommodational and laissez-faire sectors.

There may be some problems when students move out on their own; i.e. when they leave for college or university. If they have a job they can use the proceeds from that job to pay for accommodation, utilities and goods and services in the laissez-faire sectors. However, if a student needs to devote a very high percentage of his time to studying he may apply for the extra work transfer and accommodational award. In the end he will have to pay back to the government for the help it provided him during his time of need.

Clearly minors and students should be enjoying their youth as well as studying. However we should encourage minors to contribute at least a little to society. 3 – 4 hours of work a week is not excessive. If every minor and student worked this much the output of our economy would be much, much greater. Keep in mind that this system has a lot of mechanisms to eliminate unemployment. So, if a minor or student can't find a job in the natural partition, there are always opportunities in the command partition or the laissez-faire labour system.

These are the predicaments of students and minors. We discussed their situation regarding the governmental, materialist, accommodational and laissez-faire sectors. Even if students and minors contribute a little bit to the consumerist economy, both they and society will benefit.

The Stratagems of Barter

In a sense, all economic systems are based on barter. Barter can be in the form of direct trade or with the use of currency, at which time it becomes a form of market economy. Either way there are a number of fundamental rules or principles that apply to barter. These rules or stratagems are listed and discussed here.

1) Trade is necessary for fulfilling people's needs and wants

If people do not trade, they will lack certain goods that they need. If a person who is a piano teacher wants food, she cannot obtain it unless she trades for it somehow, offering her teaching skills to others. If a person has a number of chairs and has no clothes but wants to be clothed, he will not be able to become clothed unless he engages in trade somehow exchanging his chairs for clothes. Trade ensures that people are able to get what they desire.

2) Both traders are better off after a wise trade

If both traders benefit after a trade then the trade can be considered a good one. The better off the traders are, the better the trade was. Suppose a man who has 35 bicycles trades with a woman who has 10 fish. If the trade involves 1 bicycle for 4 fish, both should be better off since the man will have something to eat and the woman will have a means of transportation. Suppose a man who has 5 sweaters trades with a woman who has 10 L of milk. If the trade involves 2 sweaters for 4 L of milk, both should be better off since the man will have something to drink while the woman will have a way to keep warm. Good trades benefit both traders.

3) The getting rid of what one doesn't want and the acquisition of what one does want in exchange for this is the purpose of barter.

In every trade someone trades something away for something one wants more. If people didn't want more, they wouldn't always be seeking to find something. Also, if people did not have things they didn't need they would not be trading, they would not be trading them away for something better and there would not be barter. A trade occurs where a man trades a bicycle for 5 novels. Here he gets rid of something that he doesn't want, the bicycle. He wouldn't trade it away if he wanted it. He acquires 5 novels. Here he acquires something he wants. If he didn't want them he wouldn't take them. A woman trades a litre of milk for a hamburger. By trading away the milk she asserts that she doesn't want the milk that much or else she would keep it for herself. She also asserts that she values the hamburger since she gave up something, the milk, for it. Barter's purpose is to gain desirable things and loose undesirable things in exchange for them.

4) The obtainment of what one wants, a lot of it and the best of it, is the measure of success in barter.

To benefit from barter a trader strives to acquire what he desires. In addition a trader wants to acquire the best possible of what can be acquired and as much as possible of this. If a barterer is hungry, he would be successful by trading the things he has for a meal. The bigger and tastier the meal, the more successful he is at trading. If a barterer needs transportation he would be successful if he trades things he has for a means of getting around. He would be successful if he obtained a bicycle but even more so if he obtained an automobile. A trader, who succeeds in trading not only for what he wants but also for the most desirable and greatest quantity of that which he wants, is a successful trader.

5) At least two people are necessary to conduct barter

A man cannot trade with himself. If there is only one person, there is no one to give a good to or to receive from. A second person makes barter possible. If someone has a radio and he has no one to trade with he has no one to give the radio to in exchange for another good. If someone wants a loaf of bread and there is no one to trade with, he will be unable to get the bread from anyone. For barter to exist there must be a minimum of two people.

6) The meeting of two individuals at the same time and place is necessary for barter to take place.

If two people are not in the same place they cannot exchange their goods because they are too far away from each other. If two people do not meet at the same time they cannot exchange their goods because one appears later than the other. If a man who has 3 automobiles wants to trade with a man who has four paintings, they must be in the same place (Elm Street, New City). If the same two people want to trade, they must also do so at the same time (3:15 p.m. Thursday, May 15). The coincidence of time and space is a prerequisite to a trade.

7) Good bargaining skills are a prerequisite to successful trading

If not, then a person may make a foolish trade. Like most skills, it is to one's advantage if one knows what he is doing or has some experience in the art. If a trader has no familiarity with trading, he might make foolish trades. For example, one may trade a house for a box of matches or a car for a sandwich. The trader must know how much he can get in return for what he is trading. In the above example, the trader may have gotten much more than a box of matches for a house and much more than a sandwich for a car (maybe 1000's of sandwiches). A person skilled in trading will be more successful than one who isn't.

8) Obtaining more of a particular good is preferable during trade when trading an identical good.

If a trader is seeking to acquire a commodity, the more of the same commodity he acquires, the more successful he is. When trading pencils for notebooks, it is better to obtain three notebooks than two and better to obtain four notebooks than three. When trading televisions for radios, it is better to receive two radios than one and three radios are better to receive than two. Generally, when considering an identical good it is preferable to receive as much as possible of it during a trade.

9) Giving up less of a particular commodity is preferable during trade when trading an identical good.

If a trader is seeking to acquire a commodity, the less of the commodity he has to give up, the more successful he is. When trading pencils for notebooks, it is better to give up 1 pencil than 2 and it is better to give up 2 than 3. When trading televisions for radios it is preferable to give up 2 T.V.'s rather than 3 and it is better to give up 1 television than 2. Generally, when considering an identical good, it is preferable to give up as little of is as possible during trade.

10) The obtainment of the best trade possible should be sought during barter

All traders wish to obtain a trade that is in their best interest. This is haggling. A man has a horse, a cat and a dog. A woman has a TV, a computer and a bicycle. The best deal among the two can be obtained when one makes an offer and the other makes a counter-offer in return until a proposal stands such that both of them are happy. The man might offer a horse for a TV. The woman wants the dog also. The man wants the bicycle in return. Thus the man gives up a dog and a horse for a TV and a bicycle. A man has a soft drink, a sandwich and a doughnut. The woman has a knife, a fork and a spoon. The man offers the woman a sandwich for a knife. The woman wants the soft drink also. The man wants the spoon in return. Thus the man gives up a sandwich and a soft drink in exchange for a knife and a spoon. When engaged in barter, the participants have their best interest in mind.

11) What one needs should not be traded away unless one will directly or indirectly obtain something one needs more.

The things one trades away are those that one does not need. The things one needs are so important that they should not be traded away. Imagine two traders in the dessert. One has a TV and the other has a bottle of water. In this case, unless the other person plans to cross the dessert without any water, he would be foolish to trade away the water even if it is for a TV. Imagine two traders in the arctic. One has a coat and a hat and the other has a king size bed. In this case, unless the other person plans to survive without warm clothes, he would be foolish to trade away his coat and hat even if it is for a king size bed. The things that a person desperately needs should be the last to be traded away.

12) A commodity that one already has in great abundance should not be traded for.

If someone has a large quantity of a certain good and he has more than he can use, he really doesn't need any more of it. If one doesn't need any more of an item, he should not trade for it. If one already had four bicycles and only really uses one, he would gain little if he got more unless it was to exchange them for something else. A farmer with acres of apples would not want to trade for more apples. In fact his greatest priority is getting rid of his apples for something else. One would be wise not to acquire what one already has a lot of unless it is just to exchange for something else.

13) The same commodity may be valued differently by different traders.

The value of a good is subjective. How much a trader cherishes a commodity depends on personal preferences and circumstances. One trader may think that a TV is worth 3 radios while another may think a TV is worth only 2 radios. One trader may think that a bicycle is worth 3 hours of piano tutoring while another may think that a bicycle is worth 5 hours of piano tutoring. The value of a good is different among different people.

14) Society is better off and people are wealthier the more trades occur in a market.

A successful trade represents two things. First of all, someone obtained something they wanted and did not have before. Secondly, another person got rid of something he didn't need for something better. If Joe trades shampoo for a loaf of bread with Cindy, society benefits. Joe has a loaf of bread and he has gotten rid of a bottle of shampoo he did not need. Also, Cindy obtained a bottle of shampoo for her hair and got rid of some bread that she already had too much off. If Bob trades a car for a cottage with Jack, society benefits, Bob has a cottage and he has gotten rid of a car he values less than a cottage. Also, Jack obtained a car to drive around with and got rid of a cottage that he doesn't really use too much anyway. When both traders benefit in a trade, getting what they want, society becomes better off and the traders are more prosperous.

15) A three-way trade is a useful way to trade goods.

A three way trade occurs when a trader trades for something he doesn't desire but knows that someone else will trade this for something that he wants. If one barters for a good, not for its own sake but for the purpose of using it for a future trade, this represents a three-way trade. One has 2 fish and wants a duck. But he who has the duck doesn't want fish. However he does like a sweater. The first trades the 2 fish for a sweater and subsequently the sweater for the duck. In another example one has a dog but wants a cat. But he who has the cat doesn't want a dog. However he does like a ferret. The first trader trades the dog for a ferret and subsequently the ferret for a cat. If one can't get a good one wants directly, one might be able to get it by trading for an intermediate good with a third party.

16) Desperation is a disadvantage

When one feels a great urge to trade a commodity as quickly as possible, he often losses. Desperate traders often accept the first offer for the goods they are trying to get rid of or acquire. This may lead to a worse trade than if a trader was not in an anxious position to quickly trade. A person who is extremely hungry might give up a TV for a sandwich if the person with the sandwich is the first person he sees. If one waits longer, one may only have to give up a pillow for a sandwich. A person who is moving to a new house and has to get rid of his old furniture might give the furniture up for a pillow if the person offering the pillow is the first person he sees. If one waits longer one may have received a TV for the furniture. Traders who are desperate are more likely to make trades that they will regret in the future.

17) The perception that one's commodities are valuable and important works to one's advantage

If one owns a good and waits for a good offer from other traders he will have the opportunity to trade it for something he really likes. If one acts as if what he owns is valuable he will get a better trade than if he thought that what he had was worthless. The more valuable he makes his goods seem, the higher the other person will view them also. If one owns a bicycle and doesn't trade it for mediocre offers like a pencil, but waits, one might eventually procure a better deal such as two television sets and a radio. If one owns a bed and doesn't trade it for mediocre offers like a hamburger, but waits, one might eventually procure a better deal such as a table and chair. How a trader values that which he trades, has a profound effect on what he is able to gain in a trade.

18) Traders who have an abundance of a good are willing to accept less of another good on exchange for theirs relative to people who have less of that good to trade.

If a trader has a large quantity of a particular good, he will be less picky about what he gets for it. Furthermore, he will be quicker to complete a trade than if he has less of that commodity. He will accept less of a particular good than a person who isn't that desperate to unload. A trader who has 1000 kg of turkey meat may be willing to trade a kilogram of that turkey meat for a kilogram of apples. However if the trader only had 100 kg of turkey meat he may demand 5 kg of apples for 1 kg of turkey meat. A trader, who is also a wheat farmer and wants to trade his wheat, having a truck full of wheat, may accept a kilogram of wheat for a kilogram of beef. However if the trader only grew wheat in his back yard and had no more than 5 kg of wheat, he may demand 3 kg of beef for a kilogram of wheat. Generally the more of a good a trader has, the lower are his expectations for what he receives in return for that good.

19) How much a trader wants for his good sometimes depends on how much the person he is trading with has to trade for.

If a trader sees that another trader has a lot of goods, he will often demand more of him than if he had less. A trader always tries to extract the most possible from another trader. A trader wants a cassette. The person with the cassette asks how much the first person has to trade for. He says 10 pieces of gold. The person with the cassette demands 8 pieces of gold for the cassette. In another trade, another person wants a cassette from a trader who asks him how much he has to trade for. He says that he only has 5 pieces of gold. The trader with the cassette demands only 3 pieces of gold from him in this case. How much a trader wants from another depends on how much a trader has to trade with.

20) It is necessary to give something in order to obtain something in return.

If someone doesn't give a good or service in exchange for another he will most likely get nothing himself. An exchange in barter requires that in order to receive one must at the same time give. A trader who wants a bike will not likely get it for nothing. A trader who wants a TV will not get it for nothing. Usually one needs to give in order to obtain another good.

21) Stratagem #20 does not always apply.

Sometimes a trader may evoke enough pity to obtain things for nothing. This is the idea of begging. Someone who has nothing and looks miserable may get a loaf of bread for free from someone who empathizes with him. A trader who is very hot and thirsty may get a bottle of water for free just out of the generosity of the giver. There are instances when one need not necessarily give in order to get a good.

22) It is necessary to receive something in order to give to someone else that which they desire.

If someone does not get a good or service in exchange for something, he is unlikely to give anything to anyone else. An exchange in barter requires that in order to bestow one must at the same time receive. A trader who wants to trade a house will not give it up unless he gets something for it. If a trader wants a car, he will not give it to anyone unless he receives something for it. Usually one needs to get a good in order to give up something to another person.

23) Stratagem #22 does not always apply.

It is possible that a trader will give things to another out of the good will of his heart, if he deems that the other person is needy or has a close relationship with him. This is the idea of charity. A person may give another an apple if he sees that the person will starve otherwise. A trader may give his brother a radio for his birthday. Although in these cases the trader gains nothing materially, he does gain spiritual satisfaction.

24) The trading of something that everyone else wants to trade away is unlikely to result in a good trade.

If a lot of people have a particular commodity they want to get rid off for something better they must look even harder for those who will give them anything valuable for that good. Suppose a trader is bartering for apples and there are 100's of other traders who also wish to get rid of them. In such a case, the trader may get a book for 10 kg of apples. If there were less apple traders, he might be able to obtain 2 or 3 books seeing as those who want apples would have to go to him and offer more to him for those apples. Suppose a trader is bartering for milk and there are many other cow farmers. In such a case, the trader might get a sandwich for a litre of milk. If there were less milk farmers, he may have received 3 sandwiches for the same amount of milk. A trader who is trading something that everyone else wants to trade away is less likely to get a good deal or even trade at all.

25) The trading of something that no one wants to have will be unsuccessful.

If no one wants a commodity that one is trading for, no one will give much for it. If no one wants a commodity it becomes worthless and it is hard to get a deal trying to trade it away. A person from the arctic trying to give snow to other arctic travelers probably won't get anything for the snow. Why would anyone give him anything if they can pick the snow from the ground? Someone in a city trying to trade away banana peels probably won't get anything for them. First of all, anyone can dig into the dumpster to get them. Second of all, most people don't want banana peels. That's why they are dumped into trash cans in the first place. Trying to trade a good or service that few desire will produce bad results.

26) Being a trader with a rare commodity is an advantage

Having a commodity that few other traders have permits a trader to have the opportunity to choose better more desirable commodities in exchange for his than if more traders traded that commodity. The trader may wait as other traders offer better and better deals for his scarce commodity. If a trader has a rare spice, he will be able to trade for 3 bicycles instead of just one or for a hamburger instead of a slice of bread. A trader with ice in the dessert will be able to trade the ice for a camel instead of a bicycle. If almost everyone had ice in the dessert, the trader may have to be happy with only one bicycle. Having a commodity that everyone wants and that few or no one has is a great help.

27) Trading inferior goods is discouraged.

A trader must assure others that his goods are workable and not broken. If a trader barters useless, worthless goods, he should be avoided. One cannot trade away rotten beef or pork. A trader cannot trade away a car with no breaks or engine unless he says so when he is trading it. It is frowned upon to trade unworthy commodities.

28) The protection of a trader's goods as his own must be enforced by law

There mustn't be any steeling. If traders stole their assets then there is no sense in trading as he who steels most will have most. A person who has his bike stolen from him will have nothing to keep or trade with. A person who has his cow stolen from him would also have nothing for himself or to exchange for another good. If steeling is permitted, no one has an incentive to trade and everything falls apart. Steeling cannot exist.

29) The reputation of being a trader well known for trading a particular good is an advantage.

A trader known for bartering a particular good or service has an advantage over others. If traders know what one trades, then they are more likely to trade with him as this saves them the trouble of looking too far. A person known among society as a trader of cups, will have more traders who want to trade with him even if others also trade cups. A man known as a good doctor will probably have more people seeking to be healed by him than by more obscure doctors. Being well known for trading a particular good or service can give the trader the upper hand.

30) The offering of a discount is an effective way of trading goods.

If someone is led to believe he is getting a good bargain, he will agree to a trade he normally wouldn't. Traders get rid of commodities (for better ones) that they can't easily trade away by making others think that they are getting a good trade. A rug dealer says that that he usually wants 20 eggs for a rug but for this one customer he will gladly trade for 18 eggs. The person with the eggs is more likely to complete the exchange because he is convinced that he is getting special treatment. A man who trades milk sees someone with fur. The man with the milk says to the fur trader that he will give him 3 litres of milk for one beaver pellet and that he usually trades 3 litres of milk for 2 beaver pellets. This isn't true but the fur trader believes that he is getting a bargain by having to pay less beaver pellets and so agrees to the trade. The perception that one is getting a great bargain is a reason for many exchanges.

31) The utterance that one can get a better trade somewhere else may lead to the negotiation of a better deal than otherwise.

If a trader says that someone else has offered to give him more or receive less, he may induce another trader to lower his expectations. What other traders offer matters in trades involving similar commodities. Suppose a trader has 5 L of milk and wants to exchange the milk with someone who has apples. The person with the apples says that he will give the milk trader 10 lbs of apples for 3 L of milk. The milk trader says that someone else offered her 20 lbs of apples for the 3 L of milk. The apple trader now realizes that he must give at least 20 lbs of apples for the milk or else no trade takes place. Suppose someone has some eggs and wants to exchange them for sausage. The person with the sausage says that he will trade 10 eggs for 2 kg of sausage. The egg trader says another sausage trader who she spoke to before would give her 2 kg of sausage for 5 eggs. Now the original sausage trader must not ask for more than 5 eggs for his 2 kg of sausage if he wants to make a transaction. A wise trader looks around different traders to see who will offer him the best deal.

32) The application of pressure to force a trade increases the likelihood of the trade taking place.

Applying pressure to carry out a trade in a certain amount of time can cause someone to trade for something he wasn't going to in the first place. If someone forces another person to trade without carefully thinking about the trade, perhaps due to a lack of time, a trade may result that wasn't planned originally. A video company releases a video that is only available for 2 weeks and will never be released again. Traders who do not normally like the video might trade away their possessions for it, thinking that they might miss a great opportunity by not buying it. A sandwich trader offers a new kind of sandwich for a "limited time only". People who do not normally eat these go trade for these believing that they will miss a big chance. By putting pressure on a trader, one may cause him to trade something he wasn't going to.

33) The combination of goods into a package facilitates trade.

Sometimes a good is put into a "combo" with another. Usually one trades fast and the other is hard to get rid off for something better. If a good that is trading poorly is put together with one that trades quickly the first good can be traded more quickly than normal. A trader has a litre of milk and a chestnut. Instead of trading them separately, he trades them together and gets something for the chestnut whereas otherwise he wouldn't. A trader has steak and a piece of paper. Someone offers him 2 bananas for the steak and no one wants the paper. By putting them together into a package, the two would have to be traded together. He receives an offer of 2 bananas and an orange for the package. Thus he earns an orange more than he would normally. The combining of goods into an inseparable package to be traded may help trade goods that are slow to trade.

34) There are two good strategies of bargaining. They are stratagem #34 and stratagem # 35

The trading of a variety of goods is a successful strategy. Doing so, one is able to find at least one person with at least something to trade. Suppose that a trader wants to be sure that he will carry out at least one trade. Instead of trading just milk and tomatoes he can pursue the option of trading these and in addition to them chairs, cars, carpets, plants and spoons. Thus he will attract other traders with varying interests. If a trader is not interested in milk and tomatoes, he may be interested in a spoon or a chair or maybe a pair of pants. It is a good idea to trade a variety of goods and services.

35) Specializing in the trade of a very specific field of goods is a successful strategy.

Doing so, one is able to attract other traders who know what they are looking for. Trading one type of commodity will distinguish the trader as a trader of that commodity. A trader may specialize in meat. He trades not only beef but is also renowned for having fresh poultry, pork, mutton, liver etc. Those who want to trade for meat know where to go. Another trader may specialize in wood products. He also makes them as he is a carpenter. He has different kinds of tables, chairs, patios, stools etc. Those who want to obtain a wood product (i.e. a desk) now know where to go. It is a good idea to specialize in one specific area.

36) Goods surrounded by excitement and attention are traded more successfully

When people are very enthusiastic about particular goods, other traders are attracted to these goods. If a good is talked about a lot, more people want it than if it were obscure. A trader may hire his cousin to rave about his water filters. He would exclaim how wonderful and necessary they are and that everyone must have one. This will attract more traders to trade for those filters than otherwise. A potion seller may get his brother to exclaim how healthy he feels after drinking some tonic. This will also attract traders. Bringing attention and excitement to one's goods is an effective way to attract potential traders and carry out a good trade.

37) The accentuation of the positive is the goal of advertising

A trader emphasizes the good points about his good when he is haggling with a potential trader. If a trader hears the good qualities of a good he is more likely to trade for it. A rug dealer may point out that his rugs are made of real animal skin and that they are easily washable. A car trader will mention first of all, that his cars have four wheel drive, anti-lock breaks, air bags and so on. The most positive is mentioned first as it is this that makes a trader want to trade. When advertising his goods, a trader accentuates the positive.

38) The discounting of the negative is the goal of advertising

A trader avoids talking about the bad points regarding his good when he is haggling with a potential trader. If a trader doesn't know the negative qualities of a good, he is more likely to trade for it. A rug dealer will probably not mention, even if it is true, that his rugs will rot if they are wet and are not dried properly. A car trader will not mention, even if it is true, that his cars have really bad fuel economy. When advertising a trader discounts the negative. Negative information is not mentioned as it detracts buyers from buying a good.

39) Goods and services that are perishable are riskier to trade than those that are not.

If someone does not trade away a perishable good or service in adequate time, he loses out. This usually applies to foods and drinks. Traders with perishable goods are focused on the expiry date and trade those goods that expire first before those that expire later. Perishable goods must be consumed before their expiry date or else they lose their value. If a grocery trader does not trade away his apples within a short time, they rot and no one wants to buy apples that are rotten. He who trades with milk must trade it away soon as rotten milk is only good for throwing out. A ticket to a hockey game loses its value after the night of the game. Likewise a rock and roll concert ticket is worthless after the performance. There is more risk involved in trading goods that can expire than those that do not.

40) Barter is generally inflexible

When two traders wish to exchange with each other they must both want to receive what the other is giving. Barter involves direct exchange making it awkward for many trades. Notwithstanding the stratagem (#15) of 3-way trade, usually direct exchange is a prerequisite. A trader, who wants food and has to trade pencils, must find another trader who will give him food and accept pencils. This can be avoided with stratagem #15. A trader who wants a book and has to trade pickles must find another trader who will give him the book and who desires pickles. This can also be avoided with stratagem #15. Barter, although useful in providing things needed and satisfying wants, is very rigid.

41) The introduction of a commodity or an item that can be used as a unit of exchange and a measure of value can make barter efficient

Such an item would eliminate the need for direct exchange (or 3-way trade). For example, traders could use gold or some precious metal as a currency. This is then used to purchase goods like honey and cars. Traders would accept gold in exchange for goods. Thus a trader gives another a car for a certain amount of gold. When traders accept an item or commodity as a unit of exchange or measure of value, barter metamorphosis's into a quasi-free-market system.

These stratagems of barter are universal. Barter, as well as all economic systems that flow out of it, functions as we have just described. This knowledge is important to a complete understanding of the inner workings of an economy.

Consumerism in a Prison Camp

Here we demonstrate how consumerism would work in a prison camp. The prison camp scenario is often used to show how the free-market system works. It is useful to describe an economy in a prison camp due to the simplicity such a setting offers.

We will first look at how a free-market would function in a prison camp. Suppose that there are people in a prison camp and that they are given rations. They each have different tastes and prefer different quantities of the goods that they are rationed. How do they maximize on their preferences?

We make several assumptions here. There are 200 people. There is another prison camp nearby. Each day each prisoner receives 1 box of rations. Each box of rations has 5 cigarettes, 1 bar of soap, 2 potatoes, 2 tea bags, 3 slices of bread, 1 can of ham, 1 bottle of beer and 6 crackers.

In a free-market arrangement cigarettes become the currency. Each good becomes quoted in terms of cigarettes. When prisoners trade, they exchange cigarettes for one of the goods they were rationed. The people do not necessarily have to smoke. All that matters is that cigarettes become the universal currency in the camp. They are a store of value, a unit of account and a medium of exchange.

Let's look at two exchanges between Joe and Matt. Joe wants to have more bread and Matt wants more crackers. Joe is willing to pay 2 cigarettes for a slice of bread while Matt is willing to accept 2 cigarettes in exchange for a slice of bread. Thus Joe gives Matt two cigarettes and Matt gives Joe a slice of bread. They are both content. Matt is willing to pay a cigarette for 2 crackers while Joe is willing to give 2 crackers for a cigarette. Thus Matt gives Joe a cigarette and Joe gives Matt two crackers. They are both content.

In our camp, many transactions like the one above are carried out between prisoners in the free-market paradigm. One prisoner gives another some cigarettes in exchange for a good. In this way prisoners maximize on the goods they enjoy and get rid of the goods that they do not need that much for ones they would rather have instead. Each prisoner may value a good differently in terms of how many cigarettes it is worth. Eventually those who are buying a good (spending cigarettes) come to equilibrium with those that are selling the goods (earning cigarettes). Suppose Joe wants to buy a potato. He thinks it is worth a cigarette. He goes to Matt who has a potato and values his potato at 3 cigarettes. Joe doesn't want to pay 3 cigarettes for a potato so he goes to Paul to see how much he wants for it. Paul wants 4 cigarettes for it. Joe goes back to Matt and offers Matt two cigarettes. Matt counter-offers with 2 ½ cigarettes. Joe agrees. Thus Joe gives up two and a half cigarettes for a potato from Matt.

A prisoner who wants to buy something has two choices. He could go to each prisoner asking how much they want for the good or he can bargain. Suppose a prisoner, Sam, wants to earn a few cigarettes. He is selling soap. He wants 2 cigarettes for it. However there may be several other entrepreneurs like him. Since the soap is exactly the same, they are competing with him. Let's call his competitors Bill, Jack and John. In order for them to sell soap, they must make it known to other prisoners that they are selling soap. In order for Sam to sell his soap, he must charge the lowest price for it (in cigarettes). He charges 2 cigarettes per bar of soap. However, Bill will settle for 1 ½ cigarettes per bar of soap. John charges only 1 cigarette for it. This undercutting ends when soap buyers start competing with each other to buy soap. So suppose Sam, Bill, John and Jack each lower the price of their soap to 1 cigarette. They each have 2 soaps to sell. Now suppose that there are 10 soap buyers. Each of them will offer a price higher than the other for the soap thus raising the price of soap (in cigarettes). This ends when the price of a bar of soap reaches equilibrium. Here the equilibrium is 2 cigarettes per bar of soap.

Every day a new box of rations arrives. This means more cigarettes. The prison camp population experiences the effects of inflation. What happens is that the price of goods (in cigarettes) increases relative to the last day's prices.

That is the way a free-market economy will operate in a prison camp. Now we move onto a different type of economic system operating in a prison camp. We now look at an economy in a prison camp under consumerism. We look at the major areas where it differs from the free-market orientation.

We make several assumptions. There are 200 people. There is another prison camp with which to exchange. Every prisoner receives 1 box of rations. A box of rations contains:

- 5 cigarettes

- 1 bar of soap

- 2 potatoes

- 2 tea bags

- 3 slices of bread

- 1 can of ham

- 1 bottle of beer

- 6 crackers

- 1 bar of chocolate

Instead of an accommodation based consumerist system we have a "luxury based" consumerist system. Thus we divide all the rations into 2 groups; "necessities" and "luxuries". The reason for this will be clear a little bit later.

The necessities include:

- 1 bar of soap

- 2 potatoes

- 3 slices of bread

- 1 can of ham

- 6 crackers

The luxuries include:

- 5 cigarettes

- 2 tea bags

- 1 bottle of beer

- 1 bar of chocolate

The prisoners elect a president or accountant. We assume that he has a piece of paper and a pen. He is in charge of all transactions in the consumerist prison camp.

The prisoners put all of the rations together. They vote on the prices of each good. The top 30 prices for each good are excluded as are the bottom 30. The remaining 140 are averaged. In our example let's suppose that the outcome of the price vote was as follows. In the necessity sector:

Soap-   2.00 ☉

Potatoes-   1.00 ☉

Slice of bread- 1.00 ☉

Can of ham-   2.00 ☉

Crackers-   0.50 ☉

In the luxury sector:

Cigarettes-   1.00 þ

Tea bags-   0.50 þ

Bottle of beer- 2.50 þ

Chocolate bar- 2.00 þ

In the first sector, the necessities sector, the prices were expressed in Norses. In the second sector, the luxuries sector, the prices were expressed in Ignits.

The president finds the value of both sectors. The value of the prices of all necessary goods times their quantity is called the Gross Total Necessity Wealth (GTNW). It is expressed in Norses. The prices of all luxury goods times their quantity is called the Gross Total Luxury Wealth (GTLW)

The GTNW would be thus:

Soap- 1 x 2.00 ☉ = 2.00 ☉

Potatoes- 2 x 1.00 ☉ = 2.00 ☉

Slice of bread- 3 x 1.00 ☉ = 3.00 ☉

294

Can of ham- 1 x 3.00 Θ = 3.00 Θ

Crackers- 6 x 0.50 Θ = 3.00 Θ

The sum is thus 13.00 Θ. Since there are 200 boxes of rations, the GTNW is 2600.00 Θ.

The GTLW would be thus:

Cigarettes- 5 x 1.00 þ = 5.00 þ

Tea bags- 2 x 0.50 þ = 1.00 þ

Bottle of beer- 1 x 2.50 þ= 2.50 þ

Chocolate bar- 1 x 2.00 þ = 2.00 þ

The sum is thus 10.50 þ. Since there are 200 boxes of rations the GTLW is 2100.00 þ.

Due to the fact that there are 200 cases of rations and 200 prisoners, the GTNW per capita is 13.00 Θ and the GTLW per capita is 10.50 þ. The accountant (president) manages all of the prisoner's exchanges. There is a list of the names of all the prisoners and by each prisoner's name there is a credit of 13.00 Θ and 10.50 þ. The prisoners make two lines. When they reach the end of a line, they can exchange some of their credits for rations. Each time they obtain something, the amount the good is worth is deducted from their credit by the president. The goods (rations) are stockpiled and can be obtained by trading some credit for a good. An example should be helpful. John is in one of the lines for the goods. Upon reaching the end he is greeted by the president. He can buy any "necessity" sector good; seeing as he is in the necessity line. He can choose any combination of items worth equal or less (but not more) than 13.00 Θ. He picks two cans of ham, 8 crackers and 3 slices of bread. The president deducts 13.00 Θ from his account; i.e. he crosses out "13.00 Θ" and writes "0.00 Θ" in the space by his name on a paper. The president then hands John the goods he chose.

Upon receiving these goods, John joins another line, the luxury line. His position in this line is the inverse of the previous line. So if he was first in the necessities line he will be last in the luxury line and if he was last in the necessities line he would be first in the luxury line. And if he was 50th in the necessities line he would be 150th in the luxury line. After reaching the end of the luxury line he is once again confronted by the president who asks him how he wants to spend his money (credits). He can spend 10.50 þ. He chooses 2 bottles of beer, 2 chocolate bars and 2 tea bags. The president deducts 10.50 þ credits from his account by crossing out "10.50 þ" and writing "0.00 þ" by his name. The president then gives John what he asked for. In this setup, John can meet his preferences and he would prefer the goods he got under such a system to getting what he did in the original ration.

Matt is another prisoner. After reaching the end of the necessities line, he chooses a can of ham and 6 crackers. This only costs 6.00 Θ. The president deducts the 6.00 Θ from his account. He still has 7.00 Θ. He can spend this 7.00 Θ the next day. When the president gets ready to hand out rations the next day (assuming that a new box of rations arrives every day and its contents are exactly the same as the day before) he simply adds 13.00 Θ and 10.50 þ to everyone's name. Thus Matt would have 20.00 Θ to spend the next day however he pleases.

The president is counted as among the 200 prisoners in the camp. He also gets his own account from which he has to deduct credits whenever he wants to obtain some of the goods contained in the rations. Therefore it is important that the prisoners choose someone honest as the president.

Now we see why there are two sectors, not just one. If there was only one, the prisoners would set a very low price for the most desirable goods and a high price for the less desirable goods. The more desirable goods will be relatively less expensive than the less desirable goods and yet since the less desirable goods will be relatively high priced, a lot of credits would be granted. Thus the people at the front of the line would buy all the more desirable goods first leaving the less desirable goods for those who line up later. This can be avoided by having two sectors. In each sector the goods are relatively equally desirable compared to each other.

Prisoners can spend all their credits or some of them, but they can never spend more than they are credited with. If some prisoners spend less than they are credited with each day, then there is a natural surplus of goods. By the action of choosing and buying, the prisoners indicate which goods they want more of and which goods they want less of. We assume that there is another camp with 200 prisoners each receiving the same rations as our prisoners. They can trade with us. The only differences are that they probably set different prices for their goods and they also likely have a surplus but of different goods.

The president of our camp exchanges the goods we have in surplus (those that were not sold) for goods that the prisoners would buy a lot of. Suppose the president did not sell 12 bars of soap, 8 potatoes and 20 tea bags. These have a total value of $(12 \times 2.00\ \Theta) + (8 \times 1.00\ \Theta) = 32.00\ \Theta$ and $20 \times 0.50\ \text{þ} = 10.00\ \text{þ}$. The other camp also has some surpluses. They have 5 cans of ham, 12 crackers and 15 cigarettes. They chose to price their goods as follows: $3.00\ \Theta$ per can of ham, $1.00\ \Theta$ per cracker and $1.00\ \Theta$ per cigarette. Note that the type of currency does not matter here. The distinction between sectors at this point is irrelevant. So we will use Norses as currency and rather than our tea bags costing $0.50\ \text{þ}$, they simply cost $0.50\ \Theta$ each.

Now our president must get rid of the goods we have in surplus- 12 bars of soap, 8 potatoes, and 20 tea bags- since no one wants them. If they did they would have bought them.

In order to trade between the two camps, an exchange rate must be set. In consumerism the exchange rate is calculated and it is calculated as such. We quote our prices in Θ but we quote the other camp's prices in $. We do this to avoid the confusion we would have if we expressed real exchange rates in the same currency. The real exchange rates are: (expressed in $/$\Theta$)

Ham- $3.00/ 2.00\ \Theta = \$1.50/\Theta$

Crackers- $1.00/0.50\ \Theta = \$2.00/\Theta$

Cigarettes- $1.00/1.00\ \Theta = \$1.00/\Theta$

Tea bags- $1.00/0.50\ \Theta = \$2.00/\Theta$

Potatoes- $0.50/1.00\ \Theta = \$0.50/\Theta$

Soap- $1.50/2.00\ \Theta = \$0.75/\Theta$

After multiplying each real exchange rate by the number of goods involved and dividing by the total number of goods traded we get an exchange rate of $\$1.38/\Theta$

The president creates a trade pool. This is an entry on a piece of paper that earns money during some trades and allows subsidized trades in other cases.

We are selling 20 tea bags, 8 potatoes and 12 bars of soap. We are buying 5 cans of ham, 12 crackers and 15 cigarettes from the other camp. First we take care of the selling. The other camp pays 20 x $1.00 = $20.00 to us for buying tea bags. In terms of our currency it is $20.00 x (1.00 Θ/$1.38) = 14.50 Θ. But our price for tea bags is 20 x 0.50 Θ = 10.00 Θ. Therefore 4.50 Θ goes to the trade pool. The 10.00 Θ go to cover the cost of the tea bags. The other camp pays 8 x $0.50 = $4.00 for potatoes. This is equal to $4.00 x (1.00 Θ/$1.38) = 2.90 Θ. But our potatoes cost 8 x 1.00 Θ = 8.00 Θ. So to subsidize this trade, the trade pool must lose 5.10 Θ. The other camp pays 12 x $1.50 = $18.00 for soap. This equals $18 x (1.00 Θ/$1.380 = 13.04 Θ. But we need to receive 12 x 2.00 Θ = 24.00 Θ for the soap. Thus the trade pool must subsidize 10.96 Θ.

Now let us look at buying. We buy 5 cans of ham. We must pay the other camp 5 x $3.00 = $15.00. This equals $15.00 x (1.00 Θ/$1.38) = 10.86 Θ. But we pay 5 x 2.00 Θ = 10.00 Θ for the ham. That means that the trade pool must subsidize 0.86 Θ for this trade. We buy 12 crackers. We must pay the other camp 12 x $1.00 = $12.00. This equals $12.00 x (1.00 Θ/$1.38) = 8.70 Θ. We pay 12 x 0.50 Θ = 6.00 Θ for the crackers. The trade pool must subsidize 2.70 Θ. Finally the president buys 15 cigarettes for $1.00 = $15.00. This in terms of Norses is $15.00 x (1.00 Θ/$1.38) = 10.87 Θ. We pay 15 x 1.00 Θ = 15.00 Θ. The trade pool gains 4.13 Θ.

Now let's see the net surplus or deficit of the trade pool.

It gains: 4.50 Θ + 4.13 Θ

It loses: 5.10 Θ + 10.96 Θ + 0.86 Θ + 2.70 Θ

Thus the net result is – 10.99 Θ. The president wants to avoid a negative trade pool balance. He can do this by manipulating how many goods he wants to trade.

We have explored, in detail, how a consumerist economy would spring up in a prison camp. We saw how goods, which were divided into two sectors, would be traded. We also saw how two prison camps would trade with each other, getting rid of their surpluses and maximizing on their desires.

Quotas and Rent Control

Here we examine two pervasive features that exist in most free-market economies. They are import quotas and rent control.

By import quota we mean a limit on the quantity of foreign goods brought into our country. Such a quota raises the domestic price above the world price and therefore domestic sellers benefit while domestic buyers are harmed. This doesn't occur in accommodation based consumerism. There is no import quota and importation is encouraged. Since importation benefits the consumerists and the system is primarily concerned with aiding the consumerist (as long as it doesn't hurt the producer at the same time), there really are no limits on imports of foreign goods. There is one exception. The trade pool, which we discussed before, should be positive most of the time. Therefore sometimes it may be necessary to restrict some imports.

Now let's look at rent control. Rent control is a price ceiling placed by some governments on rent that a landlord may charge his or her tenants. The idea behind it is to help the poor receive affordable housing. However this is inefficient. Rent control does not exist in an accommodation based consumerist society. However landlords are not able to set the price they want on their housing either. Rent prices are determined by the Rental Equivalence Duration (RED). This is set by the central bank. A tenant pays how many years it would take to own the building.

To help those not working, the consumerist government has an approach different than rent control. In consumerism, absolutely everyone is entitled to an accommodational award. No one at all should be homeless. However these individuals must pay all, none or some of the value of this accommodation as soon as they find work in the natural or governmental partitions. Also, these people are usually employed in the command partition or the laissez-faire labor system and they can use their extra-work transfer payments to pay for rent.

Rent control and import quotas are found in the free enterprise system. They do not exist in accommodation bases consumerism. These are the advantages that this system has over the first.

Investment

By investment we mean the purchase by a firm of inputs, land, capital and material often to expand or start operation. Investments are associated with the accommodational sector. Therefore transactions concerning investments involve Ignits.

The four main types of investment are in land, labor, capital and R & D (research and development). By land we mean territory on which, for example, a factory may be built. By labor we mean workers that convert inputs into products. These include janitors, cashiers, clerks, technicians, analysts, etc. By capitol we mean equipment that can be used to convert inputs into products. These include cash registers, mops, actual buildings, paper pressers, knives, tolls, computers, motors, etc. By research and development we mean better methods of turning inputs into products using new know how. These include new patents and new inventions and innovations of technology.

All these forms of investment have a price or wage function set by the central bank. For example a janitor may be paid 6.00 þ per hour and commercial land may cost 50.00 þ/m^2. The accommodational markdown does not apply to labor or R & D or capitol. It does apply to land.

Let's do some examples. We use our hypothetical Bob's doughnut shop. Bob wants to expand by buying more land and building another doughnut shop on it. The land costs 40.00 þ/m^2. He buys 500 m^2. This is 20 000.00 þ. We assume in this section that the accommodational markdown is 25 %. Now he has where to build his shop. The former owner of the land receives 15 000.00 þ.

Now Bob builds the actual store. It costs 100 000.00 þ and it is built by our hypothetical Super Plus Construction. Bob pays 100 000.00 þ for it while Super Plus Construction keeps 75 000.00 þ. To encourage investment in firms located in a consumerist nation the government sets a Capital Investment Transfer (CIT). Let's say it is 3%. In this case Bob would be given 3 000.00 þ.

Bob also needs a cash register, a mop and bucket, a doughnut rack, seats and tables, washroom sinks and stalls, light bulbs, carpets and other things that a doughnut store needs. They cost 40 000.00 þ. The firms from whom Bob bought these earn a total of 30 000.00 þ split among each other. Assuming a CIT of 3%, Bob would be given 1200.00 þ.

Bob also hires 3 employees; 1 baker and 2 waitresses. The waitresses earn 10.00 þ/hour and the doughnut baker earns 9.00 þ per hour. For these workers there is no accommodational markdown although they are technically in the accommodational sector. Wages are the incentive for anyone to produce goods and services. If there was an accommodational markdown on wages there would be a disincentive to work much like a heavy income tax discourages productivity in a free enterprise economy. Bob is rewarded by the government for hiring these workers. The government pays a percentage of their wages so as to encourage employment. So if each worker earned 1500.00 þ per week and the Employment Reimbursement Transfer (ERT) was 2%, Bob would be given 90.00 þ for hiring these workers.

Bob does an investment in research and development. He tells his baker to experiment with dough and chocolate to come up with two new flavors of doughnuts. For this time the baker is paid 50.00 þ. There is no accommodational markdown so he keeps all of it.

We saw what investment is. We encountered the three areas a firm can invest in. Using an example, we saw how a firm would go about investing in itself. We did calculations involving the ERT and the CIT.

Advertising

Advertising is as important for the economy as it is for the business that is advertising. By advertising we mean letting one firm's products be known through some kind of medium. There are many ways to advertise. Examples include through television, radio, newspapers and bus stop signs. Advertising is in the accommodational sector and is manipulated by Ignits. It is affected by the accommodational markdown.

The central bank sets the price for advertising through the different types of media. For example, advertising through television may cost 2000.00 þ/minute and through radio 500.00 þ/ minute and through newspaper, 10.00 þ/ word.

In the case of television, the more entertaining it is, the more viewers watch a program, usually. However the more viewers watch a program and the commercials during it, the more people will see a firm's commercial and the firm will earn more money selling its products. Therefore there is a certain type of selection for televisions broadcasting companies to come up with more entertaining programs. Similar arguments apply to radio and newspaper firms. Advertising should be encouraged as much as possible so that consumerists have more TV stations showing entertaining programs.

Here is an example. Let's suppose a hypothetical Joe's Crispy Cookies wants to attract more buyers to their cookies. They make a 30 s add on TV. To put a commercial on TV it costs 2000.00 þ/minute. They must pay 1000.00 þ to the TV station (let's call it Channel Super Plus) to air their commercial. Due to an accommodational markdown of 25 %, Channel Super Plus earns 750.00 þ,

A firm could also advertise through the radio. Let's use Joe's Crispy Cookies again as an example. To put a commercial on the radio it costs 700.00 þ/minute. This is set by the central bank and is the same regardless which radio station airs the commercial. They want to put on a commercial for one minute. Thus Joe's Crispy Cookies puts their commercial on a radio that has the most listeners (let's call it Super Radio Station Plus). Due to an accommodational markdown of 25 %, Super Radio Station Plus earns 525.00 þ/ minute

Another option for Joe's Crispy Cookies to advertise is through bus stop ads. Suppose that the central bank sets that it costs 400.00 þ per bus ad/ 2 weeks. So if Joe's Crispy Cookies puts a bus stop ad for 4 weeks they would have to pay 800.00 þ for that service. Since these bus stop shelters were put up by the government, this 800.00 þ goes to the government (usually municipal). The same would happen if a firm placed an ad on the side of a bus.

A question that comes up is this: should some products be banned from advertising, i.e. cigarettes? This is a question left to the government as it is essentially a political rather than an economic question.

We saw that advertising is important. We saw how a firm would go about advertising its products. With advertising a firm can increase its revenue and earn a higher profit, benefiting society, itself and all consumerists.

The Underground Economy

The free-market system has a tendency to induce the development of an "underground economy". By the term underground economy in this sense we mean business operations that are not officially reported. They include lawn mowing, selling goods without a vendor's license (i.e. selling chocolate bars door to door or lemonade at a street corner). They also include operations in the so called black market where illegal or prohibited goods are exchanged secretly. Furthermore there is a tendency for people to do jobs like house renovations or eye exams secretly using cash as a payment for their services. The reason these spring up is that if these transactions are not reported, the entrepreneurs do not have to pay taxes; they are keeping everything they charge.

In the communist system, there is a different kind of underground economy. In the communist system all the means of production are in the hands of the government. However some enterprising develops, where buyers and sellers exchange goods and services for currency in the free-market sense. This is the extent of the communist system's underground economy. That is the development of a merchant sector. Citizens buy jeans for money. They buy soft drinks for money. They buy running shoes for money. All of these would not normally exist in a purely communist system.

Now let's look at the consumerist underground economy. What do we do regarding small jobs like mowing lawns, baby sitting or selling lemonade? The simplest solution is to put these services and goods in the laissez-faire sector. Since there isn't any income tax, sales tax, corporate tax, etc... these services will no longer be "underground" and there really won't be any serious problems. So mowing one's lawn or babysitting will be dictated by the laws of supply and demand. Then, mowing someone's lawn is just as legitimate as teaching French although mowing someone's lawn and teaching French are in different sectors.

Suppose a 10 year old, Jack, wants to make some money. He decides he will mow his neighbor's lawn. They agree that mowing the lawn is worth 5.00 f/hour. It takes Jack about an hour to mow his neighbor's lawn. His neighbor gives Jack a check for 5.00 f. Jack takes his check to his local bank. At that time the bank credits Jack's laissez-faire account with 5.00 f and deducts 5.00 f from Jack's neighbor's account. The same reasoning applies to other "underground" transactions such as selling lemonade, selling hot dogs or shoveling driveways.

In the consumerist underground economy, we have the existence of dollarization. That is people start to use dollars instead of the other 3 consumerist currencies. This is clearly a major problem. When a tourist comes to our nation he will have to exchange his dollars for Ignits and Fortals. The private bank takes his dollars and opens up for a him a bank account in terms of Fortals and Ignits. He is then given a book of checks. Every time he wants to make a transaction in a consumerist nation, he simply writes the place of business a check and receives a good or service in return.

Another type of underground economy arises where people begin to oversell or undersell a good or service. This means that they start to sell goods and services for prices that are above or below that set by the central bank. Of course, this is totally benign in the laissez-faire sector but it does present problems for the other 3 sectors.

We saw how an underground economy develops in a free-market system. We also saw how an underground economy develops in a communist system. Finally we saw why it is unlikely that there will be an underground economy in the consumerist system.

Gratuities and Charities

The question arises: what are the circumstances regarding a tip? A gratuity is a payment for a service that is not official but the buyer pays if he thinks the service provider did a good job or in other words saying "I appreciate the fine job you did". Waiters, hair dressers, taxi drivers and newspaper couriers rely on gratuities. People also receive gratuities from helping someone out as in the case of assisting someone across the street or helping someone with their groceries.

Gratuities fall under the laissez-faire sector. When someone gives a tip, they do not give a bill or a coin since these do not exist under our system but rather they write a check in Fortals. The peculiar thing about gratuity payments is that the payer is not obliged to pay anything but rather he pays as a way of saying "thank you" to someone. The amount of the gratuity is determined by the person giving the gratuity and there is no price function for tips. Therefore the payer can give as little or as much as he wants for there is no accommodational markdown on a gratuity payment.

The idea of a charity exists to give people or others who are in desperate need of assistance and help. These people usually cannot make money on their own and their living conditions are horrible. Charities exist to help people who are afflicted by war, children starving in third world countries, people recovering from bad weather conditions like a tsunami or mistreated dogs that were abused by their owners. All these types of charities can be supported in consumerism.

What if someone wants to give a gift to a charity to help poorer people in another country? Suppose someone sees starving kids who cannot write in a far off place and wants to help them. In such a case the person can give a donation to the poor people. The donation must be in Fortas not Ignits or Norses. Furthermore the donation can be of any size the donor wants.

We saw the circumstances regarding gratuities. We also saw the circumstances regarding charities. With these two forms of money transfers, people can earn tips and poor people who need help can get assistance.

Free Goods and Services

This section is about free goods and services. These include birthday presents, Christmas presents, wedding gifts, in store free samples and surprises in cereal boxes. They are characterized by the fact that the recipient receives the goods without paying for them.

Many grocery stores offer free samples of foods to taste for customers. This free sample may help the firm in its operation. Although the customers do not pay for the free sample, if they like what they try, they may be more willing to buy the product. Free samples are a great way to promote goods and help the firm make profit.

Let's take the case that occurs when a free product comes with another good. For example a juice maker comes with a set of knives. The problem is that in the transaction of the juicer, the knives are not counted towards the GDCP. The benefit is that the consumerists receive more goods. Also, the firm is able to sell its products more quickly. Since the system is designed with the consumerist in mind the benefits outweigh the costs. The consumerist is helped directly; i.e. he receives free goods. And the consumerist is helped indirectly; i.e. the firm achieves its aim of selling goods.

It is necessary to allow for giving and receiving of gifts for special occasions (i.e. birthdays or Christmases). The difference here is that the gift is paid for- the gift giver bought the gift from a store (a radio from an electronics store for example). Since the gift giver bought the present, it is now his and he has the right to give it to anyone he wants as a present. The gift receiver thereby receives the gift for free.

There is a very important stipulation regarding free goods. When a firm gives a free product to a consumerist along with the things he bought during a transaction, the good must be of a different family (taxon). For example, when someone is buying a battery, he cannot receive another battery for free. This injures quality selection as a different quantity of the good, in this case batteries, is given than set by the price function. Likewise, when someone buys a set of 5 knives, he cannot get a 6th knife "for free". He could receive however, a free juicer.

Sometimes the giving of free goods takes a different form. For example, a coffee store gives free milk, cream or sugar to someone who buys a cup of coffee. If the coffee outlet does this voluntarily, it should be fully encouraged. The extra cost of the milk or sugar is so small yet it makes the coffee more enjoyable than if someone had to drink the coffee without anything or pay extra for the milk and sugar.

The giving and receiving of free goods and services is not to be discouraged. Although free goods and services are not recorded in the GDCP, consumerists benefit greatly from their availability. The economy benefits from the existence of free goods.

Pre-owned Goods

We must know what to do with used goods. By used goods we mean those goods that are not new as they have been enjoyed by a previous customer. Examples of used goods include old cars, pre-owned computer games or used hockey skates. We do not include houses or living accommodations in this as these are of a somewhat different nature.

Let's talk about a concrete example. Let's use cars. All automobiles have the same price function. Let's say that it is 10 000.00 Ө/car. It would seem logical that there should be some sort of "pre-owned markdown" on used items since they are clearly at a disadvantage in their goods family. That is used goods should cost less than new ones. However this leads to absurdities. A used economy car with not too many features would cost less than a limousine. A used sofa would cost less than a new one. If a used limousine costs less than a new one people would buy the used one. Consumerists would then not be receiving goods of the highest quality but will settle for worse quality ones. There will be competition in price rather than competition in quality. Thus quality selection would be jeopardized and we must do away with the "pre-owned markdown". All goods in the same family cost the same regardless of how old they are (except in the laissez faire sector).

So what to do with used goods like worn hockey skates or used cars? One option is to make used goods more competitive in a quality oriented market. This might mean painting the car, changing the seats, engine or tire or repairing broken parts. For hockey skates this might mean changing the lasses or mending worn parts.

Another option is to break the goods into parts and sell the parts to a manufacturer. The owner of a used car might still earn a lot of money selling the engine, tires, or glass to someone who needs it. In the case of hockey skates, the blade might be sold and used to make another new hockey skate.

The idea of the recycling-for-pay program may become useful. One can sell the parts of a pre-owned good to the government for profit. For example if someone has used hokey skates, he can take the skates to pieces- plastic, metal, rubber, upholstery- and sell these to the government for some money. The government then sells these items to firms that make use of inputs.

There is yet another thing we could do with used goods that we do not want but are not necessarily garbage. We could export these used goods to poor countries where the country's people could make use of them. For example, an old bike may not be of any value to us but in a third world country it could be very highly prized. Giving our used items to other countries may be a great way of improving our relationships with those countries.

We have in consumerism exportation firms. Essentially, producers of poor quality goods or consumerists who own used goods can sell that used good that they no longer need to an exportation firm for less than the good would cost normally in a fixed price system. The exportation firm then sells the used good to another foreign nation for the consumerist price, thus making a profit. In this arrangement, the consumerist trade pool is made use of.

We talked about pre-owned goods. We explained why pre-owned goods must not cost less than new ones; i.e. there mustn't be a "pre-owned markdown". We saw the options that exist for owners of pre-owned goods to trade away their goods.

Hard to Price Items

We come into a difficulty in pricing some goods and services. How do we price something like a painting or a book or art? How do we compare the "Mona Lisa" or the "Last Supper" with a stick drawing some first grader drew? What about books? Do we price them in terms of the number of pages or number of words or subject or what? We must find a coherent way of pricing everything.

We can compare the prices of cars, TV's, fruit and soft drinks using the consumerist approach. The reason is that they have the same essence. But the same is not true for art.

To price books we use the laissez-faire sector. The price of a book is determined by the laws of supply and demand. So some books cost more than others. The price of a book has to cover the cost of printing the book and give the author of the book some type of profit. There is no retail markup as the price set at that the bookstore where the book is sold already incorporates a profit for the bookstore. Suppose that to publish a book it costs 20.00 ₤. The author of the book receives a certain percentage of this called a royalty. A royalty is a percentage of the earnings from selling his or her work of art. It is set by the interaction of authors and book buyers. Let's assume that it is 20%. The bookstore has a mark-up is 35 %. Thus for a certain book, the publisher will sell his or her book for 20.00 ₤+ (0.35 x 20.00₤) = 27.00₤. The author keeps 27.00 ₤ x 0.2 = 5.40 ₤/book. The book store sells the book for (27.00 ₤ x 0.35) + 27.00 ₤ = 36.45 ₤. Here a mark-up is used twice; once for the publisher to make a profit over the publishing costs; secondly for the bookstore to make some money. The transaction is in Fortals, which is the currency in the laissez-fare sector. To convert Ignits to Fortals and vice versa, one would use the Ignit/Fortal exchange mechanism.

Now let's turn to the production of CD's. To make a CD costs, for example, 8.00 ₤. The royalty is 20% and the retailer earns a mark-up of 35%. Thus the retail distributor makes 8.00 ₤ + (8.00 ₤ x 0.35) = 10.80 ₤. The artist earns 10.80 ₤ x 0.2 = 2.16 ₤ per CD. The CD distributor earns 8.64 ₤ per CD. The CD store sells the CD for 10.80 ₤ + (10.80 ₤ x 0.35) = 14.58 ₤. The transaction involves Fortals as it is in the laissez-fare sector.

How about paintings? They are dealt with in the same way as in the free-market. Painters are allowed to sell their paintings for as much as they want to. This involves the idea of auctioning to the highest bidder. It is one of several instances of such a solution. Also under such a method of selling are antiques, collector's items and memorabilia. They are under the laissez-fare sector.

Jewelry is another kind of hard to price item. It is hard to put a good price on a gold or diamond ring or necklace solely using the consumerist pricing method. It makes much more sense to price the various types of jewelry using the laws of supply and demand. So, jewelry is in the laissez-faire sector and the price of jewelry is quoted in fortals.

We saw that some goods are hard to price. We demonstrated how a book and a CD are priced and sold. Furthermore we saw that some other items more notably paintings have to be exchanged using the method of auctioning as in the free-market system.

Trade via Internet

The world is being continuously more computerized. The internet has connected people from all over the world and has opened up new dimensions of trade. Now people can buy things without leaving their homes. They simply click the mouse button a few times and they are the proud owners of a new desk.

Under consumerism, internet trade is encouraged as it helps the consumerists. It provides a wider range of products for a consumerist to purchase. It also makes it easier for certain firms to sell their products.

Internet trade must however fit the parameters of the economic system. The prices of all products must be the same as those set by the central bank for that family (in the GAM sectors) whether they are sold over the internet or not. The goods sold over the internet are treated as if they are sold at the retail level. Therefore the prices of goods sold over the internet have to have the retail mark-up included in them. This means that it is the internet retail company that pays for the shipping and handling. Here's an example. Suppose a company on the internet is selling a microwave. They bought the microwave for 200.00 þ as this is the price set by the central bank for microwaves. The retail mark-up is 25%. Suppose Joe buys the microwave off the internet. The shipping and handling costs 5.00 þ. Joe pays the company 200.00 þ + (0.25 x 200.00 þ) = 250.00 þ. The internet company keeps 250.00 þ – 200.00 þ – 5.00 þ = 45.00 þ. The microwave is in the accommodational sector so all exchanges are in Ignits.

Trade over the internet could involve either the accommodational, materialist or laissez faire sectors. It could involve firms in either the command or natural partition. As discussed above trade over the internet in the materialist and accommodational sectors is under certain constraints set by the central bank. After these constraints are fulfilled, trade over the internet is simple, convenient and easy.

Trade over the internet is even simpler and easier when it is done through the laissez-faire sector. Here the price of goods and services sold over the internet is totally set by the interaction of those firms selling their products over the internet and those buying their products over the internet. There is no AMD or tax of any sort whatsoever. Who pays for the shipping and handling is also determined by the interaction of buyers and sellers. Internet trade through the laissez faire sector can be in either the command or natural partitions.

Trade over the internet is desirable under the consumerist system. Such a trade operates as any other form of trade, adhering to the parameters set by the government and the central bank. We gave an example of a trade carried out on the internet.

Budget Deficit and Surplus

By deficit we mean having less money to spend than required. One spends more than earning in revenue. By surplus we mean having more money than able to spend. One earns more in revenue than spending on services and goods. We deal with the budgets of governments in particular. That is the federal, provincial and municipal levels of government.

The government (all levels) has several sources of income, one being the GCT. They have several others which we mentioned previously. The central bank grants the GCT to them. Each level of government receives 1/3 of the GCT. The federal government earns the entire 1/3 while the other two levels of government earn income based on population.

In this section, for simplicity, we talk about the budget of the federal government. The budgets of the other two levels are similar.

The actions taken during surpluses and deficits are simple. If there is a surplus, there are 3 choices. One is to provide more services and increasing spending. Another choice is to cut the GCT. Also, the government can buy stocks and bonds and have a stream of income for the future. If there is a deficit there are also 3 choices. One is to raise the GCT another is to cut services and spending. The government can sell Consumerist Savings Bonds- this depends on the level of government in question.

Let's do some calculations. The GCT is 30%. The output of the materialist sector is 1 000 000.00 Θ. The government gets 0.3 x 1 000 000.00 Θ = 300 000.00 Θ

The federal government gets 1/3 x 300 000.00 Θ = 100 000.00 Θ. The provinces/ states and municipal governments get 1/3 of this amount each depending on the population each state or municipality has.

If the government made 100 000.00 Θ and spent only 80 000.00 Θ, this would represent a surplus. This would leave purchasing power for the future. Sometimes having a surplus is useful as having money to spend in the future is good when the money may be needed more.

Deficits are possible. The government can earn more money than through the GCT. It operates in the governmental sector using Norses. But it can raise money by selling Consumerist Savings Bonds (whether federal, provincial or municipal) which are parts of the accommodational sector or expanding the role of the command partition. Then, the Ignits are directly used to purchase government services and goods. If the government wants to make more money it ought to raise the GCT or sell even more Consumerist Savings Bonds. In case the government suspects it will not make enough money to cover its expenses, it must start to cut the least essential services. Other ways of raising money quickly include the selling of licenses and permits as well as the selling of land and building more casinos.

From time to time, surpluses also occur. The government has more purchasing power than before as they have higher revenue than their expenditures. Consumerists love a budget surplus because then the government can do three things each of which benefits the consumerists tremendously. One option is to lower the GCT. This means that more of the GDCP will be going to the General as well as Non-working Consumerist Grants. So consumerists have more purchasing power. The other option is to increase spending on social services. The government could build another hospital, school, library, roads or pay doctors more for their services (assuming we have ultra-universal health care). The third option is very subtle. During times of surplus, the levels of government should buy stocks and bonds- whether of the consumerist or speculative kind. This creates an alternative stream of income for the levels of government. Let's do some calculations. Suppose that the federal government had a revenue of 100 000 000.00 þ and spent 80 000 000.00 þ leaving a surplus of 20 000 000.00 þ Now a hypothetical firm RFVB issues Consumerist General Bonds with a CGBIR of 5 % and a CGBIRF of one month. The maturity is 5 years. If the federal government uses its surplus to buy these bonds it will make money every month and after 5 years it will get all their investment back.

We talked about budgets and deficits and surpluses that are related to them. We saw how budget deficits and surpluses are caused. We saw how a government deals with a surplus and finally we saw how a government deals with a deficit.

Gambling

It should be possible to gamble in a consumerist society. We look at two types of gambling; lotteries and casinos. By lotteries we mean opportunities to win a large sum of money by buying a lottery ticket and picking the right numbers. By casinos we mean institutions where consumerists get together and play games in which they can make money or lose money. Games played at casinos include poker, black jack, roulette and slot machines among others. Gambling is in the laissez-faire sector and involves Fortals. However the proceeds from gambling go to the three levels of government to pay for social services, although some lotteries are operated by particular government jurisdictions. The accommodational markdown does not apply to gambling.

First let's look at lotteries. Scratch-and-Win cards are sold for a markup in the laissez-faire sector but the proceeds go to the government. Suppose the government sets the price of a lottery ticket at 2.00 ₤. It sells these tickets to firms in the laissez- faire sector who charge gamblers a higher price in terms of Fortals. Let's suppose here it is 3.00 ₤. If a gambler, Bob, buys a lottery ticket for 3.00 ₤, he has a chance to win the lottery. All lottery gaming is owned and operated by the government but works in conjunction with the laissez-faire sector. In this case 1.00 ₤ goes to the firm in the Laissez-faire sector that sold Bob the ticket. Assume for simplicity that 1₤ = 1þ. Then 2.00 ₤ = 2.00 þ go to the government to pay for social services.

Not all tickets cost 2.00 ₤. Some may be 1.00 ₤ and others may be 15.00 ₤. The rewards of winning are set by the lottery company run by the government. The higher the grand prize or the greater the chances of winning smaller prizes, the more it can charge per ticket, the more tickets the lottery company sells and thus the more profit it earns. If Bob wins the lottery and the jackpot is 1 000 000.00 ₤, he keeps 1 000 000.00 ₤ (because there are no taxes or accommodational markdown to worry about). If the government run lottery company earns a profit of 10 000 000.00 þ (after giving out prizes), it keeps 10 000 000.00 þ.

As stated lottery tickets are operated by the levels of government but they are sold directly to consumerists in the laissez-faire sector. Firms in the gambling industry of the laissez-faire sector could be either of the command partition or natural partition type. If they are from the natural partition the profit from selling the lottery ticket (price minus what goes to the government) goes to profit maximizing firms. If firms selling lottery tickets are from the command partition, then there is even more revenue going to the government for socials services. For example, if the government sells a lottery ticket for 2.00 ₤ to a command partition-laissez faire firm and this firm sells the ticket for 3.00 ₤, then 3.00 ₤ total go to the government to pay for social services (2.00 ₤ + (3.00 ₤ – 2.00 ₤)) = 3.00 ₤

Also, laissez-faire firms in the command partition dictate, somewhat, the price of the lottery ticket. If a command partition-laissez faire firm charges 4.00 ₤ for a ticket and another natural partition-laissez faire firm charges 5.00 ₤ for the same ticket, most consumerists would buy the 4.00 ₤ ticket.

Now let's look at casinos. Casinos are owned, managed and operated by the government. Gambling in a casino closely resembles gambling in a free-market economy in that gamblers can wage any amount of money on games and machines. The accommodational markdown does not apply to the winnings of the casino. Suppose Bob plays poker and wins 10 000.00 ₤. He gets a check from the casino for this amount and keeps 10 000.00 ₤. If a casino earns 100 000 000.00 ₤ in a year, it keeps 100 000 000.00 ₤. After being exchanged to Ignits through the Ignit- Fortal exchange mechanism, this also goes to the government to help pay for social services.

The idea of gambling has a negative side, however. Excessive gambling can lead to gambling addiction. Lives can be hurt and personal savings can be ruined if a person's gambling leads to addiction. Gambling addiction hurts lives personally and it hurts society. Thus the consumerist government should embark on programs designed to help those with gambling issues. Support groups, counseling and help lines should be made available for those struggling with gambling addiction

Gambling is a part of the consumerist system. We saw how a gambler would play the lottery or enjoy the casino. Gambling exists as a method of entertainment or as a way to become instantly rich. It is also beneficial as the proceeds from gambling go to the government to pay for needed social services.

Vacations, Time Off and Maternity Leave

Every working consumerist should be entitled to a vacation. By vacation we mean some time off from work. Consumerists need time to appreciate the things they have or go to a place to relax, enjoy themselves and have fun. Working consumerists should be paid during their vacation.

How long should a consumerist's vacation be? It should be based on time per year and this should be set by the government. The amount of time in a year that a consumerist is entitled to spend as a paid vacation is called the *Yearly Vacation Duration Period*. Suppose it is set at one month. If this is the case, every consumerist working for at least a year can spend 1 month off from work with pay. What about jobs where a worker works less than a year, like a job contract for 6 months? In this case the worker can have half a month of vacation as 6 months is half a year. What if the job contract is for 1 month? In this case the worker is entitled to have a vacation for 2.5 days as 1 month is 1/12 of a year.

The timing of the vacation is set by the bargaining of the workers and the employers. Usually when a worker signs a contract, it will say when he can take his vacation. Also, if a worker wants a vacation at a particular time, i.e. to see his family for a wedding, he may ask his employer for some time off for vacation.

Being able to take a long, pleasant, restful vacation is just as important as making a lot of money. Having some free time and the opportunity to enjoy life make life so much more meaningful. If a man worked hard all his life, amassing a considerable fortune, without taking any time for vacation he will probably really regret it when he is very old. Therefore, in Accommodation based consumerism it is highly encouraged for workers to take enjoyable vacations. Although, usually, the longer the length of the vacation the better, we must balance this with 1) a worker is not doing anything productive for society on vacation and 2) the employer usually has to pay for the vacation (in terms of lost income)

Sick leave is similar to the Vacation Duration Period. The difference is that a worker doesn't get paid when he gets sick. The amount of time off for sickness is called the *Sick Leave Exemption Period*. It is set by the government. It is usually much shorter than the Yearly Vacation Duration Period. Suppose that the government sets it at 12 days per year. Thus a worker who works at least 12 months is entitled to have 12 days off for sickness.

If a worker is sick, he must first use up his sick leave for time off. If his sickness is longer than the length of the Sick Leave Exemption Period, he can stay off work during his Vacation Duration Period.

It is reasonable that a worker, from time to time, will get sick. He may have the flu, the cold or an infectious problem. The employer ought to give him or her some days off to recuperate and get better. This is obviously better than the worker spreading the flu to other employees. However, there should not be any pay for taking days off- unless this illness is prolonged or prohibits the worker from being productive and effective. If workers were paid for being sick, we could anticipate an abuse of the system where people would just take the day off because they don't want to work and they would still expect to get paid.

What if a worker becomes injured on the job and cannot work anymore? For example he cuts off his fingers while cutting meat. In such a case, the injured worker receives a severance package from the work he used to be employed in. This is set by the central bank and reflects the extent of the injury, i.e. how severe it is and how career ending it is. This is called the *Injury Severance Payment*.

What about maternity leave? Should a pregnant woman or new mother be paid while she is carrying her baby and taking care of the baby? A mother to be should be paid during her time off. The length of the time she can take to take care for her baby is set by the government.

We discussed in this section the circumstances regarding vacations. We also mentioned time off, sick leave and injuries. Finally we talked about maternity leave.

Tourism

Tourism is the visitation of foreigners in another country for a while. Many tourists come to relax on a holiday while others come to places of historical or cultural importance. Others visit foreign countries because they have relatives or friends there. In every case a foreigner comes to a country for some time but does not stay there permanently. In every instance, a tourist needs to buy things in the country he is visiting. Thus he must spend money and the local economy prospers. Let's look at tourism as it applies to accommodation based consumerism.

We have two types of tourism. 1) Our citizens visit other countries and 2) Foreigners visit our country. First case 1. Our citizens can only spend Ignits when visiting other countries. Tourism belongs to the leisure industry which is in the accommodational sector. These tourists cannot use Norses. However they must exchange Ignits for foreign currency in order to buy things there; i.e. resort, hotels, meals at restaurants and passes to museums and galleries. We assume for the purpose of this section that our tourist is visiting the U.S. Thus he must exchange Ignits for U.S. dollars. This is easily accomplished when we know the nominal exchange rate. Using the nominal exchange rate, Ignits are converted into dollars and dollars into Ignits. We have already discussed how the nominal exchange rate is set (using calculations involving real exchange rates and their weights in trade at the consumerist trade pool). So suppose someone has 500.00 þ. The nominal exchange rate is $1.50/þ. This tourist can exchange his Ignits for 500.00 þ x $1.50/þ. While in the U.S. our tourist sees a movie, goes to a museum, eats a meal at a restaurant and stays at a hotel. These cost respectively, $12.00, $20.00, $60.00 and $400.00. Thus he spends $492.00 on his trip. Usually a tourist must have transportation to his destination. We have not incorporated this into our calculations yet. We do so now. In order to get to the U.S. and to comeback our tourist must take a plane. This trip costs 300.00 þ. Our tourist must pay 300.00 þ to go to the U.S. and return.

Now for case 2; where a visitor comes to our country. This visitor is from the U.S. and has $500.00. The nominal exchange rate is $1.50/þ. His trip and return ticket cost him $ 200.00. So now he has $ 300.00. This is equivalent to $300.00 x 1.00 þ/$1.50 = 200.00 þ. He wants to buy the following things: a stay at a hotel, a trip to an art gallery, a movie and a meal at a restaurant. The stay at the hotel costs 70.00 þ for 3 days. Tickets to the art gallery cost 15.00 þ. Visiting the art gallery belongs to the leisure industry that is part of the accommodational sector. The chance to see a movie also belongs to the leisure industry that is part of the accommodational sector. There is a problem with the restaurant meal as it is in the hospitality industry that is part of the materialist sector. The materialist sector operates with Norses but Norses must not be exchanged for dollars or vice versa. What happens is that the tourist can use his foreign currency, in this case dollars, in the form of a check. Keep in mind that 1.00 þ is always equal to 1.00 Θ but that they cannot be exchanged directly for one another. So suppose that the meal cost 50.00 Θ. The American tourist gives the waiter a check for 50.00 þ x $1.50/þ = $75.00. When the restaurant takes the check to the bank, the bank credits the restaurant with 50.00 þ and deducts $75.00 from the American visitor's account.

During tourist activities, bank deposits are used as opposed to actual cash. When our tourist visits the U.S. he has 500.00 þ. The nominal exchange rate is $1.50/þ. The bank turns the 500.00 þ in his account to $750.00. When in the U.S. he can sign checks on his account in dollars. This money is transferred from his account to the business owner he dealt with in the U.S.

Suppose a tourist from the U.S. visits our country. He has $500.00. Cash is not acceptable. He must pay with check. If he spends all his money $500.00 is deducted from his account and the right amount of Ignits is put into a domestic Ignit account belonging to the firm he had a transaction with.

We saw that tourism is good for both the tourist and the international economy. We looked at the case where a visitor from our country visits another. We also looked at the case where a foreigner takes a trip to our country.

The Institutionalized Population

Here we talk about the institutionalized population. This refers to the part of the general population that is separate from the rest as they are specially cared for or are in a special situation. Who is counted as being in the institutionalized population? Those in jails or correctional facilities, the people in hospitals or group homes, those in retirement homes and those in the army.

How is their welfare taken care of? These people are taken care of by the government spending through the tax (GCT) and other sources of revenue like profits from the command partition.

Those in jail do not get paid the consumerist grant. Neither do they get welfare money. Their food and clothing is paid by the government. The care of inmates is the responsibility of either the federal or provincial governments. The same applies to those in correctional facilities.

People that are in the hospital for a short time (i.e. a few days) still receive the consumerist grant. However those in the hospital long term do not receive the general consumerist grant as they are not working. The functioning of the hospital is paid by the government and the government provides those in the hospital long term with what they need (food, bed, clothes). The same is true for those in group homes and retirement homes. All their food and accommodation is paid for by the government. Thus they do not receive the consumerist grant; either general or non-working.

The situation is different for armed forces personnel. They are paid by the government but are given the general consumerist grant since they are working. Since those in the army, navy, air force do a tremendous service protecting us and serving our country it would be disrespectful if they earned the Non-Working Consumerist Grant as opposed to the General Consumerist Grant. Since they give us so much of their selves and their time they certainly do deserve the General Consumerist Grant.

There is a special program for inmates of prisons and correctional facilities. Basically they perform some sort of work in exchange for a shorter prison sentence. For example, they can be made to mop the floors, cook meals for other inmates or sort garbage. These jobs must be such that no one can be injured nor can the inmate escape. They must be low-risk jobs. In exchange for this work the inmates have time taken off their sentence. So, for example, if an inmate worked 10 hours sweeping the floors of the prison, he would have 4 hours deducted of his sentence. The idea behind this is that it will increase the output of the economy while leaving more demanding jobs for more skilled workers, i.e. those outside bars and with some education. This is called the Work for Freedom program.

Those in institutions are treated differently from the rest of society. Their welfare is ensured by the government. Save for armed forces personnel, they do not usually receive the consumerist grant.

Retirement

As workers age, they will reach a point where they will not be able to work anymore. After having contributed to society for so long, society should help them in their time of need. Accommodation based consumerism makes sure that those who reach an age where they can't work are still well cared for. Retirement is the concept of society helping those who contributed to society by working but who are now no longer to work due to old age.

First of all, those that retire need not be concerned about services from the governmental sector. If a retiree needs knee surgery, eye surgery, assistance from a dentist or protection from the police or service from the fire department, he, like everyone else in consumerism, he can get it. These public services are provided publicly by the government and are funded through various ways including the GCT.

Workers, even though they may be old, continue to be granted Norses to spend on the materialist sector. Instead of a general consumerist grant, they are granted the non-working consumerist grant. Since they aren't working they are granted less than those that do. When they stop working they still need Ignits to spend on the accommodational sector.

The government sets a minimum age at which a worker can retire. This is called the *Minimum Retirement Age*. If workers cherish their jobs and want to work past that, they can.

The government- not the central bank- grants those beyond the minimum retirement age a sum of money in Ignits. The government determines the amount of each payment. This is called the *Retirement Pension Allowance*. The money for this grant is obtained through the tax system and other sources of revenue we discussed previously.

A retiree may still want to buy goods and services in the laissez faire sector for example jewelry or antiques or books. The laissez-faire sector uses a different currency- fortals. To buy things in this sector, the retiree must exchange the Ignits he was given through the retirement pension allowance into fortals at the private bank using the Ignit-Fortal exchange mechanism.

Past a certain age, a worker can retire. Those that retire are cared for by our society. The government grants money to retirees to spend on the accommodational sector while retirees still receive a grant from the central bank for materialist goods.

Distribution of Income

In this section we compare several philosophies of distributing income. Basically, "distribution of income" refers to how the economic pie is divided. We compare utilitarianism, liberalism, and libertarianism. Then we contrast these with consumerism. (Kneebone, R.D. et al, 2002)

Libertarianism is the idea that income is created by individual people of a society not society itself. Distribution of income by the government takes some people's money and gives it to others. The idea that the final distribution is just regardless how unequal it is, is based on a process of determining the distribution of income that is fair. Libertarianism was founded by Robert Nozick. Libertarians claim that it is more important for opportunities to be equal than for income to be equal. The government's objective should be to safeguard individual rights and that all people should have the same chance to utilize their talents. Besides this, the government has no right to change the final distribution of income. (Mankiw, 2002)

Utilitarianism was founded by Jeremy Bentham and John Mill. The objective of this philosophy is to use the logic of individual decision making in the context of matters regarding public policy. The government's goal is to maximize the utility or level of happiness and satisfaction of everyone in society. It is based on diminishing marginal utility. The government must strive to attain a more equal distribution of income. The redistribution of income increases utility. The argument for utilitarianism is this. John and Bob are two workers. John earns $200 000.00 and Bob earns $100 000.00. By taking a dollar from John and giving it to Bob, Bob's utility increases but John's decreases. Utilitarians do not want completely equal distribution of income because this would take away the incentive to work. (Mankiw 450-451, 2002)

Liberalism was created by the philosopher John Rawls. It tries to find a "just" distribution of income. It is hard for people to set rules of a just society because people's point of view is distorted by how much they have now, whether they were born into a poor or rich family, their education, whether they are lazy or hard working, etc. Liberalists propose an "original position". This is a position where all people get together before they are born to determine the distribution of income. In this scenario they would be indifferent about where they would end in life. If people before they are born do not know whether they will be well off, badly off, or medium off, they would naturally be concerned about being poorly off. Liberalists thus propose as public policy trying to increase the welfare of the poorest individual in society. The maximin criterion is to maximize the minimum utility. Liberalism advocates public policy directed at equal income distribution because this increases the standard of being of the worst off. This doesn't lead to a total egalitarian society since it would kill incentive. (Mankiw, 2002)

Another important concept is the productivity principle. It states that all people should receive the monetary equivalent of that which they personally produced through human resources and non-human resources. The harder one works, the greater his productivity. Therefore the greater his reward should be.

Finally let's look at consumerism. Consumerism stresses that it is important that people have a strong incentive to work. There shouldn't be any redistribution of income. What a worker earns he can decide to spend on things that enhance his quality of life. Under consumerism it is also important to eliminate poverty. There should be no poor. But what does it mean to be "poor"? In the free-market system whether a person is poor or not depends on his income or the combined income of his family. Analysts use cost of living analyses and other measures. Yet most economists agree that there are problems with this type of definition of poverty. Suppose that the poverty line was $20 000.00. If there was a massive deflation and one could buy a 3 storey house for $1000.00 then this person would be rich, even though he had little money, as his ability to own assets increases, In Germany 1n 1919, a person with a billion Marks was considered extremely rich. There came about such a massive hyper-inflation that in 1923 a trillion Marks was worth $1.00. This person was now a beggar. Again suppose someone had $20 000.00 and suppose that this was low enough to call him poor. If this person moved to an impoverished nation like Rwanda, Chad or Cameroon, with $20 000.00, this person would be among the wealthiest in the country.

Consumerism defines poverty in another, better way. The definition is more qualitative, subjective and relative than it is quantitative, objective and absolute. A person who rides a bicycle is poor relative to a person who rides a limousine who is rich. A person who walks around in dirty rags is poor relative to a person who walks around in a business suit with a tie who is rich. A person who eats potatoes for dinner every day is poor relative to a person who eats lobster whenever he wants who is rich. A person who sits on a 3-legged 60 year old wooden stool is poor relative to a person who relaxes on an armchair who is rich. A person who is entertained by a ham radio is poor relative to a person who is entertained by a home theatre who is rich. Poverty is a function of the quality of the assets a person owns as well as the services one has access to. If we want to eliminate poverty we need to give all people goods and services of the highest quality. This is accomplished through the idea of "quality selection". Firms, for the most part, compete to give customers goods and services of the highest quality as the prices they can charge for them are set by the central bank. This has the effect that only goods of high quality are produced and goods of high quality are bought. This eliminates poverty as we have defined it.

In consumerism there is not a single economy like the other 3 philosophies assume. There are 4 sectors; the accommodational, materialist, laissez-faire and governmental. In order to eliminate materialist need, all individuals, with some exceptions, receive from the central bank income equivalent to the output of the materialist sector. With this money consumerists can purchase materialist goods and services. All working consumerists receive a grant of the same size.

To encourage people to contribute to society, they earn another currency which they can spend on goods and services in the accommodational and laissez-faire sectors. The more they contribute to society, the more money they earn. Therefore there is at the same time a large gap between the rich and not-so-rich in the accommodational sense and no gap between the rich and not-so-rich for working consumerists in the materialist sense.

Those consumerists who do not work or contribute to society earn less money to spend on the materialist sector so as to encourage them to work. For those who cannot contribute to either sector of the economy, the government provides accommodational welfare (housing, utilities) and money. Absolutely no one is homeless as everyone is granted the Accommodtional Award if they desire it. However this is hardly redistribution as those on welfare have to pay back a portion of everything the government provided them while on welfare. This is another incentive to discourage idleness.

We examined 3 different philosophies of income distribution. We talked about utilitarianism, liberalism, and libertarianism. Then we contrasted these with the consumerist philosophy of income distribution.

Externalities

An externality is a situation where one person affects another without compensating him. An externality can be positive or negative. An example of a positive externality would be a mathematical formula. Once a person finds it, everyone else benefits from it for free. An example of a negative externality would be pollution. If a company dumps toxic waste into a river without paying for it and the pollutant harms the river users, then this is a negative externality.

free-market economists acknowledge that there is a trade-off between externalities and production. In order for some businesses to prosper, they need to pollute; i.e. a paper mill makes pollution as it creates jobs and paper. They contend that some pollution is necessary to have a strong economy. In the free-market economy, the solution to the pollution externality is solved using quotas. Each firm that pollutes has a right to dump a certain amount of pollution into a river. Firms can trade quotas with each other so that companies that pollute more have a right to do so and those that do not can sell their quotas. However this can be a poor solution. Suppose that there are two firms. One has dumped 100 L of ooze into a river and firm 2 has dumped 200 L of ooze into a river. The river is polluted with 300 L of ooze. So the government sells quotas to the companies that restrict only 10 L of ooze to be dumped into a river by a company in a month. The two companies trade their quotas so that firm 1 can dump 3 L of ooze and firm 2 can dump 7 L of ooze. The consequences are counterproductive. In 30 months, there will be exactly the same amount of ooze in the river (300 L) as the government tries to prevent. All quotas do is that they delay the polluting process.

The consumerist solution to externality is based on the proposition that there does not necessarily exist a trade-off between an externality and productivity. The solution strives to eliminate pollution while maintaining a high standard of firm functioning. It is not impossible to promote a healthy environment as well as a strong industry. The concept can most easily be grasped using the negative externality of smoking. Smokers like to smoke. Non smokers on the other hand can't stand the smoke. We segregate a small section of a building and set it aside for smokers and we leave all other sections for non-smokers. In the smoking section the smokers can smoke all they want. However, the non smokers are not harmed or interfered with. Thus an externality has been destroyed without hurting output or smoker's functioning (smoking).

Let's apply this logic to the case of river pollution we examined above. Rather than aim for a policy that slows down an externality, the government should try to completely eliminate it. The polluting firm can buy a portion of land around its facilities where it can pollute all the solid waste it wants as long as this waste does not go into other areas sectioned off for non-polluters.

A polluter can buy a river or a section of a river where it is free to dump all the waste it wants. It can't buy major rivers that others want to enjoy; i.e. for fishing, drinking or swimming. If the polluting firm's pollution spills over to other areas beyond their pollution jurisdiction, they must be ordered by the government to perform a complete clean up of that area. The company that produces waste ought to find a way to get rid of it without polluting at a cost to the polluter. This is prescribed by the government and may involve using waste storage facilities or the destruction of waste. Polluters of ooze can dump their ooze into their private disposal units especially suited for getting rid of ooze. To combat this dumping of pollutants there should be a government agency or ministry that oversees that all waste is either destroyed or disposed of safety.

In many industrialized nations there is a tremendous negative externality problem where factories (e.g. steel makers or car assembly plants) emit dirty toxic smoke into the air. Certainly our quality of life would be compromised if we were to completely eliminate these pollution creating institutions. On the other hand we are forced to breathe in polluted disease causing smoke. In consumerism, we remedy the situation thus. The factory is made to emit all of its smoke into a large dome. This dome collects all the smoke the factory can ever produce. As a safety precaution the dome should be made of three separate layers. With this arrangement, the factory can expel all the smoke it wants to as none of it is going into the atmosphere. Clearly, common people are not harmed by pollution while the factory can still maintain its current level of productivity. Meanwhile the factory should strive to find a device (something like a catalytic converter) to break down the pollution-smoke into harmless particles.

Suppose a scientist working for a university comes up with a new theory of the universe. This leads to teleportation. How does this scientist gain from the invention of teleportation? The university pays him to teach and think there. They also pay him to write articles. If John Smith produced a new mathematical formula and wrote an article about it, he would receive money for the article (a price function set by the central bank). Those who read the article are free to use the knowledge provided in the article to advance the cause of humanity. The problem in this case is that the scientist does not get paid by the people who use his theory directly. There are other ways he can benefit. This involves the idea of special rewards. In the consumerist society there should be "achievement awards" where certain people are honored, receiving money, fame and recognition. Thus in each industry or profession there should be some kind of achievement award. For example, there should be awards for most heroic police officer, most helpful doctor and in the case of the physics community there should be an award for most respected physicist. In this way many positive externalities are overcome.

By-standards benefit from historic buildings without paying those who restored them. Suppose there is an old hut where the city's founder lived his life. The land could be used to make parking space. However to preserve the building, the government does not allow its destruction. Another option is that the local museum buys the building and offers the building for viewing to interested citizens who are curious about their town's history.

Let's see how we would apply consumerist reasoning to the problem of traffic congestion along a highway. In many major cities, Toronto, New York, Chicago, for example, there is commuter gridlock as people try to go home or go to work. During "rush hours" people can expect to spend some time on the highway. Is there a way to solve this problem? The best solution is to drastically increase the number of lanes in the highway. There may still be traffic congestion with 4 or 5 lanes. Perhaps some with 8 or 9. But if we built our highways with 17 lanes then the chances of traffic are almost not existent. On the positive side, commuters will be able to get between point A and point B much quicker. On the downside the highway will be a little bit bigger. Yet if we built the highway in the right place- a good distance from residential housing and commercial businesses- this shouldn't be a major problem.

We talked about both positive and negative externalities. We saw the solution to the dumping of ooze- a negative externality. We also saw the solution to the restoration of historic buildings- a positive externality.

Prostitution, Drugs and Illegal Commodities and Services

There are several goods and services that arise naturally in a free-market society that we may not want to have. They include prostitution, drugs, illegal weapons and other things. They arise in the free-market economy because the people that provide these things can earn money from people who want these things. These activities sometimes go hand in hand with poverty. Whether we want some of these things or services may be considered a political question concerning the government. For example, should we legalize marijuana or prostitution? Which drugs and weapons, if any, should be illegal or prohibited?

Prostitutes do not usually sell their bodies as a first choice. In many cases they are driven to this type of work because they are poor and have little food. If they could find another job paying just as much as a prostitute earns, they would surely chose that job over prostitution. Nevertheless we may, under some circumstances allow some form of prostitution to be legal in some places (like brothels) if the government or society decides there are any benefits to legal prostitution.

The same applies to people who sell drugs. Drug dealers are forced to sell drugs to make money. They are usually stricken with poverty or see selling drugs as a very quick and lucrative way of making money. Given a choice of a job that paid as much as drug trafficking, they would also choose it over drug selling. But we may want to legalize some drugs (like marijuana) so as to control all sales of that product. One of the advantages of legalizing a drug like marijuana is that we can make all sales of marijuana under the control of the government. Thus this would provide another source of revenue for the government in addition to the GCT.

Poverty does not exist to the same extent under consumerism as it does under the free-market system. All non-institutionalized consumerists are granted money from the central bank to spend as they wish. Therefore they are less likely to resort to prostitution or drug selling.

It's hard for prostitutes and drug dealers (assuming that we don't want them in our system) to operate in a cashless society. Since consumerism is a cashless society, it is easier to monitor all transactions as they are carried out by banks in bank accounts.

We talked about the major types of illegal businesses that form in a free-market economy. We saw that poverty is usually the major cause. Finally we saw why these would not be as prolific under consumerism.

Research, Development and Technology

Here we talk about three related concepts; research, development and technology. By research we mean the investigation into the knowledge of how things work; whether this relates to innovations, inventions or more theoretical things. By development we mean the application of knowledge to attain progress. By technology we mean the level of sophistication of our methods of doing things that promote progress.

Research can be carried out by institutions of higher learning; i.e. universities or colleges, or by private institutions; i.e. firms and corporations. Whether it is carried out in a knowledge or private institution, research has a positive externality. It is in the best interest of our consumerist society that a maximum amount of research is carried out. Almost everyone in society benefits from research.

The carrying out of research is in the accommodational sector if it is done by private institutions and it is in the governmental sector if it is done by universities. The funding of research at the governmental sector is done through the GCT. The funding of research in the accommodational sector is done through firm's payments from their profit. It is not covered by the accommodational markdown. It is included in the firm's "reinvestment in itself". Research done by firms is similar to an investment like hiring more workers, buying more machines or opening another outlet. When a corporation is paying its shareholders their dividends, the amount invested in research is deducted from the profit.

Firms develop when they use knowledge gained from research to expand their firm. This is a form of investment. Firms are encouraged to develop as much as possible. Development involves Ignits as it is in the accommodational sector but there is no accommodational markdown on it. Here's an example. A car factory spends 5 000.00 þ on research on a new motor. The research scientist working for them designs a new type of motor that makes the firm's car 1.8 x faster. The research scientists are paid by the car firm. Like all jobs, theirs is set by the central bank as a wage function. With this new knowledge, the car firm makes their new car with the new motor just invented. They pay 100 000.00 þ to apply the new knowledge of the motor to the cars. Their sales increase by 45% and they make 450 000.00 þ in the first month of introducing the new car. Obviously it was worth researching and developing this new motor.

Technology or the level of sophistication of industry is a measure of how well off a society can be. The level of technology is affected by research and development. The more research done and the more ideas developed, the higher the level of technology. In consumerism a high level of technology is an important goal as it is a factor that affects quality selection. The higher the technology level, the better the quality of products sold and bought. Since all goods and services in the same family are equally priced, it is the level of technology that has the biggest impact on quality and thus wealth, as wealth is measured by the quality of assets owned by consumerists.

It is important that our society tries to raise the technology level. The government can do this by employing professors to do research. If the knowledge gained from this is utilized, the technology level rises. Also, firms can increase the technology status by investing in research and development; i.e. car firms can perform tests on their tires to achieve a better tire for consumerists. Restaurants can experiment with flavors and ingredients to come up with the perfect rib sauce. Clothing makers can investigate the composition of their t-shirts to come up with a more comfortable t-shirt. Also, cell phone designers can investigate their products by trying to find a cell phone that is low weight, small and with maximum features. If these ideas are implemented, the level of technology of a society increases. And everybody wins.

We talked about research and its attributes. We talked about development and its characteristics. We talked about technology and its effects. These three concepts are key to a prosperous consumerist system.

A More Complex Demonstration of the System on a Larger Island

We justify this section by recognizing that if our system can work at the micro level, it should work at the macro level. A system that functions well on an island should function equally well on a national scale.

Here we also make a few simplifying assumptions but we abandon some of those that we made during our discussion of the smaller island. There are a limited number of people but there are more than before. People also sell what they make. There is no non-working consumerist grant markdown. Actually the non-working consumerist markdown is 100% so those who do not work are granted the same amount as those who do work. In this analysis producers need inputs but not all inputs are required. Although unrealistic, producers can make their goods very quickly. To simplify things, there are two currencies. The ratio of accommodational to materialist product prices is better balanced. We add more factors such as a private bank, interest rates and a neighboring island with which to trade. We examine how a command partition worker would operate. Finally to calculate interest we use simple interest not compounded interest.

Let's begin our analysis. There are 26 people. Each person has a name that begins with a different letter of the alphabet. We do this to simplify our task. Our islanders are: Alfred, Betty, Charlie, Daryl, Emma, Fred, George, Hariotte, Ivona, Joanne, Kristine, Lucy, Mickey, Nathan, Oscar, Posy, Quennie, Richard, Susie, Troy, Uma, Vanessa, Wes, Xiu, Yolla and Zlatko.

The size of the island is 500 km². The islanders have a neighbor island about 10 km away. The name of their island is Aulesia and the neighboring island's name is Fraunica.

The first thing the islanders do is elect a leader. How they chose him is a political rather than an economic question so we will avoid answering it. The people elect Alfred as the president. Alfred then creates the central bank and appoints Betty and Charlie as chairman. Another task that that Alfred has to perform is to divide the land for uses. He sets:

-15 % for agriculture

-15% for industry

-10% for conservation

-15% for residential

-15% for commercial

The rest is set aside for division later. Therefore,

-75 km² is for agriculture

-75 km² is for industry

-50 km² is for conservation

-75 km² is for residential

-75 km² is for commercial

Daryl sets up his own private bank. All he needs is paper and a pen (which we assume he has)

Betty and Charlie now set up price functions and wage functions. Although they cannot calculate them they can make a coherent system by voting. This is the economic constitution. They set the interest rate that Daryl's bank can charge per loan at 5%. After voting on price functions, their values are averaged. There are 2 currencies- Ignits and Norses. Final goods in the materialist sector are bought with Norses (Θ) and final goods in the accommodational sector are bought with Ignits (þ). Also all inputs are paid for in Ignits from the profit of producers. The central bankers make the retail mark-up = 25%. The following is a list of the price and wage functions they derived:

Wood-	0.50 þ/kg
Shirts-	1.00 Θ/shirt
Shoes-	1.50 Θ/ pair of shoes
Root vegetable-	0.25 Θ/kg
Tree fruit-	0.25 Θ/ kg
Berries-	0.20 Θ/kg
Stone-	0.75 þ/kg
Tree cutting tool-	2.00 þ/each
Textile material-	0.25 þ/kg
Animal hide-	0.25 þ/kg
Beef-	0.25 Θ/kg
Cow-	9.00 Θ/cow
Steel-	0.20 þ/ kg
Cotton-	0.20 þ/kg
Central banker-	5.00 þ/day
President-	5.00 þ/day
Agricultural land-	30.00 þ/km²
Industrial land-	25.00 þ/km²
Residential land-	20.00 þ/km²
Commercial land-	25.00 þ/km²
Building-	x0.10 þ +y2.00 þ + z1.50 þ + a2.00 þ

Where x-   # of square feet of space

    y-   # of bedrooms

    z-   # of washrooms

    a -   # of floors

Work in the command partition   2.00þ/day

At this point all the islanders choose occupations. Emma, Fred, George and Hariotte all work in the accommodational sector. They use stone and wood to make houses. Ivonna makes axes. Joanne and Kristine cut wood. Lucy makes linen. Mickey and Nathan make shirts. Oscar chooses not to work in the natural partition but works in the command partition. His job is to walk around the island to make sure there is no garbage. Posy makes shoes. Richard harvests potatoes. Susie harvests carrots. Troy harvests apples. Uma harvests plums. Vanessa picks blueberries. Wes picks blackberries. Xiu picks cotton. Queenie mines for stone. Yolla raises cattle. Zlatko mines for steel.

We follow the progress of our islanders for a period of several days. Firstly, Joanne, Kristine, Richard, Susie, Troy, Uma, Vanessa, Wes, Xiu and Yolla must buy the agricultural land they need to make their goods. To buy this land however, they must borrow from the private bank run by Daryl. The interest rate is 5% (simple interest). They each buy 5 km^2 of land. So they each pay 5 km^2 x 30.00 þ/km^2 = 150.00 þ + 5% interest. Since initially all the land is owned by the government, all the money from the purchase of agricultural land goes to the government.

Ivonna, Lucy, Mickey, Nathan, Posy, Queenie and Zlatko have occupations that require industrial land. Each islander buys 5 km^2 of land with the money they borrow from Daryl and the interest rate is again 5%. The money goes to the government. They each pay 5 km^2 x 25.00 þ/km^2 = 125.00 þ.

At this point we see that some land has already been bought. 50 km^2 of the original 75 km^2 of agricultural land has been bought. Also 35 km^2 of the original 75 km^2 of industrial land has been bought.

It's visible that some of the producers on the island require inputs. Namely, wood cutting requires axes and axes require steel. Shirts require linen and linen requires cotton. Shoes require leather and leather requires cattle. Houses require stone and wood. Thus those islanders that make something that requires inputs cannot manufacture them unless they acquire these inputs.

Before the islanders can produce anything they need inputs. They borrow from the bank money to buy from the island of Fraunica. The price per cow is 8.00 þ/cow on Fraunica (in our currency) and 9.00 þ/cow on Aulesia. Yolla buys 3 cows from Fraunica. She pays 27.00 þ + 5% interest which is 27.00 þ + 1.35 þ = 28.35 þ. This she borrows from the bank. The Fraunicans receive 3 x 8.00 þ = 24.00 þ and the trade pool gets 3.00 þ. The bank run by Daryl gets 1.35 þ in interest.

In the cases of Richard, Susie, Troy, Uma, Vanessa and Wes, we assume that either they have the seeds for the vegetables that they are planting or that these foods are naturally occurring. The same applies to Xiu who picks cotton. Although in reality it would take months to grow potatoes or apples, we make the simplification that the island can make these goods in a day. With regards to Joanne, Kristine, Queenie and Zlatko we assume that there are a lot of trees for wood and many mines for steel and stone.

In the first day the following was the output of the economy:

Richard grew 20 kg of potatoes

Susie harvested 20 kg of carrots

Troy harvested 15 kg of apples

Uma harvested 20 kg of plums

Vanessa picked 25 kg of blueberries

Wes picked 20 kg of blackberries

Xiu picked 25 kg of cotton

Yolla bred 2 cows and slaughtered 2, each weighing 200 kg; therefore there are 200 kg of leather and 200 kg of beef

Queenie mined 10 kg of stone

Zlatko mined 10 kg of steel

Now it's time to calculate the Gross Domestic Consumerist Product per capita. The GDCP per capita is equivalent to the general consumerist grant since the non-working consumerist grant markdown is 100%. The GDCP is calculated by taking the total output of all final goods in the materialist sector and multiplying this by the price per quantity set out by the central bank. We factor in the retail mark-up. On the first day we only count the production of potatoes, carrots, apples, plums, blueberries, blackberries and beef. All other things (the steel, stone, cotton, leather) are inputs

The GDCP is:

- Potatoes-   20 kg x 0.25 Ө/kg = 5.00 Ө + (5.00 Ө x 25%) = 6.25 Ө

- Carrots-   20 kg x 0.25 Ө/kg = 5.00 Ө + (5.00 Ө x 25%) = 6.25 Ө

- Apples-   15 kg x 0.25 Ө/kg = 3.75 Ө + (3.75 Ө x 25%) = 4.69 Ө

- Plums-   20 kg x 0.25 Ө/kg = 5.00 Ө + (5.00 Ө x 25%) = 6.25 Ө

- Blueberries-   25 kg x 0.20 Ө/kg = 5.00 Ө + (5.00 Ө x 25%) = 6.25 Ө

- Blackberries- 20 kg x 0.20 Ө/kg = 4.00 Ө+ (4.00 Ө x 25%) = 5.00 Ө

- Beef-   200 kg x 0.25 Ө/kg = 50.00 Ө + (50.00 Ө x 25%) = 62.50 Ө

The total is 97.19 Ө

At this point, Alfred, the president, has to announce the tax on the GDCP. However since the government has already made a lot by selling land, he feels generous and levies a tax of 0% for the day. This is a boost to the economy and the people are extremely happy.

To find the GDCP per capita, we divide the GDCP by the population. So 97.19 Ө/26 = 3.74 Ө. Therefore regardless of how much each member added to the economy, everyone is granted 3.74 Ө. Let's round this up to 3.75 Ө because this is easier to work with and simplifies our calculations yet it is very close numerically. This money is not paper money or coins. It is all entries in the private bank run by Daryl.

Now those that produced goods (apples, potatoes) are able to sell their goods for Ignits. In our island scenario this is done as such. Suppose that Alfred wants a kg of apples. Troy gives Alfred the apples. At the same time, Troy is credited with 0.31 þ (including the retail mark-up) and 0.31 Ѳ are deducted from Alfred's account by Daryl. A Norse and an Ignit have the same numerical value except that they are used to buy different things. So again if Venessa wanted a kg of beef, Yolla would give her this while Daryl adds 0.31 þ to Yolla's account and subtracts 0.31 Ѳ from Vanessa's.

A curious case occurs when someone wants to buy from himself. If Uma wanted a kg of plums, she would gain 0.25 þ and loose 0.25 Ѳ at the same time.

At the end of the day, let's see what everyone bought. Here is a summary:

- Alfred bought 24 kg of beef

- Betty bought 1 kg of potatoes and 2 kg of carrots

- Charlie bought 5 kg of carrots and 2 kg of beef

- Daryl bought 3 kg of carrots and 9 kg of plums

- Emma bought 12 kg of potatoes

- Fred bought 12 kg of beef

- George bought 5 kg of carrots and 7 kg of apples

- Hariotte bought 15 kg of blackberries

- Ivonna bought 15 kg of blueberries

- Joanne bought 5 kg of carrots and 7 kg of potatoes

- Kristine bought 12 kg of beef

- Lucy bought 5 kg of blueberries and 5 kg of blackberries

- Mickey bought 1 kg of apples and 1 kg of plums and 10 kg of beef

- Nathan bought 1 kg of apples, 1 kg of plums and 10 kg of beef

- Oscar bought 1 kg of apples, 1 kg of plums and 10 kg of beef

- Posy bought 1 kg of apples, 1 kg of plums and 10 kg of beef

- Queenie bought 1 kg of apples, 1 kg of plums and 10 kg of beef

- Richard bought 1 kg of apples and 11 kg of beef

- Susie bought 1 kg of apples and 11 kg of beef

- Troy bought 1 kg of apples and 11 kg of beef

- Uma bought 1 kg of plums and 11 kg of beef

- Vanessa bought 1 kg of plums and 11 kg of beef

- Wes bought 1 kg of plums and 11 kg of beef

- Xiu bought 1 kg of plums and 11 kg of beef

- Yolla bought 1 kg of plums and 11 kg of beef

- Zlatko bought 1 kg of plums and 11 kg of beef

Now everyone has spent their money and we assume that they spent all of it. We record the income of the producers in day 1:

Richard-   6.25 þ

Susie-   6.25 þ

Troy-   4.69 þ

Uma-   6.25 þ

Vanessa-   6.25 þ

Wes-   5.00 þ

Yolla-   62.50 þ

The other islanders also want to make some money. They do so by borrowing money to pay for inputs which they use to turn into finished goods. Left over from the first day are the following: 200 kg of leather, 25 kg of cotton, 10 kg of stone and 10 kg of steel.

Ivonna buys 5 kg of steel by borrowing from Daryl at 5% interest. For every kg of steel, Ivonna can make 2 axes. Since steel costs 0.20 þ/kg, Ivonna borrows 1.00 þ from the bank and must pay 1.05 þ to Daryl at a later date.

Since Lucy makes linen she needs cotton. For every kg of cotton she can make 3 kg of linen. She needs to buy 15 kg of cotton which costs 0.20 þ/kg. So she borrows 3.00 þ and at 5% interest she must pay 3.15 þ in the future to the bank.

Posy makes shoes. Thus she needs leather. For every shoe she makes she needs 2 kg of leather. She needs about 30 kg of leather which costs 0.25 þ/kg. She borrows 7.50 þ from Daryl at 5% interest which is 8.25 þ.

Now we list the output for day 2:

- Richard-   23 kg of potatoes

- Susie-   20 kg of carrots

- Troy-   15 kg of apples

- Uma-   18 kg of plums

- Vanessa-   30 kg of blueberries

- Wes-   25 kg of blackberries

- Yolla-   slaughtered 1 cow- 100 kg of leather and 100 kg of beef

- Xiu-   20 kg of cotton

- Queenie-   15 kg of steel

- Zlatko-   15 kg of stone

- Ivonna-   10 axes

- Lucy-   45 kg of linen

- Posy-   15 shoes

Today we have a little more output since we have islanders who were able to convert certain inputs and turn them into finished products. Today we have shoes for the first time.

Now we calculate the GDCP

- Potatoes-   23 kg x 0.25 Ө/kg = 5.35 Ө + (5.35 Ө x 0.25) = 6.69 Ө

- Carrots-   20 kg x 0.25 Ө/kg = 5.00 Ө + (5.00 Ө x 0.25) = 6.25 Ө

- Apples-   15 kg x 0.25 Ө/kg = 3.75 Ө + (3.75 Ө x 0.25) = 4.69 Ө

- Plums-   18 kg x 0.25 Ө/kg = 4.50 Ө + (4.50 Ө x 0.25) = 5.63 Ө

- Blueberries-   30 kg x 0.20 Ө/kg = 6.00 Ө + (6.00 Ө x 0.25) = 7.50 Ө

- Blackberries- 25 kg x 0.20 Ө/kg = 5.00 Ө + (5.00 Ө x 0.25) = 6.25 Ө

- Beef-   100 kg x 0.25 Ө/kg = 25.00 Ө + (25.00 Ө x 0.25) = 31.25 Ө

- Shoes-   15 shoes x 1.50 Ө/shoe = 22.50 Ө + (22.50 Ө x 0.25) = 28.13 Ө

This gives us a total of 96.39 Ө

Thus the GDCP is 96.39 Ө. Again, Alfred the president announces a tax of 0%. This is because the GDCP is a bit smaller than the previous day's. This is due to less beef. Only half as much beef was produced today relative to yesterday.

The GDCP per capita is 96.39 Ө/26 = 3.71 Ө. Now the islanders purchase goods with their 3.71 Ө. As an islander takes a good, its value is deducted from his Norse account and its value in Ignits is added to the seller's bank account. This is all on paper that Daryl is in charge of keeping records on.

Thus the islanders make purchases. Some of the islanders did not spend all of their money and thus they have a surplus. Fred has a surplus of 3.50 Ө. Harold has a surplus of 2.35 Ө. Lucy has a surplus of 0.65 Ө. Oscar has a surplus of 1.15 Ө. Queenie has a surplus of 0.73 Ө. The total surplus is 8.38 Ө. In terms of goods, the surplus is 5 kg of blackberries, 1 kg of blueberries, 4 kg of beef and 3 pairs of shoes.

Now let's recap the income of the producers in day 2.

- Richard-   6.69 þ

- Susie-   6.25 þ

- Troy-   4.69 þ

- Uma-   5.63 þ

- Vanessa-   7.25 þ

- Wes-   5.00 þ

- Yolla-   30.00 þ

- Posy-   22.50 þ

- Oscar   2.00 þ

The islanders would now like to open up trade with the island of Fraunica. They have blueberries, blackberries, beef and shoes to trade. The people of Fraunica have gooseberries and radishes to trade. According to the economic constitution set up by Betty and Charlie, a kilogram of gooseberries, like any berry costs 0.20 Ө/kg and a kilogram of radishes like any root vegetable, costs 0.25 Ө/kg. On Fraunica, a kg of gooseberries costs $0.50 and a kg of radishes costs $0.15. The Fraunicans use dollars as their currency. Also, on Fraunica the goods which we wish to trade – blueberries, shoes, blackberries and beef- have a price. This price may be set by a market economy on Fraunica or by a consumerist economy headed by a central bank. Over there, blueberries and blackberries each cost $0.25/kg, shoes cost $0.25/pair and beef costs $0.25/kg

The central bank operated by Betty and Charlie must operate a trade pool. The trade pool gains money during certain trades and must subsidize other trades in order for them to occur. Thus Betty and Charlie must find the value of the Ignits relative to the dollar that will maximize the trade pool; i.e. make it positive. Although the above prices were expressed in Norses, the trade pool operates in Ignits rather than Norses, 1 Norse being equal to 1 Ignit.

Suppose that Betty and Charlie set the price of the Ignit exactly equal to one dollar. Let's see what the trade pool would look like in such a scenario. First the exporting. We sell 3 shoes for 1.50 þ. The Fraunicans give us $0.75. We sell 4 kg of beef for 1.00 þ and receive $1.00. We sell 1 kg of blueberries and 5 kg of blackberries for 1.20 þ. We receive $1.50 Thus we receive $3.25 and give up 3.70 þ. Now the importing. The Fraunicans sell us 10 kg of gooseberries. We pay $5.00. To us this is worth 2.00 þ. They sell us 20 kg of radishes for $3.00. To us this is worth 5.00 þ.Thus we pay $8.00 and they give us 7.00 þ.

The central bankers, Betty and Charlie, must pick a common exchange rate. The real exchange rates factor in. The real exchange rates are:

Importing-	Gooseberries-	$2.50/1 þ
	Radishes-	$0.60/1 þ
Exporting-	Berries-	$1.25/1 þ

Beef- $1.00/1 þ

Shoes- $0.50/1 þ

Suppose that Charlie and Betty set the exchange rate at $0.75/1þ. We sell beef at 1.00 þ and the Fraunicans must pay us $1.00 x 1 þ /$0.75 = 1.33 þ. Thus we receive 1.33 þ. 1.00 þ goes to Yolla and the trade pool earns 0.33 þ.

Again suppose that Betty and Charlie set the exchange rate at $0.75/1 þ. We sell 3 shoes for 1.50 þ and the Fraunicans pay us $0.75. So the Fraunicans would pay $0.75 or $0.75 x 1.00 þ/$0.75 = 1.00 þ. Now Posy would get 1.50 þ but 1.00 þ would come from the Fraunicans and 0.50 þ from the trade pool.

In setting the exchange rate, Betty and Charlie must strike a balance. When importing it is better for the trade pool to have a higher exchange rate and when exporting it is better to have a lower exchange rate. The exchange rate is expressed as foreign currency in terms of domestic currency. If the exchange rate were equal to the real exchange rate there would be no need for a trade pool.

There is a way for Betty and Charlie to calculate the optimal exchange rate for their trade pool. The method is as follows. List all the real exchange rates of all the goods being exported and imported. Next multiply these values by how many units are being traded. Then divide this number by the sum of all the units being imported and exported. The calculations follow:

Units	Good	Real Exchange Rate
10	Gooseberries	$2.50/ þ
20	Radishes	$0.60/ þ
6	Berries	$1.25/ þ
4	Beef	$1.00/ þ
3	Shoes	$0.50/ þ

The ideal exchange rate is given by (10 x 2.50/þ) + (20 x $0.60/þ) + (6 x $1.25/þ) + (4 x $1.00/þ) + (3 x $0.50/þ) = $50.00/þ

($50.00/þ)/43 = $1.16/þ

Now we use the exchange rate, $1.16/þ to calculate the trades occurring between Aleucia and Fraunica. First the gooseberries. We import 10 kg of gooseberries (actually Richard buys them). The Fraunicans get paid $5.00. This is equivalent to $5.00 x 1þ/$1.16 = 4.31 þ. However Richard pays only our price for the gooseberries = 2.00 þ. They are considered a final good. The central bank pays the other 2.31 þ. For now the trade pool balance is negative. Now Richard can sell the 10 kg of gooseberries to the other islanders to enjoy. The central bank sets the retail mark-up at 25%. The retail mark-up is the profit gained for retailing a good versus the original price. Thus Richard can sell his gooseberries at a price of (0.20 Θ x 0.25) + 0.20 Θ = 0.25 Θ

Now the radishes are imported. Each kg costs $0.15 and there are 20 kg of them. So they all cost $3.00. In Ignits this is $3.00 x 1þ/$1.16 = 2.59 þ. Vanessa chooses to import them. She pays 2.59 þ to the Frauncian islanders and 2.41 þ (5.00 þ – 2.59 þ) to the trade pool as the domestic price of radishes is 5.00 þ.Vanessa can sell her radishes for (0.25 Θ x 0.25) + 0.25 Θ = 0.31 Θ

Now the exporting. The berries are sold (exported) to Fraunica. Since they have the same price, blueberries and blackberries are treated as one. There are 6 kg of berries. They cost the Fraunicans $1.50. In terms of Ignits, they are $1.50 x 1þ/$1.16 = 1.30 þ. 1.20 þ is given to our berry growers and (1.30 þ – 1.20 þ = 0.10 þ) goes to Charlie and Betty's trade pool.

Now beef. We sell 4 kg of beef. The Fraunicans must pay us $1.00. In our currency this is $1.00 x 1þ/$1.16 = 0.86 þ. Yolla, the beef producer, earns 0.14 þ from the central bank as a subsidy and 0.86 þ from the Fraunicans.

Lastly, let's take care of the shoes. We have 3 pairs of shoes and they sell for $0.75 per pair. In our currency this is $0.75 x 1þ/ $1.16 = 0.65 þ. The trade pool must add 1.50 þ – 0.65 þ = 0.85 þ to the shoe maker, Posy's, income. Posy receives 1.50 þ; 0.65 þ from the Fraunicans and 0.85 þ from the central bank.

Let's see how our trade pool managed. It loses 2.31 þ, it gains 2.41 þ, it gains 0.10 þ, it loses 0.14 þ and loses 0.85 þ. Thus the central bank loses 0.79 þ. This brings a negative trading pool balance. It is possible that there could be a positive trade balance if the exchange rate was somewhere between $3.00/þ and $4.00/þ. But if we do the calculations for this exchange rate, it turns out that only one good that is traded will give a surplus and the others will have to be subsidized. Yet with an exchange rate of $1.16/þ, we end up with the least differences between subsidies of goods exported and imported relative to each other. Thus, although this value doesn't give the most positive result, it gives the most equal result for all trades.

The islanders would like to have accommodation (huts, houses), but to build these the builders require stone and wood. In day 2 there is still no wood made. In day 1, 10 kg of stone was mined and in day 2, 15 kg of stone was mined. So we have 25 kg of stone. Buildings are made of wood and stone. For every house, 1 kg of wood is needed for every bedroom and 1 kg of stone is needed for every floor. To recall, the price function for a building is:

x 0.10 þ + y 2.00 þ + z1.50 þ + a 2.00 þ

Where: x is the number of square feet of space

y is the number of bedrooms

z is the number of washrooms

a is the number of floors

The islanders would also like to have shirts. To produce 1 shirt it requires 1 kg of linen. In order to cut wood, Joanne and Kristine need axes. They need 1 axe for every 10 kg of wood cut.

Now it is day 3. Mickey and Nathan make shirts. There are 45 kg of linen left over from day 2. They cost 0.25 þ/kg. Mickey buys 20 kg and Nathan buys 25 kg of linen. They borrow from Daryl with 5 % interest. Thus Mickey pays 20 kg x 0.25 þ/kg = 5.00 þ + 5% interest = 5.25 þ and Nathan pays 25 kg x 0.25 þ/kg = 6.25 þ + 5% interest = 6.56 þ. So Lucy who owns Linen earns 45 kg x 0.25 þ/kg = 11.25 þ. There is no retail mark-up on this since linen is an input.

Joanne and Kristine produce wood. Joanne and Kristine buy the axes (5 each) by borrowing from Daryl's bank. Each axe costs 2.00 þ. The interest rate is 5%. Each wood cutter pays 5 x 2.00 þ + 5%